BOWLES.

BLAKENEY.   1946.

ESCAPE TO DANGER

A rest in a blizzard. Some of the 10,000 allied Air Force prisoners-of-war from Stalag Luft 3 sink exhausted in the snow during a ninety-five kilometre forced march following the evacuation of the camp in the face of the oncoming Russian armies in January, 1945. For the ill-nourished and half-frozen prisoners the march was one of the grimmest episodes of their captivity

ESCAPE TO DANGER

by
F/Lt. PAUL BRICKHILL
and
CONRAD NORTON

illustrated by
LEY KENYON

FABER AND FABER LIMITED
24 Russell Square
London

First published in Mcmxlvi
by Faber and Faber Limited
24 Russell Square London W.C.1
Printed in Great Britain by
Purnell and Sons Limited
Paulton (Somerset) and London

Preface

———

'. . . Some of our aircraft failed to return.'

So ended the story. It always ended that way. Aircraft took off and flew into silence. Invariably, inevitably they earned that same terse epitaph—'failed to return'.

By its very briefness and lack of emotion it stirred imaginations at first and men could see the visions of those savage air battles, the sickening fall of flaming aircraft and the tragic sequels. But repetition through years of war soon had its numbing effect and men no longer saw those visions. They had become commonplace, and so they lost reality.

Yet beyond the silence which followed the take-off, another story was just starting—the story of a few who lived when 'some of our aircraft failed to return'. It was the tale of one in ten who survived and for courage and blood, pain and misery and sheer sustained drama, it dwarfed the wildest flights of fiction.

All of it so far has remained among the great untold adventures of the war because these one in ten who knew it have been exiled for weary years behind barbed wire in the midst of the enemy.

During the war in Europe, some 100,000 young men fell with their aircraft over hostile soil. Of them, about 10,000 lived. And in 10,000 ten-to-one chances for a man's life in air battle, there are going to be some fabulously slim chances that came off.

There were. Hence this story of miracles.

*   *   *

There is one thing more.

These 10,000 who lived paid for their survival by drear imprisonment behind barbed wire and the years they spent in those barren, cramped compounds were numb misery. It was such an indefinite purgatory. Life marked time, but despair and emotion didn't.

They did the obvious thing. They tried to escape.

In the North Compound of Stalag Luft III, near Sagan, there was a secret association of escapers known as the 'X Organization'—a team of young officers of the Royal and Dominion Air Forces who did fantastic things. On the night of the 24th of March 1944, seventy-six of them broke out of a tunnel called 'Harry' that was 350 feet long and 30 feet deep—the longest prisoner of war tunnel ever dug.

Most of them were caught and, you may remember, fifty were murdered by the Gestapo.

We were writing this book in North Compound at that time, in barrack block 103, next to block 104 from which the tunnel 'Harry' was dug, and we give here also the first full account of that strange and dramatic affair.

For fairly obvious reasons we had to hide our manuscript for a year from the Germans; sometimes in a secret wall panel, sometimes down another tunnel called 'Dick' and sometimes by the simple expedient of putting it in the barrack block that the Germans had searched last, knowing that it would wait its turn before being searched again. Much of the story we did not dare to write. We had to remember it till we got back, but that was not so difficult because the incidents of those days are still vividly with us.

Eventually we lugged our manuscript on two refugee marches across Germany, cursing its weight during the day that made us throw away precious food and using it by night as a pillow. Liberation began to seem like a lovely dream that could never come true.

But one day it did. So here is the manuscript. We can carry it no further.

PAUL BRICKHILL
CONRAD NORTON

Contents

Illustrations

Notes on the Illustrations

The drawings of the tunnel in this book are the only authentic records of the tunnel in existence. The work of Flight-Lieutenant Ley Kenyon, D.F.C., who was in the camp with the authors, they have a chequered—almost a romantic—history.

It was impossible to get flashlights for photographs, so not long before the mass break took place, Kenyon, one of the leading camp artists, was sent down the tunnel 'Harry' to make a pictorial record of it. The results were the pictures Nos. 5, 7B, 8, 9, and 10.

He sketched under extremely difficult conditions, sometimes lying on his back in the cramped space and using the tunnel roof as drawing desk. A flickering flame from a pyjama-cord wick floating in margarine in a sardine tin gave him light for the job. Immediately after the drawings were done they were packed away in an airtight canister made of old milk tins, and hidden away in the disused tunnel, 'Dick'.

Months later, in January 1945, all the prisoners were suddenly evacuated from the camp on a forced march as the advancing Russians were only thirty miles away. The drawings had to be left behind. There was just time to flood 'Dick' as a precaution against the drawings and other documents hidden there being found by the Germans. Though the Germans used the camp for a while as an advanced depot, they never found the tunnel cache and eventually the Russians over-ran the place.

The drawings were eventually recovered by a British officer who was too sick to be evacuated with the main body of prisoners and was left behind in the camp hospital. He descended into the flooded tunnel, found much of the water had seeped away, discovered the drawings and other documents undamaged in their sealed containers, and brought them back to England.

The other drawings in the book are also by Kenyon whose sensitive perception and touch has given them the authentic atmosphere as well as detail of the camp and the refugee march.

Glossary

In the backwater of captivity, a little world of their own, prisoners of war developed their own 'slanguage'. We make use of the following:

KRIEGY: A prisoner of war (from the German 'Kriegsgefangener').

KRIEGYDOM: The world of kriegies, or, as the Germans put it so succinctly, 'Kriegsgefangenenschaft'.

FERRET: German security guard, usually in blue overalls, who patrolled compounds constantly to counter our escape activity.

STOOGE: One of our own sentries to warn escape workers whenever ferrets approached.

PENGUIN: A cunning specialist who disposed of sand excavated from tunnels so that the ferrets could not find it.

THE CIRCUIT: The worn track round the compound, just inside the warning wire, which kriegies 'pounded' or 'bashed' (walked) for hours at a time to get away from their own thoughts.

PURGE: A newly arrived batch of kriegies from Dulag Luft, the Luftwaffe interrogation centre. From this, also, the passive verb, 'to be purged'.

PART I

___

THE DOWNFALL

___

*By strange ways they arrived
in prison camp*

Chapter One

BARBED WIRE—FOR FIVE AND
A HALF YEARS

─────

That sunny Sunday morning when war was declared the handful of young men who flew the operational aircraft of the R.A.F. knew they were in for it. There was no real fear. The placid, prosperous days of peace did not train one to accept death as an everyday commonplace. They knew most of them would die, but did not really comprehend it. A man might look at Johnny or Pete and think, 'Hell! those chaps might be dead in a week', but could not quite apply it to himself. In point of fact about 75 per cent of them were to die, but they did not know that; nor did they care greatly.

When they considered it, which was not too often, they thought a few would get through with a whole skin. Good show! And the rest would die. Bad show! The prospect of becoming a prisoner did not occur to them, which was not surprising as very few of them did, in fact, become prisoners.

Though there was a certain relief in having the job plonked down squarely in front of one at last, the chief emotion was a simmering excitement. No one knew what modern war would be like and it was all vastly intriguing.

There wasn't much to occupy their minds. They had been busily preparing for months. Dispositions had been made and they were ready, just waiting for the first job. So they sat in the sun outside the messes and drank quite a lot, even more than usual, and laughed and talked with their wives and girl friends who were paying week-end visits. It was almost like a prolonged party in a dentist's waiting-room. Everyone was gay and stimulated, though it wasn't quite a natural effervescence. It was the restless spirit of 'eat, drink and be merry, for to-morrow we die'.

On the morrow, some of them *did* die.

Blenheims went out to bomb the pocket battleship, *Admiral Scheer*, in Wilhelmshaven. It was the first raid of the war, a low-level attack through low cloud and mist from about a hundred feet, because they thought in those days that you could attack heavily defended warships in harbour from that height.

The first wave of five aircraft caught the Germans napping. They whistled across the *Scheer* at mast height, dropped their bombs, scored some hits and four got back. It wasn't bad. The second wave of five went in a little later, ran into a roused defence and the result was reversed. Four didn't get back. One crashed on the deck of the *Scheer*, one went into the sea, and God knows what happened to the rest. Of the missing crews, who amounted to seventeen, two were saved. Sgt.-Observer Booth and Wireless Op.-Air Gunner A.C.1. Slattery found themselves in the water after their aircraft had gone into the sea. The Germans picked them up and they became the first British prisoners of war, with a pretty deadly five and a half years in front of them.

Back on the squadron which got one aircraft back, the fellows who had been wondering what war would be like were rather shaken. They considered there was no future in two or three years of this sort of thing.

The first officer prisoner went into the bag two days later, and at this early stage the first of a long run of freak escape stories was chalked up. He was Pilot-Officer Ted Edwards, a stocky, cheerful lad with wavy blond hair which gave him the nickname of 'Locks'. He was a New Zealander and had been an All Black trial as an extremely nippy wing threequarter. He would have got his international rugger cap if he hadn't left home to take an R.A.F. short-service commission.

On September the 6th, he was flying a staid, respectable old Anson on a Coastal Command recce over the North Sea, near the Bight of Heligoland. They sighted another aircraft, which for a moment, they couldn't identify, because nobody was very experienced in aircraft identification in those days. Then Ted's observer claimed he knew the type and swore it was French, thus producing the first 'famous last words' of the war. It was not French. It was German—a Blohm and Voss seaplane. Ted discovered this when a hail of machine-gun bullets came rattling into the Anson. The controls were shot away, the tanks were hit, and the wood and fabric Anson, burning like a bonfire, curved down in a crimson parabola that ended in a mighty, sizzling 'ker-dumph' of white foam and black smoke. The crew was still inside.

When Ted woke up he was floating alone in his Mae West. There wasn't any Anson, and there weren't any of his crew. He didn't know how he got there, or why he didn't go down with the aircraft, and he still doesn't know. He was just floating, half-drowned, concussed, and somewhat burned. The heel of one of his shoes was shot off and another bullet had pierced the shoulder of his shirt, but he himself had not been scratched by them.

He would have floated there and died unpleasantly in normal circum-stances, but the pilot of the Blohm and Voss, all agog over this first victory, wanted confirmatory evidence to take home, so he went down and landed, and a bedraggled, bemused Ted was hauled on board over the floats and haled off to Germany and Wesermunde hospital, where he met Slattery and Booth, also recovering from injuries.

It was only two days later that Squadron-Leader Wank M—— and Pilot-Officer Tommy Thompson (later, much later, one of the lucky few who escaped Gestapo bullets in the mass escape from Stalag Luft III) and their crew set out in a Whitley on their last trip. It was a night leaflet raid and they were on their way home about 4 a.m. when one engine packed in. Then the other one started to cough and drop revs., and the Whitley began to sink. They hung on till there was obviously no future in it before they baled out. Searching Germans rounded them up at dawn and they were locked in cells on an aerodrome near Gotha. Their captors took from them anything with which they might hang themselves, braces, shoe-laces, belts, and ties, and they spent several hours rather on edge because there had been reports that the Germans were shooting people for dropping propaganda.

Early in the afternoon an interpreter came in and said something which shook them considerably.

'Have you a last wish? You are going on a long journey.' His voice seemed to be fairly steeped in sepulchral menace.

Wank and Tommy were startled and speechless, and then the inter-preter walked towards Tommy, carrying his tie, holding it forward stretched between his hands as though he were going to bandage his eyes. Stiffly, to cover their nerves, they asked the interpreter what the devil he meant, and innocently he made himself clear. He wanted to know if they would like anything to eat before they set off by car along the autobahn to Berlin. At 3 p.m. they started for Berlin, where they arrived at about 9.30, and spent the night in a hospital just outside the city—a rather disturbed night as they were woken at 2 a.m. and interrogated till 4.30. This was not at all pleasant, because no one knew what to expect from German interrogation in those days.

About lunchtime they were taken for a walk to meet a very important German. After about a mile they came to a wood, where they waited for a while, rather mystified, until a messenger arrived and beckoned them on. They entered the wood and came to a siding of railway lines and a string of carriages across their path. They were led up into a carriage and out the other side, where they came upon a strange sight.

In front of them stretched a pleasant grassy clearing, with a huge spreading tree in the middle. Under the tree was a large dais on trestles, about four feet high and ten yards across. On the dais was a solitary large table desk—and behind it sat an almost legendary figure. There was no mistaking the gorgeously immaculate bulk of Hermann Goering, directing his Luftwaffe, then smashing through Poland, under an open sky. Wank was beckoned forward and walked across soft grass to the dais.

As he mounted the steps, Goering rose to his feet and waited while Wank marched up to the desk and saluted stiffly. Goering formally returned the salute, offered Wank a handshake, and motioned him to sit down at a corner of the desk. The Nazi chief was resplendent in a magnificent uniform of pale blue, perfectly cut, with the cross of the highest German order, '*Pour Le Mérite*', glinting at his throat. Round his heavy shoulders hung a great cloak of soft, pale blue leather, under which Wank caught the gleam of other badges and decorations. In spite of his prejudices Wank could not help being impressed. He thought Goering looked fit and well and he seemed quite friendly. Though the Reichsmarschall understood a little English, he spoke to Wank through an interpreter.

'I am not going to ask you questions of a military nature. I know you are not permitted to answer them.' It was a promise he kept throughout the interview, which lasted for twenty-five minutes.

'What do people in Britain think about this war?' was his first question.

'They were naturally reluctant,' said Wank, 'but they have faith in their leaders, and as our leaders have decided that the war is unavoidable, the people will see it through.'

Goering nodded and asked, 'And what do you think of it?'

'I'm not a politician,' said Wank soberly, 'I'm an Air Force officer.'

Both men were being punctiliously correct in their behaviour. Surprisingly then, Goering gave Wank some startling inside information.

'I can tell you that Russia is coming in on our side in two days,' he said, 'and the Polish campaign will be over in a week.'

He was more or less right in both, as the Russians marched into Poland a few days later, but in his next forecast he was pathetically wrong.

'You may be home again in time for Christmas,' he told Wank. 'When Poland is defeated, Britain will have done all she can to fulfil her pledges and there will be nothing left to fight about.

'My main point in seeing you, however, is to tell you that the Luftwaffe policy is to look after you Air Force prisoners well. I know myself that men who fly are by nature least adaptable to imprisonment.'

He told Wank he would try to give them as many sporting facilities as possible during their captivity, and when the interview ended, asked if there was anything more he could do for them at the moment. Wank immediately said there was. The Germans had taken their leather Irvin jackets at Gotha. Could they have them back?

'Certainly,' said Goering. 'I'll see to it.' And within twenty-four hours Wank and Tommy were handed back their jackets.

They went the next day to Itzehöe, a Polish prisoners' camp about thirty miles east of Hamburg, where there were about 1,200 Polish officers and some Polish soldiers. In accordance with the Geneva Convention, the Germans were paying Wank and Tommy the equivalent pay of a German major and lieutenant, and for a time they lived moderately well. Germany was not short of luxuries in those days and they were able to buy plenty of fruit, soft drinks and so on. They were rather lonely as the only British people there until Ted Edwards left hospital and joined them on September the 30th.

About the middle of October, kriegy life started in earnest when they were taken to the old fortress castle of Spangenburg, a drab, dilapidated old pile standing aloof on a hill near the town of the same name, a few miles south of Kassel. There was a lovely view from there, but that was all. The captive officers and a few N.C.O. prisoners had to live there on German non-working civilian rations. As non-working civilians were not encouraged in Germany, the ration was not much more than a formality, and they were always hungry, and grew thin and peaked.

They were depressing days, as most of the prisoners were realists. They tried not to think too much about the length of the war. When they did, they candidly estimated that it would last at least three years, but this was rarely referred to. They retained such a confidence in final victory, that the Germans could not help being impressed by a morale that was pretty commendable.

They kept this up even when France collapsed and the handful of kriegies, sick with dismay, found life rather horrible. Even then morale did not falter. They said, 'Well, this might make the show last a bit longer, but we'll still win, so what the hell!' To the Germans, who were cocky as hell and twice as patronizing they presented the usual bland front of casual confidence, and it brought them grudging respect.

By November 11th, there were thirteen R.A.F. officers at Spangenburg, including Wing-Commander Prickie Day,[1] who was a more than average good type, and who later was very nearly like Tommy Thompson, among the fifty Gestapo victims after the epic Stalag Luft III mass break. Also in that thirteen was Flight-Lieutenant Mike Casey, and Mike *was* among the fifty victims, after a pretty heartbreaking four and a half years of waiting for the end.

[1] Later to become Group Captain H. A. Day, D.S.O., O.B.E., M.C. The M.C. for his part in the first world war, the D.S.O. and O.B.E. for a gallant record of escape and other activities in P.O.W. camps in the recent scrap.

20

Chapter Two

THE FAMILY GROWS

Of course even in those days, it wasn't just the dolorous gaggle of Air Force people who were turfed into Spangenburg and subsequent air-crew prison camps in Germany. With Teutonic inelasticity of intellect, the Nazis took the naive view that anyone who had any remote connection with flying should go into an Air Force camp, be he Army, Navy, Marine or Air Force. So from time to time we took to our bosoms a sprinkling of naval and marine types from the Fleet Air Arm, who were both fish and fowl, so to speak, and later—much later—there was also a leavening of paratroops.

As the Fleet Air Arm was fairly promptly in action during September 1939, it was not long before Wank and his cohort at Spangenburg gave their woebegone welcome to the Navy, in the persons of a couple of Skua pilots, Lieutenant Dick T—— and Captain Guy G——, the latter, incidentally, being a Marine. They won, respectively, the dubious honours of being the first Fleet Air Arm and Marine types to taste the dregs of captivity, and their downfall was a quirkish mixture of misfortune. It was one of those game, sporting efforts, which, with even nominal support from Lady Luck, often result in the most sparkling of successes, but as it was, every atom of luck was obstinately against them. The bombs they dropped to eliminate a German U-boat brought about their own, literal downfall in a rapid double-play of calamity, and the same U-boat they had intended to sink, took them, instead, under the waves with it and back to Germany.

It was in the second week of the war that the renowned *Ark Royal*, before she was sunk—even for the first time—was cruising about northwest of Ireland on anti-submarine patrol, with four destroyers in her brood. Everyone was on their toes because a terse message had just been received from the Admiralty to the effect that the Germans were already resorting to unrestricted U-boat warfare. Had anyone been in doubt as to what that meant, their doubts were violently dispersed about September 13th, when the *Ark* passed a spot where the grey Atlantic was bubbling restlessly as great gouts of air vomited turbulently up from the depths. It was the spot, where, nine days earlier, the *Athenia* had gone down—the war's first famous victim of the U-boats.

Over her grave the sea was still in festering torment, as though the ship, even in death, were sending up a protest against man's inhumanity. It was a sight that depressed, and at the same time produced a thirst for revenge.

Next day they got the desired first chance for action. Early in the afternoon an electrifying message crackled over the *Ark*'s radio receiver: 'S.O.S. s.s. *Fanad Head*. Am being attacked by U-boat. . . .'

And there the message dramatically stopped. But there had just been time for the *Ark*'s radio men to position her by R.D.F. bearings, and they pin-pointed the harassed *Fanad Head*—she was a British freighter —roughly more than a hundred miles west of the *Ark*. Long months of training bore fruit as the carrier's crew moved smoothly into its first action. Though the flight deck was heaving over a long swell, three Skua fighter-dive-bombers were scrambled to attack the U-boat, a squadron of Swordfish torpedo-bombers was lined up to follow and two destroyers swung away from the *Ark* and threw up great twin shields of curving white water from their bows as they raced to the rescue. The three Skuas were flown by the C.O. of the squadron, Dick T——, and Guy G——, and they set out on slightly divergent courses for the approximate position of the *Fanad Head*.

Dick, who is a sensitive, rather slight young man had been flying about half an hour at about 3,000 feet, just under the base of heavy, grey cloud that sagged like a soaked blanket over the Atlantic, when he saw a thin, black shape directly in front of him. He promptly pulled up into the cloud to cover his approach and kept on course until he judged he was near the spot where he had seen the black shape. Putting down his nose, he rocketed out of the cloud, and dead ahead and just in front he had a bird's-eye view of the *Fanad Head*. She was lying stopped, heaving in the swell; but much more interesting was another, much slimmer, dark shape lying at right angles to the freighter, almost touching it. It was undoubtedly the U-boat. Hung in his bomb-racks, Dick had a 100-lb. anti-submarine bomb and four 20-lb. anti-personnel bombs. Too close to bomb from where he was, he veered away for a few seconds then swung back again and shoved his nose steeply down for the bombing dive, approaching the U-boat broadside on, so as not to hit the *Fanad Head* if his bomb fell short.

Dick had just the one bomb of respectable size, and therefore only one chance, and as it was his first, tingling taste of real action he concentrated solely on getting the U-boat, ignored the danger to himself and dived as low as he dared before he pressed the button to release his bomb. His aim was good, but not quite good enough, and the bomb fell just a few feet short, not quite close enough to settle the submarine, though its flying fragments dented the conning-tower.

As he pulled up and around, Dick looked back and saw the boiling, white patch where his bomb had landed. He still had a faint chance left —the four 20-lb. anti-personnel bombs. He knew they wouldn't settle a U-boat, but thought that if he could drop them down or on her conning-tower, he might prevent her from submerging until the destroyers or Swordfish could arrive for an easy kill. There wasn't much time, as the U-boat, considerably perturbed, was flooding her tanks and submerging. Already her decks were awash.

Dick peeled off and dived again. This time he came even lower. He was pretty determined, and when he was almost over the U-boat he pressed his button four times in quick succession, to release every bomb. His aim was fine, but his luck was dead out. Two bombs fell on one side of the target, and two on the other side. Even less lucky was the sequel. As he pulled up his nose again he got a little tingle of shock to see a flame shoot up in the bottom of his cockpit. Apparently a bomb splinter, malignantly aimed by Fate, had pierced his unprotected petrol-tank. Almost before his mind could register the fact, the flame, fed by leaking petrol, multiplied and leapt up to blaze around the controls. Strapped in his bucket seat, Dick could not move his legs out of the way and was agonizingly burned through his thin uniform trousers. Flame surrounded the control column and burned his hand and wrist through the gloves he was wearing. If it had not been so painful and serious, it would have been comical to see him jerking his hands on and off the stick like a man juggling a hot potato.

He was only two or three hundred feet up and promptly shoved the stick forward to get to quenching water as soon as possible. The Skua smacked into the crest of a wave, bounced about fifty feet into the air, dropped and hit again, then ploughed to a foaming stop, with water cascading over the cockpit. Dick and his navigator tossed off their straps and flopped out on to the wing as the nose dipped under. A week previously they had seen another Skua crash-lob on the water and explode into flame for twenty yards around. With petrol-tank already split and flame in the offing, Dick didn't wait for the same thing. The navigator could barely paddle, but as they tumbled into the water, Dick grabbed him and pulled him with him out of the danger zone.

The navigator had omitted to pull the dinghy release toggle and though the Skua didn't explode, it sank, dinghy and all, and left them there. About a mile away, Dick could see the *Fanad Head*, still motionless and lifting in the swell. Though the navigator was kept afloat by his Mae West, he could do little about propelling himself, so Dick grabbed him in the orthodox life-saving method and started off to swim to the ship, dragging the navigator with him.

After about ten minutes, it was obvious that they were getting nowhere fast. They had made practically no progress and would never reach the *Fanad Head*, which might move off at any moment. There was only one thing to do, and Dick had the commonsense to do it. He told the navigator to keep on making what progress he could, and then struck out alone for the *Fanad Head* to get help for both of them. He struggled on for about an hour until he was about 200 yards from the ship, when the cumulative effects of shock, burns, and cold immersion took effect and he passed out.

For once, he was lucky. The U-boat had captured the *Fanad Head* before the Skua arrived on the scene and a prize crew was on board. A German sailor saw Dick's unconscious body, jumped overboard with a line, swam to Dick and he was hauled on board. Dick woke up a little later in the ship's saloon to find brandy being poured down his throat, which was quite pleasant. The ship's crew had already been sent away in the boats, so Dick gasped out to the Germans standing around him that his navigator was still in the water, requiring assistance.

In the meantime, the U-boat had surfaced again, and the conning-tower had barely been opened when Guy G——, in another of the Skuas, hove in sight. He came up on the other side of the *Fanad Head* to the submarine and didn't see it at first, as he was flying low over the water. He was trying to read the name on the freighter's bow when, with his approach, the other side of the ship was revealed to him and with surging exhilaration he, too, saw the submarine. He pulled up his nose instantly, selected his 100-lb. bomb, swung away for room to manœuvre then swung back, put his nose down and dived to bomb. When he was as low as he dared, he pressed the button.

After that there seemed to be a shattering explosion and the Skua's tail was apparently blown off. All Guy knows of the next few seconds is a vague memory of diving into the sea with no small violence, and he had to rely for the rest on what the Germans told him. Somehow, he doesn't know how—just another of those inexplicable, freakish things that happen—Guy found himself, considerably dazed, a few seconds later floating on the surface by the foaming, white cauldron where his Skua had gone in. There was no aircraft; not even a sign of it, apart from that bubbling white patch. Luckily he was not far from the ship and before long, he, too, was hauled on board, wet, bedraggled and crestfallen, like Dick.

The U-boat, of course, had submerged again when Guy first arrived, but presently there was a great cry from the anxious Germans on the *Fanad Head* as she surfaced again. Naturally the Germans were not taking any more chances on Skuas arriving, so Dick and Guy were promptly bustled over the side again into the sea near the U-boat. Rough hands lugged them both on board the submarine and they were more or less poured down the conning-tower. Without wasting time, the U-boat slid away from the *Fanad Head*, pooped a couple of torpedoes into her and began to submerge, just as the drone of engines heralded the arrival of the Swordfish squadron. They were just too late to get that very lucky U-boat. Dick, barely conscious and shivering violently, was lifted into a bunk in the bowels of the submarine and dimly remembers hearing reverberating explosions in the water as the Swordfish dropped their eggs all around the area in a vain effort to force the craft to the surface again.

A fortnight later, the U-boat berthed at her base in Wilhelmshaven. Dick and Guy were taken off and shortly after were whistled away to join the exiles in the grim old castle a few miles south of Kassel.

With similar occasional additions to their wretched family, 'Les Misérables' of Spangenburg passed the months of that strange period between peace and real war. A little mail was coming through by November, and in December the first clothing parcel from England arrived for Squadron-Leader Wank M——. November also saw the arrival of the early food parcels—first the odd private one and then those from the Red Cross. As an instance of how welcome the food parcels were to the lean and hungry kriegies, there is the case of Wank again, who received his first food parcel at 3 p.m. one fine afternoon, and by 6 p.m. he had polished off the lot, barring half a pound of tea and a bar of soap.

Round about March 1940, when the little family of Nazi 'guests' was growing in numbers, the Germans, looking to the future when business was to pick up, opened up Dulag Luft, a sort of transit camp for Air Force prisoners. It was at a little town called Oberursel, a few miles outside Frankfurt-on-Main, and consisted at first of a large house and a couple of small huts. In the house, apart from the German administrative staff, were some small cells, about ten feet by six, which a lot of Air Force prisoners got to know. Dick T—— and Guy, and also Wing-Commander Prickie Day were among a few officers taken from Spangenburg and sent to Dulag to act as British staff, where they did what they could to help the new boys after they had first been put through the German official welcoming machine, which consisted of a few days cooling the heels in solitary confinement in one of the cells, with next to nothing to eat, followed by an interrogation of varying menace and cunning.

After all that, the new boys were passed out and lived for a few days in the huts before being taken off to the permanent camps. They were not elegant, those huts, but at least, in them, the forlorn new boys thankfully found British company again—often old friends would meet there sometimes without knowing the other was shot down. They also found cigarettes there which they were usually craving for, and, for the first year or so, adequate supplies of 'hard likker' in which to drown their sorrows. After about a year, the grog supplies ran pretty dry and eventually petered out. A lot of it before it was finished, was pretty good stuff too, pinched by the Nazis in the rape of France, but after that had gone about the only stuff available in any camp in Germany was a pale, innocuous fluid called 'flieger' (flyer) beer. It was good exercise for the bladder, but a dead loss for anything else. Even then we only got a small issue of it about twice a year. It was an awful travesty of beer. So kriegydom, taken by and large, was a distressingly dry affair.

In April there was a rumbling of things to come, when the Norway campaign started. Inevitably, out of the vortex of the struggle eddied a few lost souls to augment kriegydom's Fleet Air Arm population.

But the R.A.F. took the grand award of all the stories from Norway, and the lone man who lived to tell it did not get away like the others, but duly arrived, somewhat damaged, at Dulag. You've probably often thought what a poor thing it would be to fall from an aircraft without a parachute. Well, Leading Aircraftsman George —— actually did it, and got away with it too! It was from no mean height, either, if 14,000 feet means anything. As blessed unconsciousness blacked out unpleasant

26

feelings for him, he is one of a select few in the world who can boast of a free fall of nearly three miles without a parachute and without turning a hair, or, for that matter, without considerably denting himself in the process. In point of fact he did suffer some hurts, but, with fitting craziness, they came from incidental sources.

He was a shortish, slim Welshman, with a jocund outlook that never seemed to waver, and when the Norway business started George was rear gunner in a Sunderland flying-boat. He was only an L.A.C. in rank then because that was before the days when all air crew became at least sergeants. One morning in that disturbing April of 1940, George was sitting quietly in his rear turret as the Sunderland took off for a long recce trip over Norway.

They were flying eventually about 14,000 feet over the wide white carpet of Norwegian snow, drawing quite a bit of attention from German flak. There were lots of dirty little stains of black smoke appearing magically in the air near them, and then an ominous tremor ran through the heavy flying-boat as a shell punched into her hull. Apparently they were hit in a vulnerable spot, for the airman's greatest enemy, fire, broke out. Before much could be done about it the flames were beyond control and spread with alarming swiftness through the hull. As was normal most of the crew were wearing standard observer type parachute harness, and some of their actual canopy packs were in a rack in the hull, right in the path of the spreading fire, so George pulled himself out of his turret and crawled back up the hull to try and save their last lifelines.

Unfortunately, the flames beat him to it and the canopy packs were quickly engulfed in crackling flame and choking smoke which spread inside the narrow, confined hull and drove George, coughing and with smarting eyes, back along the catwalk and into his turret. There wasn't much more he could do then, except sit there and twiddle his thumbs while he waited, helpless and considerably hopeless, for the sticky ending. Even an unremitting optimist like George would have sold out then, but there was more to come.

There was a blinding flash and a hefty explosion which blew George's turret, with him still inside, clean off the aircraft. Though it also burned off a lot of his face, George doesn't remember much about it, for he was in blissful oblivion. So down he fell, in the disintegrating fragments of his turret, down through the abyss of unresisting air, down and down and down.

The story should end with a sickening thud and spattered, mangled flesh, but it doesn't. At terminal velocity, George sank into a deep drift of heavy snow in the side of a steep mountain.

Some Norwegians had watched his sickening drop with horror and set out to find the body to identify it and give it decent burial. Hours and hours later they found it, still breathing gently in carefree unconsciousness many feet deep in the soft embrace of the drift. Bits of the turret were scattered in the near vicinity, also deep in snow.

George was doubly lucky when he was blown off, because the Sunderland piled into the deck a few miles further on in a welter of flame and the rest of the crew were killed instantly.

The Norwegians hauled George out of his snow bed and carried him back to hospital, where he eventually recovered consciousness, to find, ironically, that he had been both burnt and frozen. Ironically again, the snow that saved his life with one hand, so to speak, gave him one of his worst hurts with the other—frostbite. And that is how George lost bits of his ears.

Even though his good looks were somewhat moderated by his burns and frostbite, George never seemed to be noticeably abashed when he was at Dulag. He still had lots of energy and bags of cheerfulness. To help pass the time, he organized quite a successful mouth-organ band, and used to play football in long woollen underpants, like a relic of the Naughty Nineties, just for the fun of it. At Dulag, he became firm friends with a Sergeant D——, who had been gunner in a Blenheim. D—— was so impressed by George's story that he used to laugh at his own yarn and treat it as merely funny. His Blenheim had piled into the deck at about 250 m.p.h. and D—— had been tossed clean out. The sum total of his injuries was a broken little finger.

Maybe D—— was right at that. It certainly *was* funny.

Chapter Three

FRANCE COLLAPSES

O n the 10th of May 1940, the *adagio pianissimo* prelude to war ceased, and the Germans crashed into a full-throated first movement, *con grande moto*. They flung their massed might against the flank of the Maginot Line, near Sedan, broke through, and the show was on. The curtain was soon rung down on the first act, the Battle of the Bulge. It brought France to her knees; it brought Britain to the brink of defeat, and to the few lost souls in kriegydom, it brought stunned despair.

Inevitably, interwoven into the main theme of the crescendo of battle, were the sub-themes of miraculous escape, like capricious *cadenzas* of fantasy.

Take the case of Capitaine Larmier, who should have won a '*Croix de Bois*' on the first day of the battle. He was a fair-haired Frenchman, plump and aged a little over thirty. An artillery observation spotter attached to an *escadrille* of the French Army of the Air near the Maginot Line, he was therefore intimately concerned when the open season for total war began.

Low over the embittered fighting that morning swept a Potez 63, Type 11, a handsome and fast little twin-engined, French general-purposes aircraft. In the rear seat sat Capitaine Larmier, busy noting the course of the battle and not taking a great deal of notice of the hail of fire sizzling up from the ground. The Potez suddenly shuddered as a light flak shell slammed through the tail assembly, leaving this vital section somewhat bent. The pilot found he could not fully control his aircraft, which, already low, started to nose towards the ground.

Capitaine Larmier did not wait for the inevitable. At about ninety feet he threw himself over the side and immediately pulled his rip-cord.

It was, of course, a vain hope: parachutes don't even half open from ninety feet, but he pulled his D-ring just the same because he had nothing else to do.

The silk canopy was just streaming out of the pack when he hit—the top of a haystack, bounced a little, and then stayed put. He was winded, shocked, dumbfounded and semi-stunned. His mind went from a numbed hiatus to fumbling confusion as he wondered what sort of death this was. Then he sat up and saw where he was, and mere words just can't cope with his thoughts.

However mixed his feelings were then, they became a violent vortex a moment later when he saw his late aircraft. Relieved of his weight, the trim of the Potez was apparently restored, and the mortified and desolated Capitaine Larmier watched the machine pull up over the trees and vanish towards the French lines.

After being let down so lightly, his luck couldn't hold any longer. Haystack or no haystack, Capitaine Larmier was no needle, and the Germans soon found him. They took him back to five years 'in the bag', when there were times he cursed that fortuitous stack.

*   *   *

Out of the cauldron of the Battle of the Bulge came another strange story. It concerns a certain Flight-Lieutenant Paddy Byrne, who went to Dulag at that time, and its beginnings go back for quite a time—back to the years before the war.

On a grey London day in December 1935, two young men, aged about twenty-two, who had never seen each other before, climbed into the same compartment of a train in Paddington Station. Despite a dank fog that shrouded the platform like a wet blanket and the cold that was turning their ears blue, a bubbling joy was burning warmly in each of them.

One, who was tall and hefty and tanned, looked at the other and thought what an unlucky earth-bound mortal that other must be, as he, the tall and tanned one, had just joined the R.A.F. and was on his way to start flying training. And the other, short and nuggety, was thinking pityingly much the same of the tall and tanned man, because he, too, had just joined the R.A.F. and was also on his way to start flying training. Eventually, after a few cranky jolts and jerks, the train grudgingly got under way and went clickety-clacketing over the rails towards Bristol. They ran out of the fog into green country and grey skies, and, as is proper in English trains, first class, were about half way to Bristol by the time youthful enthusiasms had loosened tongues and they talked. There was a moment of comic surprise and pleasure when each discovered the other was also bound for the same flying school, on the same mission. And in that same moment started an association that merged strangely into one pattern and lasted for five and a half years, till it was broken by a shot that missed its target, but hit another—which was lucky for one of these two, unlucky for the other, and horribly unlucky for a lot of Germans.

The name of the short, nuggety one was Paddy Byrne, and he was the unlucky one. The tall, tanned young man, who was the lucky one, was A. G. Malan. You should know him very well, because he is now a famous man. He is more commonly known as 'Sailor', and he wears a lot of braid and 'gong' ribbon. Sailor had been in the Merchant Navy, hence, of course, his nickname, and came originally from South Africa. Paddy was obviously Irish and had one of the ripest brogues that ever came out of County Wicklow.

The two of them went on to Filton, the aerodrome of the Bristol Aeroplane Company, where they did their *ab initio* training at the civil flying school there. From Filton they both went together to the service flying school at Grantham. And in the same course at Grantham they met a slim, debonair young man called Bob Tuck, whose life thereafter became closely associated with theirs. Like Sailor (and for the same reason) Bob Tuck eventually became famous and also wore a lot of braid and ribbons. And like Paddy, he was eventually hacked down and went behind the same barbed wire.

In due course they passed out of Grantham as pilot-officers with short-service commissions, and all three went to the fighter station at Hornchurch, where Paddy and Sailor still stayed together. They went, not only to the same squadron, but also to the same flight of this squadron, which was distinguished by a well-known tiger's head crest and a dazzling record in the 1914–1918 war. This squadron enhanced its record considerably a few years later by top scoring in the Battle of Britain, led by none other than Sailor himself.

But that is another story and is going too far ahead. There were still three years of peace before war, and in these years Paddy and Sailor became very capable fighter-pilots. Then war broke out, and though the squadron was flying Spitfires there was no real business for them for quite a while, until eventually the storm broke on the 10th of May 1940, and the Battle of the Bulge thrust an ugly snout into France and began to nose towards Calais.

31

It was decided to send England-based Spitfires across to help in the struggle. So on the morning of May 21st, six Spitfires from the Tiger squadron took off from Southend and flew across the Channel to patrol over the retreating B.E.F. between Ostend and Calais. They flew in two independent vics of three. One of them was led by Flight-Lieutenant 'Sailor' Malan, and the other by Flight-Lieutenant Paddy Byrne. Apart from the trip a day or two earlier when they had escorted destroyers bringing the Dutch Royal Family out of Holland, it was their first real flight against the enemy and they were bubbling with exhilaration and expectation. Towards the end of the patrol, however, they had seen nothing and were feeling rather let down, so Paddy half expected it when he heard Sailor's voice over the R/T.

'Formate on me, Paddy, and we'll go inland and find some Jerries.'

Forthwith and gladly, Paddy swung his section across into the box position, just behind and below Sailor, and the six fighters headed south towards St. Omer. They were travelling fast and low, barely three hundred feet over the trundling, tenuous columns of the retreating army, when they came to a wood whose green expanse was suddenly pierced by brilliant crimson flashes, and then shells were whistling about them and they knew that for the first time they had crossed the front line.

In a few moments they were past and away, with no one hit. They ranged about over enemy-held territory for as long as petrol permitted, but saw little on the ground and no other aircraft in the air. Eventually they had to turn for home, and, still flying low and fast, they came, after a while, to what appeared to be the same wood, and once again bright jabs of red split the green and light flak came whistling up.

This time, one of the Spitfires rocked a little, streamed some black smoke and dropped behind the formation, nosing down. It was Paddy. Three light shells had slammed into the belly of his aircraft—one into the engine, one into the tail section, and a third which hit dead centre, came up into the cockpit, smashed the rudder-bar and scored a deep gash in Paddy's left leg. He felt the warm gush of blood as his Spitfire headed down in a steep glide which he could not check as both fore and aft controls and rudder had gone, owing to the hits in the tail and rudder-bar.

The aircraft, travelling at about 250 miles an hour, hit a clear field and bounced steeply up again. Because of its momentum it climbed to about 300 feet once more, and then again headed down. Helpless in the cockpit, Paddy had decided to jump for it and had undone his straps, but then he had to give up the idea as he was too low. The Spitfire hit again in another clear field, and as it ploughed a spectacular furrow both wings snapped off as she kicked her tail into the air. Paddy was thrown forward and out, bashing his face *en route* on the windscreen, which is the reason Paddy's nose is now a little dented.

He lobbed in a dazed heap near the twisted wreck of his Spitfire and before he could do much about anything was surrounded by Germans from the flak battery who had hurried to the spot on motor-cycles. They took him back to the battery, where he was given some rather galling information. After the customary greeting, as 'For you the war is over', and 'So glad you weren't killed', the officer in charge apologized for bringing Paddy down, because, as a matter of fact, he explained, they had been aiming not at him, but at the leading aircraft.

That, of course, was Sailor, who got back to base unscathed, who then went on to brilliant success as a fighter-pilot with over thirty victories, who rose to command the Tiger Squadron during the Battle of Britain, who rose then to command a wing, then became a group-captain, and was deservedly five times decorated for gallantry and skill.

And Paddy went on to a nearby house to have his wounds dressed and to four years of quiet hell. The association that had seemed unbreakable was severed, suddenly and brutally, and Paddy became the first Spitfire fighter-pilot shot down over enemy territory.

The house to which they took him for dressings had recently been shelled, and in the room they took him to was the dead body of a woman, and the body of a man lying half under the pile of bricks and debris of a collapsed wall. A dog, with its insides hanging out, was scrabbling around, whimpering in agony. It was a cruel introduction to war.

For two days after that Paddy travelled with a fleet of about thirty ambulances, which stayed with the front-line troops until they were filled up, and then he was taken back some miles into Belgium and placed in a temporary field prisoner's cage—just a bare field, with a single strand of barbed wire around it and soldiers with machine-guns on the outside.

They were bringing hundreds of wounded men in—mostly Belgians —and a couple of overworked Belgian doctors were doing what they could for them. They had a crude operating-table fixed up in the open air. It was just a door standing on two barrels, and on it they were doing major operations, including a lot of rough amputations. Men were dying in hundreds and the bodies were laid out in rows in the adjoining field.

Paddy decided immediately that he had had the place and did not wish to stay. There was a short, stocky young Belgian who brought water into the compound in buckets, and on the second day Paddy saw his chance. The Belgian had taken off his coat in the heat while he gave out the water, and Paddy, who was about the same size, tried it on. It fitted well, so he picked up one of the empty buckets and headed for freedom. At the gate the guard stopped him, but Paddy, who could blarney his way past Saint Peter, convinced the German in schoolboy French that he was the Belgian water-carrier and passed out and away.

He headed immediately for the coast and the British lines, along roads and through villages scarred with the passing of war. From deserted houses he dressed himself in abandoned civilian clothes and found scraps of food. In one of them he had a stroke of luck and found a torch and a bicycle, which he cheerfully mounted and rode away along a main road choked with German tanks, infantry and heavy transport.

As he rode, however, dozens of Germans shouted angrily at him. They shook their fists, and, though he couldn't make out what they were saying, seemed to be cursing him and waving him to stop. With a tremor of dismay he looked over his clothes and bicycle and wondered how he had given himself away, how they knew he was British. Was the game up again? Yet no one seemed to be chasing him, and no one actually tried to stop him. So he rode on and ignored the shouts and shaking fists. And as he rode the cries and gestures continued to be hurled at him, but still no one actually tried to stop him. He covered five miles like that in nervous bewilderment, until suddenly, comically, he saw the light.

As befits a good British subject, he was riding sedately on the left of the road, and on the Continent one keeps to the right. Amiably he doffed his cap to the cursing Germans, veered to the right and rode cheerfully on.

After three days Paddy neared a village on the banks of the Somme River and heard firing. Parking his bike in a ditch, he hid himself near the village, which he later learned was Bray-sur-Somme, and saw German machine-gun detachments firing across the river. He had found his objective. Once across the river he would be safe again.

When darkness fell that night, Paddy crawled up to the village and snaked his way over the back wall of a house which fronted a main street. The river bank was only a few hundred yards away across a field and he wanted bearings to get to an unfrequented spot on the bank for his swim to safety. He also wanted food. With his torch, he crept into the house, which seemed to be empty, and found the kitchen. Then he quickly stepped back in fuming frustration. Inside the room a huge dog, chained to a cupboard, grinned in hateful fury at him, snarled and broke into sustained, deep-throated barking.

Paddy tried his infallible blarney again and the dog barked louder and longer. The racket aroused the suspicions of Germans near the house and the first warning Paddy received was a banging outside and a crash as the front door gave in. Silently and swiftly he hared up the stairs as heavy footsteps thudded into the passage.

He heard them moving downstairs, and then heard their jackboots thumping up the stairs. With a helpless, cornered feeling he sidled into a front room. There was a bed there and Paddy dived under it, with the sinking certainty that it was just a gesture. The footsteps halted on the landing, moved uncertainly for a few moments, then clumped into Paddy's room and walked straight up to the bed.

Pop-eyed and quaking, Paddy saw two heavy jackboots stop about six inches from his nose, and resigned himself to capture. The German thumped the bed, muttered something in German to a comrade in the doorway, turned and walked out again.

Slightly dizzy with relief Paddy heard them leave the house and emerge into the street before he left the shelter of the bed. He crawled out, then in a cupboard of the room found a handsome new jacket which fitted him, so he took it and discarded his old one. He gave up the idea of food and determined to swim the Somme forthwith. Then he found a bucket of water and plunged in his hands for a wash. In the water he felt something hard and round, and pulled it out. It was an egg: the bucket was half full of them. God seemed to be standing by, so raw though they were, Paddy made a weighty meal, had a wash and set off for the river.

He snaked his way back over the fence of the house, and with bearings he had taken from the upper storey, set a creeping course across the field and came eventually to a small embankment, just on the other side of which he could hear the gurgling water of the river. At that point he stopped, lay doggo without moving a muscle, and listened tensely for several minutes. There wasn't a sound, so he quickly pulled himself to the top of the embankment and slid down the other side—right into the arms of a German machine-gun detachment.

There was no escape this time. Rough grasping hands held a horribly shocked Paddy before he quite realized what had happened. The machine-gunners must have heard his early approach, because they had made not the slightest sound for some minutes as they waited for him.

They promptly escorted Paddy to their barracks, where, sick with disappointment, he made a game last stand. In his shaky French, which was better than the Germans could do, he declared he was a French farmer who was trying to get to his wife, stranded across the river. The Germans reserved strong doubts and took Paddy to a nearby château, which was some sort of an H.Q., and where there was a French collaborationist. There was no hope of sustaining his story before a real Frenchman, so Paddy grudgingly gave it up and told his true story of being shot down. He was thereupon locked in a small, bare cellar for the remainder of the night.

Next morning, he was haled into a fine, sunlit room of the château before a stiff German general, who looked the approved Prussian type, complete with monocle. There was a touch of farcical unreality when an interpreter was produced—a German soldier who had lived most of his life in Golders Green and who spoke with a classic Cockney accent.

But Paddy wasn't amused. Dispiritedly he told his true story again, while details were checked with his previous account of a few hours earlier. Then the general spoke a few words and the interpreter turned to Paddy.

"'E says they've rung the flak battery and they sye they've never 'eard of you,' he said, disapprovingly.

'Oh, don't be damn silly,' said Paddy wearily. 'Ring 'em again. You probably had a wrong number.'

The general spoke a few more curt words, and the interpreter turned to Paddy again.

'They got the right battery, orl right,' he said, 'Yer in a spot, myte. If yer carn't tell a better story than that, they're a'goin ter shoot yer.'

A cold fear settled on Paddy. Wildly, vainly he protested, but they wouldn't listen and he was abruptly returned to his cell, bewildered and shaken. Something had gone wrong. It was absurd. Why should the flak battery deny his downfall? They should be boasting of it. He thought, and thought, and thought, until a tired brain revolted in confusion and the only emotion left was a sickening, helpless fear that lasted through an endless day and a longer, grimmer night.

Next morning, a guard, holding a drawn revolver, opened his door and beckoned Paddy to accompany him. Paddy braced himself, took a deep quivering breath and walked out to meet death. He was put into a car with guards on each side, and one standing just behind—all with drawn Mausers pointing their hollow ends at Paddy's ribs. He thought it was the end.

The car took them for some distance, with Paddy expecting them to pull up at any moment, give him the 'works' and toss the body out. Eventually, however, they pulled up at a courthouse which was being used by the Germans as an H.Q. Paddy was ordered out and once more haled before a general—a different one, this time, with a full field court of inquiry.

With a slight dawning of hope, he told his story again, while the general sheafed through some papers. Then the general looked un-emotionally at Paddy's guards and said, surprisingly, in English:

'Let him wait another day.'

Paddy's dawning hopes crashed, and in the reaction his agony of dread hit a new low as he was hustled away to a tiny, concrete cell. In that bare hole, with a tiny, flat grating of steel bars let into the ceiling, Paddy passed another grim day and grimmer night.

At dawn, he was lying sleepless and sweating, when he heard heavy footsteps ringing along the stone corridor, and cold fright again shook his abject wretchedness. There was the clink of a key in the lock, and then the door swung open and a stern-faced German officer faced him.

'Komm mit,' he said.

No other word was spoken, and for the second time in twenty-four hours Paddy went out to meet violent death. Two soldiers with rifles and bayonets were waiting in the corridor. Wordlessly they fell in on each side of him and the silent four walked out of the courthouse into the road, and turned up to the left. After a hundred yards they came to a bridge over a canal, and Paddy thought, with tightened lips:

'This is the spot. Here it comes.'

And suddenly he didn't feel frightened any more. He didn't care what they did. He wasn't even faintly perturbed. He didn't give a tuppenny damn if the whole German Army turned on him and smashed him with every bullet, bomb, and shell they had—which in those days was considerable. He felt placid and carefree, and then a little exhilarated. He was even amused when nothing happened at the bridge and they turned off up the bank of the canal. After a time the officer halted, and Paddy, with detached calm, thought again that this was 'it'.

Again he was wrong. The officer moved off again, turned into a

37

nearby wood—and this time Paddy was certain. And still he didn't care. He even thought, as they tramped through the undergrowth:

'God! What fools these people are. What absurd pains they go to.'

And then they came to the far edge of the field, and the officer, who was in front, pointed ahead. Peering past him, Paddy saw a Fieseler Storch, light German communication aircraft. The pilot was waiting by it, and before he quite knew what was happening, Paddy was bundled in and they had taken off.

The Storch landed at an aerodrome in the Siegfried Line, and Paddy was taken to another H.Q., where he spent a tedious, but not terrified twenty-four hours in another cell. Next day, ragged and dirty, with a week's growth of beard and dressed in the shabby, stained civilian clothes he had purloined, he was brought before another court of inquiry and yet another German general, who browsed through a file of papers, then looked up at Paddy and said in English:

'When we first investigated your story, we got in touch with the flak battery you mentioned. Unfortunately, they had split into two parts for operational purposes and we spoke to the wrong part. Since then we have been in touch with the other part, which was moving up on Dunkirk, and they have confirmed your story. You will henceforth be treated as an officer prisoner and go into Germany.'

So, without much emotion either way, Paddy was taken back to the Storch and flown to Dulag Luft at Oberursel, where he had another strange experience.

At Dulag, there was a room that was rather well known among Air Force kriegies as the 'operations room'. Around the walls are rather smart paintings of a variety of French dancing girls—very attractive, very colourful, and slightly naughty. They were done by a Frenchman who signed himself 'Nicol'. He had been a test pilot at the big Potez factory near Bray-sur-Somme before he was caught in the battle.

Nicol was at Dulag when Paddy arrived, and in due course, as new kriegies do, they swapped stories of their capture. Paddy came to the part where he reached Bray-sur-Somme and Nicol looked extremely interested. He told how he had crawled into a house, and Nicol broke in curiously:

'What house was this?'

Paddy told him, and described the house, and Nicol laughed delightedly.

'Mon Dieu! That was my *pension* when I was a test pilot,' he said incredulously.

Paddy described his narrow escape under the bed.

'What room was that?' asked Nicol excitedly, and Paddy told him.

'Nom de Dieu! That was my old room,' cried the Frenchman amazedly.

'Well, for Pete's sake,' said Paddy. 'I pinched a coat from the wardrobe in that room.'

'Show me, show me,' yelled Nicol, hopping with excitement.

So Paddy showed him, and it really was Nicol's coat.

*   *   *

About this stage of the war, business in the prisoner of war line was expanding rapidly in Germany. Stocks of both British and French of all three services were in glut supply and storage premises obviously had to be enlarged. To cope with the increasing numbers of R.A.F. prisoners, the Germans opened a new camp at Barth, on the Baltic Sea near Rostock, to which they moved fifty R.A.F. and Fleet Air Arm officers from Spangenburg.

The camp was under Luftwaffe control and from that time on Air Force prisoners invariably lived under the watchful eyes of Luftwaffe guards, not only at Barth, which grew to be quite a big camp, but also at a series of other camps that were later opened.

There were a lot of pretty ripe hard-luck stories among the new kriegies anent the way they were shot down, and the little word 'if' figured largely in quite a few. There was, for instance, a slim youth who became tangled up with the spearhead of the advancing Germans in France and had a hectic time trying to race ahead of them for nearly a month before his luck gave out. At one stage of his flight, the Germans unwittingly gave him a lift; at another, they nearly shot him.

He was Eric Jones, a pleasantly spoken young Hurricane pilot whose tangled thickets of brown hair tumbled over his eyes like a Skye terrier. A couple of 109's hacked his Hurricane down near Montreuil on the 10th of June 1940, and Eric jumped from his pranged kite and ran for it, finding himself in the middle of the advancing German spearhead. He got hold of some civilian clothes and a tattered old French smock from a farmhouse and joined a party of refugees trudging along the road for Arras. He plodded along with them for several days, begging food in a variety of villages passed on the way, met three Tommies, also trying to get back, and with them reached the Somme River.

They hid up in a deserted village for three days waiting for a chance

to cross the river and penetrate the German lines, and eventually purloined a German officer's motor-launch and reached the other bank.
As they were scrambling out of the launch, German soldiers opened
fire on them from a nearby road and almost the first shot neatly severed
the heel of one of Eric's shoes. They got away, crawling through long
grass, but shortly after that, Eric became separated from the three
Tommies and continued on alone, making, now, for Cherbourg, where
British troops were still holding out, according to a farmer who
directed him.

From another farmhouse, Eric bought a bicycle for 370 francs, rode
it for about one kilometre and then it collapsed under him. He dis-
gustedly threw it into the ditch and walked on. At a village near
Lisieux, a German guard suddenly confronted him and asked for his
papers. Eric told him in schoolboy French he lived in a nearby house
and the guard let him walk into the house to get his papers. Eric
walked straight out through the back and away again.

He went through Lisieux and Caen, and at Bayeux went into a small
café for a meal. A minute later, a motor-cycle pulled up outside and a
German Obergefreiter (lance corporal) entered. He was a friendly,
voluble soul and sat down beside Eric while waiting for his meal. Eric
pretended he was French, and got away with it, though the German
spoke better French than his schoolboy version. They chatted uncomfortably for a few minutes and the German pulled out photographs of
his wife and children which Eric tactfully admired. On the subject of
politics, the German soldier said what a brute Chamberlain was and
wanted to know why he should have to fight because of Chamberlain's
warmongering. Eric discreetly agreed again. He was posing as a de-
mobilized French soldier returning to his home at Cherbourg.

After his meal the German soldier went back to his motor-cycle to
resume his journey. He kicked the self-starter and nothing happened.
Again he kicked, and again and again, and still nothing happened. Eric,
who was rather an authority on motor-cycles, wandered out and told
the German he was probably having carburettor trouble. Between
them the two soon had it fixed and the engine chortled away happily.
The grateful Obergefreiter beamed warmly at Eric.

'I, too, to Cherbourg am going,' he said. 'On the back jump, and I
the lift to Cherbourg will give you.'

So Eric nipped on the pillion and eventually the German dropped
him on the outskirts of Cherbourg, by which time, of course, Eric
realized that there were no free British soldiers left in the city. He

branched off down the west coast of the Cherbourg Peninsula, his plan then being to 'win' a boat from somewhere and cross to Alderney, in the Channel Islands. He was nearly caught trying to purloin, single-handed, a large coastal barge at St. Valerie, and then scuttled off down the coast to Cartaret, where he succeeded in commandeering a small fishing-smack, rowed it outside the harbour, raised the sail and set course for Alderney. It took him fourteen hours, and his twenty-second birthday dawned while he was in the boat.

At sunrise there was an enormous number of aircraft flying overhead out to sea, and Eric wondered vaguely what it was all about. He found out when he arrived at the islands. He had seen the airborne invasion of the Channel Group and found himself in enemy-held territory once more. Again he was lucky, received help from the inhabitants and hid up in a barn for a week, but on the 7th of July, twenty-seven days after he had been shot down, Germans suddenly entered the barn and the game was up, Eric was captured and went on into kriegydom.

Not long after that little sidelight of sorrow, Charlie Bowman added another rather harrowing tale to the lugubrious list of gall. Luckily, he had the temperament to take it, mostly with a grin, though after four years of rather unnecessary captivity the grin was occasionally a bit lop-sided. Still, Charlie was essentially a cheerful bloke, with a full, round face that beamed cordially on friend and stranger alike. He was a pilot-officer and gunner of a Hampden that went to bomb Kiel on the 21st of July 1940. About 5,000 feet over the harbour, they were well caught by several searchlights and went twisting and turning all over the place until they were down to about 500 feet and still the searchlights held them and flak was bursting all round them in a venomous and accurate concentration, kicking up quite a din.

They must have been hit several times when the pilot's voice came over the intercom. to Charlie.

'Jump! Bowman! Jump for it!'

They were dangerously low and there wasn't much time, but Charlie found he couldn't open his hatch to get out. He called back over the intercom. that it was jammed but there was no reply from the pilot, so Charlie heaved at the hatch again in a sweat until suddenly it opened and he tumbled out. His parachute just opened in time but he landed heavily and broke his left leg.

The Germans who found him told him the Hampden had dived into the sea just after he had baled out. There was no sign of the rest of the crew, so during the next few weeks in hospital, Charlie miserably thought they had all bought it. Then he went on to Dulag and about the first person he met there when he came out of his cell was Tim Muir, navigator of the Hampden.

'Why, hullo, Tim,' beamed Charlie gladly. 'So you got out of the kite, O.K. It's good to see you. What happened to the rest?'

Tim looked as though he were seeing a ghost.

'Got out of the kite?' he echoed. 'Gosh man! The skipper got the kite back under control just after you'd baled out and we all got home that night. I joined another crew then and was shot down on a later raid. The rest are still in England.'

And that is why Charlie sometimes gnashed his teeth in the following five years.

Chapter Four

HERMIT OF THE OASIS

With all hopes of victory and freedom toppling about their ears in that doleful spring, the early kriegies naturally developed a fulsome hatred of Italy for her 'stab in the back' entry into the war. This general hatred was a drop in the ocean compared to the bitterness felt by Flying-Officer James M——. He considered—and with undeniable justification—that Italy had given him a personal and private stab in the back, for he was captured by the Italians eleven days before Mussolini declared war on Great Britain, and was condemned to become, for four and a half months, the loneliest prisoner of war in the world. His concentration camp was a tiny oasis on the Libyan-Saharan border, with 1,000 miles of desert between him and the nearest point of civilization.

James had seen active service long before war broke out, for his squadron was engaged in helping suppress the revolts in Palestine. When the peace barometer began falling in '39, his squadron, caught in the flap that was general at that time, was moved no fewer than fourteen times, before finally coming to rest near Mersah Matruh, where James, who had been recovering from an appendicitis operation, rejoined them. His late arrival made him odd man out for a time, so it happened quite naturally that when Middle East Air H.Q. wanted a recce made for landing-grounds in the desert east of Matruh, James was given the job. It had to be done by truck at a time of the year when violent, blinding sandstorms swept the desert.

He set out with a little caravan of trucks and traversed the dreary desert for weeks on end, looking for suitable stretches of firm flat ground. He returned eventually, but in April was sent back to the desert to explore the region around Sollum. This time he came upon a salt-pan that would be suitable for six months out of the year. He was ordered to go ahead and make it serviceable for aircraft, and for the next three weeks he supervised the activities of a gang of Arabs.

That job done he was told to recce more territory around Sollum, so on the 31st of May he and his driver were bumping blissfully over the empty, undulating sand when a fusillade of rifle shots brought them to a sudden and astonished stop. The next minute they were surrounded by an Italian military patrol and without further ado James and his driver were taken to Fort Capuzzo and officially 'interned'. That evening James was taken to Bardia and lodged in a noisome cell in the local jail. Later he was transferred to a half-completed building and locked in a room containing only a bed and a chair. The curtains were drawn across the only window and he was ordered not to open it. For eight days he remained in this bare, semi-dark room.

He was beginning to get more than a trifle soured off when he was suddenly taken out at midnight, put into a tiny Fiat car together with two enormously fat Italian officers who took absurd precautions to ensure he did not escape, and driven off into the desert. All night they travelled and the next morning, tired and stiff, he was taken out at Derna and given food. Then back into the car and another uncomfortable journey across the desert. They ended up at Benghazi, where he spent the night in a cavalry barracks. He was befriended by an amiable Italian colonel who showed him his horses, but studiously avoided discussion of the political situation.

Later James became a passenger in an Italian air liner, making its last civilian journey from Benghazi to Tripoli. He arrived there on the 10th of June. For him the day had no special significance, until exactly six hours later when he was taken from the military barracks to Italian H.Q. Here he was ushered into the room of the official interpreter, who, with a self-important air, said to him in clipped, precise English,

'I have to inform you, on behalf of the Governor of Libya, General Balbo, that, Italy having declared war on Great Britain at 6.30 this evening, you are now a prisoner of war. The General, as a fellow-pilot, wishes to express to you his sympathy, for he can understand your feelings at being prevented so early in the war from flying against us. Have you any last request?'

If the strange developments of the past eleven days surprised James, he did not show it, for his startled mind was wondering just what the significance was of the words, 'last request'.

'I would like my family informed and also Middle East Air Headquarters,' he replied mechanically.

'That will be done,' said the interpreter, and then surprisingly, handed him ten pounds in lire and 400 cigarettes—'to help you until your country is able to support you.'

Early next morning a black civilian car arrived at the barracks and James, heavily guarded, together with his driver, set out across the desert in the direction from which they had come. At Misurata they turned due south and for the whole of that day they jolted across a desert track, leaving all traces of civilization behind.

At evening they arrived at Bu Ngem, a fort of medieval design, standing absolutely alone in the desert. They spent the night here and next morning continued the mysterious journey, farther and farther south. After hours and hours of acute discomfort they reached the oasis of Hon, which lies on the border of the Saharan Desert and which was a headquarters of the Italian Carabinieri, who policed that desolate wasteland.

The oasis itself was a beautiful, cool, green smudge on an endless expanse of scorching sand that shimmered and danced in eternal heat. James was taken into a small mud fort and shown a sparsely furnished room which, he was told, was to be his. It looked out on a small courtyard, beyond which lay the main fort, while on the other side was an Arab village.

Utterly alone—his driver was lodged in some other part of the fort —James surveyed his future. It was not cheerful. He had not the slightest clue as to how long he was to remain here; the sum total of his reading matter comprised a pocket Shakespeare; his companions, other than his driver, were a handful of Italian soldiery, separated from him by the wide gulf of language. As far as the world was concerned he had disappeared, completely and utterly.

Man has an infinite capacity for adapting himself, however, and it was not long before James was winning the battle against boredom and loneliness. He found endless entertainment in watching insects, of which there was no lack in this forsaken corner of the world. With all the zest of a professional naturalist he made an intense study of their habits and started collecting specimens; one of them—a hideous outsized scorpion—remained with him until the end of his kriegy life. He learnt his pocket Shakespeare off by heart and to keep his English from going rusty started declaiming long passages aloud, choosing for an audience an unresponsive palm-tree. He never regarded this part of his life as wasted for the experience he gained made him, later, a valuable member of kriegy theatrical companies. The smallest deviation from the deadly daily routine was a landmark in his life and James remembers, with deep affection, two gazelles, prisoners like himself, which he was able to befriend. Feeding them with tit-bits became the major pleasure of his life.

For four and a half months James lived at Hon. He was beginning to despair of ever returning to civilization, he had only the vaguest idea of how the war was progressing, and the little he knew didn't make him particularly happy. Britain was facing invasion—the war seemed as if it were going to last a lifetime.

One day, however, he was informed that he would be leaving the next morning. He was given no hint of his destination but that was the least of his worries. The journey across the bumpy desert trail, normally a nightmare, was an exciting adventure to James and when he arrived once more at Tripoli he felt as if he had been reborn. He was taken to the local gaol where he met a group of British officers who had been captured in recent desert fighting. With them James sailed for Italy and helped to establish the first prisoner of war camp in Italy at Sulmona in the heart of the Apennines.

He rusticated with quiet fury in Italy for the next three years and then at last, just when freedom was within his grasp on the collapse of Italy in September 1943, his luck maintained its usual rock-bottom standard and he was grabbed by the Germans along with many others and haled off to Stalag Luft III in Germany.

As a matter of fact, James' luck *did* change when, about a year after that, he managed to bluff his way past the Medical Repatriation Board and got himself sent back to England.

But way back a bit, just about the time when he was first getting used to the lonely oasis of Hon, the shouting and the tumult was dying in France. Dunkirk came and went and then the French were wriggling under the German jackboot and Italian dancing pump. As kriegy food parcels and mail used to come through France, via Switzerland, there followed a rather dreadful hiatus in the arrival of both mail and extra food that lasted for a year before the Red Cross could get organized and send the stuff regularly through other channels to Switzerland, and so on to the starved kriegies in Germany. It was mid-1941 before prisoners' mail and parcels services were properly restored, and it was high time, too, for by then mild scurvy was rife among the wretched young men whose ribs were sticking through their skin. Hair was falling out and teeth were loosening in gums. They suffered from extreme lassitude, and experienced dizziness and black-out spells if they got up too quickly from their bunks, where they lay apathetically for most of the day.

So much for the Geneva Convention according to Nazi interpretation. Under its provisions, the Germans were supposed to give prisoners the same rations as their garrison troops, but the garrison troops never seemed to suffer from malnutrition. We worked out once that they fed us on 1s. 2d. a week. The ration was usually a sixth of a loaf of bread a day (about four slices), a few potatoes (though not always), less barley and a token offering of jam, sugar, and margarine. About once a month there would be a little meat, and occasionally a few scrawny vegetables. All in all, serving a long and indefinite sentence in a barren, barbed-wire jail on little hope and less food was not very funny.

(Towards the end, incidentally, these rations were cut even further —and then things really WERE unpleasant.)

If you've ever known hunger, not just keen appetite, but real gnawing hunger, you'll understand why the stoppage of food parcels gave an added zest to the attempts by prisoners to escape. Not that they needed any extra incentive. It was about the first thing all of them thought of when they first came down and it was never very far from the thoughts of all prisoners.

Just about the time then when hunger was becoming not so much a nuisance as a nightmare, the first heartening success in the escaping line of business occurred at Dulag Luft near Frankfurt where Wing-Commander Prickie Day and his staff, in addition to welcoming new R.A.F. kriegies, were taking surreptitious steps to deprive themselves of the hospitality of the Third and Last Reich. They had formed themselves into several teams and set to work at the old kriegy custom of digging tunnels. About three tunnels were attempted, quite simple and elementary jobs in those inexperienced days, but the Germans were also inexperienced at finding them and one of the tunnels was a success. Guiding lights of that little effort were Paddy Byrne (you heard all about Paddy in Chapter Three—the incident of the Spitfire, Sailor Malan and the Frenchman's coat) and Mike Casey, whom we have also mentioned before as one of the first thirteen R.A.F. prisoners and later murdered by the Gestapo in the mass break from Stalag Luft III in 1944.

One night in July 1940, this first Dulag tunnel was broken out into the open on the right side of the wire and twenty-four of the Dulag Luft prisoners crawled through and away in a bid for freedom. As well as Paddy and Mike, some notable gentlemen of the escaping business were among them. Prickie Day was there and also 'The Dodger', an Army major with a D.S.O. and M.C. from the last war who had been caught in this war in France, but only after he had swum nearly half-way across the Channel in a very game bid to get away, a pretty sound effort as the Dodger was no chicken. The Dodger was for a time, another of those missing from the Stalag Luft III tunnel in 1944. Jimmy Buckley was another of the twenty-four. He was one of the first to organize escapes on a big scale. A naval lieutenant-commander, he got away again from a camp at Schubin a couple of years later with a Danish R.A.F. officer. The Dane's body was later reported washed up in the Baltic and Jimmy Buckley's ultimate fate is a mystery.

But the most notable member of those first twenty-four escapees was Squadron-Leader Roger Bushell, South African born former London barrister and commander of the R.A.F.'s most successful fighter squadron until he was shot down over the beaches of Dunkirk in May 1940. He was a genius. It was Roger Bushell who, from 1942 to 1944, organized and commanded the Stalag Luft III 'X' Organization in which 500 men worked for fifteen months to break out a tunnel over 350 feet long and 30 feet deep. Under his leadership those 500 did fantastic things, not only in the tunnelling, though details of that are fantastic enough, but also in such allied illicit pursuits as forgery, security, map and compass production, tailoring, and so on. He was unquestionably the greatest organizer of prison camp escapes in the war.

However, getting back to that first simple tunnel at Dulag Luft, the full fruits of success were not plucked at all on that occasion.

When Roger Bushell got out that night, he and a comrade made their way as far as the Swiss border. The comrade was recaptured, Roger Bushell was nearly trapped in a marsh, evaded his pursuers, was shot at and finally recaptured. All the rest of the twenty-four were rounded up and turfed smartly behind barbed wire again. Still, it was a start. Valuable experience had been won, and probably more than anything, the kriegies had tasted blood. Strange things were to follow.

Meantime, prisoners were still starving.

Chapter Five

ORDEAL BY FIRE

―――――

They were pretty haggard with hunger and misery when news of a couple of classic suicide bombing raids in the next couple of months let in the first ray of sunshine. They were the raid on the Dortmund-Ems Canal and the pranging of the *Tirpitz*. Details were brought to camps in Germany by the odd survivor—men who survived those shows *had* to be odd.

The *Tirpitz* affair was the first. It came in July 1940, just after France had collapsed and there didn't seem to be any future in things. Back in the thick of the war a lot of situations had suddenly cropped up demanding considerably urgent attention and an R.A.F. that was still quite small had to rely more on dash and cunning than on brute strength. So it became the season of the 'shaky do'.

One of these situations requiring attention was the question of sea-power. Even in their barbed wire backwater, kriegies could see what would happen if Hitler got his hands on the French Fleet. In point of fact they were in an unpleasantly good position to have the consequences emphasized to them. German morale was never, could never be, higher. They thought, with no small cause, that with France fallen and England about to fall, the war was already over, and made loud noises of rejoicing. Prisoners got the full blast at short range, which was disconcerting.

Nazi newspapers spread their front pages with screaming black banners, bells pealed, whistles hooted, and processions marched and capered. It was all rather like Boat Race Saturday. Everybody beamed except the prisoners, and for all their outward confidence they were only human and couldn't help feeling shaken. Sometimes it *did* seem as though it really were the British swan song they were carolling outside.

Some of the Germans who were in contact with prisoners were arrogant and offensive, and others were boisterously good humoured and pitying, which was even more maddening and humiliating. Such for instance as the Feldwebel (sergeant) who said:

'Of course it's such a pity you're going to try and fight on in England: such a waste of your time and lives. We thought you had more sense.'

So it was no wonder this question of sea-power was worrying. And if it worried kriegies so much, they thought it was a safe enough bet that the Admiralty people would also be having the odd headache, because with the French and Italian Fleets and their own, the Germans would have something like numerical naval parity, or even superiority over the R.N., which was already grossly overworked. As communications were our flimsy life line, the result would be the obvious one. According to prisoners' reasoning, there must be a limit, even to what the R.N. can do. The policy clearly appeared to be—'Smash as much of the enemy navy as possible, and at any cost.'

And that was where Dave D—— came in, and why he went to Wilhelmshaven, and eventually into Kriegsgefangenenschaft (which means kriegydom) after he had put up a dazzling effort.

He went to Wilhelmshaven to deal with the *Tirpitz*, brand spanking new Nazi battleship. To start her off well she had just been officially blessed by Adolf Hitler himself and some of the bunting she wore for the occasion was still draped about her superstructure as she lay in her dock at Wilhelmshaven.

It was decided to drop mines under her: such a simple solution, except that defences were so arranged that that sort of thing couldn't be done. Which was where the dash and cunning came in, because the R.A.F. powers-that-be thought that maybe it could be done.

Three Hampdens were loaded with mines timed to explode an hour after being dropped. Dave D——, a serious young man with a lean and brown face, was to skipper one of them. At twenty-seven, he was quite a veteran, having become discontented with accountancy back in 1935, when he joined the R.A.F. with the first batch of direct entry sergeant-pilots. He was one of the odd couple of original pilots left in his squadron which was formed in 1937. Shortly after war broke out he was commissioned and developed a rather imposing moustache. It was one of those bushy black jobs and hid a considerable area of lip. With his grave brown features it made Dave look like a cabinet minister of no small importance and dignity.

About the only way to make sure of dropping mines right under or against the *Tirpitz* was to do it from nought feet, and the three Hampdens were briefed accordingly. It sounded like an elaborate method of suicide because the *Tirpitz* and surrounding harbour were almost smothered in flak guns, but it was here that the cunning was produced. Other aircraft were briefed to attack the harbour from high level to engage the flak, and under this side-show the Hampdens were to go round to the north of the city at nought feet from the sea, and then pelt up to the *Tirpitz* in the docks over the rooftops of the town, getting, in that way, as much cover as was possible from the flak. On paper it looked just barely possible.

So at eight minutes past ten on the 20th of July 1940, Dave D——— took off from Hemswell aerodrome with two heavy mines in his bombracks, and soberly headed into a bright, moonlit night.

Luck was against him early in the piece for unexpected wind conditions upset the co-ordination of the raid and the diversion raid, and when Dave swept in from the North Sea just a few feet over the white lace of the shore and swung the Hampden south over the northern part of Wilhelmshaven towards the basin, the diversion raid was finished and the concentrated flak batteries were again watchful on their main task—protection of the valuable ships in the docks.

They located Dave's Hampden just as he straightened up for the sticky run up to the *Tirpitz* across the rooftops. Within a few seconds every gun that could be brought to bear was throwing a vicious barrage low across the roofs, right in his path, and Dave's lips tightened under his heavy moustache. He looked more serious than ever, and possibly not quite so brown. There was no missing those shooting, searing lines of red tracer, and as the Hampden, travelling fast on full bore, swept into the thick of it, shell after shell slammed into her. There was a dreadful jolting and a bedlam of jarring explosions in the narrow fuselage.

By some sort of a miracle the mines didn't go off, but the petrol-tanks did—not with a deafening bang, but with the tearing, husky 'whoosh' that riven tanks give. Shooting runnels of liquid fire sluiced along the main spar and sprayed upwards, cascading into crimson flower inside the fuselage. From Dave's armour plate towards the tail everything suddenly seemed to dissolve into masses of flame.

The cockpit was suffocating with searing heat, which Dave, in his concentration, almost ignored as he held the Hampden stoically on his last course towards the *Tirpitz*. Then the rooftops dropped away just under the belly and flat, oily water appeared instead. Just ahead the battleship spread her black length like a solid barrier, rapidly growing in fearsome size for the hurtling Hampden was below funnel height. After an almost endless last few moments, Dave pressed the bomb-release button and heaved back on the control column. Freed of the weight in the bomb-racks, the Hampden, trailing a fiery tail like a rocket, shot up just over the ship.

Dave was going for height to try and bale his crew out, but the Hampden had answered her controls for the last time. When Dave tried to steady her there was no response and the stick was slack. The connections to the control surfaces were either shot or burned away, probably the latter. Dave let the stick go and it flopped forward against the instrument panel. There was nothing more he could do. He yelled over the intercom. to his crew to take the slim chance and jump for it, and then, in case the intercom. had gone, turned to shout to the navigator.

It was then that he got the full blast of the heat. It hit him unbearably, unbelievably, as flames licked round his armoured seat. A sharp smell of burning seared his nose. It was a distastefully familiar smell, strong and sharp. With a vague shock he saw that it came from his moustache. It was smouldering and the black hairs were smoking. He scrubbed a smothering gauntlet against it and noticed then that the aircraft was rolling a little to starboard. He struggled out of his Sutton harness, and fiercely pulled at his sliding cockpit top till it jerked open. His mind was clear, almost detached as he pulled himself over the edge of the cockpit and flopped on to the starboard wing root, where he crouched against the cool slip-stream which carried the flames away, and clung to the cockpit edge with his left hand.

Distinctly he felt that the slip-stream was not as strong as it should be and knew that the Hampden was almost stalling.

'It was just then,' according to his record of the affair, 'that I saw shipping masts in front of me at about the same level. My parachute didn't seem any good at that height, but I pulled the rip-cord anyway —I thought I might as well do something.

'It opened and I hit something as it pulled me off the wing. It seemed in the same moment I saw railway lines behind my left ear, and a moment later I hit on my side.'

Dave landed heavily and found he couldn't move to get up. He saw that he was lying on the edge of a stone mole just a few feet from sluggish water. Without much emotion he noticed that his moustache was still smouldering, and brushed a glove against it till it seemed to go out completely. Through his daze he became aware, after a while, of a glow from the harbour, and painfully turned his head towards it. Fifty yards away he saw his Hampden, a floating torch protruding from sullen heaving water that reflected a red glow for hundreds of yards. She was sinking rapidly.

Two German soldiers were the first to arrive, their steel-shod jackboots ringing sharply on the stone mole. With their help Dave was able to hoist himself to his feet. He spoke the only German he knew 'Nicht sprechen Deutsche pas.' The 'pas' always amused him later on, but not then. He stood there, groggy and bemused, and didn't look like a cabinet minister any more. His face was still lean and solemn, in fact more solemn than ever, but a singed and tufted moustache had lost its effect. Not that Dave cared a damn. A small crowd collected and showed spiteful hostility, so Dave's captors hustled him away to a small wharfside building.

He was still there about an hour later—his mines were set to an hour's delay—when two deep explosions in the harbour shook the buildings. After that they promptly whipped him off to the barbed wire. But during the five weary years of captivity that followed, Dave had the consolation of knowing that the *Tirpitz* was moved just after the raid to dry dock, where she stayed for many months, and that he had saved his life by probably the lowest parachute jump on record.

Which is some consolation at that.

It is major modern history now that the Germans didn't get the French Fleet after all, though this question was still undecided in the following month and kriegies still felt horribly depressed over a military situation that was undeniably grim. It was in the natural course of events, therefore, that the suicide season was crowned by another classic raid—the destruction of the Dortmund-Ems canal.

Mull Mulligan brought in the details about the Dortmund-Ems show. Like most of the characters in this book he should never have told anyone, anything, any more, after his part in the raid. He was a slim Australian with a short-service commission in the R.A.F. and captained a Hampden in the squadron chosen to smash the canal at the point where it crossed the Ems River, north of Munster, in a sort of viaduct. Along this canal the Germans were sending huge barge-loads of material to the invasion ports. Hence the need for pranging the canal; and that right swiftly.

The raid was smartly planned along the lines of guile and audacity. An expert who had helped build the viaduct was in England and he vowed that bombs wouldn't dent it. So it had to be mines, dropped from about fifty feet. Not so good. The vulnerable crossing was naturally plastered with flak. Five Hampdens were laid on for the actual job, including Mull's. A scale model of the viaduct crossing was made. The boys studied it and spent a couple of weeks whistling at nought feet over canals in Lincolnshire, practising dummy runs.

Came the 12th of August 1940, and the hour of nine p.m., when Mull took off from Scampton with a high heart—so high it was practically in his mouth. With him were four other Hampdens, and each carried one 1,500-lb. mine. Number one had to drop his in the narrow viaduct from about fifty feet at eleven p.m. sharp. The others were to drop theirs at exactly two-minute intervals. The mines had a ten-minute delay exploding device, so the boys had to be strictly on time. As a diversion for the flak like the *Tirpitz* raid, nine other Hampdens were to drop bombs a few hundred yards away to keep the flak around the canal interested.

Mull arrived nicely on time and by a plump, three-quarter moon could see his target some 5,000 feet below, gleaming and placid. Although they were to drop their mines from very low, Mull was at 5,000 feet because the idea was to come down in a steep dive along the canal and bolt at full bore across the target and away.

All of which he did except the 'away' part. He was number two on the target, and timing his approach nicely shoved his nose down a few miles back from the Ems crossing at just about eleven o'clock. The Hampden built up speed quickly and was hitting about 300 m.p.h. when he straightened her out at twenty feet over the canal and went rocketing up towards the target, half a mile in front.

Unfortunately the first man in had roused the flak, two batteries of which were grouped around the viaduct, with searchlights at each end. Mull's first warning of his reception was a searchlight that hit him right in the eyes from dead ahead at the near end of the viaduct and robbed him of sight. Skipping a bare few feet above the water, he was blind flying by pure instinct and terse directions from his semi-blinded navigator, lying in the nose.

Light flak was flying at him from all directions—and a beautiful target he was—as he swept up to the viaduct and pressed the button to drop his mine. Out of the corner of his eye he saw wicked flashes as shells ripped ugly gashes in his port wing and the aircraft shuddered as impact after impact pounded the life out of her. Mull and another of the crew were hit by shell splinters, and then the starboard engine caught fire and cut dead and the ailerons jammed.

Without lateral control and with one engine dead and ablaze, Mull coaxed the mortally wounded Hampden up to 200 feet and then the port engine started to cough and surge. The aircraft wouldn't hold her height but Mull nursed her under control as she sank towards a belly landing.

They had one stroke of luck before they hit. Unaccountably, the fire in the starboard engine seemed to shrink, flickered a little, and suddenly went out.

Crash landing at night is a hit-and-miss business, but Mull was able to put the battered Hampden down on fairly level ground. As she slid to a rending, twisted stop, the shot-up starboard engine wrenched bodily from solid mountings and flung sideways against the fuselage. Sharp, heavy, metal propeller-blades crashed through the flimsy fuselage shell. One instantly killed the navigator trapped immediately below Mull. The other thudded down an inch in front of Mull's nose and stopped suddenly, pinning his left leg to the bucket-seat like a powerful vice. Another inch or so further down and it would have crushed his legs. Another inch or so further back and it would have crushed his head.

So much for that. And in the dazed silence that followed, a finger of flame shot up once more from the starboard engine and flickered in devilish dance beside the cockpit. Wild eyed and sweating, Mull struggled in frenzy to free himself, but he was pinned with cruel tightness. There wasn't a hope. His navigator was dead in a shambles of blood, the gunner was unconscious and dying, and the wireless op. was helpless, white with pain on the floor of the fuselage with a broken leg.

The flame multiplied and lengthened, blazed over the top of Mull's cockpit, and the fuselage stank of petrol. Mull managed to drag his seat parachute from under him, but it didn't relieve the crushing pressure on his leg. It was immovable.

'God,' he thought. 'This is it.'

His helpless eyes turned, fascinated, to the flames again. There was a spluttering crackle. They flickered, danced uncertainly, shrank a little, sank below the cockpit, and then went out. A pop-eyed Mull looked unbelievingly, and quietly fainted.

He recovered consciousness after a while, felt the numb ache in his leg, and shouted for help. There was no answer for a long time, until two German peasants arrived, and stared from a safe distance.

'Bomben, bomben,' they said, and went away.

It was four and a half hours after the crash that German soldiers from the flak battery arrived to cut Mull free and tell him another of the Hampdens had been blown to pieces in mid-air by their fire. And it was nine months before Mull got feeling and power back into his leg, though that was a small thing beside the fact that the viaduct was well dented and he was still alive. Because it's not often an engine catches fire in the air and goes out of its own free will. Still less often does one catch fire twice and go out voluntarily again—in fact Mull's is about the only case on record. And when it happens while the pilot is trapped by a heavy propeller which should have killed him anyway, it's just another ruddy miracle. So Mull well and truly earned his D.F.C.

It is worth mentioning that Babe Leroy who was skipper of the fourth aircraft on the target got a V.C. for his part and Pitt Hill, who led the raid, got a D.S.O.

It was that kind of a job.

Chapter Six

MICKEY MOUSE (POLISH)

I f anything more were needed at this stage to strengthen the impression among kriegies that the war was not quite proceeding according to plan, the deficiency was supplied by the Battle of Britain, which was just about the last straw. It was bad enough to be turfed out of one's homeland and away from one's people into a pretty drab sort of indefinite, long-term captivity among the enemy, but it was worse still to know that after all the other crushing reverses suffered outside England even the homes and families one longed to see again were being systematically disintegrated by H.E. and incendiaries. Consequently, the dim view taken of things became positively opaque.

To make it worse, there was only the German version of the Battle to go on, because, as it was fought out over England, there were no new kriegies coming in to give us the other side of the question. According to the German version, of course, the whole battle was a stupendous victory for the Luftwaffe. The R.A.F. was apparently being decimated, truncated, decapitated and, in fact, just about eliminated, and a pulverized England was on the point of sinking beneath the waves she used to rule. German claims of R.A.F. aircraft destroyed were astronomical and their own losses were in inverse ratio of distortion. As there was no precedent to judge by, it was quite disconcerting for a while until reason jibbed at the German claims and kriegies developed a system to get a true perspective of the battle.

It was decided that our own losses, as reported by the Germans, be divided by three and that German losses, as admitted by them, should be multiplied by four. Check-ups, later on, showed this system to be remarkably accurate. The greatest number of aircraft the Germans ever admitted losing in one day in the Battle of Britain was 45. Multiplied by four this comes to 180, which is as near as dammit to the 185 aircraft the Germans lost on the 15th of September 1940.

Kriegy anxiety about the battle vanished overnight as soon as new purges arrived from Dulag with accurate information as to how affairs were going.

Later on, when the Luftwaffe was thrown back and British fighters again took the offensive and ranged out over the occupied territories and Germany itself, it was inevitable that the odd Battle of Britain Old Boy would be hacked down, escape death and land in our cages. In the ensuing years quite a sprinkling of these types came in. Among them were some of the stars of the battle, like Wing-Commander Douglas Bader, who was legless and of whom more anon, Wing-Commander Norman Ryder, and Wing-Commander Bob Tuck, who was mentioned a few chapters ago as a training contemporary of Sailor Malan and Paddy Byrne. When Bob Tuck landed behind the wire he had a D.S.O. and D.F.C. and a couple of bars to indicate a long string of confirmed enemy aircraft, mostly shot down during the Battle of Britain. Somehow or other he always managed to look immaculate among the ragged hoi-polloi of kriegydom where a behind visible through shabby shorts and ragged tufts of beard were the usual sartorial form. Maybe, though, Bob only looked immaculate by comparison.

One of the most entertaining of these Battle of Britain types who trickled in by dribs and drabs later on, was Mickey Mouse. He was a Pole, not the Disney offspring. His real name was Michal Macie——, oh heck—a surname that is a baffling conglomeration of Continental consonants. It makes an impressive euphonic ensemble if you can pronounce it but is a bit beyond the gymnastic capacities of the normal English tongue. For that reason way back about the time when Michal got a 109 on his first op., a rather famous R.A.F. fighter pilot, Group-Captain Victor Beamish, dubbed him 'Mickey Mouse'. The nickname was remarkably apt because it conveyed all the sense of a diminutive knight errant, chockful of guts, skill and a puckish, appealing wit—which was Mickey all over. He was a bare 5ft. 4 ins., topped by a close-fitting cap of dark, wiry hair, and built like a baby tank, sprouting knotty muscles from hefty shoulders and slightly bandy legs. He had the most mercurial eyes of a dark, dark brown with black rings edging each iris and they positively sparkled with liveliness. When he became a kriegy, he grew a wiry black beard that made him look like a benevolent anarchist, but later on he shaved it off to reveal a solid jaw and a mouth that was curved upward in perennial good humour.

Though he was thirty, and therefore no chicken to be flying fighters, he was temperamentally ideal for the game, a fact which was confirmed by his row of ribbons, which, incidentally, he never bothered to wear in kriegydom. From left to right, they were the Virtuti Militari, which is practically the Polish equivalent of the V.C., the Polish Cross of Valour, the D.F.C. and the D.F.M., not at all a bad collection. He had eleven and a half confirmed victories, three probables and several damaged, and his fighting career was quite spectacular until a stroke of fiendish luck put him behind the wire.

Mickey came from a little village near Lemberg, and when war broke out he was a corporal flying instructor in the regular Polish Air Force. He got out of the country into Rumania and caught a ship through the Black Sea and Mediterranean to France. From there he crossed to England and joined the R.A.F. in February 1940. They put him on fighters and as a sergeant-pilot he went to an R.A.F. Hurricane squadron at North Weald early in October, when the Battle of Britain was raging furiously.

Early one morning, shortly after his arrival, Mickey was sitting at readiness when several Me 109's whistled out of the low cloud that hung like a pall over the aerodrome and made an ugly dart at them with cannon fire. Mickey's section was promptly scrambled and they got off the deck just as the 109's finished their job and popped back into the cloud.

Mickey vanished into the cloud after them. He was inexperienced at the business of air fighting but soon saw there was no hope of finding anything in the grey opaqueness of the cloud, so he dropped his nose and a few moments later broke out into the open again. Right in front of him, like a piece of cake on a silver platter, were two 109's, blissfully scooting for home. Mickey was so close he was almost formating on them and it was just too easy. He opened his taps and gave a well-considered squirt to the leading 109 which flickered over like a startled bunny and dived straight into the Blackwater River, not far below. The other 109 saw what was happening and shot up into the cloud with discreet celerity. It was Mickey's first op, and first victory.

In those days, the boys used to sleep in the dispersal huts so as to be ready for business at any time. It was life at pretty close quarters and for Mickey, rather difficult, as his knowledge of English was strictly limited. About all he knew were a few of the essentials, like 'yes,' 'no' and 'good morning.' A couple of days after his first victory he had cause to regret this.

About 5 a.m. on the 15th of October, just when the sky was beginning to lighten in the east and the boys in dispersal were still either asleep or drowsily half awake, the ops. phone rang and a moment later a shout of 'scramble' cracked across the silent room. There was a mad rush and Mickey was sprinting out to his Hurricane, pulling on his Mae West. The rest of his outfit consisted of flying boots and a pair of violently striped red, white and blue silk pyjamas that had recently cost him £3 10s. A few seconds later they were in the air with orders to patrol from Manston to Dover at 'Angels 26', or 26,000 feet.

When they topped the 20,000 feet mark, Mickey was shivering like a pneumatic drill with cold that sneered at silk pyjamas. He was acutely miserable until they saw a gaggle of 109's break out of the top of the cloud layer beneath them. The squadron immediately dived to attack and Mickey forgot his cold as he singled out a 109 and gave it a nicely judged squirt. It seemed that almost in the same moment the German pilot jumped out in a sudden white blossom of silk parachute. Mickey swung round to find another target and his engine gave a series of ragged explosive pops and died.

In the strange silence, he dropped his nose and headed down for a crash landing. They were not far from Dover at the time and as it was invasion season the only fields Mickey could see were covered with ugly-looking poles specifically put there to prevent aircraft from doing what Mickey wanted to do with his. He was getting quite low with Hobson's choice for a landing-field when he saw a clear field beside some huts with only four poles in it. He turned for it, dropped his wheels and glided in to make a smooth landing on a large football field. Forgetting to switch off his 'pip-squeak' (radio contactor), Mickey climbed thankfully out on to the wing just as an army officer and several soldiers came dashing towards him brandishing revolvers and rifles.

Forgetting what a queer sight he presented in his violent silk pyjamas, Mickey turned to greet them. The return greeting was not so cordial. No chances were taken in those days and the lieutenant who arrived first, faced with the weird vision of a pilot in pyjamas, took no chances and assumed he was a German flying a captured Hurricane. Mickey found himself looking at hostile faces and the hollow ends of a revolver and several rifles. Incomprehensible questions in English were barked at him, and unconsciously he tried to explain in Polish. It was fatal, of course. The sound of a foreign tongue cleared up any doubt that existed in the minds of the men behind the guns. The strange vision must be German. The position dawned on Mickey and he tried in broken English.

'Polski, Polski,' he said, pointing at his chest. 'Engleesh squadron.'

The lieutenant made a rude reply which Mickey later identified as 'Oh yeah,' and beckoned him down from the wing.

Then Mickey remembered he hadn't switched off his pip-squeak.

'Pip-squeak, pip-squeak,' he said helplessly, pointing to the cockpit, not quite realizing what the effect might be on an Army man who knew of 'pip-squeak' only as comic strip characters. Mickey turned back to switch it off when he felt a powerful hand grab him by the seat of his gaudy pyjamas and yank him on to the ground, completely lacking in dignity. They hustled him away, protesting in garbled English and fluent Polish to a nearby hut, where he was locked in a small room.

A little later, a major came in and spoke to him in German. Here, at last, Mickey was on sounder ground, for he knew a little German and told a faintly staggered major in not very good German that his name was Mickey Mouse. Then he explained more fully, and after the Army people had checked with his squadron by phone they welcomed him warmly, produced a double whisky, and, as Mickey hadn't eaten since the previous night's supper, gave him a huge breakfast.

A few months later, after the Luftwaffe had been thrown back, Mickey Mouse took part in the first of all the famous sweeps by which the R.A.F. again took the initiative. He got two 109's on that show and one of them didn't cost him a single bullet. It was towards the end of February 1941, and they were led, incidentally, by Wing-Commander Douglas Bader, whose name keeps cropping up everywhere. Spitfires and Hurricanes escorted Blenheims into France and they were near Boulogne when 109's came up to attack. Mickey got one of them at 19,000 feet and then on the way back they dived right down to strafe an aerodrome. As they dived on the target, Mickey saw a 109 just taking off and swung his Hurricane towards it. The 109 pilot evidently saw him coming and tried to turn away sharply. As he turned, he ran slap-bang into a tree, hit the deck, burst into flame and went somer-saulting across the fields like a fiery comet. They gave Mickey a D.F.M. after that.

He got another 109 on his second sweep. At the same time he also had his throttle connecting rod shot away and had to land at Horn-church by cutting his engine switches. It was his fifth victory and they gave him the Polish Cross of Valour.

Chronologically, the rest of Mickey's story is a little premature at this stage, but must obviously be told here. He later transferred to a Polish Spitfire squadron and his next momentous day was the last day of 1941. The squadron was escorting Halifaxes to Brest with evil intent for the German battleships *Gneisenau* and *Scharnhorst*. They were top cover at 20,000 over Brest when some 109's made passes at the Halifaxes. Mickey's squadron was diving to the attack when Mickey, conscientiously having a final look behind, saw more 109's diving out of the sun at them. Shouting a warning over the R/T and cursing in fluent Polish, he swung round just as one of his squadron mates, the first to receive the 109's' attentions, baled out of his flaming aircraft. The 109 responsible pulled up steeply according to the inevitable German tactics and Mickey pulled up after him. He squirted carefully and a couple of seconds later the German pilot was also hanging from his parachute. Mickey finished by suddenly spinning off and vanished into a heavy bank of cloud. By the time he had pulled out, he was down to 9,000 feet and below the cloud.

Some little way away he saw one of the Halifaxes, escorted by two smaller aircraft heading towards England, and according to the fighter boy's axiom of safety in numbers headed in their direction to join up. When he was still about 500 yards short of them he got a shock to see the two escorting aircraft were neither Spitfires nor Hurricanes, but 109's, and they weren't escorting the Halifax either, but were shooting in a very business-like manner. Completely unnoticed, Mickey slunk up behind them. The Halifax had been forced low over the water when he opened fire and one of the 109's did a lightning flick roll into the drink with a mighty fountain of foam. The other one must have got an eyeful and did a quick vanishing trick back into France. Mickey flew up alongside the Halifax which was in a pretty bad way. Two engines were out of action, the fuselage looked somewhat ragged and ventilated and she was smoking a little. The crew clustered round the cabin windows making loving signs to Mickey, blowing kisses and other salutations.

The Halifax was labouring a little on two engines but waffled on towards England under Mickey's paternal eye until they were about sixty miles from the English coast, when a third engine cut out and the Halifax sank soggily down to an unpremeditated ditching in a slather of milky spray. Mickey climbed up over her to broadcast a radio fix for the air-sea rescue people. He thumbed his fuel button and found he had only twenty-five gallons left, which is little enough for a powerful fighter engine that fairly drinks petrol. With propeller back almost to fully coarse he stooged slowly over the spot for some time at low revs, broadcasting over the R/T till he was certain the air-sea rescue people had a good fix, then set course for the nearest land, which was Plymouth. After an anxious few minutes he made a good landfall and slapped his wheels down in the circuit of a nearby aerodrome just as his petrol gauge was flickering on the zero mark. He landed, and the engine cut as he was taxi-ing in.

One of Mickey's most treasured possessions now is a fulsome letter of thanks from the Halifax crew who were picked up shortly after. He then had nine confirmed victories and received the Virtuti Militari and a commission.

The day of Dieppe, in September 1942, was the day that Mickey came back from a period of leave. They wouldn't let him fly on the squadron's first trip that day because his leave wasn't officially up, but he begged and pleaded and finally insisted and they let him go on the second show of the day. He got a 109 when they arrived over Dieppe and a couple of minutes later when they dived down to strafe he came upon a JU 88 returning low from the sea. He gave it a solid burst and its port wing seemed to blow up and it smacked into the beach near some British tanks. Mickey's dark brown eyes were sparkling like champagne bubbles when he got back.

In the afternoon, he took off again. They were escorting the attacking convoy back to England when Mickey saw flak bursting below and to port. Where there was flak, he reasoned, there was probably an enemy aircraft and peeled off to investigate. A Dornier 17 saw him coming, jettisoned his bombs and high-tailed back towards France, diving low over the sea. Mickey, with his No. 2 close behind, caught it easily. First Mickey gave it a burst, then his No. 2 had a shot and then Mickey flew right up close to the Dornier and gave it a solid burst of cannon fire. The Dornier dropped its nose and smacked into the sea in the usual cloud of spray. Mickey's Spit was so close behind that his windscreen was completely drenched by the water.

On the way back to base, mercurial Mickey Mouse was bouncing up and down in his cockpit with delight. He was so excited that he went in and landed with his wheels up and felt very foolish when he found himself sitting in his pranged Spit with a crumpled belly.

Mickey only claimed half the Dornier, giving the other half to his No. 2. It brought his score to eleven and a half, and it was the last victory he scored. He had a long spell away from ops after that and then went back to his squadron again about the middle of the following year, where he found one of the newly joined pilots was one of his oldest friends from his former flying school in Poland. His name was Leszek and as he had just finished his training, Mickey took him under his wing and began to instruct him in the finer niceties of air fighting. Leszek, who was tall and slim, in contrast to Mickey's nuggety short-ness, had a keen intelligence and was an apt pupil. He showed fine promise and Mickey always had him in his section on sweeps. Eventu-ally he became Mickey's deputy section leader and Mickey felt pretty safe when he knew the faithful Leszek was tagging along with him.

On the 8th of August they went off for a sweep over St. Nazaire. Patrolling near the port Leszek was flying out on Mickey's right. They were about 27,000 feet when the squadron did a turnabout to port. Half-way through it, Mickey felt a sharp crash just behind his cockpit, had a brief vision of Leszek's Spitfire falling away, almost within arms' reach behind his right shoulder, and then he was spinning down viciously, minus starboard wing and all the fuselage and tail behind the cockpit. He got out at about 23,000 feet and floated down by para-chute. Leszek did not get out at all. His aircraft crashed close to Mickey's.

Chapter Seven

EUROPE BECOMES A FORTRESS

In the months that followed Mickey's early adventures in the Battle of Britain, the general war situation, though not exactly healthy, was at least a little less sickly—which was more than a little reviving to kriegies. Much of the change was due to Wavell's first advance into Libya—really our first offensive victory and a classic one at that. At any rate it showed that one end of the Axis was more ludicrous in war than fearsome and kriegies took fresh heart accordingly.

The first retreat from Libya, of course, was another story and kriegy hopes took another right to the chin, though it was realized that diversion of large chunks of our Middle East Forces to Greece was largely responsible. It was in this retreat that one of the finest little epics of the war occurred. For quiet guts and drama it deserves the halo of immortality, but as the star and his driver went on into captivity the story went with them and never leaked out. We tell it here now for the first time, as told by the driver and grudgingly confirmed by the star, Humphrey B——. We feel very tempted to give his full name, though he would hate it.

This, incidentally, is not an Air Force story, but is wholly to the credit of the Army. Strictly speaking, it doesn't come within the scope of this book but it is a story of a kriegy who lived with Air Force prisoners and it's such a damned good story that it's worth an honoured place anywhere.

Humphrey B—— was a captain in the Tank Corps and belonged to a hard-bitten desert tank unit. To look at, he was not the stuff of which heroes are made. He was short, slight, with thick-rimmed glasses and as shy as a desert gazelle. He had dark hair, and, as a concession to the Army, a dark, wiry moustache that was the only outwardly fierce thing about him. His father was a vicar near Oxford and Humphrey himself was a law student till they gave him a gun, or rather, a tank.

The outstanding thing about Humphrey was his brain. It was almost inhuman in its penetrating efficiency. Before he became a prisoner he was an accomplished Latin and Greek scholar and also spoke French. After a few months' captivity he had mastered German, Italian, and Arabic, even to the point of writing in Arabic characters. He was an accomplished pianist and also learnt the piano accordion in captivity with ridiculous ease. Therefore, taken by and large, Humphrey was potential material for almost anything.

He took part in Wavell's epic advance to Agheila, and then, when the Greek campaign started, the Powers-That-Be took nearly all the tanks from Humphrey's unit, which then had to help hold the fort in the desert with some captured Italian light M13 tanks taken between Agedabia and Agheila. Like all things connected with the Italian war effort the tanks were pretty ropey. When they went, which was not often, they could not be trusted to keep going and as a fighting weapon they were easily dealt with by German tanks, so when Rommel started to liquidate Wavell's advance it was not long before the Italian tanks were all either knocked out or broken down.

One day, as the Eighth Army was pulling back towards Tobruk, Humphrey was rattling over a rough, Libyan desert track in a truck, accompanied by a driver and a young signals officer, on their way back to rejoin the main body of the unit which was taking part in the rear-guard actions. They could not know for certain where the forward elements of the Afrika Korps were owing to the fluid nature of the battle, but realized they might have infiltrated anywhere.

A couple of clouds of dust appeared way off in the desert, moving swiftly towards them. Relentlessly nearer they drew until the cores of the dusty swirls clarified into the ungainly, buff-coloured shapes of two armoured cars, each bearing black crosses. Neatly they intercepted Humphrey's bouncing truck and forced it to a grudging stop. Hatches on top of each armoured car snapped open and the dusty forms of a German N.C.O. and several German soldiers clambered out and dropped on to the side of the track. A pistol and a couple of tommy-guns covered the silent three in the truck and reluctantly, in response to an imperative wave of the N.C.O.'s hand, Humphrey and his two companions also climbed down on to the desert.

The German soldiers formed a silent circle round them. The N.C.O. —he was a Feldwebel (sergeant)—stepped forward and rammed a heavy Luger into the stomach of the signals officer. He spoke passable English.

'You will tell me,' he said, 'what is your unit and where is it?'

The signals officer gave the brief and standard answer.

'Can't possibly tell you that,' he shrugged.

'You will tell me or I will shoot you,' said the German.

'I'm not allowed to tell you and I won't tell you,' said the signals man.

'I'll give you three seconds to change your mind,' said the Feldwebel. 'If you are still obstinate then, I'll shoot you. I'm not bluffing.'

The signals man clamped his mouth shut.

'One!' said the German. 'Two! Three! Now where is your unit?'

'Go to hell,' said the signals man.

There was a heavy explosion and the signals man collapsed on the sand. He writhed a little and shortly lay still. (His grave was found some months later.)

The smoking muzzle of the Luger swung till it prodded into the pit of Humphrey's stomach.

'You have seen what happened to your obstinate comrade,' said the Feldwebel unemotionally. 'Be sensible and tell me where your unit is.'

Now if it had been a Hollywood epic with the script and everything else nicely arranged beforehand and a toy Luger pistol, Humphrey would have declaimed some dramatic lines giving a false position and led the Nazis into a trap. Unfortunately it was real life, with no script but a real pistol and it is considerably harder than somewhat to make up a convincingly watertight story on the spur of the moment, particularly as the German had a map and a rough idea of where forces should be. As a matter of fact, Humphrey cannot remember that the idea of faking a story occurred to him then. He gave the Feldwebel a look that contained none of his normal mild benevolence.

'I will not tell you,' he said decisively.

'You have the usual three seconds,' said the German. 'Then you know what to expect. One!'—Humphrey stood motionless, tensed, shoulders hunched a little—'Two! . . .'—a long, unnerving pause. . . . 'Three! Well?'

Eyes behind Humphrey's thick glasses were unblinking. The atmosphere was slightly terrific.

'No,' said Humphrey. 'Nothing doing.'

There was the tiniest of pauses—and then a ragged burst of sound. The circle of tough Nazi soldiers was clapping and cheering and a couple of times Humphrey caught the international word of approval, 'Bravo.'

The dusty, set face of the Feldwebel slowly cracked into a hard smile.

'You are too brave to shoot,' he said, and tucked the Luger away in its holster.

And that is the story of how Humphrey B—— won his life and lost his freedom. He has no medal.

*   *   *

Though the epic of Humphrey B—— was a sparkling vignette in the sorry story of the war, the broad perspective of events had further shocks in store for prisoners about this time. As though the Libyan retreat had not deflated sudden hopes enough, the calamities of Greece and Crete shook those hopes right down to the foundations and kriegy optimism everywhere hit a new low. They couldn't understand it. Wherever the Germans appeared we didn't seem to be able to cope. The loss of Greece and Crete had a deeper significance to the vitally interested arm-chair strategists behind the wire. We had lost our last foothold in Europe. What the hell could we do about it now? And what was more to the point, how many long, wearying years would it take? To prisoners serving an indeterminate sentence, neither question produced any kind of acceptable answer. And still morale survived the blow. However low kriegy spirits sank, their confidence in ultimate victory would have shamed many of their people back home. Faith always told them we would win eventually, but how it was to be done was where logic conflicted with faith.

A great crumb of comfort was that the U.S.A. would be forced to enter the war eventually, and it was considered in the perennial kriegy confabs that this extra strength would somehow enable the Allies to turn the tables.

But, oh God! How long? The whole of Europe was an Axis fortress.

And as if these what might be termed 'foreign affairs', were not sufficiently galling, there was at the same time as all this another cross to bear in the shape of what might be termed 'domestic' trouble. Through Swedish quarters came a report to the Nazis of the life of German prisoners of war at Fort William in Canada. God only knows the original source of the report but the Nazis believed it, which was unfortunate, for the extent of the hardships it revealed was only equalled by its all-embracing inaccuracy.

At any rate, the Nazis considered that the honour of the Third Reich could only be satisfied by inflicting similar conditions on the helpless kriegies in their hands, in much the same spiteful spirit as the manacles they put on prisoners after Dieppe.

So were born Thorn and Posen—'comparative camps', the Nazis called them because they reproduced the alleged harsh conditions of Fort William in Canada.

Both Thorn (about 100 miles north-west of Warsaw) and Posen were grim old forts in Poland, two of a system of five such forts built by Bismarck in 1871 on the Vistula as a defence against Russia. They were quite a few miles apart and allegedly connected by hidden tunnels. Posen became a prison for Army officers, but to Thorn, in addition to several hundred Army people, were sent some 200 Air Force officers from Spangenburg, Dulag Luft, and Barth.

It was an old stone and brick place, sunken so that the roof was at ground-level. After being discarded as a fort it was used as a prison and then the Poles made it into a cadet school and barracks. It had a moat about fifty feet deep and a tiny square of courtyard used as a parade ground, recreation centre and sports field for nearly 1,000 men.

The boys arrived at Thorn towards the end of February 1941 and were met by armoured cars, searchlights, and tommy-guns. The first item on the programme was for the whole crowd to be herded together and told what they were in for. In a blurb which he read out a German officer enumerated the alleged harsh conditions of Fort William and told kriegies they were to have the same conditions.

They were sixteen in each small, low-ceilinged room. They were locked in from 8 p.m. to 8 a.m. with total sanitary arrangements consisting of a bucket. They were in darkness most of the time as the barred windows were boarded up as well and the Germans weren't giving much away in the matter of electric light. Ventilation was practically nil and the atmosphere was invariably stifling. There were practically no cooking facilities. A room of sixteen could get half an hour on the stove every three days. Prisoners were not allowed to lie on their beds during the day. (Perhaps that was just as well as the straw was so wet you could practically wring water out of it.) The only washing facilities were a few trickles of water from a pipe with holes punched in it.

As parcels were still not coming through everyone was suffering from malnutrition and many from wounds, so a lot of the prisoners were constantly ill. The Germans also deliberately fenced off part of the tiny parade ground to make it smaller still and made it clear that they wouldn't hesitate to shoot any trespassers into the forbidden area. All the guards carried rubber truncheons as well as their arms. The camp was full of lice and the prisoners had to attend three roll calls a day, plus an individual photograph check.

After a month of this rather acute misery the Germans suddenly found the reports of the Fort William harshness were all wrong, so without a word the restrictions were suddenly lifted.

Shortly after this, the boys at Thorn began to see some most interesting—and inexplicable—things. One of the main Polish railway lines passed only a couple of hundred yards from the camp and as soon as the restrictions were lifted and the kriegies were allowed up on the ramparts and earthworks so that they could see outside the camp, they noticed a fabulous amount of traffic on the railway line. All day and all night long trains of box cars and flat cars were rumbling along the rails —all loaded with war material and all going the same way, from west to east, towards Russia. Streams of empty trains filed back, heading west.

The boys couldn't understand it—those being the days when we were still cursing Russia with earnest and prolonged eloquence. No one—and who could blame him—thought for a moment that Russia was to be in the war on our side. It was never dreamed either that Russia would attack Germany or that Germany would attack Russia.

Still the trains kept rumbling through and the nights were a bedlam of noise from Thorn railway junction. Traffic on the line became heavier and heavier till at times trains were whizzing by every two minutes— long lines of tanks and guns and lorries perched on flat cars and scores, hundreds, then thousands and thousands of troops cheerfully squatting in the open doors of box cars, laughing and cheering. Poor fools.

There were two roads nearby too; not main roads, but good respectable roads running up towards north-east Poland. And after a while military transport began to flow along them, all heading east. The stream grew till it was a flood, till there were just two long lines of traffic as far as the eye could see, heavy transports and guns, nose to tail, all rumbling east, and a pall of dust hanging over the roads.

It went on growing for day after day that lengthened into week after week and extended eventually into months. Then the prisoners heard that the main roads were even more choked and the traffic on the two lesser visible roads was just the overflow.

It was queer—damned queer, and the German guards were no nearer the solution. They were all convinced of the friendship between Russia and Germany, and kriegies had no evidence to the contrary, either. Eventually, a theory was produced that afforded a possible explanation. It was considered that Russia was probably giving free passage to German troops through Russia down into Iran and the Middle East; not an encouraging theory, but what else could they think?

Then the position was complicated further by the appearance of fighter patrols over the military columns and rumours of frontier clashes came through, then more rumours of troops massing on each side of the Russo-German frontier. A rigid black-out was imposed at Thorn but still the boys couldn't logically consider a Russo-German conflict, as Germany was still supposed to be getting vast quantities of war material from Russia (though, as a matter of fact, she wasn't). Everyone looked for a deeper meaning to the puzzle, and, of course, couldn't find one.

Towards the end of May the kriegies were taken from Thorn and the Air Force boys went back to Spangenburg. For a few short weeks they received no more clues as to what was happening in the east until suddenly and without warning one day they heard the unbelievable news that the Germans had marched into Russia, 'to forestall the Russians', the Nazis glibly said.

Kriegies had a sudden upward surge of joy. This might be the end of Germany, though Russia was militarily such an unknown quantity. For a week there was little news—and then the Germans produced their first claims of a bewildering advance and astronomical figures of Russian dead and prisoners, and of material captured. They were so vast they staggered the imagination, but photographs in German newspapers went far to confirm them. They showed enormous columns of prisoners, badly equipped and not comparing well with the German front-line troops. Many of the Russians didn't even have boots, many had had no arms and all of them seemed tattered and torn. Other photographs showed the Russian weapons—pitifully old and obsolete most of them.

However, all of this, combined with the undoubted veracity of German announcements of captured Russian towns, rapidly forced dejected prisoners to the conclusion that Russia would go the way of France, and liberation would not come from that direction.

A month after the Germans attacked Russia, the pendulum of optimism had swung right back and you would hardly find a kriegy who would bet that Moscow wouldn't fall within a few weeks.

Chapter Eight

BADER ARRIVES

D oubly welcome at this time were new purge people who still kept trickling in. They were such a vital contact with the life that had been. It was so reassuring to know from them that there *was* an outside world still, with flying and popsies, pubs and people. And freedom, too. Prisoners had heard so much about it before but never stopped to think it had any value till they lost it. Odd how much interest they took in the war who could do so little about it. Not so odd, really, because the end of it concerned them so deeply. God, how deeply!

It was slightly cheering to know in summer, '41, that the fighter boys had the sweeps taped and that some of the lads were knocking up sizeable scores.

Many others, of course, were stopped before their scores were so big, like 'Dapper' Dougall, who was shaping pretty well, even for his squadron which was top scoring for the R.A.F., when he came down.

He was once described as a 'dapper young man' (hence, obviously his nickname) before he left on his last sweep. He was minus a leg when he arrived behind the wire. Later he received a D.F.C. which was some slight compensation.

Dapper didn't let the loss of his leg worry him much. Or if it did, he didn't show it.

Pat must take a lot of the credit for that. She was the girl in England, rather a wistful, winsome-looking lass according to the photograph that Dapper cherished. She had heard from the Red Cross about Dapper's leg, and when his letters didn't reach her for a long time she thought he was giving her a chance to forget their engagement. She wrote promptly expressing her views.

After two years, Dapper was repatriated to England. Pat married him a week later and they went back to Montreal, Dapper's home town, where he used to be a bacteriologist.

Feminine fidelity was not always so enduring in regard to prisoners.

But getting back to the new purges. Sometimes kriegies had an idea of who was coming in with them. Whenever an R.A.F. personality was killed or hacked down and taken prisoner, a jubilant paragraph usually appeared in the German papers and we knew that sooner or later the new exile would find his way through our rusty, barbed-wire gates.

Kriegies therefore weren't surprised one autumn day in 1941 to notice among a new purge the broad-shouldered figure of a rather famous wing-commander. If his D.S.O. and Bar and D.F.C. and Bar and solid square jaw were insufficient proof of his identity as a phenomenal sort of fighter pilot, his jerky, lurching walk left no doubt. The whole world knew of Wing-Commander Douglas Bader who lost both legs in an aircraft crash way back in the early 'thirties and was able to pass, with 'exceptional ability' a war-time flying course and then went on to knock down Huns and win promotion and decorations with rare speed.

Prisoners knew from the papers that he had been shot down in a sweep over France, and as they might have known, the story behind it was typical of the man. He was leading his Canadian squadron when German fighters from St. Omer came up to attack, and in the busy party that followed, Wingco Bader found himself opposed by an enemy as obstinate as himself. In a head-on attack neither gave way and Spitfire and Me. 109 met in a glancing, rending crash that left both aircraft shattered and torn and one of the pilots—the German—dead.

In his Spitfire, spinning down, Bader found that one of his legs was jammed immovably in the wreckage of his cockpit.

Now, to the normal man that would be decidedly fatal, but the God-knows-how-many-million-to-one chance occurred. Bader was not the normal man. He simply unstrapped his trapped metal leg, hauled himself over the cockpit rim, let go, counted three and pulled his D-ring. As simple as that.

It is the only time the Wingco had ever thanked his lucky stars he had lost his legs.

He came back to earth in a field—with rather a nasty bump—was picked up by German soldiers and carried to St. Omer aerodrome.

Oberst (Colonel) Galland, later to become major-general, was in charge of the station. He was one of Germany's greatest fighter aces, with ninety-five victories claimed, and on hearing who his prisoner was, went to see him. It was a strange meeting, more like a cut from a film than actual reality.

Each knew the other by reputation and each regarded the other with considerable interest.

Galland gave orders that the Wingco was to be taken to the officers' mess and must be shown every courtesy. Then followed the incident—recounted in every newspaper in the world at the time—that was to shed a gleam of chivalry on the black bitterness and hatred of war.

Bader was helpless without his other leg. Galland offered to arrange for one to be sent from England. That night the German radio broadcast news of the Wing-Commander's predicament and offered to allow a British aircraft to fly over St. Omer with a spare limb. The R.A.F. declined any immunity, declaring that they would drop it in the course of an ordinary bombing raid.

Accordingly, a day or two later, a squadron of Blenheims set off from England on a raid and, when over France, a machine detached itself from the squadron and flew over St. Omer. The Germans did not open fire nor did any fighters take off. A parachute floated down from the Blenheim, and shortly afterwards a black box containing the leg was handed to Bader. Stuffed in the metal limb, he found hundreds of cigarettes and other kriegy necessities.

There was a celebration in the German mess that night, one of the entertainments for the benefit of the once again mobile Wingco being the screening of a film of Galland's ninety-fifth air victory.

Next day he left for kriegydom. Galland wished him good-bye with the words, 'If ever you are ill-treated as a prisoner, don't hesitate to write to me.'

Thereafter the Wingco lost no time in making himself a thorn in the Germans' side. So troublesome did he become that after one unsuccessful escape the German threatened to remove one of his legs. They didn't do so but later, in a final attempt to curb his activities, they ordered that he go to Lamsdorf Hospital where he would receive 'more skilled attention', they declared, and in June 1942, he arrived at the hospital which served Stalag VIIIB, then the biggest British other-ranks camp in Germany.

In less than a month the Wingco had devised a new plan for escape. It was a typical Bader plan.

On the morning of the 31st of July, a working party of twenty British other ranks gathered at the gate to go to an aerodrome not far

74

from the Polish border. While waiting to file out, one of them stupidly allowed his suitcase to fall open and in the confusion that followed the attempts to gather up the articles no one noticed a man who walked with a strange jerky movement change places with one of the members of the party.

Quite unsuspecting, the Germans marched the party to the station a half-hour's walk away, an ordeal which caused agony to Bader.

He had to be lifted on to the carriage, but so carefully had everything been planned that the suspicions of the Germans were never aroused, despite the fact that twice during the journey they had to change trains and each time the Wingco had to be lifted off and on.

The aerodrome lay a good hour's walk from the station and at the end of it Bader was on the point of collapse. He had achieved the first part of his plan, however. What remained was to get a German aircraft before his escape from Lamsdorf became known.

But if Providence had been generous to him so far, it turned sour now. Nothing he could devise could get him nearer than a few hundred yards from those aeroplanes. The desperate expedient of rushing the machines and overwhelming the ground crew suggested by the R.A.F. sergeants who comprised part of the working party, was turned down by the Wingco because of the consequences it would have for those who were caught.

After four days on the aerodrome with success no nearer, the British working party was suddenly called on parade and a German security N.C.O. who knew Bader personally, appeared.

Bader made one last-minute attempt to avoid detection by dodging behind an orderly and changing places with another, but it was no use and he was identified.

This time the Germans were taking no more chances and Bader was sent to Kolditz, the officers' 'strafelager' (punishment camp) where rigorous precautions made escape almost impossible.

Bader wasn't the only kriegy trying to escape. Everyone else was trying too, and a variety of weird and wonderful plans were put into operation all over the place. Barth, the Baltic camp for Air Force kriegies opened in the previous year, was by this time a hotbed of general escape activity.

People tried to make audacious breaks, cunning breaks, breaks in ones, in twos and threes and also in organized teams. The Barth camp population contained many of the pertinacious escape gentry from the early tunnel at Dulag Luft in the previous year, like Squadron-Leader

Roger Bushell, the genius who got to the Swiss border from the Dulag tunnel and who later planned and commanded the 'X' Organization at Stalag Luft III. Also there was Lieutenant-Commander Jimmy Buckley, also ex-Dulag and later to be posted missing after an escape from Schubin with a Dane.

Tunnelling was the favourite sport at Barth, as at nearly every camp, but Barth presented peculiar difficulties. It was very close to the sea and as a result only about six feet below ground-level, tunnellers struck water that seeped into all their shafts and caused general havoc. As a result tunnels had to be very shallow and could therefore be located by the Germans with probes, particularly as the Germans were getting a few more clues in the anti-tunnel business.

Just as in the bigger conflict outside, new and ingenious developments in kriegy escape methods were countered by improved anti-escape organization on the part of the Germans. The kriegies designed and built beautifully camouflaged trap-door entrances to their tunnels. The Germans instituted more exhaustive searches, found a couple of them and got a better idea of what to look for and how to do it.

They even took to driving wagons round camps and by this means collapsed a couple of shallow tunnels. Eventually the Germans brought in a powerful weapon. For about a week the Barth prisoners were daily removed from their camp and locked in a hut from which they could not see outside. With this secrecy, the Germans installed sound-detector apparatus round the barbed-wire fence with a complex listening switchboard that could plug in and listen to any part of the perimeter and kept a constant listening 'watch'.

The kriegy intelligence system soon discovered the details of this and a system was worked out whereby they dug at points during times the listener-in had his attention concentrated elsewhere. It was a serious handicap all the same as kriegies, because of the water seepage, could not dig deep enough to get out of the range of the sound detectors. They did discover that the detectors would not record digging operations about twenty-five feet down and it was this that led to the phenomenal thirty-feet-deep tunnels later on at Stalag Luft III.

As a matter of rather startling interest, the kriegies attempted forty-eight tunnels at Barth between July 1940 and March 1942. This was before the days of large-scale organization. Mostly they were the private attempts of comparatively small teams, without very much security, and for this reason only one of the forty-eight was a success. Three kriegies escaped from it but all were caught and two of them were purged to Kolditz, the 'strafelager' where Bader was sent, as punishment.

But tunnelling was not the only escape method. There were a lot of trick jobs. Pat Leeson, for instance, got out disguised as a chimney sweep with a grimy face and a painted cardboard top-hat, like those favoured by sweeps in Germany. In his hat, incidentally, he hid his forged papers as he talked his way through the gate. Pat's escape is a good indication of the cunning and patience required. He had to wait three months for the sweep to come into the camp. When this happened, he got some Polish officers to engage the sweep in conversation in an out-of-sight corner of the camp and then, with only about ten minutes' notice all told, put on his sweep's kit which he had had waiting all these months and blarneyed his way out of the gate with a special forged pass he had also kept ready for the occasion.

When this chance came it was the middle of winter with an unpleasant blizzard blowing, and a couple of days later Pat was recaptured, exhausted from exposure.

Other escapees hid in rubbish carts and trusted to luck that they would not be stabbed by the vicious pitchforks that the guards on the gate stuck through all the rubbish carts, looking for the odd, hidden body. More than one kriegy was stabbed unpleasantly in those circumstances.

Another favourite trick was to sneak out to the wire and cut one's way through at night time, every moment expecting a bullet to come whistling along. In the escape line at least, there was never a dull moment at Barth.

One of the people who got out temporarily was Squadron-Leader Ken Doran, who led the first raid of the war on Wilhelmshaven (mentioned earlier here when Slattery and Booth were captured) and who received the first D.F.C. of the war for it. He was shot down and captured on a later raid.

The general escape blitz at Barth resulted in several naughty boys being purged to Kolditz punishment camp.

Another prison camp was established in Germany during 1941 which a lot of Air Force kriegies came to know. It was at Lübeck, on the Baltic, and a pretty barren spot it was, with wretched facilities. Army people were mostly imprisoned there but quite a few Air Force kriegies spent several months there during that year They were hungry months as Red Cross parcels were still pretty scarce: so hungry that one day, in desperation, the fellows in one room sorrowfully bumped off their cat, roasted it and it went the way of all flesh. They said it was 'Very good; rather like rabbit', and from time to time, when food became more than ordinarily scarce, there were several imitators of this dolorous expedient. Cats were always in fairly good supply at prison camps. For some unknown reason nomadic felines drifted into camps in scores and settled down there. Lord only knows what the attraction was. It couldn't have been food, for there was little enough of that to spare for pets.

Days at Lübeck were incredibly dull, but happily, nights were often enlivened by the passage of British aircraft overhead, *en route* to Berlin and other hot spots. Lübeck flak always opened up and they were the only times when prisoners did not mind having their sleep disturbed.

On one occasion a bomber passing over jettisoned a stick of incendiaries. One of them fell on one of the living blocks, went through the roof and landed on the bed of an Army major. He was injured so badly that one leg had to be amputated. Others of the incendiaries dropped on the German officers' mess and completely gutted it.

One of the kriegies purged to Lübeck when it opened from Barth was Squadron-Leader Roger Bushell, whose escape proclivities were always bringing him under notice. Again he was purged from Lübeck late in 1941 to another camp, and on the way in the train, he, a Czech, and a third officer, jumped off the train. The third man was killed immediately by a train coming the other way, but Roger and the Czech made their way by devious means to Prague. Both spoke fluent German, which was very helpful, and in Prague the Czech had many friends, who were even more helpful.

While they waited for a chance to get completely clear of German-occupied countries, the two lived in a flat in Prague—a delightful change for a man just escaped from P.O.W. camp—for three months. Then Czech patriots 'got' Heinrich ('Butcher') Heydrich, Himmler's murderous lieutenant in Czechoslovakia, and the S.S. turned on a mass search for patriot elements in the country. In the course of it, S.S. men burst into Roger's flat one night and Roger paid for his three months' freedom with a rather shaky three months in a Gestapo cell before he was sent back to prison camp. He just escaped being purged to Kolditz by the skin of his teeth.

The camp at Lübeck, from which Roger had come, was cleared of Air Force prisoners late in 1941, most of them being sent to a big new officers' camp that was opened about October of that year between Warburg and Dössel, north of Kassel and not very far from Spangenburg. Practically every able-bodied British officer prisoner was sent there, both Army and Air Force, about 3,000 in all, including about 400 Air Force. It was the normal, barren sort of camp—huts with sixteen to a room, etc., and far too few facilities for any degree of comfort for the crowds of people there.

One interesting feature of the place was that the camp was on the site of the Battle of Warburg of Napoleonic days, in which British troops took part. One day a prisoner was digging in his little patch of garden there and his makeshift spade hit a solid obstruction. He dug round it and finally brought it to light. It was a cannon ball, undoubtedly a relic of the battlefield.

Chapter Nine

THE FRENCH UNDERGROUND

M eantime, outside the monotonous backwater of prison camp life, the war was still going on.

Towards the end of the year, when 'Gucio' Gutowski was shot down, the Germans were putting their new fighter, FW 190, on the market in France to counter the Spitfire sweeps. With lots of speed and four cannon, the 190 was the real tabasco and sent quite a few lugubrious souls to kriegydom and lots more to the happy hunting grounds of fighter boys who fight no more. Gucio was probably the first man to shoot one down, but didn't get back to claim it because a couple of minutes later—and busy minutes they were—he was down himself. The fact that he wasn't also out is thanks to another one in umpteen million chance and the French sugar-beet industry.

Gucio was a Pole, straight and slim as poles should be. He was rather a sound type with an arresting sort of face that was a complete justification of the description 'clean cut'. His name, Gucio, was a nickname, an abbreviated corruption of his surname, and it was pronounced 'Goocho'—almost like 'good show', and therefore not inapt.

He was twenty-three and belonged to the Regular Polish Air Force when the show started, and when his country was overrun he got out through Rumania, like Mickey Mouse and so many other Poles, and then through the Black Sea and Mediterranean to France. When France was being overrun, he was flying a fighter on the Italian sector in the south, where he found the Italian pilots would not come up and fight. He waited for them in vain until the last moment and then took off in his fighter and flew to North Africa, caught a ship at Casablanca and went on to England, where at last he found a firm base for operations. He joined a Polish Spitfire squadron and got in quite a lot of ops.

Gucio's evil and lucky day was the 8th of November 1941. His squadron was close escort to Blenheims and the target was a power station near Lille. They duly arrived, dropped their load and turned for home. Quite a few German fighters were making wary passes at the outskirts of the fighters, but none came in to attack Gucio's squadron. Mostly they edged up into the sun and waited for stragglers, so Gucio, stooging home for lunch at about 18,000 feet, felt that the excitement was almost over, though puffy clouds of flak intermittently stained the sky around them.

His Spitfire suddenly shook as though it had been clouted by a steam hammer. It was a direct hit from flak, and Gucio just had time to see a gaping, raw hole open near the port wing root before the Spit flicked over sharply and tumbled into a vicious, left-hand spin, trailing a dirty black stream from the oil radiator, which was ripped open like a burst sausage. Automatically Gucio applied correction, stick forward and right rudder. The spin slackened, then stopped and Gucio eased her out of the dive. A couple of miles ahead and a couple of thousand feet above he saw his squadron cavorting around the bombers and going rapidly away.

Still streaming oil, Gucio opened the taps to overtake them, knowing perfectly well he was just the target the enemy fighters were waiting for. Weaving extensively and craning right round to keep a watch past his tail, he didn't have long to wait for what he knew was coming. In a matter of seconds he saw a 190 slant down and point a blunt nose at him in an incipient port quarter attack. Just as it came into range and opened fire, Gucio pulled a very old, but very effective trick. He yanked his throttle right back, threw his prop into fully fine pitch and slipped steeply to one side—making a most deceptive target. As his speed slackened off, the 190's shells from four 20-mm. cannon shot past like angry red ping-pong balls just above and in front. The 190 travelling fast, in the attack, also overshot him. It passed just over Gucio and tried to break away, diving below and to starboard. Gucio shoved his throttle wide and went down after it, getting a nice target. From barely 100 yards he gave the 190 a solid, four-second burst and immediately its smooth round engine cowlings flew off in great chunks and then the 190 heeled over to starboard and went down in an ever-tightening spiral dive to the right.

As Gucio pulled up again, a 109 attacked him from behind and below. Again Gucio slipped steeply out of the way, but before he could repeat the dose to the 109 there were enemy fighters on him from all directions like a swarm of flies round a sore toe. It was the busiest few minutes he ever had as he turned and slipped in the scrambling, lightning confusion of air battle. They came at him again and again and were gone in the next second. Several times he had a quick snap squirt at a momentary target that flashed by in front but there was no chance to observe results. Inevitably his Spitfire was hit several times. He copped it in the wings, the tail and engine cowlings, but the Spit hung together and the engine ran sweetly, though she still streamed a dirty trail of oil and Gucio knew he couldn't last much longer. He ran out of cannon ammunition and then exhausted his machine-gun trays, though not before he observed strikes on another 109. When his guns would fire no longer he half-rolled, pulled his nose steeply down and tried to out-dive the 109's, which had the reputation of not holding together very well in a prolonged dive.

At 6,000 feet Gucio pulled out and went scooting towards England. A few seconds later there was a heavy explosion out on the already battered port wing as accurate German flak scored another hit. Gucio saw his left wing-tip and aileron disappear and then the Spit was thrown on her back and flicked into an inverted spin until Gucio's eyes were sticking out like organ stops. He tried to correct for it but found his controls were slack and useless so he finally gave it up. He tried to explode his secret I.F.F. radio but found that the detonating button had been blown away, then opened his cockpit top to bale out. As it slid back the Spit twisted out of the inverted spin and continued spinning normally. Gucio unclipped his Sutton harness and as he dived over the side had a shaking glimpse of the ground, just below him. In point of fact he was a bare 150 feet up as he left the aircraft and pulled his rip-cord. He knew he didn't have a chance, but pulled the D-ring just the same, automatically.

'Jesus Maria,' he half-prayed, half-swore. 'Konies Zemna!' The equivalent in English is 'Christ! I've had it!'

White silk was just streaming out of his seat pack when he hit, or rather squashed soggily into a pile of sugar-beet leaves stacked in a field by a conscientious French farmer. In the same moment, he had a split-second glimpse of his Spitfire hitting the deck with a mighty wallop about ten yards away. Gucio bounced gently then rolled off the side of the stack on to the ground. Fifty yards away a badly shaken French peasant left his plough and bolted off in the opposite direction. He was probably responsible for the pile of leaves, which was about six feet high and ten feet across, like a midget pyramid. There was nothing else like it in sight.

Gucio did not linger to meditate. With a brief, farewell glance at the crumpled, smoking wreck of his Spit, he hared away from the spot. A couple of minutes later, incidentally, another Spitfire crashed about 400 yards away and its pilot was caught by the Germans examining Gucio's aircraft where he had gone to see if he could help its pilot. But Gucio was well clear and went to earth in a wood about three kilometres away near a small village. The Germans must have traced him to it for they were out there in strength that night looking for him. Gucio heard them trampling about near his lair in a dense thicket. Then he heard a blood-curdling sound, the baying of dogs which were helping in the search. He kept very still and prayed for luck. Twice he heard German jackboots tramping heavily past his thicket.

After a while there was a light pattering and rustling, and in the darkness he saw the lean shape of a dog push through the undergrowth towards him. The dog saw him too. He was a medium-sized, smooth-haired pooch and eyed Gucio suspiciously, but, luckily, did not bark. He sniffed, but stayed motionless and Gucio, his heart thumping against his ribs, held out a coaxing hand towards it. The dog cautiously approached, craned out its neck and sniffed. It was its last sniff. Gucio made a lightning lunge and in half a moment had both hands with all his strength clamped round the dog's throat, while his body lay on its body and smothered its struggles.

The dog wriggled furiously for half a minute before it suddenly relaxed and lay still. Gucio held his grip for quite a while before he dared loosen his hands. He lay stiff, cold and silent where he was for the rest of the night and when he saw the coast was clear at dawn, stepped warily out of the wood and went to a small farmhouse on the outskirts of the village.

They gave him food and shelter there and later, near the village, Gucio contacted 'The Organization' for getting people like himself back to England. They hid him and fed him while he laid plans for purloining an aircraft from a nearby German aerodrome and flying it back to England. 'The Organization' also put him in touch with a German Unteroffizier (corporal) from the aerodrome who was fed up with the Luftwaffe and wanted to escape to England.

This Unteroffizier instructed Gucio in the finer points of cockpit drill of the German aircraft at the nearby unit and one dawn they slunk together to the perimeter track of the local airfield as Gucio had promised to fly the Unteroffizier back with him. Low mist cloaked their approach, but unfortunately it refused to go away for the rest of the day. It made flying out of the question and they had to postpone the scheme.

A couple of days later they tried again, but on the edge of the aerodrome a German patrol stopped Gucio and wanted to see his papers. He tried to bluff it out as a French civilian and almost got away with it until an officious N.C.O. interfered. In a last-minute attempt to save the day, one of Gucio's French helpers offered to vouch for him, but as it might have cost him his life if Gucio had succeeded in making his escape, Gucio had to decline the offer and was taken to the Gestapo for questioning. There, of course, his bluff fell down and he finished up behind the wire.

Chapter Ten

'BY THE SEAT OF HIS PANTS'

———

Only the line-shoot flying epics churned out by Hollywood could have produced the legend of the pilot who flew 'by the seat of his pants'. The phrase is pretty high in the 'famous last words' class. Of course Hollywood was only talking metaphorically, but even so Air Force pilots don't fly like that, and if there ever was one his kit has long since been handed over to the Standing Committee of Adjustment and the usual form letter sent off to his people, saying what a good fellow he was.

But once upon a time—and this is no fairy story—there really was a man in the Air Force who literally—not metaphorically—flew by the seat of his pants. We put it forward as the first and only time that an aeroplane has been flown by a man's behind on the stick as the controlling element for half an hour. Yet possibly an even more fantastic twist to this incident is the fact that the man who owned the behind had never before flown an aircraft in his life. He is, incidentally, still alive and unmaimed. And this is by no means all. There were, in some respects, two men flying the machine—and neither of them had ever flown an aeroplane before. They did it in conference, by trial and error—one man putting the weight of his behind on the stick and attending to the engines, and the other looking after the rudder and trying to steer a course.

To make it all the more remarkable, they did the whole thing at night by instruments over hostile territory, and just to lift it completely above human credibility it was done almost completely on one engine, with half the controls shot away—one elevator was missing, the port aileron was flapping down crazily from one hinge and the tail trim didn't work. Then, after all that, they managed to set down such a

85

smooth crash-landing in the darkness that a critically wounded rear gunner was not disturbed.

It's a lot to swallow, but it all happened just like that to a couple of English air crew, Flying-Officer Freddy Ivins, a wireless operator-air gunner, and Sergeant Denny Dean, a navigator. They belonged to a Whitley squadron and had been in the war pretty well from the beginning. Freddy, who owned the historic behind, had wanted to be a pilot, but at thirty was declared to be over age, a fact which scarcely detracts from his performance. He was dark, and rather neat, and despite eyes that carried a tinge of green, was a most tolerant and likeable sort of chap.

It was his third close shave. On one of his early trips in 1941, they had bad engine trouble, expecting to go into the drink any tick of the clock and the pilot just managed to make the beach at Skegness for a crash-lob. The crew piled out, but some Army people appeared a couple of hundred yards away making frantic signs. The boys caught the word 'mines', so they piled back into the kite again right speedily. They found the aircraft had pulled up a few yards from the edge of a minefield and soldiers later had to escort them through the tortuous gaps in it.

Not very long after, they were coming back from another trip when the starboard engine packed in and they eventually had to ditch in the North Sea. The pilot was drowned but the rest were picked up some hours later by a naval auxiliary after a rather frightening time. Their second pilot that night was Pete Kingsford-Smith, nephew of the famous Australian airman.

Nine weeks later, on the 30th of November 1941, Freddy had his third and classic experience. The target was Hamburg and they very nearly didn't go at all. First there was trouble in getting one engine to start, and then, as they finally taxied out, they became bogged. After they got clear of the mud, the navigator's table collapsed, and by the time they were eventually ready to go they were about half an hour behind the other aircraft. Freddy called up control, told them the position and asked if it were worth while going, as they were so late they would probably be alone over the target, and targets were not a good place to be alone over. There was a slight hesitation from control, then the voice came back.

'Yes, H for Harry. You might as well go. Shake it up.'

So they went, which was a pity. It was a bright, moonlit night, and, if they had had eyes for that sort of thing, rather beautiful, with a rippled sea shining softly far below. There was a further slight mishap on the way when Denny's oxygen tube slipped from its socket and he almost passed out before Freddy noticed the trouble and plugged it in for him again. They pushed the old Whitley along to make up time, but even a pushed Whitley is not very fast, so they were probably the only bomber over Hamburg when they arrived at 16,000 feet about 10 p.m.

They had the obvious reception, of course. Everything went for them as there was nothing else to go for. No sooner had they arrived than a big concentration of searchlights caught and held them. No matter how they twisted and dived, there was no getting away from these blinding lights which made them feel like a naked Aunt Sally. Then the flak came whistling up, heavy and accurate from the undivided attention of massed batteries.

They'd never known such flak. There were masses of it, exploding all round them in an erratic intermittent profusion of brilliant orange and red flashes. They heard the 'crack' 'crack' of the nearer ones and time and again the heavy Whitley shivered and shook as the blast of near misses flung against her ungainly shape. Several times she was holed by pieces of shrapnel and it was then that the elevator, aileron, and tail-trim were badly damaged.

Freddy left his wireless cubby hole and started to crawl down the confined tunnel of the fuselage to let off the flares towards the tail for photographs of the effects of the raid. He was thankful he couldn't see the flashes of flak around them any longer, but could still hear and feel the jolting explosions. Then there were two very, very near 'cracks' and then he heard one engine falter. The Whitley seemed to lurch a little, and then began to shake and shudder ominously. Freddy plugged in his tail-position inter-com. and bawled—

'Looks like we've had it.'

'Yeah.' It was the voice of Denny, up in the bomb-aimer's position. 'We've copped a packet somewhere.'

Freddy called up the first pilot.

'Hullo, No. 1! What goes on?'

There was no answer, so Freddy called again, but still there was no answer.

'Damn this,' said Freddy. 'Drop the cargo and I'll come up front.'

He unplugged his inter-com. and started to crawl back up the fuselage. Just then, the flak suddenly stopped and for a few seconds there were no more bangs. Then Freddy heard the Brownings in the rear turret open up and knew what it meant.

'Oh crumbs! Night fighter,' he muttered. 'What a b—— party.'

He was almost back to his radio position when hell broke out just in front of his nose as a stream of incendiaries came sizzling and crackling through the slab-side of the fuselage. It smashed his receiver, just missed the auxiliary tanks and would have got Freddy if he had been where he had meant to be in two seconds' time. Then the firing ceased, and the rear turret Brownings were silent too. Freddy crawled on past the navigator's position towards the pilots' cabin to see what the position was. He got there and his mouth sagged open with shock. There was no one there. Both first and second pilots' seats were vacant and there was no sign of them.

Just then Denny the navigator, crawled back from the bomb-aimer's position in the nose. On the way he noticed that the hatch in the floor was incomprehensibly open but, too preoccupied to worry about it, he clambered across the gap and stuck his head into the pilots' compartment to see what the score was. His face was towards Freddy, only a couple of feet away as he looked up to the pilots' seats, and his mouth too, sagged with shock as he took in the pilots' absence. Pop-eyed, they looked at each other ; Denny found tongue.

'Christ! Where are they?' he shouted.

'Damned if I know,' bawled Freddy. 'They're not down my end.'

Freddy hauled himself upright and looked out of the cabin. From the starboard engine, which was surging and popping, a tiny flame was glowing.

'Let's get out of this,' he shouted to Denny. 'There's no future in it.'

'O.K.,' answered Denny, and they both grabbed their parachute canopy packs and clipped them on. Then they noticed that the flame in the starboard engine cowling was flickering faintly and almost out.

Denny grabbed Freddy and spoke into his ear.

'What say we try and get the kite back home?'

Freddy looked a bit startled, started to shake his head, then wavered.

'Hell! There's nothing to lose. Let's have a go,' he said.

So Denny climbed into the first pilot's seat and Freddy into the second dicky's place, and the show was on. The only thing they knew about flying was what they had picked up from their pilots—which wasn't much.

First of all they noticed the air-speed indicator. It was flickering down towards 80 m.p.h. and they could feel the Whitley was on the verge of a fatal stall and spin as she ploughed soggily on, shuddering menacingly. Both of them threw their weight forward against the dual sticks and Denny tried the tail-trim, but the trim didn't have the slightest effect and was obviously U/S.

So then they had to get the nose down by sheer strength, without the help of the tail-trim, and if you don't know anything about flying you might as well understand that it requires colossal strength to handle a heavy aircraft when the trim is not properly set. In fact it's almost impossible, but by using all their strength they finally got the stick a little forward and the sluggish, shuddering Whitley began to drop her nose and pick up speed. It was a very narrow squeak. They found that presumably because of the damaged port aileron, the Whitley wanted to drop her port wing, and only by holding the wheel almost hard over to starboard were they able to keep her on a moderately even keel.

As the Whitley became properly under control, Freddy opened the port engine throttle until she was howling at full bore. He tried to get the starboard engine to run evenly but it became progressively worse until she was no more than ticking over and not supplying any power. Meantime Denny, who knew his course home, was trying to get the aircraft headed in the required direction by a series of skidding flat turns against the weak engine, as there was very little aileron control. Despite their continued pressure on the control column, the nose of the tail heavy aircraft was rising again and the air speed dropping alarmingly once more.

Denny was still feeling rather sick, probably from his earlier lack of oxygen, and couldn't put much sustained pressure on the stick, so Freddy got up on his seat, put his feet on the back-rest, balanced his behind against the half-wheel of the control column and heaved back hard, like an oarsman in an outrigger putting all his weight behind a stroke. Again they were only just in time, and the Whitley, shuddering very near the stall, dropped her nose slowly and then one wing and fell away again, picking up flying speed and losing a lot of height. They got back to an even keel again and back on course and then Freddy left his seat for a few moments to try and tap out a message to base, telling them they probably wouldn't be back, but were trying hard. As he tapped the Morse key just behind the pilots' cabin, he kept an anxious eye on the instruments, as the nose was rising again and the air speed, conversely, dropping. Once he had to drop his key and rush back to throw his weight on the stick again, but finally he got his message out. There was no answer, of course, as the night fighter had smashed his receiver. He got his behind back on the stick just in time to prevent another threatened stall.

So it went on. Despite Freddy's weight on the stick, the nose kept on rising, until, with the slackened speed, the stick became easier to push and Freddy, heaving back like an oarsman till the blood rushed to his face, would just get the nose down again. Every time it happened, though, they would fall away in a sickly lurch that seemed to cast their stomachs loose from their moorings, and lose a lot more height that they could not build up again. The erratic behaviour of the Whitley made it almost impossible for Denny, who was giving most of his time to the rudder, to steer anything but a rough course. Despite his weakness, he was also shoving on the stick, trying to help Freddy, particularly at those moments when the aircraft was quivering near the stall, and at other times when Freddy's legs grew tired and he had to turn round and lean his chest on the stick.

That the Whitley flew at all in these circumstances is a tribute to her inherent stability. Freddy and Denny knew nothing about a lot of the instruments and knobs so they just left them alone. Most of the things they did they talked over first to see who knew most about it. They flew the whole time by instruments, which is not the easiest way to fly, but the only way they knew. There were times when the dummy horizon of the lurching aircraft was almost vertical, but somehow they always managed to get it back at least near the horizontal. Occasionally they saw the dark shadows of a town below them in the moonlight, but couldn't pin-point themselves as there was no time for map reading. They just flew their rough course as well as they could and hoped for the best.

After a time Freddy called up the rear gunner to see if he were still there, but there was no answer. He turned on the fuselage lights then and looked back. Far away, down the long tunnel of the fuselage, he saw the turret doors open and the figure of the rear gunner huddled motionless over his guns. It didn't make him feel any more cheerful.

At one stage another flak battery opened up on them but missed them by hundreds of yards. Freddy and Denny, a little light-headed with excitement and reaction, laughed like a couple of schoolgirls because it would have been a pretty freakish shot that hit that crazily lurching and weaving aircraft. They realized they were involuntarily doing some of the best evasive action ever flown.

They had been going for about twenty-five minutes, losing height all the time, when they hit the coast, and as the drunken Whitley headed out over quiet water they were down to about 2,000 feet. Freddy looked from the water to the altimeter with a troubled eye, the memory of his last ditching still painfully fresh in his memory. He knew it was a matter of only a few minutes before they would be in the drink and had no chance of getting close enough to England to be rescued. He stuck it for nearly five minutes before he turned to Denny.

'Listen,' he yelled. 'We haven't got a snowball's hope in hell of making it. We're only making it tougher for ourselves. We'd better turn back and bale out over land. I don't want another ditching just for the fun of it.'

'I think you're right,' Denny yelled back. 'Here goes.'

Gingerly he prodded the rudder-bar with his foot and in a series of skidding lurches the Whitley made a laborious, sickly turn against the useless starboard engine. Freddy was still shoving with his rump to keep the nose down, but it was a tricky business and they continued to lose height. When they eventually staggered over dry land again the altimeter showed a bare 700 feet.

'This is too damn low to jump,' Freddy said. 'We'll have to try and put her down. Maybe Biddy's still alive. We might be able to save him.' (Biddy was the rear gunner, huddled silent and still in his turret.)

'O.K.,' said Denny. 'Here goes again.'

Almost ahead of them, they saw in the moonlight a large field. It looked pretty good for a crash landing, so Denny pressed on the rudder-bar till the sluggish Whitley swung her nose towards it. Freddy shoved harder against the stick and they throttled back a little. The Whitley headed down towards the field.

An airline pilot couldn't have judged it better. They lumbered heavily just over the edge of the field and when they were about ten feet from the deck, Denny cut the throttles, Freddy, who had taken his behind off the stick, switched off the engines and then Denny eased the stick, which, for once, was acting their way, back into his stomach. The Whitley hit, bounced a little, then hit again and skidded to a rending stop. Incongruously the noise all died away except for the under-cart klaxon which blared jarringly in their ears.

'Crumbs. Good landing, Denny,' said Freddy.

Denny opened the top hatch and they both climbed out, flopped on to the wing and scrambled off on to good, solid earth. There was a small silence, then:

'Thank God that's over,' said Freddy in a voice that was one long, throbbing sigh.

'Yeah,' Denny sighed back. 'Got a cigarette?'

They each lit up and inhaled thankfully, luxuriously. There was another silence, a longer one. Each was trembling slightly, and a little sweaty. Then Denny said:

'Christ! How about Biddy?'

'Hell, let's look,' said Freddy, and they ran round to the turret. Dimly through the perspex in the moonlight they could see Biddy's body still crouched motionless over his guns. They banged on the perspex, but Biddy made no movement. Unable to open the turret from the outside, Freddy ran round to the cabin again, crawled down the confined fuselage to the turret doors and tapped the still form.

'Are you alive, Biddy?' he asked and felt like crying with relief when the gunner moved slightly and gave a faint moan. He obviously couldn't help himself, so Freddy grabbed him by the shoulders and lugged him out. They carried him a little way away and laid him on the ground. Biddy, barely conscious, moved his hand weakly to just below his shoulder and said, 'It's here.' They opened his flying suit, tunic and shirt and saw a horrid torn hole in the flesh, full of blood. Then they heard the sound of a car approaching at speed and gathered that it contained their prospective captors as it swung towards the field. Freddy ran back to the pranged Whitley and set off a flare inside the fuselage. A few seconds after he had rejoined Denny and Biddy, the Whitley was going up like a torch, and it was not long after that the Germans found them.

In those early days of the bombing offensive, the Germans had not hypocritically branded the bomber boys as several varieties of sadistic ruffians for the sort of thing that they themselves started over Warsaw, Rotterdam, Coventry, and so on. Hatred of the R.A.F. was not running so high in Germany. An ambulance was brought and Biddy taken to a nearby hospital. Freddy went with him for comfort. Biddy was placed immediately on the operating-table and when Freddy stood by him, just before the operation started, he could see Biddy's heart beating in that horrible hole in his chest. The German doctor, who spoke perfect English, took Freddy aside.

'Frankly, your friend has not much chance,' he said, 'but please rest assured I will do everything I possibly can for him.'

After that, Freddy and Denny were taken to a nearby barracks, where a Luftwaffe major told them that his men had shot them down as they passed overhead.

'You're very lucky to be alive,' he told them. 'Our machine-guns set one of your engines on fire.'

It was the first that Freddy or Denny had heard of it, but they reserved comment. The major took them into the officers' mess and played the host with a bottle of whisky and another of gin. He was intrigued with the fact that neither of the two was a pilot, and asked where the pilots were. As he wouldn't have believed the true story, Freddy and Denny just said they hadn't the faintest idea, so the major was of the opinion that they had run off from the crashed aircraft. They waited there until the telephone rang two hours later with the news that the operation had been successful. Biddy eventually recovered completely and arrived in the compound next to Freddy. Two years later, incidentally, Freddy was also joined by Pete Kingsford-Smith who was second pilot the time he ditched in the North Sea.

The mystery of the missing pilots was never cleared up, though their fate is known. Their dead bodies were found not far from Hamburg, the target for that night. But how they came to leave the aircraft without warning and without parachutes will never be known.

*   *   *

The few odd freaks among kriegies who fell or jumped out of aircraft without parachutes and lived to tell the tale had all passed out on the way down so they couldn't describe just what the feeling was—a feeling that most people have often wondered at with little tingles of horror. But there *was* one man who knew what it *felt* like. Though he hadn't exactly fallen without a parachute, he had done pretty well the same thing and certainly had the same feeling.

By sheer chance, he happened to be a journalist with an analytical mind and was able both to register and report his sensations accurately. He was Ray Silver, a dark young man from Ontario, Canada, with all the racy humour and explosive energy of a Hollywood reporter. It all happened actually in England on the way back from his first op. It wasn't until later that he came to settle with us in Germany. Ray was observer in a Wimpy[1] and in summer, 1941, forty-eight hours after arrival at his first squadron, he was off with an inexperienced crew on one of those bashings of French invasion ports that introduced new crews to ops. Those were the days when the invasion boot was on the other foot.

The trip was uneventful until they were within five minutes of land-

[1] Wellington bomber.

93

ing back at base, a couple of miles west of some 3,000 foot peaks of the Pennines. From his navigator's table, Ray had just looked over the pilot's shoulder, checking course, speed, and height. He saw that the altimeter read 3,300 feet. For a moment he watched the wireless op. winding in the trailing aerial, then turned back to mark in the last leg of his air plot. His hand was just reaching for the blue pencil when time suddenly stopped for a moment and the world went black. His private diary carries on the story a moment later.

'I felt myself riding along the ground between the sides of the aircraft, and then with the same indescribable momentum you sometimes sense in a dream I was launched upward and onward. It was no logical transition, but just like a dream. It took, perhaps, about half a fragment of a second, and in the next fragment of time I had a clear impression of flying through space.

'For the first time, I registered the nasty truth. We must have blown up. "The wireless op. must have caused a spark winding in the aerial and exploded us," I thought, quite clearly and logically.

'I had a sensation of being hurled through blackness, with bright yellow stars, like flak, flashing past me. There was a definite sensation of being propelled. I wasn't floating or flying. I was being shot like a projectile.

'I wondered how much of me was hurtling through space. Was it just my head, my mind, or was I still intact? It wasn't till then I realized my parachute canopy wasn't attached. Naturally enough it wouldn't be. And then my mind flicked back to that 3,300 feet on the altimeter and I thought of what was going to happen when I hit the ground.

'Without any doubt at all I knew I was going to be killed. In fact I was going to be smashed into pulp. For practical purposes I was already dead, and I knew it, but my reactions were quite unexpected. I felt neither fear nor regret. Purely and simply I was overcome with a feeling of absolute amazement. I couldn't quite accept the fact that this was happening to *me*. I had seen three aircraft blown to smithereens, but with the inevitable defence mechanism working to the last I told myself, "This can't possibly be happening to *me*. It just *can't* happen to me."'

Ray came to earth, literally, with his face buried in a soft mass of black, gritty muck. It was part of a bog on the side of a mountain. He rolled over and peered into the fog-wrapped blackness of an unfrequented mountain wood at night. He still couldn't grasp the fact that he was on earth, albeit somewhat sloshy earth. He wondered if he were still alive, or was this an introduction to the Other World. He couldn't believe that anyone could ever drop 3,000 feet out of an aircraft and live, let alone be blown out in an explosion.

Complete consciousness of the fact that he *was* alive returned slowly, and then fearsomely he ran his hands down his body, feeling for pulped flesh and jagged bones. He found his flying-boots had mysteriously vanished from his legs but everything else seemed all right till he came to his big left toe, where his questing fingers encountered a soft, soggy mass. He had a moment of horror and then discovered it was only a lump of mud from the bog and the reaction of the anti-climax helped to bring him round still further.

He found he was covered in a crust of mud and blood and decided he'd better do something about it, so he struggled on to his shaky legs and moved erratically forward in the darkness. After about five minutes he sat down again with a sudden fear of walking over a cliff—this in a man who thought he had just fallen 3,000 feet. He shouted into the darkness and felt the utter foolishness of a man who shouts into nothingness. Then he heard a faint answering voice.

'Keep shouting and walk towards me,' he shouted back to the voice. 'Who are you?'

'What's it matter? I've just been in an aircraft crash!' answered the voice eerily.

'What the hell d'you think I've just come out of?' Ray shouted back, aggrievedly.

A moment later, on the side of the hill—Boarsfell, in the Pennines—he met the tail gunner from his Wimpy.

It was quite a classic meeting, but both were already so numbed with shock that they took it almost as a matter of course. Neither was very badly hurt, though both were caked in mud and blood. They compared notes and found their experiences much the same, and when dawn came stumbled over the top of the mountain and found the wrecked Wimpy. It was nearly 1,000 feet from where they had landed in the bog. Both pilots were dead by the aircraft. The wireless op. was there too, but still alive. Reconstructing the scene, they realized that the Wimpy had crashed into the sloping side of the mountain at about 160 m.p.h. and they had been thrown out and over the mountain. Parts of the aircraft were found over a square mile, and one engine was over a quarter of a mile away. Ray and the gunner had landed in different patches of the same bog which had saved their lives.

Ray was out of hospital a few weeks later and his second trip—with a new crew—went without incident. The third stopped before it properly started, with what Ray described as 'engine trouble'. The aircraft swung on take-off and they collected a dispersal hut round one engine and about 100 yards of barbed wire around the other. The fourth trip didn't count either. They iced up over the North Sea and went into a spin. Some fancy stick-work coupled with jettisoning the bombs got them out of it, and they arrived back safely.

The fifth trip was a comedy of errors that ended up in a crash-landing with fire on board and a kite that was written off as soon as the engineering officer saw it. The sixth trip, now on a four-engined aircraft, went off smoothly enough, though they had to land on an aerodrome too small for the big aircraft and pulled up a few yards from the bomb dump. The seventh trip passed off quite smoothly, but on the eighth trip a night fighter ripped them open and Ray finished up with us behind the wire.

Chapter Eleven

STALAG LUFT III

The entry of the U.S.A. into the war on the 7th of December 1941, was a matter of no mean rejoicing among prisoners in Germany. It came just at the time the Germans were pulled up short in front of Moscow and then began to fall back in the historic first Russian winter. The combination of those two things produced the first glimmer of real hope that the tide was turning.

In some respects the jubilation was not quite so pronounced as might have been thought, though this was not because America's potential aid was underestimated. The reason was that her entry had been expected for some time by kriegies, particularly in the fortnight just before the Jap attack on Pearl Harbour. The increasing build-up of hate in the German Press against the U.S.A. at that time was sure evidence that something was cooking and kriegies knew it was only a matter of time before the American man-in-the-street realized that it was *his* war too. From the wails of German papers, too, kriegies considered that the U.S.A. had been neutral in name only for some time before her official entry.

Then Pearl Harbour and Singapore occurred and kriegies were severely shaken. Possibly even worse for them was the loss of the battleships *Prince of Wales* and *Repulse*, but with all that their reinforced confidence in the ultimate end did not waver. They realized the Allies had had little to spare for the Far East to meet the initial shock of the Jap attack, and realized, too, that the Japs would be stopped eventually, held, then pushed back in due course.

As far as their captors were concerned, never once did the kriegy attitude change from the easy air of bland condescension—an attitude which at times drove the Germans to quivering rage. In some sort of retaliation to soothe their punctured vanity, the Nazis often imposed miserable reprisals on prisoners for a variety of petty things, but the only reaction these reprisals ever evoked were sardonic cheers which were infuriating to the stiff-necked captors and rather spoilt the effect of the reprisals.

The Germans never seemed to be able to understand the reactions of kriegies either to reprisals or to bad news. It was never as laid down in the Nazi book of rules, and therefore it came under the generic heading of decadence. The trouble with the Germans was that one could pull their legs easily enough—they would stretch for yards—but no amount of effort could infuse any similar elasticity into their intellects.

There was the time that quite a well-meaning German officer (who, incidentally, had a name for hypocrisy) walked into a roomful of kriegies and with a certain amount of ostentatious sympathy, said:

'Gentlemen, I am sorry to have to inform you that Singapore has fallen.'

The answer came in shouts and screams of well-simulated mirth and a lazy voice which said:

'Don't worry, Herr Pieber. It's only a loan. It's a trap, you see.'

Pieber could not see.

After America's official entry, kriegydom became more cosmopolitan than ever, though there were already a few Americans of the R.A.F. in captivity. Prison camp life in Germany had been cosmopolitan from the start—there being so many countries of the world that hated the collective Nazi guts. It was quite normal to have ten different mother-tongues in the compound at the same time.

In nearly every purge there used to be the odd foreigner or two, wearing familiar R.A.F. blue and not looking particularly different from the rest of us. Closer inspection would reveal a flash on the shoulder reading 'Poland', 'Norway', or 'Belgium', or something like that, and often there was a strange ribbon under the brevet. Most of these boys had a private, personal hate to work off because nearly all of them had first-hand knowledge of the Procrustean protection of the Nazis.

Joe S——, a Czech, was typical. He had been trained in the Czech Air Force as a navigator and wireless operator, but had had no chance to put his training into practice in his Motherland. After that he just wanted to fight Germans, and, as a running exile, he chased the war fantastically all over Europe looking for a fight, and eventually caught up with it. Maybe he got more than he bargained for, but not before he had had a very good innings and satisfied his ambition.

He escaped into Poland when his country was bloodlessly conquered. From Poland, with many of his countrymen, he made for France. As that country was not yet at war and there were neutrality complications, Joe joined the French Foreign Legion. A few days before he was due to sail for the Legion's headquarters at Sidi Bel Abbas, France declared war on Germany and it looked as if Joe was going to get his chance.

Fate said otherwise. Joe joined one of the French bomber squadrons that did not see any action and when France collapsed, Joe had to get out again. He made for Toulouse, boarded a small Danish schooner there and arrived at Oran. From there he went to Casablanca, recrossed the Mediterranean and landed at Gibraltar. A few days later he was in England, and finally got cracking with his ambition. He joined an all-Czech squadron, and during the sticky days of 1940 and 1941 played a worthy part in Britain's fight for life.

He flew on ops. all through 1941, piling up a respectable total of operational hours until the very eve of the old year. The climax came on the 28th of December, at a time when Europe was wrapped in the bitterest winter that had been known for 120 years.

On an aerodrome in Norfolk that night, Joe and three of his countrymen were preparing to make their thirty-fifth—and last—trip together. It was to be Kiel, and it was also to complete their first tour of ops. After that it was to be leave, and for Joe, the realization of a dream he had hugged from boyhood. They had promised him a pilot's course.

A full moon shone fitfully through racing black clouds as the crew of six, including the four Czechs, grouped around the Wimpy and adjusted their thick flying kit. Rarely had they been so cheerful. Even a last-minute change of target from Kiel to Wilhelmshaven provoked nothing more than cheerful shrugs and a couple of sarcastic cracks. In the same spirit they accepted the rear gunner's: 'I've had this. I won't be needing it, anyway, on the last trip,' and he tossed aside an ill-fitting Mae West which he had wrestled to put on.

A few minutes later they were one of a series of black shapes streaming in ghostly procession through heavy cloud, headed for the North Sea.

It was an uneventful journey—uneventful, that is, in the opinion of a crew who had seen the fireworks over Cologne and Essen and the rest of Happy Valley. Wilhelmshaven was burning from the incendiaries of the leading aircraft when they arrived and they went in, stoked up the good work, and then turned for home. There was flak, of course, but it seemed lighter than usual. There weren't any of those sickening, thudding thumps that made you catch your breath and wait for the kite to fall apart. They were over the North Sea again. England, and all that it meant, was less than three hours away.

And then, 'Paul! Paul!' Joe heard the strained voice of the navigator calling over the intercom. to the pilot. 'The starboard motor seems to be packing up.'

A reassuring reply from the pilot. 'The instruments show nothing. Everything seems O.K.'

There was placid peace again for a few moments. Then the pilot's voice again, on a high, shaken note.

'Christ! Look! The bloody port engine.'

Joe felt his heart jump suddenly and looked out of the window by the navigator's table. He saw jets of black smoke shoot from the port engine fairing, and then the propeller visibly began to slow up. It became slower and slower until only the pressure of rushing air made it revolve spasmodically. Joe had risen to his feet for a closer look. Suddenly the propeller leapt off the shaft, and before a bewildered Joe could register this fact it had crashed back into the belly of the fuselage immediately under his feet.

It sheared through pipes of the hydraulic system, and the undercart and flaps flopped down. That was all they saw of the port propeller, but it was quite enough. Paul, the pilot, poured the coal on to the starboard engine until it was roaring at full bore, but it was not enough. With wheels and flaps down the Wimpy could not hold her height, and began to sink.

There could be only one ending. As the Wimpy sank lower and lower through the darkness, and the North Sea, cold and black, rose up, Paul ordered the crew to ditching stations.

They were fairly firmly braced, but scarcely enough to withstand the terrific jolt as the Wimpy ploughed into a surging, almost unyielding wall of water. Paul was thrown forward, hit his head, and collapsed unconscious over the stick held limply by his harness. Joe had much the same experience, and lay senseless where he had crouched.

Freezing, numbing water revived both of them. Only Joe's head was above water when he recovered his senses, almost trapped in the waterlogged fuselage. Both he and the pilot had their Mae Wests to thank for the fact that they were not completely submerged. The rear gunner, who had been so nonchalantly confident that he would not need his Mae West on his last trip, was not seen again.

Joe and the pilot struggled to the escape hatch and climbed out, to find the collapsible dinghy already bobbing on the sea with three other members of the crew already in it. The two scrambled in and the dinghy was immediately cut adrift, to be clutched by raging, heaving water and sent tossing and twirling into the unknown blackness.

They tried to paddle but it was useless. The cold bit into them until their whole bodies ached and their hands were so numb that their baling could barely keep pace with inrushing water as wave after wave broke angry crests over them. A nauseating sickness overtook them and the night seemed endless as the dinghy lurched and tossed in inky blackness.

Dawn did come eventually. It brought a wan light that did not much relieve them, for it showed a scene terrifying in its desolation. Dirty grey sea and a long heaving swell had replaced the mountainous black waves of the night, the sky was heavily overcast and the cold bit as cruelly as ever into their numbed, stiff bodies. Lashing spray had formed white icicles of brine on their blue faces, giving them a streaked, unearthly appearance.

How anxiously they scanned the heaving horizon for a sign of land. Time after time one of them shouted joyfully that he had seen the white line of the shore, but always it was only the white horses of the waves, and after a while some were just hallucinations induced by their vigil of misery.

Drinking water became an urgent necessity. They examined their hard rations, and sickening disappointment awaited them. Of the four water-bottles, two contained water that was undrinkable through neglect. Paul, who was captain of the aircraft and in command of the dinghy, imposed an iron regimen—one mouthful per man per day, one biscuit and one cube of chocolate.

The dinghy tossed helplessly all day. Nothing they did could make the slightest difference to its aimless, heaving motion. Sometimes, caught by a rushing wall of water, it would gyrate madly, pitching and dipping down into the trough, bringing back that awful nausea to its crew. At other times it would race forward in great wide sweeps on the crest of a wave, and then again it would remain in one position, but never did it stop bobbing up and down, and all the time the unbelievable cold froze them to the marrow and sapped their strength.

They guessed from the sun's position that it was about midday, when one of them let out an exultant yell—'Aircraft!' They listened tensely and then they all heard it, a steady, ever-deepening drone. One of them held the Very pistol in readiness and a few seconds later three Lockheed Hudsons of Coastal Command swept into view, flying low and close to them. The man holding the Very pistol fired it, fired until every one of the cartridges had exploded in soaring rockets of coloured light, and they poured the green fluorescene liquid into the sea to mark their position. Futilely they shouted and whistled at the three swift shapes until they were exhausted and their voices were hoarse croaks.

Then with a relief that no words would describe they saw one of the Hudsons detach itself, sweep down and circle a few feet above them. Round and around it flew—'Pin-pointing our position,' they told each other happily. A bulky packet fell out of the Hudson and dropped ten yards from them, floating on the surface. In it was food and water. In a frenzy they struggled to get the cumbersome, circular dinghy to move towards it. It was hopeless. Caught by the swell the packet was floating further and further away, and impotent, frustrated and sick with disappointment they were too numbed with cold to dive in and swim for it. They watched it disappear into the grey mist, but their despair was lessened by the vision that each of them now cherished—of British destroyers, called up by the Hudsons, racing to their aid; or of a Catalina flying-boat landing alongside and picking them up. It would only be a matter of an hour or so now and the nightmare would be over.

Night came and there was no sign of the destroyers or of the Catalina.

The second pilot was the first to crack. He started shouting and crying and they had to hold him down in the lurching dinghy all through the following night that seemed to stretch into eternity.

Yet dawn came again. This time it was wrapped in a cold grey mist and a drizzle that merged sky and sea into a dull monotone of drear desolation. Again and again they thought they saw and heard the aircraft and the ships that were coming to save them, but they did not hail these illusions any more. They could hardly speak. Their dry throats ached with pain and their bodies were frozen stiff. Day passed once more into night—almost imperceptibly, for the cold grey mist still clung tenaciously to the sea.

When again the sun shone palely through the never-ending mist it was the last day of 1941, and their friends back at the station would be preparing for the New Year's eve party. In the irony of it they sank to a new low. The second pilot had grown worse, and his sobbing—he was too weak to rave—racked the nerves of his companions. Their tongues were swollen with thirst. And then another torment was piled on. Numbed hands were totally incapable of undoing their clothes to urinate, and the combination of salt water and urine produced an agony of burning on their bodies.

They drank their one gulp of water and ate their one biscuit and their solitary cube of chocolate, and watched the sun cross the sky once more and dip under the horizon.

Then in the rapidly fading light they saw the silhouettes of two ships. Forcing their anguished minds to believe they were real, they whistled and shouted and waved, but the ships moved steadily away, and then were gone. If only they had had ONE cartridge for their Very pistol.

The second pilot died on New Year's Day. Their water had given out and in desperation some of them had tried to ease their parched throats by drinking sea water into which they had put aspirin tablets, in the futile hope that they would purify it. The captain and front gunner tried to persuade them not to, but the thirst-crazed others were no longer rational. Joe, the navigator and the second pilot, had drunk great gulps of the salt water, and for a few moments felt better. Then excruciating pain tore at their insides. The second pilot collapsed and died and four weak men had to struggle to roll his body over the side into the sea.

Then the navigator became delirious. He writhed in the bottom of the dinghy, screaming in a hoarse, inhuman voice, and shortly fell unconscious. It was never known whether he died then or during the night. He never moved or uttered a sound again.

Joe himself became unconscious on the fifth day. It was a blessed relief. The pilot and the gunner, the only two who had fought successfully against the overpowering desire to drink sea water, remained conscious. They had their reward, because it was they who experienced the indescribable emotion of seeing, next day, just as the sun was dipping below the mist-shrouded horizon again, a lacy fringe, with a dark background that was land.

With its cargo of one dead man and three others dying, the dinghy was met by two German soldiers who waded into the surf and covered them with loaded rifles and fixed bayonets. When they realized their prisoners were more dead than alive, they brought some nearby villagers and the men were carried to the local hospital of Altmark, a small town a few miles from Amsterdam.

They were to have one stroke of luck. The German doctor who attended them had studied at Prague University and spoke Czech perfectly. Joe eventually recovered consciousness, and with two others who had survived those grim six days remained in the village hospital for six weeks, tended by the Czech-speaking doctor. After that they spent another six weeks in an Amsterdam hospital. In April 1942, Joe, who was the only surviving officer of the Wimpy crew, went on to a new prison camp at Sagan. They had to carry him through the gate and for weeks he lay in bed, gradually regaining his strength.

This new camp at Sagan was to become one of the most notorious of the Nazi prisoner of war camps. It was Stalag Luft III and it grew into the largest Air Force officers' camp in Germany, with a population of about 10,000, including several thousands of Americans, but its notoriety did not come from its numbers. It was from the later established North Compound of Stalag Luft III that the mass tunnel escape occurred that ended in the massacre of fifty of the escaped R.A.F. officers by the Gestapo.

The location of the camp was about half-way between Berlin and Breslau and also about midway between the old Polish and Czech borders. In view of its bloody history, Stalag Luft III had a modest beginning—though the advance publicity from the Germans was anything but that. The Nazis told kriegies at Barth that they were to be transferred to Goering's luxury camp and hopes were therefore high, but when the first purge of 100 officers arrived at Sagan from Barth on the 21st of March 1942, they found no luxury but just a collection of six ramshackle huts in a tiny compound of barren, sandy soil, surrounded by the usual rusty barbed wire and machine-guns and searchlights in sentry boxes. As usual, washing or sanitary facilities were very bad.

On the way in the train from Barth there were several escapes. One of the escapees—all of whom were recaptured—was a badly burned but perennially cheerful Canadian called Scruffy Weir, another was Paddy Byrne, whom you met in Chapter Three, and a third was 'The Dodger', who also had honourable mention a few chapters back as one of the escapers from the early Dulag Luft tunnel in 1940. Though he was an Army major, the Dodger always managed to stick with the Air Force and became an almost indispensable feature of life at Stalag Luft III. He was an energetic and persuasive organizer of political and economic discussion groups, and, as an unrepentant Tory, had to find answers to a lot of banter from the large Leftist section of the camp.

Facing this page: Newly shot-down airmen filing through the double barbed-wire gates of Stalag Luft III

The Dodger was largely responsible for engineering the International Relations Group at Stalag Luft III to unite even more closely the dozen or so different nationalities represented by the prisoners there. Almost two years later to the day after his arrival at Sagan, the game old Dodger was among those who crawled out through the historic tunnel.

Luft III was only about half a mile from Sagan itself, a town of about 25,000 people with no especial claim to fame, apart perhaps from a fairly important railway junction from which prisoners, night after night, heard the clanking of laden goods trains trundling to and from the Russian front. Sagan was well inside the German 'dust bowl' area in Silesia and the dry, dusty soil, though rather trying from the living point of view, was easy to dig for the inevitable tunnelling operations. It was also dangerously crumbly.

Another point of interest about the place was that the site of the camp marked the furthest point of advance of the Russian forces in the last war, and later on, when North Compound was opened, kriegies saw a little wooden cross on a pedestal just outside the wire which had been erected to mark the occasion. That cross was the only interesting thing kriegies ever saw because thick belts of scruffy pine-trees obscured all sight of the town and railway, and in fact everything further than about twenty yards from the wire. It all added to the claustrophobic effect of Goering's 'luxury' camp.

The first section of the camp opened was the East Compound, and a few weeks after the arrival of the first hundred from Barth, the rest of the Barth people were sent on to Sagan till there were about three hundred all told in East Compound.

On one of these later purges was a Flight-Lieutenant Johnny W——— D.F.C., another notoriously persistent escaper. While crates containing the kriegies' equipment were being loaded on to transport at Barth, an amiable German interpreter standing by, commented jokingly to the kriegies doing the loading.

'Be careful with those crates. Maybe Flight-Lieutenant W——— is nailed up in one of them. You know how fond he is of trying to get away from us.'

The boys all laughed dutifully and said, 'Ha ha! Yes, how funny that would be!'—but later on the German must have felt decidedly queer because, as all the boys knew, Johnny W——— WAS nailed up in the next crate to be loaded. He broke his way out on the journey to

---

Facing this page: The prison camp from the 'outside'

Sagan and escaped. He was eventually caught again, and being a persistent offender was sent to Kolditz punishment camp to join Bader and the other naughty boys.

The night that Johnny W——'s purge arrived at Sagan, a commendable escape attempt was made by three of the people already in the East Compound. One of them was Wing-Commander Prickie Day. He, a squadron-leader and a Czech dressed themselves as German soldiers and tried to bluff their way through the gate. Unfortunately, they were detected and marched off to the 'cooler'. The cooler, like Grandmother's castor oil, was the Germans' universal remedy for difficult behaviour on the part of kriegies, and solitary confinement in a German cooler, is, like Granny's castor oil again, not so damn' funny. Even the Germans called it 'the cooler' incidentally, an expression they picked up from us.

Another incidental point raised at this stage is the question of how kriegies with insufficient clothing of their own and no spare cloth, managed to rig themselves out as German soldiers in almost authentic uniform. The story of 'how' is another fascinating angle on kriegy escape activity and we will lift the veil on it slightly in due course.

In the weeks that followed at Sagan, new arrivals came from Lübeck and Spangenburg and a new compound was opened, to be known as Centre Compound. To it were brought several hundreds of N.C.O. air crew from the big general camp at Lamsdorf. Living conditions for the N.C.O.s were even worse than those for the officers. They had no rooms in their blocks but just big, barren dormitories. Lots more N.C.O.s were crowded into Centre Compound until 1,600 were squeezed in by June 1943, when the whole lot were transferred to the new Air Force N.C.O.'s camp at Heydekrug, just south of Memel, near the Lithuanian border. Centre Compound, after the N.C.O.s went, contained both American and R.A.F. officers.

Meantime, East Compound was also filling up rapidly and Stalag Luft III obviously had to expand, so construction was started on another new compound. This became the notorious North Compound, but as the Germans had to rely mostly on slave labour from the overrun countries, the construction took many months and it was not occupied until more than a year after East Compound was opened.

It was in North Compound, shortly after it opened, that Joe the Czech, who had survived the grim North Sea dinghy ride, met a friend.

When he landed behind the wire at Sagan, Joe had completed almost full circle in his travels, for his home in Czechoslovakia lay less than

160 miles to the south of the prison camp. To a despondent Joe, who could see only barbed wire and armed guards when he gazed in the direction of his homeland, he might as well have been 1,000 miles away. He forgot to take into account, however, his determined young sister who, when she heard in the following December of his whereabouts, visited the Camp Commandant and asked to be allowed to see Joe. Her visit was to have been a Christmas surprise, for Joe had had no word from his family, but the permission was refused.

A year passed. Joe, fit once more, had transferred to the North Compound. One December day, while walking around the circuit, he noticed a girl in the roadway. Like all kriegies he stared at her. The sight of a woman was a rare event in kriegy life and rarer still was a woman who stopped to wave at kriegies, as this one was doing. And then it dawned on Joe that the muffled figure standing outside the barbed wire was his sister. She had made another attempt to obtain permission to see him and when this was again refused she persuaded a sympathetic German soldier to take her round to the fence in the hope of getting a glimpse of her brother. A tolerant sentry gazing down on them from his box allowed them to carry on a shouted conversation, and for ten minutes Joe felt he was back in Czechoslovakia.

Chapter Twelve

A DAY IN THE LIFE OF A KRIEGY

Round about the time Stalag Luft III was forming, there occurred another freak escape which, as in the case of Joe the Czech, also embraced the air and the sea. This time the setting was in the Mediterranean. The lucky man was known as John Willy, and for sheer novelty his little effort ranks high in the scheme of things.

His real name was one of those double-barrelled jobs, and on two occasions he had been sole survivor of bad crashes. Ordinarily that's not bad going, but the point is that on the second of those occasions John Willy had figured in another of those cock-eyed freaks where fact goes haywire and squashes fiction and fantasy with a wild and irresponsible abandon. He not only fell into the sea a hundred miles from land without a parachute, but did it already wrapped up in a solid, makeshift 'coffin' of steel and perspex. And still he came up—though not smiling. Houdini would have turned green with envy.

John Willy was a Londoner, and looked as an Englishman is supposed to look in books—tallish and fair, with the clear smoothness of youth in his face and carriage. He had tired of the quiet life at the early age of eighteen and entered the R.A.F. to train as a wireless operator-air gunner. That was in 1938, and by the time war came he was regarded benevolently by his seniors as a very likely lad. So it was in the natural course of events that he was swiftly commissioned and became a gunnery leader. When the war wasn't funny any more in May 1940, he was training other gunners in Wales.

There was a day in June when he was stooging quietly over the Irish Sea in a Blenheim, somewhere off Wales, showing a pupil what to do with a machine-gun, when one engine caught a ragged cough and died. The pilot turned the crippled aircraft towards the land. He made it, but the Blenheim was handling soggily and he decided he would have to force-lob near the coast. On his one sound engine he waffled into a small field and touched her down. Unfortunately, across the field ran one of those sturdy stone fences so beloved of the Welsh, and the Blenheim trundled slap into it with no small vigour. She dug in her nose, kicked her tail into the air, turned turtle into a crushed heap and exploded into flame.

The other two were killed instantly, but John Willy, in a semi-conscious daze, with a broken arm, dislocated neck and shoulder, and bleeding freely from the head, was just able to drag himself from the wreck.

He left hospital eventually with a neck that wouldn't turn in any direction, and it was not for many weeks after the crash that doctors, to whom he had complained, found that a couple of his vertebrae had jumped the rails and not been returned. When these were clicked back into position and his neck would turn again, John Willy did a tour of ops., and eventually, early in 1942, found himself attached to a Welling-ton squadron which was to be sent to the Middle East. John Willy was not going with them, but when the C.O. asked him to accompany him on a preliminary flight out there to arrange for the squadron's reception, John Willy amiably agreed.

So it was that he was sitting in the rear turret of a lone Wimpy that took off from England one night early in 1942, bound on a long and risky trip across France and Italy to Malta. Hours later, in the fresh golden Mediterranean dawn, they found themselves droning over a deep snowy carpet of billowing clouds, through an occasional gap in which glinted the jewelled surface of a quiet sea. Through one of these gaps they went down to look for the rocky microcosm of land that was Malta.

For a while they saw nothing, but after a time the pilot picked up a speck on the horizon, then more specks, and finally lots and lots of them. They magnified into a huge convoy—merchant ships, tankers, cruisers, a couple of battleships, and slim destroyers curving about on the flanks, leaving bubbling trails of white. The crew of the Wimpy thought it was probably a friendly convoy, dropped to about 2,000 feet and cautiously approached to investigate.

Momentary jabs of red light appeared from several of the ships, and a few seconds later the sky just behind the Wimpy was suddenly stained with a dozen puffy little clouds of dirty black smoke. Flak! And as the Wimpy dived and turned away there was a tremor as a light shell punched a hole in the wing. John Willy ignored it. He was watching the air over the convoy, where he had seen a couple of glints. There they were again. Damn! Fighters! He checked the four Browning guns in his turret as the glints materialized into three JU 88 long-range fighters, swiftly overhauling the portly Wimpy.

It was not a long chase, as the 88's are fast and a Wimpy is not. There was no hope of regaining the shelter of the clouds before the 88's were on her. They came in on both quarters, and from astern, and poured cannon shells that banged home with sickening jolts as the Wimpy twisted, turned and dived in hunted despair. Great chunks flew off her and she was driven low over the water.

One of the 88's came in right astern, firing long bursts. A shell smashed against the rear turret and John Willy, whose guns were already hot, found he could barely swing his turret any more. The 88 broke off steeply to starboard, presenting its pale, slim belly, and John Willy, who was not a gunnery leader for nothing, delivered himself of a careful squirt. His deflection was nicely timed. Greasy black smoke streamed from the 88's starboard engine and the aircraft slipped in towards the sea, which was a bare hundred feet below.

John Willy had no time to gloat. Another 88 was coming in on his quarter and his Brownings were rattling again. He heard the pilot over the intercom. calling to other gunners to guard against a front quarter attack. Again and again he called, but only a stony silence followed, and John Willy realized then that he and the pilot were probably the only ones of the crew still alive or unwounded. From nose to tail the Wimpy showed gaping wounds and was barely hanging together.

Sitting almost helpless in his damaged turret, John Willy could see from the corners of his eyes the slender wing-tips as they rose and fell in the despairing turns which were now almost their only defence. Another 88 returned to attack the battered tail, and in the fusillade of shells that followed, a dumbfounded John Willy suddenly saw one of the wing-tips veering towards him. His mind couldn't grasp it. It was too fantastic. Wings weren't supposed to move. Before he could think any more he lost consciousness.

He must have been 'out' for just a few seconds. It was dark when he woke up, and cold and wet, and with a choking breathless shock he realized he was under water and still in his turret. They must have dived into the drink. He couldn't turn his damaged turret away from the fuselage to open his doors into freedom. He would have to get out into the tail and crawl up the cramped, water-filled catwalk through the long fuselage to the main hatch in the cockpit, fifty feet away. There wasn't a hope of course. His lungs were already bursting, but drowning men are reputed to clutch even at straws, so John Willy pushed his twin turret doors open and crawled out.

He got a shock. He didn't emerge into the catwalk. His floundering mind grasped the fact that he had emerged into gloriously unrestricted water only as the cold darkness was lightening from above. His lungs were straining, suffocating, and he was sick from mouthfuls of sea water when he shot through the green surface and drank in heavenly lungfuls of fresh air. During the next few minutes, black seconds of unconsciousness blotted out feeling from time to time, but gradually full senses were returned.

Then with a queer shock he saw the wrecked Wimpy. It was semi-submerged, about 500 yards away. Her nose was under and her tail was in the air. It was the tail that caught John Willy's fascinated eyes—or what was left of the tail. It pointed skywards like the ugly stump of a maimed limb. There was no fin, no rudder, no tail plane, no turret. And then John Willy understood. That last fusillade of shells had sheared the whole empennage neatly from the fuselage and it had dropped like a plummet, with him still inside the turret, into the sea, while the aircraft itself crashed further on. It was the simple but shaking explanation of why he had not emerged into the death trap of the fuselage catwalk when he had crawled under water through the turret doors.

After that it was almost an anti-climax when his luck held still more. With the help of his inflated Mae West he swam over towards the wreck and found, as though God had provided, a rubber dinghy that had floated clear of the crashed aircraft. He was in this when an Italian destroyer, detached from the convoy, arrived to investigate the wreck, picked him up and took him to Messina. They told him there that the JU 88 he had hit had not since returned.

From the Wimpy there were no other survivors. John Willy had done it again.

*   *   *

The first few minutes after being shot down sometimes seem pretty unreal while the grey matter is trying to adjust itself to violently changed conditions. Nicky Pollock felt this sense of unreality to a ludicrous extent when he received a phone call from a friend a few minutes after being shot down in enemy territory. Nicky was twenty-four, came from London and was a gunner in a Manchester returning over Denmark from a visit to Rostock on the 23rd of April 1942. The flak was quite troublesome and suddenly the port engine caught fire and started to burn determinedly. Bits of the wing started to break off and the end was obviously coming, so Harry, the pilot, told the crew to hop out.

Nicky duly 'hopped' at about 4,000 feet and eventually came to earth in a field where he slipped out of his harness and began walking north, hoping to reach the coast and nip across in the ferry to neutral Sweden. After a while he came to a rambling old farmhouse and saw a light in the stables. Looking in he saw two men in the act of delivering a mare of a foal. He discreetly made his presence known and the two Danes, who had seen the Manchester crash earlier and realized who he was, took him into the farmhouse where the farmer's wife appeared and produced coffee, bread and honey for him.

None of them spoke English but they all maintained a friendly 'conversation' in sign language and in a conscientious endeavour to be hospitable, the Danish housewife indicated to Nicky that he had her full permission to try his musical skill on a big church organ in a corner of the living-room. Nicky politely declined and conversation languished somewhat, when an ornate wall telephone in the room rang shrilly into the silence. The housewife answered it and an excited conversation ensued in Danish. Then she turned and beckoned Nicky to the phone, and rather staggered and without the faintest idea of what it was all about he took up the receiver and said 'Hullo' into the mouthpiece, feeling rather foolish. He got the shock of his life when a voice answered:

'Wotcher! Is that you, Nicky?'

'What the——! Good God! Yes. Who the devil's that?' said Nicky weakly, as a numbed brain slowly took it in.

'Tim here,' said the voice. (Tim was the second pilot of the Manchester.) 'Are you all right?'

'Yes. I'm O.K. Where the devil are you?' asked Nicky, getting a grasp on things now.

'I'm at a farmhouse,' said Tim. 'Apparently you are too. The people here rang up their friends at your farmhouse to tell 'em the strange news of my arrival, and heard the same thing in return.'

'Well, I'm damned!' said Nicky, and thereafter was able to maintain an intelligent conversation. Between them they pieced together the fact that everyone barring the pilot had been able to get out of the burning Manchester. Unfortunately, as neither Danish family spoke English, they couldn't sort out their relative geographical positions, and get together, so they agreed to try for the coast independently and join up in Sweden. They rang off then and Nicky was having a hard job trying to explain what he wanted in the way of food and clothing to carry on when a Dane who spoke excellent English arrived, and Nicky was explaining what he wanted when a car pulled up outside and Danish police and an officer for liaison with the Germans were in the room before Nicky quite realized that they were looking for him. The police were very courteous and friendly, but explained that they had to take him into custody as the Nazis would take pretty grim reprisals on themselves and their relatives if they let him escape.

So that was that, and Nicky went on into prison at Stalag Luft III and did not feel any better, either, when Tim was picked up by the Germans too.

*   *   *

From time to time we have mentioned the atrophying stagnation of a prisoner of war's life. It's something that has to be experienced to be believed. It's not so much the actual hardship. The Red Cross ameliorated much of that and one could take what was left equably enough. It was not so much the negative features of the life, but the complete lack of positive elements. It was the demoralizing monotony of a life that did not vary one iota from day to day for years, a life that utterly lacked any spot of colour or brightness, just drab existence that went from a ramshackle hut to a small sandy desert of compound, enclosed by barbed wire, and back into the hut again.

One lived for years in a barren radius of 200 yards and never got beyond it. Consciousness and time became almost intolerable burdens. There was no date to look forward to for release; it all seemed to be going on eternally and always there was the humiliation of being under enemy control.

Intelligent young men do not go nuts for nothing. Nor, for no apparent reason, do they commit suicide by gashing their wrists or rushing in frenzy at the barbed wire and being shot as soon as they crossed the warning area which ran ten yards in from the fence. But these things happened.

Yet a typical day in the life of a kriegy does not sound so terrible. We took the following example from the diary of Peter Gardner, D.F.C. and Bar, who did rather well in the Battle of Britain. He makes it sound quite amusing, and, incidentally, one of the characters should be easily recognized.

This was Pete's typical day:

'7 a.m. Wake up to sound of Dave knocking the fire about. Cautiously put hand out into fresh air to feel how much ice there is on blankets.

'7.05. Stretch, curl up into ball and submerge.

'7.10. Come up for air.

'7.10½. Submerge, fighting blankets to make them air proof.

'9.00. Strident shouts of "Pete! Pete! Get up, Pete! You lazy ——"

'9.05. Crawl from under blankets and look over side. Floor looks long way down from top bunk. Scream to Dave to bring a stool so that you can get off on to the floor without jumping into deep dirt.

'9.10. Get dressed, hunt for shoes. Find them cunningly hidden among food boxes.

'9.15. Breakfast. Search for clean cup among last night's dirty crockery. Give it up, find one half filled with coffee, pour away and fill with tea.

'9.20. Breakfast interrupted by screams from Wingco for his legs. Hunt for legs. Dave finds them hidden under the linen bag.

'9.23. Watch Wingco washing, while hunting for margarine to put on cold toast.

'9.28. Rush out for appel (German counting parade.)

'9.30. Appel. Hit next-door neighbour in stomach to keep circulation going. Receive snowball down neck, others doing likewise.

'9.40. Feel ears to make sure they are there. Comfort self by thinking it all helps the East Front.

'10.0. Rush off appel to get dregs of tea and only chair. Wonder whether you can get up, find cigarettes and get back before others get in. Decide you can't so stay put.

'10.05. Others come in and shout abuse because you have finished the tea. Try to think up some snappy retort but can't.

'10.12. Seize basin and water and start washing up. Try to make Dave feel he has nothing to do, hoping he will help.

'10.15. Massage bloke arrives. Panic in room. Bill looking for powder, Dave for his pipe, me for dishcloth. Wingco taking his legs off. Jock trying to get out of room with bucket. Chaos.

'10.20. Pete again—massage in progress. Basin, hands, towel, crockery covered in grease. Dave still looking for pipe.

'10.25. Stopped washing up. Listen for chance to make clever remark thought of last night into usual argument of Army v. Air Force.

'10.30. Dave finds pipe. Everyone sitting down. Start to sweep floor.

'10.31. Massage finished. Wingco looking for legs, Dave for Spanish books, Bill for his sweater.

'10.40. Climb up and make bed. Finish sweeping floor. Sort clothes out of food locker, cigarettes out of clothes locker, food off bookshelf.

'10.50. Admire floor. Others return. Floor covered in mud and snow.

'11.0. Go for water to start laundry. Find there isn't any. Collect snow and start thawing on fire.

'11.15. Ten people arrive for brew. Fight your way over dozens of legs, push three people off the table and start in on laundry.

'11.25. Wingco screams for milk for his brew. Start sulking and tell him to wait.

'11.30. Finish washing. Climb up on to bed. Get down again to make milk for Wingco. Climb back up again.

'11.40. Listen to usual argument, bombers *versus* fighters. Think up some frightfully clever remarks.

'12.30. Someone says it's time for lunch. Promptly forget clever remarks as everyone dashes off. Feel despondent. Collect basin and fetch soup. Remark on its frightfulness.

'12.40. Finish soup, climb on to bed and settle down to read.

'12.45. Wingco suggests cup of tea. Silence. Watch Dave furtively to see what he is doing. He starts moving so you say you think it's a good idea. Lie back and watch him make it, then drink it.

'1.15. Prepare for Spanish lesson. Open book, begin.

'1.20. Start wondering where you can borrow some skates. Decide it's no good and you can't skate anyway. Interrupted by "Carlos has the pen of my aunt." Wonder what you can do this afternoon.

'2.00. Spanish finished. The usual argument. Army *versus* Air Force.

'3.30. Settle down to sleep.

'3.35. Screams of "It's time to make tea". Climb down off bed and prepare to make tea.

'4.00. Have tea.

'4.10. Letters arrive. Don't take any notice, imagining that it will enlarge your chances of getting some. Say "Good show, Dave. Glad you got some." Curse yourself and ask whether there is any justice in the world. Then sulk.

'5.00. Listen to argument as to when war will be over. As you can't see any end, just feel depressed.

'5.40. Rush out for appel. Arrive last, still pulling on boots, gloves, scarf balaclava and hat.

'5.45. Another snowball fight during appel.

'6.00. Rush back to room to thaw out.

'6.40. Melt snow and wash up.

'6.50. Peel spuds and start frying them. Lay table and sit down with a determined air. Suggest to Dave that meat roll needs frying. Watch Dave cooking.

'7.15. Have supper.

'7.30. Wingco suggests some coffee. Say you don't want any and watch Dave make it. Then change your mind and have some. Ugly murmurs from others.

'8.15. Room empty. Collect cigarettes, book-stool for feet, stoke up fire, seal windows, settle down to read.

'8.20. Interrupted by very senior officer coming in. Pretend I haven't seen him and make some caustic murmurs about noise until there is silence.

'10.00. Make bed, drop pyjamas on dirty floor and curse the camp, the Germans, the war, everything.

'10.30. Get into bed and seal all air holes.

'10.35. Remember haven't cleaned teeth. Start muttering, get out of bed, brush teeth, visit bucket in passage, remake bed and get in, still muttering.

'11.10. Dave opens window one inch. Screams from others. Finally opened half inch.

'11.15. Lights out. Listen to Dave tripping over stools, tin legs and shoes on way to bed. Laugh and receive thump in stomach.

'11.30. Submerge. Think out wonderful escape and heroic return to England. Think of yourself at home getting V.C. Go to sleep contented.'

Chapter Thirteen
U-BOAT PASSENGER

───────

After kriegies had been bundled into the bag and mixed with their fellow drabs for a while, they, too, found it such a hum-drum affair to hear of fellows being shot up, shot down and practically killed that no one was interested in hearing how the 'sprogs' of any new purges were hacked down, except, of course, the 'sprogs' themselves, who thought they were still front-page stuff. Yet kriegies did not completely lose their sense of the sensational. Now and then through the gates would wander some lugubrious soul who had got his guernsey to kriegydom with such irrational unorthodoxy that even the blunted wits of the blasé 'gefangener' were mildly stirred.

Frank Penman was one of the unorthodox types. He came into the bag after an elaborate process of catching diphtheria, pranging in the desert, being torpedoed, being bombed and depth-charged by our own aircraft, finishing up with a grand tour in a couple of enemy submarines, one of which sank under him. It was unorthodoxy, *par excellence.*

A rather pleasant-faced young New Zealand pilot, well built on tapering lines, Frank was attached to Ferry Command, and towards the end of March 1942, he took off in a Wimpy from England to deliver it to the Middle East. First stop was Malta and he spent ten days there while the island was being blitzed. He began to feel rather off colour in his last couple of days there, and eventually took off for Fayum, near Cairo, the 11th of April, with a raging sore throat. For hours and hours he had to stick to the controls, feeling like death warmed up, and then to make matters worse petrol began to run low and they realized they wouldn't make Fayum. Eventually, Frank set the Wimpy down for a belly landing in the desert. Help was sent out to them, and though no one was injured, Frank was carted off to hospital at Heliopolis where they found he had diphtheria.

He recovered, in due course, but was told he wouldn't be fit for flying again under twelve months, and in the meantime would be sent back to England. So Frank caught a boat to South Africa and in Capetown transferred to the 20,000-ton Cunard-White Star liner *Laconia* for what was to be her last voyage. She sailed early in September and in addition to Air Force and Army passengers and some women and children being sent back to England, there were about 1,200 Italian prisoners on board, with Polish guards—roughly 2,500 souls in all.

Being a fast ship, the *Laconia* was travelling solo, with no escort, and was making commendable time up the West African coast towards Freetown until the 12th of September. At 8.15 that night she was throbbing steadily through hot, tropical darkness, about 800 miles from the nearest land, when the blow came, without warning, just forward of amidships.

There was the usual, movie-like scene in the lounge; women in light evening frocks, men in uniform, after-dinner coffee and liqueurs, and lots of laughter and gaiety. Frank and some friends had just dealt the first hand for bridge and a steward was mixing the first round of drinks when there was a sickening earthquake of an explosion and the whole ship seemed to leap several feet, and then lurched over to one side as the torpedo blew a gaping wound in her side.

The movie-like *motif* continued. For a moment there was a stricken, awful hush, then as stunned people came to life again the piano slipped its moorings on the listed deck of the lounge and went charging across the room. Tables and chairs went crashing in its path, books, bottles and glasses came splintering down in chaotic confusion and a chiming clock toppled heavily to the deck. Everyone was scrambling to find the lifebelts they always carried near them, and then there was a jittery, mass exodus for the door and lifeboat stations as heavy cordite fumes drifted through the room.

Frank was on the stairway in a seething mass of people trying to go both ways when a second shattering crash and mighty jump from the ship indicated the arrival of another torpedo, followed by panicky cries from women and children. The position wasn't improved when Frank arrived at his boat station near the bridge to find that his boat and a lot of deck had been thoroughly dispersed by the torpedoes that had hit almost immediately below. Some of the other boats had been lowered, but had apparently been so badly damaged that they hardly stopped on

118

their downward path when they reached the water before continuing on below the waves.

With the help of a friend, Frank was able to get the women and children from his boat station to other boats, and then began untying a pile of rafts to throw overboard when an unpleasant diversion arrived. Heralded by hysterical shouting, the Italian prisoners broke from their guards and forced their way on deck in a panic-stricken mass. As ever with the Latin hordes in a crisis, there was immediate pandemonium and the Italians pushed aside a few remaining women and tried to take charge of a boat station. Polish guards bayonet-charged them to try and restore control, but the fear-crazed Italians could not be impressed by anything. Some of them launched the boat and the rest of them jumped overboard.

Taking their shoes off to walk on the sloping deck, Frank and his friends helped to get another boat launched and then, as the *Laconia* settled deeper by the bows, they threw over their own last raft and slid down a rope to join it. To avoid the maelstrom when the ship sank, they struck out to get clear, considerably hampered by yelling Italians. It was not the popular conception of a raft, where one could sit in mild comfort. It was just a tiny wooden affair which would keep one afloat if one hung on to the side.

From a couple of hundred yards they rested and watched the *Laconia* slowly roll and lift her stern in the air. Little figures could be seen jumping off her as she slid underneath fifty-five minutes after the first torpedo had hit, to be followed by a series of heavy, under-water explosions. After that they just waited wearily in the darkness, continually pestered by babbling Italians. Several times they tried to reach lifeboats, but could never make it, so they just hung on to the side of their raft, and after a time the agonizing strictures of cramp came upon them. They found they could stave them off if they kept continually moving, but it was a wearying business.

The Italians were becoming a serious menace. In their frantic panic they were floundering up to the raft and grabbing anyone they could by the back of their lifejacket for support. The poor devils so grabbed were dragged under and several were drowned. Frank, himself, had a lucky escape from them, being able to kick his way clear of one who grabbed him.

To their surprise, towards dawn the cause of the disaster surfaced— a German U-boat. It stayed only a few minutes, but just long enough for all the Italians to let go and try and swim to it. They didn't make it, which was unlucky for them, but a good thing for those on the rafts because they didn't come back.

Dawn didn't help much when it came because it emphasized their position rather brutally. Dozens of dead bodies were floating about in lifebelts. They were mostly Italians, and the weary wretches hanging on to the raft, who could hardly keep their eyes open, knew they had drowned in their belts, after falling asleep. It was not a pleasant thought. Nothing else could be seen but a limitless heavy grey swell, and occasionally, far out of reach, a lifeboat would appear momentarily on a crest. The sea was getting higher and the clumsy little raft insisted on turning over with every big wave. It was all highly unpleasant, though at least it kept them awake.

They hung on with dull patience till about midday, when another raft came floating by with three men, a woman and an Italian clinging to it, and after that they all kept together. No one had thought of sharks until a filthy-looking purple jelly-fish was washed on to the raft and stung the woman badly. She was almost sobbing with the pain and they began to wonder what else might be cruising around in the sea with evil and felonious intent. Combined with the sea water, a blinding tropical sun was raising huge blisters on exposed parts of their bodies. An orange came floating by and was grabbed and shared around. Frank had just about enough kick left in him to wisecrack about how the devil oranges grew in the sea.

It was not long after that the inevitable happened and everyone started to go a little crazy and see things that weren't there. A friend of Frank's thought he saw another raft, let go his hold and started to swim for it. He was never seen again. Spells of giddiness were overtaking them all, and then Frank had the prize delusion of them all. He thought he saw Father Neptune wading chest deep in the water towards them. By each hand he was leading a child. It was such a vivid vision that Frank can remember the details distinctly. He still claims that Neptune hasn't got a flowing beard, but a short, black, spiky job. What he probably saw was a dead Italian floating in his lifebelt.

Late that afternoon, two submarines appeared nearby, and neither of them was a delusion. An R.A.F. squadron-leader hanging on to Frank's raft tried to swim to one of them with a rope, but couldn't make it, so they resigned themselves hopelessly again. The sun was low on the horizon when one of the submarines swung towards the raft and then slid alongside and they were hauled on board, too weak to stand alone. They had been twenty-two and a half hours in the water.

The German crew treated them well. Frank was given hot coffee, wrapped in a coat and taken below. There were five of the *Laconia*'s women passengers in bunks there and the rest of the interior of the U-boat was crowded with survivors. The commander told Frank that, excluding his own crew, there were 269 of them on board. He added there there had been two other submarines waiting for the *Laconia* too. They had expected her the previous day.

'How did you know we were coming?' asked Frank.

'Oh, from spies in Capetown,' said the commander laconically. He added that a French cruiser was coming from Dakar to take care of the survivors.

They passed the night curled up in the cramped confines of the U-boat, half of them lying tangled up with pipes and levers of various kinds. They were allowed on deck for fresh air next day, and towards evening the submarine commander called for volunteers to man the two remaining lifeboats floating alongside, so that others in them could have some shelter inside the U-boat. Frank and some others were put in one boat, and some Italians in the other and they pushed off into the dusk. After another miserable night the U-boat appeared, as promised, at dawn to give them water. It was then that the German doctor saw Frank's blistered and swollen face and legs and bade him rejoin the U-boat.

An Italian submarine drew alongside later on and took on many of the Italian prisoners, and then the U-boat, with lifeboats in tow, set course for the rendezvous with the rescue vessel from Dakar. It was just after they started that the alarm, 'Aircraft!' was given and a Coastal Command Liberator, presumably from Freetown, hove in sight and made a business-like beeline for them. The Germans draped a Red Cross flag over the conning-tower and one of the survivors was given a lamp and furiously flashed, 'British survivors. Do not bomb', to the Liberator. The aircraft pulled her nose up a little, stooged round in a placid circuit over them, and then headed off over the horizon.

Jittery nerves relaxed again, but not for long. A Liberator appeared again half an hour later, this time with bomb-doors open. Without wasting time, it positioned itself astern of the U-boat and started its bombing run. Frank was inside at the time and was shaken to the core by shattering explosions almost alongside. Bits of the U-boat's internal machinery flew in all directions, injuring some of the *Laconia*'s survivors, and two sick women went completely hysterical. One lifeboat got a direct hit, with the obvious result for those in it. Everyone was immediately ordered on deck, and they made a wretched spectacle as they stood there. Some of the women either lacked clothes or the time to put them on, for they were huddled there in just a pair of scanties, or a torn, bedraggled slip. No one took any notice. There are times when sex just doesn't exist and the dispirited motley was developing that glazed look of indifference that showed they just didn't care about anything any more.

A few lifebelts were tossed out of the conning-tower and then the commander vanished from sight and the hatch clanged shut. There were not enough lifebelts to go round, and those who had one were putting them on, apathetically wondering what was going to happen next, when a creamy film of foam washed over the deck and before he could quite realize what was happening, Frank was picked up by a solid wall of water, thrown against the U-boat's gun muzzle and washed aside into the sea. The submarine had submerged under them and all that remained were a few bobbing heads in the water. Frank struck out for a nearby raft and found about a dozen Italians flapping around it, so he left it and made for another one, which turned out to be a water-logged lifeboat, supporting some British survivors.

One of them was a major who felt that he had just about had the whole business. After a while he said, very quietly, 'It's all up. What's the use of hanging on now,' let go his hold and slipped unobtrusively under the water. Several times the boat almost turned turtle in the heavy swell and once Frank was caught under it and tangled in loose ropes and sail. He very nearly bought it then, but just managed to free himself and kick back to the surface, breathless and vomiting up mouthfuls of sea water.

Then someone yelled, 'Look, a ship!' Someone else saw it too, and said it was a battleship. Others saw it, and it slid rapidly down the scale till it was alleged to be a destroyer. It turned out to be an Italian submarine, which eventually approached and stood off about a hundred yards away. About fifty people set off to try and swim to it, and about twenty eventually arrived. Frank was among the twenty, but all he can remember is a dim feeling of being dragged on board. He had been six hours in the water since the U-boat had submerged under him.

The Italians, who had been summoned by the Germans, told them they would have to wait on deck all night, but fed them with cognac and biscuits, and they passed another pretty hellish night huddled on the wet deck! Their only entertainment was the spectacle of a couple of dead Italians being tossed overboard. At dawn they were given a large bowl of thick soup, more cognac and a cigarette. No more air-craft appeared, which was just as well for the Italian commander had warned them that he would have to 'leave' them if aircraft did appear. They knew what he meant.

They had to give their names and addresses, and then Frank and a Fleet Air Arm pilot were ordered below and the commander told them that he was going to look after them. Both Frank and the Fleet Air Arm lad, Arthur Boyd, were given bunks up near the forward torpedo tubes.

Two days later, the French cruiser arrived and British civilians and Italian survivors were transferred to her. Frank and Arthur Boyd, how-ever, were kept on board as prisoners. The submarine then set course for Bordeaux, her base, and days passed uneventfully as the two pilots rested and got back their strength. The Italian commander, who said he was a count, treated them quite well.

There was one unpleasant experience when the submarine pack went to intercept a British freighter named *O'Brien*. Sullen with hate, Frank and Boyd watched the torpedoes being prepared for the attack, but just as the Italians were sighting on their target an exultant yell went up from the periscope. A German U-boat in the same pack had got a torpedo home and the freighter went down in a few minutes.

Days passed monotonously until they were near the Bay of Biscay and Sunderlands, with detector gear, located them. There was a jittery four days while they were depth-charged time and again, and every day the detonations came nearer and nearer. It was not a pleasant time because depth-charges have to be heard to be appreciated. They will shake a substantial freighter from phenomenal range. On the fourth day the submarine was rocking alarmingly from the explosions and nerves were horribly on edge. The Italians, who were an inexperienced crew, were frightened stiff.

At dawn on the next day they surfaced and, guided by a tiny pilot boat, zig-zagged at full speed through the minefield at the entrance to the channel at Bordeaux. When they pulled into the dock, Frank and Arthur had had thirty-two days in the submarine. There was the usual Latin rigmarole of jubilation at getting home in one piece, in which, of course, Frank and Arthur did not feel like sharing, for they were gaped at by a gaggle of gold-braided Italian and German officers and carted off to kriegydom in Italy.

When the Italians finally collapsed a year later, Frank made a break for his freedom, but there were rather too many German machine-gun bullets whistling about his head as he ran, so he didn't get far before he was dragged back and up to Stalag Luft III in Germany.

*   *   *

Well worth a mention in this chronicle of exiles are the funny meetings that took place between veteran kriegies and old friends who meandered in on new purges. One never knew who next was going to wander sadly through the barbed-wire gates to join the motley who clustered gregariously about the entrance cynically scanning the newcomers' faces. Often there would be shouts of recognition and surprise, and also gurgles of gentle mockery, for there is always something slightly funny in finding a friend in the same boat as yourself.

About the funniest of these funny meetings at Sagan was that between two identical twins, the Barnes brothers, Dick and Eddie. To describe one is to describe the other; rather above average height, strongly built on athletic lines, with determined faces and solid jaws. Everyone confused the two until one grew a moustache as identification. They both came from Torquay and both were flying-officers when they were shot down.

Dick was the first to migrate to Germany. He was twenty-one then, a navigator in a Manchester that was hit by flak over Happy Valley (the Ruhr) on the 30th of May 1942. The following half-hour was rather hectic and culminated in a little epic of quiet gallantry that brought the pilot a posthumous V.C. It brought Dick within forty feet of death, and, of course, into the bag. The flak wounded the rear gunner, put the starboard engine out of action and set it on fire and the starboard aileron was damaged so the pilot, Flying-Officer Leslie Manser, had to hold the control wheel hard over to starboard to keep the Manchester flying. From 6,000 feet they tried to make the Belgian frontier before baling out so as to have a better chance of getting home by 'underground' means, but the Manchester would not hold her height and was sinking fast. When they thought they had reached the Belgian frontier they were down to about 600 feet, just barely high enough to bale out. The coolant temperatures of the remaining good engine were way up over boiling point and it obviously wasn't going to last much longer. Dick handed Manser his parachute canopy, but Manser shook his head and waved it away.

'No go,' he said. 'I can't let go this wheel or she'll go straight in.'

Dick had enough sense not to waste precious time and prejudice

124

Manser's chances further by haggling, but left the parachute beside him and ran back to help the rear gunner out. Eventually, dangerously low, he dived out himself, and has a shaking memory of his parachute opening just above tree-top height. He landed heavily but unhurt, and then just ahead of him saw the burning Manchester, very low now, heel over, dip sharply down and explode into the ground. Dick is not sure whether it happened when Manser let go the wheel to try and bale out or whether the remaining engine packed in suddenly. Possibly it was both.

The rear gunner died and Dick was captured. Some of the others who had been able to bale out thanks to Manser's nerve, got back to England via 'The Organization' and told what had happened. Dick sent his version back too, and Manser's memory was awarded a V.C.

Almost a year later, on the 5th of May 1943, Dick's brother, Eddie, rear gunner in a Halifax, was coming back from a night visit to Dortmund when a night fighter attacked and they came to earth with a bump. Eddie, of course, knew that Dick was somewhere in Germany, but when he was told that he was being sent to a new compound at Sagan, gave up his hopes of meeting him. He could not know that Dick had been moved to the same new compound a few weeks previously. Eddie duly arrived at Sagan and was herded sadly through the rusty, barbed-wire gate of the North Compound. The next few minutes were quite funny.

Dick didn't see that particular new purge arrive and Eddie was immediately shunted along to the adjutant's office for customary interrogation, because we never knew that the Germans weren't trying to plant a man among the new purge to collect all sorts of useful information for them.

The adjutant, burly Bill Jennens, looked up when Eddie marched in, and, of course, thought Eddie was Dick, whom he knew.

'What do you want?' he barked. 'We're busy just now.'

Naturally, Eddie was mildly puzzled.

'Well—er, umm—er. Well, I—er, I was told to come in here,' he said.

'Well, see me later,' said Bill. 'I'm busy with the new purge now.'

'Well, I—er, I'm in the new purge,' said Eddie, somewhat flummoxed.

And then Bill woke up.

'Oh, I thought you were another chap in this camp,' he said.

'Maybe he's my twin brother,' said Eddie, with sudden hope. 'Is his name Barnes?'

'For Pete's sake,' almost shouted Bill in his parade-ground voice. 'His name *is* Barnes.'

They sent someone out for Dick then, and the twins met outside the adjutant's office.

'Well, I'm damned,' said Dick, as they shook hands.

'Me, too,' said Eddie.

They went to live in the same room after that, and, of course, wrote home to their parents of the meeting. But letters took a long time to get back, and for weeks after Eddie was shot down their parents and friends wrote cheery letters to Dick, the first shot down, and studiously avoided all mention of the fact that Eddie was missing, so as not to worry him. When they heard Eddie was a prisoner, they wrote and told Dick that he would be very surprised to hear that his brother was in the bag too.

And Dick looked across at Eddie and they laughed and laughed and laughed.

* * *

We have mentioned before what a cosmopolitan place kriegydom was. This diversity was not confined merely to nationalities. There was also a most amazing variety of types and occupations. Particularly occupations.

In the same diary from which we took the account of a typical kriegy day, we also found this list of occupations followed by people whom Pete Gardner, the diarist, had met in captivity in Germany. They were:

'Tram conductor, millionaire's son, multi-millionaire, waiter, lord, publican, civil airline pilot, Indian prince, racehorse trainer, racing-car driver, postman, dance-band leader, professional dancer, professional ice hockey player, professional baseball player, professional footballer, schoolmaster, bus driver, taxi driver, cowboy, vaudeville artist, movie cameraman, actor, American night club manager, plumber, lumberjack, county cricketer, England rugger international, commercial traveller in babies' bottles, ditto in ladies' underwear, ski champion, fencing champion, cinema operator, policeman, coal miner, meat buyer, veterinary surgeon, shop walker, window dresser, fur trader, university don, smuggler, bootlegger, meat packer, newspaper reporter, barman, garage mechanic, Hollywood film agent, movie producer, Red Indian missionary, detective, man who screwed nuts on railway engines, cobbler, cooper, opera singer, diamond miner, theatre organist, dietician, bacteriologist, jockey, aircraft designer, radio announcer, Canadian mounted policeman, Disney technicolour expert, Texas ranger, professional "bouncer", Covent Garden porter, tea taster, gold miner, hide hunter, ice cream vendor, soda jerker, hotel proprietor, All-American football star, chauffeur, fireman, sheriff, professional gambler, piano tuner, bookie, film make-up man, trapper, owner of fish and chip shop, burglar, pickpocket and self-confessed pimp.'

Chapter Fourteen

FIVE MEN IN A BOAT

———

There was, among us at Stalag Luft III, a great mountain of flesh and muscle and amiability who weighed eighteen stone and measured six feet two in socks and about the same round his barrel of a chest. We called him 'Bambino', which means 'baby' in Italy, where he was first a prisoner. Like the usual outsize in humanity, Bambino had a heart to match. His tolerant blue eyes were usually half hidden by folds of flesh that crinkled his face in benign smiles of unshakeable good nature and his vast bulk used to rock with his rumbling laughter. There was a time when this gentle colossus sat in the darkness with a friend and discussed the best way to drink the blood and eat the raw flesh of another friend who was dying beside them. They themselves were dying then, and had been doing so for ten days, sitting in a rubber dinghy that was just a lonely speck on the ocean.

The big fellow was twenty-four when it all happened. Dinger, his friend of the darkness and conversation piece, was about the same age. There were four others, too, but they all died.

Bambino was officially Pilot-Officer Harold B——, and, considering he came from Barbados he was pretty quick off the mark when war was declared. At first, the bickering in Europe all seemed rather remote in Barbados, which, as many people don't know, lies just above the fat bulge of South America, up towards the Florida coast in the West Indies, and early in 1940 there was no official recruiting arrangement there for men to go to Great Britain. Bambino, who was a commercial salesman, and a few more of his cronies who took participation in the war as a matter of course, without fuss saved their money and paid their own passage to Great Britain to get into the war. The six of them were the first contingent from Barbados.

128

In a pub at Glasgow they tossed up to see what service they should join and Bambino consequently became A.C2 B———, of the Royal Air Force. He was afraid they would think him too heavy for air crew, but as eighteen stone is just a fleabite to a bomber they gave him a pilot's course and he duly got his wings, got himself a wife about the same time and went to a Wimpy operational training unit. On his last training trip, he was to go on a cross country, but on the night before the flight he went over on one ankle and with eighteen stone bearing down on it the bone snapped, so his crew took off without him. They crashed and all of them were killed, so Bambino didn't curse his ankle quite so much.

When it was better they gave him another crew and attached him to Ferry Command. In May 1942, Bambino took off in a Wimpy from England to deliver it to the Middle East. First stop was Gibraltar and they finally arrived with a burst coolant tank. Another one was fitted there and on the 19th of May at 3 p.m., they took off for Malta, on the next stage. Everything went placidly for a while until they were somewhere off Cape Bon, near Tunis, when the port engine, which had previously had coolant trouble, started to overheat. They flew on, mostly on one engine, and tried to get a radio fix from Malta. Only a stony silence met their appeals and they realized their receiver was out of order. Bambino left the controls, and he, the front gunner and the wireless operator worked on the dud receiver while the second pilot kept on course.

Thick, racing cloud mostly obscured the moon that night or they would probably have seen Malta when they eventually flew right over the island. Bambino didn't find that out until long afterwards however. As it was, they saw nothing, which was a pity. Malta had plotted their coming, could get no answer to their calls from the island radio and scrambled a Beaufighter after them. This couldn't make contact either, so the Wimpy flew blindly on. On and on and around they flew until 11.45 p.m., way past their expected time of arrival at Malta, when the moon shone palely through a cloud gap and they saw a long coastline below them which obviously wasn't Malta. By this time they had dropped to about 2,000 feet and petrol had dropped a lot lower than that. At 12.20 a.m. the fuel gauges were quivering about the zero mark and Bambino decided to ditch.

For the last half-hour he had not ventured far from the coastline they had seen, but as it was presumed to be enemy territory they did not want to ditch too close to it in the hope that help would come from

Malta, which was assumed to have plotted their course and ditching. They could see the dull gleam of a calm sea as they headed down. The front gunner was told to strap the six water-bottles they carried to his belt and the navigator stood by the dinghy release toggle. It was a fairly smooth ditching, but the belly seemed to fill quickly with a wave of water that swept through it from nose to tail, and Bambino found himself floating out through his top hatch. One by one the others appeared until five of the six were paddling around the water-logged wreck in their Mae Wests. Bambino swam right round the sinking Wimpy looking for the sixth, but there was no trace. It was the front gunner who carried all their water. The Wimpy sank after about five minutes, but there was still no sign of him.

The navigator had duly done his stuff with the dinghy release-toggle and they could make out the dark shape of the dinghy bobbing on the water a little way away. All of them were wearing Mae Wests and swam to it and climbed in. It was the ordinary bomber dinghy, a large circular affair of inflated rubber, excellent for riding out a sea, but rather a dead loss for going places. When dawn came and there was still no sign of the front gunner, they tied a shoe to a point on the circumference of the dinghy to indicate a nominal 'bow', and with an escape kit compass, set a rough course southwards, where they judged land to be.

Using the two-hand paddles in the dinghy they made just about bare headway. In the rations pocket of the dinghy they found a dozen tins of chocolate concentrate and a rubber hot-water bottle, containing about a quart of water. It had been there so long that it had been affected by the rubber and looked more like weak milk and tasted like nothing on earth. There were a couple of hollow wooden plugs for stopping up holes in the dinghy, and Bambino, who was in command, took the largest, which held about a teaspoonful, and decreed that two plugsful of water per man per day would be their ration.

Heavy clouds started to assemble overhead and the sea was getting up. They found they couldn't paddle any more, but had to bale instead. Even so their spirits were not greatly dampened because they were confident that a submarine or launch or air-sea rescue aircraft would come to their assistance from Malta. If they had known they were north of Sicily, towards the Liparian Islands, they would have lost that hope and been severely shaken. As it was, they continued in the bliss of ignorance, and on the second night the sea was very rough and they also realized how cold a Mediterranean night can be, which is very cold indeed if you are sitting in shorts in a dinghy with no covering. The second pilot was quite seasick, and the others felt seedy too.

All through the next day they saw nothing but sea, but they still kept confident in spite of their sickness and the cold of the following night. They would have a teaspoonful of water in the plug about 10 a.m., and another one about dusk. They were all feeling thirsty but not unbearably so and the chocolate was so filling that no one felt hungry the whole of the time.

On the third day the sun came out and spirits rose as they basked in the warmth. Had they only known it, that welcome sun was to aid and abet the deaths of three of the five in the dinghy. The sea was fairly smooth that day and they still waited hopefully to be rescued from Malta, but again they saw nothing but water, and the following night was just as cold as those before.

What they had been dreading all along came on the fourth day—really demoralizing thirst. Their two teaspoonsful of horrible, rubbery water did little to relieve it and for the first time their hopes wavered and nerves became a little on edge.

Again the sun beat down hotly and began to burn their exposed skin. Bambino was lucky. He was the only one wearing long trousers. The others were wearing shorts and their fair skin, straight from England, was a good mark for the sun. Bambino and Dinger, the rear gunner, were the only ones who could swim, so they stripped and slipped over the side into the cool water of the Mediterranean. The others continually damped their limbs and face with water, but still the sun burned and blistered their skin. A little later they had a bad fright. Two sharks appeared, and one of them, about seven feet long, cruised leisurely under the dinghy. They could feel his rough hide and fin as he scraped along the rubber bottom. Really scared, they did not dare show their faces over the side, but the shark seemed to know that flesh was in the offing and trailed the dinghy unceasingly for two days and nights. Possibly they needn't have worried about the sharks as Mediterranean sharks are reputed to be not dangerous. Still they didn't know that then.

The boys spread damp handkerchiefs over their heads to keep cool, but tempers were becoming increasingly frayed so Bambino commandeered the revolvers they all carried and tossed them overboard, all except his own, which he kept—just in case. That was the last night they were able to huddle together for warmth. After that they found the cold preferable to the pain of contact between inflamed, burnt skin.

Next morning Bambino tied another knot in the piece of string that counted the days for them, and while another blazing sun climbed into another cloudless sky they trailed a little more of the fluorescence that marked their position from the air with a luminous green patch in the sea. They had been doing that every day but had seen no sign of aircraft.

Round about 4 p.m., there was a hoarse shout from one of them, 'Aircraft!' With surging joy they saw a lumbering German JU 52 heading towards them from the north. It was about 3,000 feet, clearly identifiable. By the grace of God they had one workable signal in the dinghy, an international distress signal, shaped like a German hand-grenade, with handle about a foot long and in action resembling a Roman candle. Fingers that fumbled in nervous haste ignited the thing and they held it aloft as it shot out its thirteen stars of red, green, and white.

Breathless and a little sick they watched the 52 as it droned over-head, then let out a cracked cheer as an answering signal of three white stars dropped, glowing, behind the aircraft and it dipped a wing and slowly circled them. It straightened up again and headed west-south-west for about fifteen miles, and they could still make it out as it dipped down and circled again before heading off south once more. They felt certain that he had circled, the second time, over the nearest land, and their spirits skyrocketed again. With bubbling enthusiasm they brought the paddles out again and headed in the indicated direction.

Another cold night dragged by and in the morning there was still only sea all round them. Then about 11 a.m. they saw another aircraft and identified it as an Italian Cant seaplane. It was flying low, about fifty feet, and for half an hour it circled over the sea from three to five miles from them, obviously looking for the dinghy but too low for much range of visibility. Feeling almost physically sick because they had no more signal flares, they waved shirts and arms and shouted themselves hoarse, but in the end the Cant turned and flew off without seeing them and they cursed Italian inefficiency with the futile fury of despair.

Yet that afternoon spirits skyrocketed again and they thought it was all over bar the shouting, for as a haze over the horizon lifted Dinger let out a howl of, 'Land! For Christ's sake, look!' It was about the hundredth time someone had thought land was in sight, but they followed his pointing finger and by God, there really was land. It was not the traditional low line, but a dark bulk, like a sugarloaf, that humped dimly in the distance. Once again they grabbed the paddles and worked them like furies. By nightfall, they were exhausted, but

Bambino celebrated the sight of land by serving out the last of the vile, cloudy water from the rubber water-bottle, just a fraction of a mouthful each. In the knowledge that land was near they could almost ignore the pain of their burnt and blistered skin, their thirst and the cold of the night.

Dawn brought them a sickening disappointment. They woke with a light-headed feeling of lassitude that weighed down their limbs and peered anxiously out to see how much nearer they lay to the land. There wasn't any land; only a horizon of shimmering haze that rimmed the desolation of glassy water.

It was a wretched, frightening anti-climax, but it wasn't the half of their troubles. Unending thirst tormented them all as the sun climbed up, and, inevitably, they took to drinking sea water. At first they just wet their lips with it, then took the odd, tentative sip. Surprisingly, when they kept their heads damp, the little sea water they swallowed seemed to help thirst a little, but it made them sick. A couple of turtles appeared about thirty yards away and Bambino, who knew they were good eating and would have blood to drink, blazed away at them with his revolver. He was certain he hit one, but both dived and swam off. They tried to catch little fish that were swimming up to the dinghy, but the little fish were like all other little fish and maddened them by approaching tantalizingly within arm's reach and darting off again before their clumsy, grasping hands could hold them.

Desperate for something to drink, and retching when they tried sea water again, they took to drinking their urine. First they mixed a little with the unsweetened chocolate into a paste and tried that. Later, Bambino sipped a little neat from a chocolate tin, and it seemed to help, though the taste was foul and he felt sick.

The second pilot began to sob. His resistance was ebbing and so was his strength. Everyone was more or less beyond talking then, both in inclination and ability. They were living on their tissues and becoming noticeably weaker. Minds were wandering too. At one time they heard thunder in the distance and everyone swore it was a naval battle.

Throughout the day the second pilot rapidly became worse.

In the early afternoon, the haze over the horizon lifted again and once more they saw the same sugarloaf of land. They might just as well have been spared the sight because it was just as far off as on the previous day. When he saw they were no closer but a lot weaker physically even Bambino began to feel sick at heart. It was so near but so far too. He and Dinger were the only ones with enough strength left in them to paddle, and he knew that the two of them wouldn't be able to get the unwieldy dinghy as far as that land. The dim sugarloaf faded again in the evening haze, and as darkness closed them in again the second pilot's face was swelling ominously.

On the eighth dawn they tried licking a dirty film that had gathered overnight on the fat balloon sides of the dinghy. Each man took a section and licked and licked till tongues and lips were all yellow from the coating of the rubber. It seemed less salty than the sea water and for a little while it helped to relieve the awful torments of their thirst. Bambino tried to drink a little more of his urine, but by this time it was thick and foul and he gave it up hopelessly and wet his lips again with salt water.

As the sun climbed up they looked again anxiously for the land, but again the haze obscured the horizon and they saw nothing. Miraculously, four flies—they looked like the ordinary house pest type— suddenly flitted on to the dinghy in the way that the ubiquitous fly has of materializing out of nowhere in the most unlikely places. Bambino and Dinger roused from their torpor and stalked them. The flies were unwilling to leave their sanctuary in the middle of the water and one by one they were slapped down. Bambino got two and Dinger got two and they flipped them into their mouths and painfully swallowed them as well as their dry, swollen throats could swallow.

'Fresh meat,' croaked Bambino. 'Nothing like it.'

A couple of jellyfish floated by and Bambino fished one out in the mood of dogged experimentation. It was a fat, transparent sloppy thing but he squeezed it into his mouth and managed to swallow it. As soon as he got it down he retched and retched, though there was little enough he could bring up. It seemed to moisten his throat a little though, and later on he tried another one—with the same result. He concluded it wasn't even an acquired taste.

It was the same day that the wireless operator went haywire. He had ditched in the sea once before and this second experience was shaking him horribly. Suddenly he began to babble and weep. He lost all control over himself and it was nerve-racking for the others to listen to him, except for the second pilot who was almost beyond noticing anything. With inflamed, raw red face and limbs he lay silent and motionless in the dinghy. His eyes were dull and mostly closed. Once or twice he tried to talk, but there was no sound from his cracked and swollen lips —only an awful brown slime that kept on bubbling out and that Bambino and Dinger gently wiped off.

That afternoon the haze lifted as usual, and oh, the warm joy that flooded out their weariness as they saw they had drifted closer, much closer to the land. They could make out a rocky promontory and a couple of little white specks on it that might be houses. It looked pretty grim and bare, but it looked pretty good too for all that. Bambino and Dinger wearily took up the paddles again, but after ten minutes of mostly futile effort their heads were swimming and they were fagged out and could paddle no longer. Once again darkness blacked out the sight of land. The second pilot seemed to be unconscious and they knew he was dying.

That night Bambino couldn't sleep. A grim problem was weighing on his mind. Dinger couldn't sleep either and the two of them sat there in the darkness, talking with dry huskiness, while the other three lay like logs, in unconsciousness that was about half sleep and half coma, for the navigator, too, was cracking up. The two wakeful ones were the only members of the crew who were married. Both had youthful wives and were very much in love, and Dinger was a prospective father. It was of their wives that they talked, though half of Bambino's mind was on his problem. He came to his decision about 2 a.m., beckoned Dinger away from the other three and spoke in a low voice, putting his problem without hedging.

'Dinger,' he said, 'if the second dicky dies, and I think it won't be long now, we may get the strength from him to carry on and save all of us. If we can drink some of his blood and eat some of his flesh, it might give us enough strength to carry on till we make it. Otherwise we probably won't. What do you think?'

There was a short, heavy silence, then a laboured breath from Dinger.

'I think you're right,' he whispered. 'It'd be better than throwing his body overboard, wouldn't it?'

They were both shivering violently, and it wasn't only from the cold.

'We'll take it as decided then,' said Bambino. 'We both have wives and you're going to be a father. We've just got to do it. It's the only way we can save the others, too.'

'We'd be criminal fools not to do it,' Dinger muttered. 'It's horrible, isn't it?'

So then, with the decision made, they braced themselves and discussed how they should do it. It was a shuddersome, gruesome talk, and if the darkness had suddenly lifted each would have seen that the other was deadly pale and sweating a little. The only sharp weapon in the dinghy was the big knife that was stowed with it for cutting the painter that tied the dinghy to the aircraft after ditching. Obviously the knife would be the instrument to use for carving the body. Thirst was the most pressing problem, so it was the dying man's blood that was first discussed. It was no good trying to drain some into one of their chocolate tins because it would congeal. They would have to suck it from his veins, they decided, and debated the best part to suck. It would be the wrist first, they concluded, and if the supply there failed, they would have to cut into some other part and suck there. The throat was suggested.

Then the question of flesh arose, and they unanimously decided that the buttocks were the most suitable. It would have to be soft flesh, because it would have to be eaten raw.

And then it was all decided and they tried to cast it out of their heads, but it kept coming back to torment their tired minds with its ghoulish imminence and they could not take their eyes off the poor devils lying in torpid oblivion in the bottom of the dinghy. All night long they sat and shivered while cruel imaginations worked overtime for hours and hours that dragged wretchedly until the dawn of the ninth day in the dinghy arrived and dispelled the forbidding darkness.

The haze lifted early that morning and they almost sobbed with joy to see that they were still nearer to the land. They could easily see two rocky humps of land sticking out of the sea, and little white specks of houses that looked so friendly and there seemed to be little tufts of scrub growing here and there. They were, perhaps, ten miles from it. Bambino and Dinger took the paddles again but their efforts hardly moved the dinghy and sapped their strength completely. The second pilot couldn't move that morning but was still alive, and they still had to wipe the slime from his lips. The wireless operator was almost unconscious and the navigator was having spells of delirium and was very weak.

Across the water the sound of engines on the island came clearly to their ears, and it spurred Bambino and Dinger to another effort. They refused to abandon the men in the dinghy, but decided instead to try and tow the boat to land. It was rather a gallant scheme, but scarcely practicable. Too desperate to worry about sharks, they tied the painter of the dinghy round their bodies and slipped over the side. For twenty minutes they swam doggedly before they would admit that it was hopeless. The dinghy had scarcely moved and they had little strength left, so they crawled back, and after a rest decided on a last throw. The scheme was to swim the ten odd miles to the shore and send back help to the dinghy. It was crazy, but not quite so crazy as it sounded, because they still had their Mae Wests.

So about 6 p.m. they slipped over the side again and swam. They kept going for about an hour before they saw it was no good. Darkness was closing down and they would never find the island. The water was chilling them, too, so reluctantly they swam back and decided to try again at dawn. They shivered throughout another night, and at 5 a.m., in the first light of dawn, they saw one of the two peaks of rocky land about six miles away. Shedding all their clothes except Mae Wests, they slipped again over the side. The navigator was able to mutter a feeble farewell. The other two were unconscious.

Before they set off they decided irrevocably that if one should get into difficulties, the other was not to try and save him, but would go on alone and try to get help for the helpless three left behind. Mostly they swam a placid, strength-conserving breast-stroke, and occasionally turned on their backs to rest and paddled with their feet. Bambino went on and on. He had always been a strong swimmer since his days in the warm waters of Barbados. Dinger was gradually dropping behind and when Bambino looked back again after about four hours, Dinger was no longer in sight. Doggedly he stuck to the job, but was feeling very weak and the water was chilling him. There were times when he wanted to give up, for there is a limit to will power, even of giants like Bambino. In those black moments he forced himself to think of his wife, and her memory kept him plugging tenaciously on. He had not been married very long, and a young man in love like that can be a very determined creature. Involuntarily at first, he had swallowed a few mouthfuls of sea water, then decided bemusedly it tasted fine and swallowed a lot more thirstily.

He could see the white cottages clearly now and the island was looming large. Then he saw a fishing smack and pulled up his whistle, hanging on a string from his Mae West, and blew and blew till he was breathless, but they did not hear him. Dully he swam on and at last came under the lee of a rocky hill, with a smooth shelf of rocky shore.

Luckily the sea was smooth, and foot by foot he paddled in, almost at his last gasp, until he felt the glorious rocky bottom under his feet. He tried to stumble ashore but found he couldn't stand, and the rocks felt like cotton-wool under his nerveless feet. He has never forgotten that cotton-wool numbness. Splashing and floundering his way into the shallows he started to crawl on his hands and knees until he was just clear of the water's edge, where he lay like a log, barely conscious and too weak to struggle any further. It was eleven o'clock and he had been swimming for six hours—a mile an hour. Stark naked but for his Mae West, he lay there for a quarter of an hour, utterly unable to rouse himself, and then he saw a ragged old Italian fisherman climbing down the rocky hill towards him.

By the grace of God the old fisherman spoke a little broken English, and Bambino was able to make him understand about the dinghy. The ragged little man promptly turned and hurried round the shore until he vanished from sight round a rocky point. A few minutes later a little fishing boat hove in sight round the point, turned towards Bambino and beached gently by his inert form. It was all the crew could do to lift the big fellow on board, and as they headed out into deep water again Bambino grabbed a large jar of water near him and began to take great gulps.

Almost before he had started the Italian crew took it from him, with signs that he mustn't drink too much, and handed him another jar of their national vino, light red wine. Bambino tried to drink some, but just couldn't get it down. As soon as the crew's backs were turned, he grabbed the jar of water again. The fisherman tried to take it from him again, but Bambino suddenly found the strength of a maniac and clung savagely to it, until they let him go, and he held it to him and drank and drank and drank until he thought he could feel his belly sagging down between his knees. The jar must have contained at least half a gallon, but Bambino didn't put it down till he had finished the lot. He thought he had never tasted anything so delicious in all his life.

The Italians took him to the little hamlet on the island, which was one of the Liparian group, and put him to bed in the local Carabinieri house while another little boat put out to find the dinghy. They found it without a long search and then turned back to try and find the rear gunner, whom Bambino had last seen swimming behind him. For the rest of the morning and into the afternoon they combed the sea round the island, and at 4 p.m. they found him. He had been eleven hours in the water and had drifted past the island, unable to swim another stroke. Half an hour before the boat arrived he had undone his Mae West to try and sink and end it all, but after all that he just couldn't rake up the final strength to struggle out of it and let himself go.

They were all put to bed in the Carabinieri house. The Italians gave them food, but not even Bambino, who had stood the ordeal best, could keep any of it down, apart from a couple of raw eggs. They were only allowed a sip or two of water, and then permitted to suck wet handkerchiefs.

An Italian doctor arrived and started rough surgery on their burnt, inflamed skin. Using a scalpel like a fellmonger in a tannery, he began to scrape the skin from the navigator's legs. It was a nauseating sight as angry, raw flesh was revealed and the poor devil of a navigator was screaming with helpless agony, but was too weak to resist. Bambino could not stand the pitiful sight and pleaded with the Italian doctor to stop, but the doctor would not desist.

'It ees best that I do thees,' he said. 'There ees no other way.'

'Well, for Christ's sake, can't you give him an injection of anaesthetic,' pleaded Bambino.

This the doctor consented to, but not before the navigator had fainted. The second pilot was done next, but was not troubled by it. He was in a coma. The wireless operator followed, but he was half crazy and only semi-conscious, and babbled meaninglessly all the time. The doctor turned to do Bambino, but the big fellow wasn't having any.

'Don't you touch me,' he said. 'I'm an officer and prefer not to have your treatment.'

The doctor, acutely conscious of the size of the patient, agreed that maybe Bambino had better have his own way and left him alone.

After a few days in bed on the island, a fishing boat took them all to hospital at Messina, on Sicily, where doctors told Bambino that the second pilot, navigator and wireless operator would all die, as they were too far gone. He never saw them again, but both he and Dinger had recovered fairly well after three weeks and were allowed another couple of weeks of convalescence before going to a prison camp in Italy. Even after he had recovered Bambino still found he was three stone lighter than when he had started out.

Fourteen months later, when Italy fell, Bambino and Dinger were both among the kriegies down there who were rounded up and herded north into Germany by the Nazis, where he came into our select circle of exiles. He was once again his old, huge, amiable self then, though he still carried a souvenir of his sunny ten days at sea. His hands are red and scarred and cracked from his sunburns, and they will probably always be that way.

Chapter Fifteen

THE TUNNEL GAME

It is time we interrupted the stories of the war outside kriegydom and reverted to the East Compound at Stalag Luft III where the inmates were staging an ingenious and unremitting campaign of their own—the fight for freedom.

So far we have only mentioned a fraction of the escape attempts made by kriegies. It should be understood that escape activity was going on in all camps endlessly. So was counter-escape activity by the Germans. Night and day in all compounds, German security guards patrolled and snooped. Their uniforms were overalls and they carried torches and metal spikes with which they stooged in, out and under the living huts and all round the compounds, probing the ground for tunnels with their spikes, shining their torches in all dark corners and generally trying to upset things. They worked on the assumption that we would always be operating on escape activity and they were not wrong in that respect. These guards were known by us as 'ferrets', a name that the Germans, when they came to understand its meaning, did not appreciate.

After its opening, East Compound went to work with a will on escape plans and a brief account of them will indicate how kriegy escape operations were growing. As the camp was in the German 'dust bowl', the soil was light and sandy—easy to dig for tunnelling, but requiring a lot of shoring as the sand collapsed so easily.

Prisoners sorted themselves into small syndicates and a number of tunnels were started. Expecting such activity, the Germans had built the camp so that the huts were a long way from the barbed wire. This meant that any tunnels would have to be very long ones indeed as huts gave the only practical camouflage for entrance trapdoors and for working the tunnels generally.

Because of this, even the best locations for tunnelling in East Camp necessitated that any tunnel would have to be about 300 feet long, a tough project, particularly when it is considered that the huts were built off the ground so that ferrets could crawl under them in the search for trapdoors. This difficulty was largely overcome by designing increasingly cunning trapdoors leading down through brick and concrete hut foundations so that they practically defied detection.

The other great difficulty was in the dispersal of sand dug out of tunnels. Immense amounts were brought up and it was always very hard to dispose of it without leaving some traces for the watchful ferrets to find. They used to look for dispersed sand particularly. Various schemes were devised to overcome this trouble, but we were never very happy about it.

Early tunnels in East Camp were mostly shallow, some being only about three feet deep. Quite a few were started by various syndicates but one by one they were discovered. The most unfortunate was a very shallow one whose proprietors dug it a shade too near the surface, and a horse pulling the ration wagon stuck a hoof through it, to the mortification of the diggers, the joy of the Germans and the surprise of the horse.

Faced with this spate of shallow tunnels, the Germans dug a deep trench between the barbed-wire boundary fence and the warning wire to foil our efforts. It was about seven feet deep and made an opportunity for one of the most ingenious efforts of all time.

After dusk one night two Englishmen and a New Zealander risked detection and a hail of bullets and slipped across the warning wire into the trench. Once there, equipped with a little spade they began to dig their way into the side of the trench nearest the boundary fence and only a couple of feet below ground-level. As soon as they had dug far enough in they crawled into their 'blitz' tunnel, filled in the entrance so that prowling ferrets wouldn't detect it during the night, pushed a little air-hole about two feet up to the surface and then dug on towards the wire, only about twenty feet distant.

The idea was to finish their tunnel, climb out and be on their way before dawn. They worked like frenzied beavers, pushing up extra air-holes every few feet, as it was pretty stifling down there. The cream of the joke came when they were about half the required distance. Several of their friends were watching from a nearby hut window and could clearly see steam rising out of the air-holes the diggers had made in the surface. This steam always rose when men were below, digging in the close, sweaty confines of a tunnel.

The watchers were therefore vastly perturbed when two patrolling ferrets happened to spot the steam. Holding their breath, the watchers saw the ferrets approach and stare blankly at the steam. They stood there for some minutes, marvelling at the phenomenon of steam rising apparently without cause from the ground, then unsuspectingly turned and walked off.

The tunnellers kept on course, piling the sand behind them and thus filling up the shaft in the rear as they worked until about 4 a.m. when they calculated they had dug enough, pushed up to the surface just outside the boundary wire and slunk off into the darkness.

It was such a smart scheme that they deserved complete success, but alas, they didn't get it. A couple of days later they were picked up and probably out of sheer rage at having their preventive trench converted to kriegy advantage, the Germans sent two of them to the strafelager at Kolditz.

Another startling tunnel was later dug from near the wire with delightful ingenuity in hiding the tunnel mouth from sight under a vaulting-horse used for exercise by the prisoners. The three officers who escaped from it had the complete success they deserved and got right back to England.

Probably feeling that the indiscriminate tunnelling was getting out of hand, the Germans installed sound detectors round the boundary wire, as they had done earlier at Barth. That put a stop to the shallow tunnels but started kriegies off on a scheme they had been cooking up ever since the sound detectors made their appearance at Barth a year or so earlier. It was decided to dig the next shaft about thirty feet deep, which the camp intelligence staff had discovered was deep enough to evade detection from the German microphones. At Barth it had been impracticable because of water seepage, but in the dry sandy soil of Sagan the way was clear.

Two such tunnels were started about May 1942; one by a team under a lieutenant-commander known as 'Hornblower' and another team headed by such persistent old hands as Flight-Lieutenant Johnny Marshall, tall, a little thin on top and with years and years of Air Force service, 'Crump' Kerr-Ramsay, nuggety, dour and Scottish, and Wally Floody, tall, very slim and very brown skinned, who

Facing this page: A page from the German Luftwaffe magazine 'Adler'

It was on this factory chimney that the Canadian pilot got stuck after baling out. The remains of his parachute are still fluttering sadly in the wind after his rescue. Top picture: The exhausted flier after his rescue

"HELP ME! HELP ME!"

PK-Photos by war correspondent v. Pebal

All clear! Day dawns. The workers of a factory are on their way to work when they suddenly hear a strange noise above their heads. It is a human voice, that reaches their ears as if issuing from the lips of a spirit, and it seems to be coming from a great height. They stop and now they hear it more distinctly: "Help me! Help me!" In the meantime it has grown lighter and they see the cause of this apparition. On the 35 metres-high factory chimney flutter the remains of a parachute and suspended to it by a couple of cords and hovering between life and death hangs one of the enemy pilots whose machines had been shot down during the night. It was really an extremely precarious situation in which he found himself, for at any moment the cords might break. In the meantime, however, the people in the streets of the little town have become interested. They hurry along from every direction, straining their necks to see what has happened. What's to be done now? A lance-corporal undertakes the risky job of getting the man down from his dangerous position. The crowd hold their breath as he climbs up the dizzy height of the chimney, takes the enemy on his shoulders, and carefully climbs down again, step by step, to the ground. Without a word he hands the rescued man over to the authorities. That is how Germans behave

was a former mining engineer and therefore invaluable on such projects.

In addition to cunningly camouflaged trapdoors, both tunnels had a further ingenious hidden entrance. About eight feet below ground both teams dug small dummy tunnels about forty feet long and stopped there. Half-way along each dummy they sank a second camouflaged trapdoor in the floor, dropped another shaft about twenty feet and started the main tunnel from there. The idea was that if the Germans found the tunnel entrance they would not find the main tunnel, which might by then be hundreds of feet long, but would only find the dummy instead. Then the diggers could dig down to the main tunnel from another direction and carry on work.

It was a very smart idea but ferrets found Hornblower's tunnel and also, probably by accident, hit upon his second hidden trapdoor in the dummy tunnel. That left East Camp one down and one to play in the tunnel game. Johnny Marshall, Crump, and Wally Floody forged ahead on their tunnel, supported by about twenty comrades.

It was this tunnel more than any other which led to the grand-scale efforts later on in North Compound, when hundreds of men were employed. That this East Camp effort was worked with so few men is a tribute to the terrific amount of labour that the diggers put into it.

In starting it, they discarded the idea of digging from one of the huts near the wire as those huts received most attention in tunnel searches from the ferrets. Instead, they started the venture from hut number 67 in which most of them lived. It was separated from the wire by another row of huts and also the camp cookhouse. This new scheme meant that the tunnellers would have to dig the fearsome distance of about 400 feet before they could get out but they decided it was worth while as they would have more immunity from searches.

The scheme was to dig about 120 feet to a spot under the cookhouse which had a concrete floor. They reckoned on digging upwards then under the cookhouse floor, finding space under the concrete for further dispersal of sand, and then carrying on to the wire.

They built a trapdoor in the floor of their room in hut 67 and constructed a second camouflaged trapdoor in the ground which was about

Facing this page: A digger hacking at the three-foot square face of 'Harry' the famous North Compound tunnel through which the mass break was made

a foot below the floor as the living huts were built off the ground. Dispersing the sand they dug out by spreading it under the hut floor they made their first short shaft and dummy tunnel and then another secret trapdoor half-way along it. Below this they dropped the main business shaft straight down for twenty feet and at the base dug out a chamber where sand could be stored after digging for dispersal. Then they started digging their tunnel out towards the wire.

The workers were divided into three shifts and they dug all and every day and often for part of the night. As the sand was so loose and crumbly the tunnel had to be shored with wood. Consequently much of the labour had to be diverted to stripping the lower part of the double floors of the block and converting the wood so obtained into frames for the tunnel. Basins hauled along the tunnels by ropes plaited from string were used for sending sand back from the working face to the dispersers who stowed it away under the hut, raking it over smoothly so that the ferrets who periodically inspected there would not notice the level under the hut changing perceptibly.

Though only one or two people could dig at the one time, the remainder of each shift was fully occupied in dispersing, constructing shoring frames, handling the sand sled in the tunnel and keeping watch. With such a complicated system of dummy tunnel and extra trapdoor the main tunnel obtained practically no air and it was soon seen that the air supply was going to be a problem.

For the first hundred feet or so of the main tunnel, the diggers pushed up air-holes—an arduous and slow job that did not result in a very good air supply either. About twenty short lengths of wood were each fitted with a rough metal socket into which the top of the next piece fitted. One, with a rough boring device, was pushed upwards from the roof of the tunnel, then the next piece was fitted into its socket and the wood was pushed further up, then the next piece was fitted and so on until the top boring piece broke above ground where a sentry—always known in kriegy life as a 'stooge'—saw that the coast was clear of ferrets. The air shaft thus made was camouflaged at the top with a brick. These shafts gave some air, but barely enough to keep the home-made margarine lamps burning in the tunnel and not sufficient for a man working hard down there in cramped conditions.

The air position was getting critical until one of the gang happened to come across constructional details of a home-made air pump in a magazine that had somehow or other found its way into the compound. The tunnellers made a pump according to the specifications from a kit-bag and wire hoops, and with a pipe-line made of old tins they pumped air up to the working face.

Not enough wood could be found to shore the whole tunnel and in those parts left unshored bad falls were constantly occurring which were a definite risk to safety and also held up work badly by having to be laboriously cleared and packed again.

When it was judged they were under the cookhouse a shaft was dug upwards. To their bitter disappointment they found there was no space under the concrete floor for sand dispersal.

Further calamities were in store. A very bad fall of sand took place at the base of this shaft, leaving a huge dome about twelve feet high over the tunnel, and then to pile on the misfortune the ferrets discovered the trapdoor in hut 67 and the dummy tunnel. Then luck turned the way of the tunnellers. The camouflaged trapdoor in the dummy tunnel stood the test and remained undiscovered.

The dummy was filled in by the triumphant ferrets and the trapdoor in hut 67 once again became a part of solid floor.

Without losing a day, the tunnellers crossed to the opposite room, made another trapdoor in the floor and started on another blind tunnel. When this was completed another hidden trap was made half-way along it and another shaft sunk a further twenty feet below ground.

It was not realized at the time but the new blind tunnel had been built under the block foundations and at the time they were about to link up with the main tunnel, thirty feet deep, the dummy tunnel collapsed under the weight of the foundations just as Wally Floody was crawling along it. The whole shaft fell for about ten feet just where he lay, but by a miracle he had just got his head and shoulders over the entrance to the deep shaft and was able to breathe, and after about an hour's frantic digging the tunnel team was able to pull him clear.

After that, a third dummy shaft was dug, another hidden trap made half-way along it, another deep shaft sunk below that and eventually contact was made once again with the main deep tunnel that stretched out under the cookhouse.

At this stage the sand level under hut 67 was rising perceptibly and it became clear that fresh dispersal areas were most advisable. The best place appeared to be under some other hut, but the big problem was how to get the sand there without being seen by watchful ferrets.

The solution was worthy of the tunnellers. They would do that part all underground too. They dug another tunnel from hut 67 back about eighty feet to the next-door hut in the direction of the centre of the camp. Along this tunnel they were going to drag the sand dug out in completing the main tunnel which still had about 300 feet to go.

By this time the project had been going on for months and the tunnellers felt they were spending nearly all their lives underground. There was so much work to do that their organization was growing as more labour volunteers were engaged. A 'duty pilot' system was started, consisting of sentries constantly posted round the camp sending back information as to numbers and locations of all Germans in the camp, particularly of course in respect of the ferrets. At this stage the original twenty-four workers had grown to about sixty.

A special organization formed in the camp to assist all escape schemes was lending valuable help. Specialists were starting the first factory for forging papers and passports; others were concentrating on metal work and carpentry for the construction of such things as shoring frames for the tunnel, and yet others were starting a tailoring shop and similar institutions for producing aids to escapers. At the head of this organization was Lieutenant-Commander Jimmy Buckley, who had figured prominently in the early escapes from Dulag and Barth.

This growing organization to help all escapers formed the model of the future giant 'X Organization' in North Camp the following year and which we are going to describe in greater detail in later chapters.

Digging on the main tunnel which had reached the cookhouse was now resumed with renewed vigour. The great dome left by the heavy fall of sand at the base of the shaft under the cookhouse was utilized and an extra air pump installed there after the dome had been shored with wood. Digging carried on in the main tunnel towards the wire and, apart from minor falls, proceeded fairly smoothly.

Week after week they carried on at a cracking pace and the tunnel grew to an encouraging length. By this time the whole project, with the first blind tunnel found, the second blind tunnel discarded, and the third blind tunnel used, plus the dispersal tunnel and main tunnel, was like a gigantic rabbit warren, and ton after ton of sand had been excavated and hidden from the Germans.

But the level of dispersed sand under the new dispersal hut had risen by nearly a foot and it began to look a little obvious, no matter how smoothly they raked it over. It was going to be a race to beat the prying eyes of the ferrets.

The main tunnel was nearly 200 feet past the cookhouse, more than

300 feet all told, and there was less than 100 feet to go when a team of ferrets suddenly entered the camp one morning in September, five months after the project had started. They turned all the kriegies out of the new dispersal hut and gave it an exhaustive going over. They found fresh sand over the exit to the dispersal tunnel, found the trap-door and then it was all up. The most ambitious of all kriegy tunnels to date was unceremoniously blown up.

It was a sad disappointment after all those months of back-breaking work, but the history of escape in Germany will never write off that tunnel as a loss. It was the undoubted father of the lusty offspring which grew to a length of 350 feet later on in North Camp. The organization had grown up and was waiting for the chance to try its strength.

Chapter Sixteen

A DENT IN CREDIBILITY

B ehind the wire prisoners took far more interest than other people in the bombing of Germany—except, possibly, those who were hanging around when the bombs landed. The reason, of course, was that the vast majority of them had been on bombers before being forcibly diverted to kriegydom.

So that when the Air Ministry reported, 'Some of our aircraft did not return', they did not say, 'Fancy that', and let it slip into the uncomprehending vacuum induced by repetition. As a matter of fact they were inclined to be rather flippant about it, because the facetious point of view had always been the fashionable way of relieving the strain of ops. and debunking the glamour of the business, and the fashion still held in captivity.

Yet behind the wisecracks there was a fraternal and full understanding of the efforts of the bomber crews who were still on ops. The growing weight of the bombing was noted with grim satisfaction as fresh purges brought news of more and heavier aircraft and more and heavier bombs. Then came the first 1,000 bomber raid, and it was music to kriegy ears. Even the fighter types admitted it was something, which was no mean recommendation.

All this growing activity meant many more aircraft shot down and correspondingly more freak experiences for some of the lucky few who weren't 'chopped'. Some of them thought their stories sounded so wildly improbable that they wouldn't be believed, but they needn't have worried. Prisoners were quite blasé about such things. The day that Bren Hooper, who was five-feet-five and built like a pocket battleship, walked into our midst, we chalked up a narrow escape that stood in a category all of its own as a crazy mixture of the best and the worst that could happen to man.

Bren was Irish, and therefore more or less at home in a fight. This may have accounted for his war record, which wasn't at all bad. In 1938 he became fed up with distributing talkie films in Dublin, so he applied for the R.A.F. He achieved this heart's desire in 1939, and entered with a short-service commission, to emerge as a pilot-officer in 1940. By June 1942, he was a squadron-leader, with sixty-three bombing trips to his credit, not to mention a D.F.C.

That was very nearly more ops. than anyone else in Bomber Command had done at that time. Bren had been backwards and forwards over Germany so often it was just habit. He had dropped his bombs on Berlin and Kiel, and Hamburg and Wilhelmshaven and other news-making names. And he had done the Happy Valley excursion so many times that taking a navigator there was almost a formality. He knew all the best targets, all the best ways in and all the best ways out, and so far had never been seriously disturbed, either by flak or fighters. He had one more trip to do to finish his second tour, and after that he was earmarked for one of those delightful jaunts to America, where he was to hand his experience on to others and live at ease without black-outs. It was a pleasant prospect.

Bren was to make his last trip on the 27th of June, but on the 26th a squadron pal of his who was up on the board for a raid on Bremen had a bad hang-over and asked Bren to swap trips with him. Bren amiably agreed in the soft brogue that had never deserted him, and in that moment his guardian angel, who had stood by so long and so loyally, turned a frigid shoulder on him.

The first part of the trip went off all according to Hoyle. Bren took his laden Wimpy off into a soft, moonlit night, with quivering shafts of the Northern Lights flickering agitatedly over the sky. He stooged placidly to Bremen, had his usual charmed run through vicious flak, made his conscientious run over the target, dropped his bombs and turned for home. Because a couple of pals were waiting up for him in the mess to celebrate his last mission and the coming trip to America, Bren edged his throttles forward and the lumbering Wimpy began to draw a little ahead of the main bomber stream. They made good time at about 12,000 feet and before long the navigator reported the Dutch coast coming up. In a few minutes it was going to be all over bar the shouting. Amiable meditations were shattered by the rear gunner's voice, terse and tense over the intercom.

'Fighter to port, Skipper. He's just....'

The rest was blotted out in the sickening, jolting clangour of pneumatic drills as a stream of cannon shells ripped, clawed and blasted through the fat side of the Wimpy. The night fighter-pilot was no mean shot. His first burst positioned Bren neatly in the centre of his cone of fire. Two feet from his nose his instrument panel shivered into fragments before he could blink, spattering him with vicious splinters, and just behind his seat the wireless operator's neat radio set-up disintegrated with similar speed.

The same thing, of course, should have happened to the wireless operator, but it didn't. He was bending down fiddling with God knows what on the floor and wasn't even scratched; though the front gunner had a shell rip through the soft flesh of his side.

The intercom. went dead as the fighter's attack finished. Then the port engine faltered; its steady roar split into explosive, ragged pops, and it cut dead. Under its cowling spread a rosy glow, and Bren, watching it, felt his stomach turn over as the glow flowered softly into crimson fire, fed by petrol from split wing tanks.

With a dead intercom. Bren couldn't bale out his crew, but his reflexes were equal to the occasion. He swung his half-wheel to starboard, shoved the control column forward and kicked on the rudder. Like a skittish matron, the Wimpy dropped her starboard wing, flicked her tail into the air and peeled off into a howling dive.

There was just a chance that this would put out the blaze as well as get them away from the night fighter, but the fire was too well served by petrol and areas of the wing were quickly alight. Long banners of flame streamed out to the tail as the Wimpy plummeted down. Not far below, Bren made out a layer of cloud, presumed the ground was just below, and eased back on the stick to jockey the heavy aircraft out of its headlong dive.

Nothing happened. He pulled back harder. Still no response, and he felt his stomach somersault again as he realized that the fore and aft controls were gone. (From a shaken rear gunner they gathered later that flames and petrol, streaming back from the burning wing, had burnt the fabric off the elevators.)

There was one slim chance—the tail-trim. Bren's hand was reaching out for it when, what with hits from shell splinters and one thing and another, he passed out. With an unconscious pilot at the controls that were useless anyway, the hurtling Wimpy was swallowed up in the layer of low cloud.

Putting it mildly, there was no future in the position, but just then Nature took a hand; or maybe it was Bren's guardian angel relenting.

One of the basic facts of aerodynamics is that the faster an aircraft travels, the more lift is developed by the wings—a fact that is fairly obvious. And if the wings give more lift, the nose rises and the aircraft changes direction in the vertical plane. If the aircraft is in level flight when the speed is increased, it will climb. If it's heading downwards, it will tend to level off; which is why a diving aircraft, if left to its own devices, will usually level out, because it accelerates automatically in a dive.

And that's what Bren's Wimpy did. It was as simple as that.

But it was mighty low. As it shot out below the cloud layer, trailing flame like a rocket bomb, there was about 2,000 feet to hard, uncompromising earth. The nose of the hurtling aircraft was gradually coming up. But so was the deck. It was going to be close, and a pop-eyed front gunner had a paralysing view of a grotesque race between earth and aerodynamics.

The result was a dead heat.

In a howling swoop, travelling at about 300 m.p.h., the rocketing Wimpy just about got her nose horizontal. She touched flat fields in a screaming skid that ripped up her plump belly like a gutted fish, slapped her tail on the ground, which snapped off the whole tail assembly—turret, gunner and all—leapt a few feet in the air again with lift from the wings, smacked the earth again, lifted again, hit again, left most of her wings behind this time and went charging across flat Dutch lowlands near Groningen as only a 20-ton, 250 m.p.h., amorphous mass of battered, blazing aircraft can charge. A fearsome sight, it crushed everything flat in its path until it finally shuddered to a flaming standstill more than half a mile from the touch-down point. It was proved to be that far because the tail, with rear turret and gunner, was found half a mile behind. It hadn't had wings and weight to help it along.

The silly sequel to the story is that the four men left in the clumsy juggernaut were still alive—not even really injured, apart from bruises and cuts. Bren's crew smartly pulled him out of the blazing wreck and he woke up later in the ambulance.

The sillier sequel is that the shaken gunner in the snapped-off rear turret was alive too, and not badly hurt.

Silliest of all, he staggered out of his turret when it stopped, fell heels over head into a nearby canal and was damned nearly drowned.

Doubt the story if you like, but there are five men living to-day who will steadfastly swear to it.

* * *

Pilot-Officer Freddy Bist was another who should never have come to us. They should have buried him where he fell; which would have been easy because he made quite a hole when he hit.

Fred is another of the freaks who won't get a Caterpillar Club badge, even though he was blown out of his aircraft at 500 feet. His parachute wasn't clipped on and he came down all alone. Probably his case is the most illogical of all such cases, because, as far as he knows, he didn't land on anything soft. The fact that he lived rather strengthened his faith in the Almighty; of which he already had considerable as he is going to be a Protestant minister in the U.S.A. when he has finished his interlude with a machine-gun. He got over a broken neck too, and a few other things, so, all in all, he considered that God had stood by to some extent in the good old hour of need.

Which is about the only way of explaining what happened.

Being an American citizen, an incipient man of God, and over-age to boot, one would not expect Fred to be personally involved in the early days of the war. But there is no accounting for tastes and long before his own country entered the turmoil, quiet, slim, reserved Fred packed up his theological training and started training as a wireless operator-air gunner with the R.C.A.F. instead.

He didn't have any trouble about his age, because, although he was rising thirty-four, he looked only about twenty-six. He emerged from his training with a commission, crossed to England and joined a night-intruder squadron equipped with Bostons. On a black night in September 1942, he was located a few hundred feet over France on business, which consisted of picking-off odd enemy aircraft over their own bases as they were landing after returning from ops., dropping 500-lb. bombs here and there, and generally beating hell out of the place. It was quite entertaining as a rule, but on this night there was a heavy entertainment tax.

They were strafing a German aerodrome at the time, sweeping in low while Fred, in his mid-upper gunner's position, conscientiously sprayed soft-skinned targets, briefly glimpsed in the dark. Light flak was spitting back with angry fervour, but Bostons are fast and hard to find at night. They've usually gone almost as soon as they've arrived. There were lots of lines of luminous ping-pong balls, but most passed well behind.

However, you can't fool all the tracer all the time, and one shell hit them just forward of amidships—a neat bullseye. On the heels of the blast came a thunderous 'whoosh' as the petrol tanks blew up and the sorely tried Boston snapped in two, just about in the middle where Fred was sitting. He was smartly ejected into space, rather like a champagne cork, to find himself without any visible means of support. He was wearing observer type 'chute harness, and, as usual, his actual canopy wasn't clipped on.

At such trying times, Fate is sometimes mildly kind to her playthings, inasmuch as she relieves them of the distressing meditations of consciousness. Freddy was so blessed for he promptly passed out.

It's difficult to write the next part of his story because it sounds so fantastic. It's none-the-less true. He fell about 500 feet, and landed—not, as far as he knows, in a hay stack, nor a snow drift—but on ploughed *terra firma*, thereby making a deep impression, both in the earth and on credibility. He believes it was a ploughed field, though he doesn't know for certain.

Let us at this stage dispense with superlatives and talk of miracles, and state baldly that Freddy wasn't killed.

At the very best he should have been unconscious for a long, long time, but he wasn't even that. Surprisingly quickly he recovered consciousness, to discover, rather dazedly, two German soldiers bending over him. They muttered incomprehensible words in German and soon brought medical aid. Freddy was carted off to hospital with a broken neck, a steel splinter of shell embedded near his spine, a shattered hand and severe burns. The Germans told him he made quite a dent in the field he lobbed in.

The front part of the aircraft, incidentally, crashed to earth half a mile from Freddy's alighting point. The tail half was not so far from him and the rest of the crew were very dead. Somewhat shaken and rather intrigued by Freddy's escape, but forced to believe by possession of the details and the still living body, the Germans made a special point of giving the shattered gunner every possible chance of recovery. They cared for him really well and Freddy pulled through.

After six months of hospital, plaster casts and dressings, he arrived among us, with a stiff neck, a hand that was three-quarters unserviceable, and a huge patch on the back of his pants stretching from the hips to the knee. He made himself quite a reputation as a practical joker in due course, but that patch on his pants hid a bigger joke than any he ever planned.

The petrol blast that blew him out of his aircraft also burned the seat off his pants and large chunks out of his behind. They more or less rebuilt it for him in hospital but Freddy sits down even now on rather a home-made job.

He has taken it with him back to his theological college at Montreal.

Chapter Seventeen

A FATHER—KRIEGY STYLE

In this same month a new Air Force officers' camp was started at Schubin, just south of Bromberg in Poland, to which practically all Air Force officers from Warburg were sent. Eventually Schubin housed about 1,000 prisoners in conditions of invariably acute discomfort.

Some of the huts were of brick, with concrete floors, bitterly cold in winter as adequate supplies of fuel were never a feature of the Nazi programme. There would be maybe two tiny stoves with one burner each to cook for upwards of 100 people and never enough coal for the cooking alone, apart from the question of infusing a little warmth into the huts. Schubin, therefore, was a good place to stay away from and escape activity was consequently brisk.

Hard work of this nature paid dividends early in 1943 when a successful tunnel about 150 feet long was dug from one of the huts. Nearly forty prisoners got away through it (at least, temporarily) and the break wasn't discovered until appel (counting parade) the following day. It was almost missed by the Germans even then.

Normally prisoners paraded in five ranks to be counted, but on the first appel after the escape and before the Germans had wind of what had happened, some of the sections of kriegies fell in in four ranks to try and conceal the deficiencies in their numbers for a little longer and so give the escapees a little more precious time before the hue and cry started. The German officer had almost finished counting the appel before he suddenly noticed that the fives he was counting were not fives but fours. His face turned almost purple and he was practically speechless.

A tremendous flap followed. The Germans turned out about 5,000 troops to help in the search and eventually all the escapees were recaptured. After that there were five appels a day at Schubin, one of which was a 'floating' appel and might take place at any time. These appels might take half an hour or more each and that sort of thing five times a day did not make life any the pleasanter for kriegies there. It is quite a tribute to their nuisance value that they had to be counted so many times a day to ensure they were all there. A couple of kriegies eventually got right back to England after other individual escapes from the compound—the sort of thing a kriegy dreams about, but it is considerably easier said than done.

About the time that Schubin was opened, the number of air-crew prisoners in Germany, both officer and N.C.O., ran into several thousands in various camps, and it might be pointed out that not all the strange stories that lurked in this pot-pourri of Kriegsgefangenenschaft concerned the blood and thunder of escape from death. There were stories of a quieter, more human nature—such as the tale of a young man who was called Cherub. He was pink and plump, with curly fair hair so that the name of Cherub seemed to fit. Withal he had been captain of a 28-ton, four-engined Halifax, and a veteran on his second tour.

Cherub was one of the quietest people in our North Compound at Stalag Luft III, but had been in the war as a pilot right from the beginning. For all his seeming stolidity—which was not so much stolidity as solidity—he was dead keen on flying and long ago he had made up for the dry routine of his office by learning to fly under the Civil Air Guard scheme. When war came he already had his 'A' licence and made a bee-line for the R.A.F.

Cherub had come from a little country village and had been a civil servant. He had to endure a lot of ragging about his bowler hat and red tape, but he bore it patiently, just as he bore his nickname patiently. He was so shy that he had only ever taken out one girl in his life. Her name was Olive and she was tiny and frail, but rather cute. She stood about four feet eleven and seemed absurdly young to be grown up.

As life was somewhat uncertain, they married, like so many others, and were quietly happy. Then Cherub went back on ops. and Olive found out she was going to have a baby. It was rather worrying.

One night in November 1942, Cherub was driving his heavy Halifax at low level across France, bound for Happy Valley. From a hundred feet he could see the dark mosaic of fields and ditches and little farmhouses and the trees that rose out of the deeper gloom like ghostly milestones that came and fled almost in the same moment. They came then to what seemed like a larger field, with a couple of criss-crossed, wide, straight roads through it. It looked like an aerodrome. It was— and heavily defended at that.

Protecting darkness was split by the shooting fingers of searchlights, the flashes of guns and well-drilled processions of rosy bulbs that rushed madly at them. Both searchlights and shells converged on a target so low and visible that the white beams were hardly needed. The Halifax looked naked and defenceless, as, in fact, it was. There was the usual jolting cacophony of pneumatic drills and the usual awful shuddering as shell after shell blasted gaping tears in the matt black metal of engine cowlings, wings and fuselage, and machine-gun bullets punched patterns of neat scattered holes here and there.

Then the Halifax was through the gauntlet with two engines silent and rosy ribbons of fire pouring back from one of them, spreading and lengthening. Like a wounded hippo the stricken bomber floundered: Cherub, fighting with controls that were slack and soggy, knew there were just a few seconds left.

You can't bale out from a hundred feet or less. You have to crash-land. And you can't get rid of your bombs for the crash-landing either, because they go off just under you, and that is undesirable. You just have to pick as good a spot as possible and put the kite down there and hope the bombs don't do anything.

If it's dark, you can't even see to pick a good spot, so Cherub was not to be envied. The only spot he knew of was the one he was in, and he knew that was a bad spot.

He prayed a bit, eased the heavy kite lower and prayed a bit more as masses of black earth rose out of the gloom. There was a rending, grinding, slithering—then silence but for crackling fire which lit the broken hulk of the wreck it was cremating. Cherub and five of his crew struggled out, dragging another who was dead.

They had a hunted forty-eight hours before searching Germans caught up with them and they went into the bag. So Cherub came to Dulag and in the next few months he learnt something.

Of course lots of kriegies learnt things. They studied German and French, and architecture and navigation, and accountancy. But it wasn't these things that Cherub learnt. Others did a lot of deep thinking (there was plenty of time for that) and learnt wisdom from their thinking. But it wasn't so much those things either that Cherub learnt. Shy, silent, reserved Cherub learnt how to mix, and how to come out of his shell.

After he left his cell at Dulag, he wandered into the messroom, where other just-shot-downs were discussing their adventures with animation, as just-shot-downs are wont to do. He sort of appeared unobtrusively, sat down near the fire, and didn't say a word. He looked as though he wouldn't say 'boo' to a goose; and at that time he probably wouldn't have. He felt pretty low. There was Olive. She wouldn't know he was O.K. for weeks yet; bad time for her to be worried. She seemed too tiny and frail to have a baby.

It so happened that Ted E—— was there then. He was a whimsical-looking Welshman, and had come down on his way back from a target in Italy. He spoke a cheerful word to Cherub, who looked so alone and depressed. It was a somewhat stilted conversation at first. They agreed, just as all other just-shot-downs, about what a bad show it was and anyway they were still alive, which was something. Cherub's contributions were mostly monosyllabic.

'Rotten time for this to happen,' volunteered Ted. 'My wife's going to have a baby.'

Cherub showed a reaction.

'Gosh. So's mine,' he said.

'Good Lord!' said Ted. 'Well, I'm damned! Isn't that a coincidence. We're in the same boat all right.'

Cherub, with a rare smile, agreed that it was and that they were.

'I'm rather worried,' Ted said. 'We lost our first and my wife had a tough time.'

'So'm I,' said Cherub. 'My wife's very small.'

It was natural, later on at Sagan, that Cherub and Ted should be in the same room. Cherub slept in the bottom bunk and Ted was in the top. The weeks passed, and Cherub was quiet and depressed. He stayed well and truly in his shell; hardly ever opened his mouth. He was described as 'N.I.', which means 'not interested' in anything. Mostly he just lay in his bunk all day.

Then the months passed and the time came when Cherub's baby was due on earth, and a couple of weeks later Ted's baby was scheduled. But of course, their mail, which was just coming through, was two or three months behind events in England, so they just had to wait. All the time Cherub was quiet, like a country mouse, and we knew he was badly worried though he didn't mention it.

Then a letter came from Olive, written days after the big event was expected, and nothing had happened. More days of unnerving suspense. Then Ted got a letter, grabbed it and read it, and looked up with a silly, fatuous grin spread all over his face.

'Hell,' he said. 'It's a girl, I'm a poppa. Wow!'

There was a lot of noise, and there was Cherub congratulating him too. It made it all the harder when the mail arrived next morning. Again, nothing for Cherub.

We were coming in from a few brisk circuits round (inside) the wire that same afternoon, when someone hailed us. It was an American in the R.A.F., Danny, who lived in the next room.

'There's a letter for you, Cherub,' he said.

'Oh yeah,' said Cherub, who knew the only mail delivery of the day had come round hours and hours before.

'No kidding,' said Danny. 'One of the boys swiped some from the censor's bag when he was in the *vorlager* (the German administrative compound) getting a tooth fixed this afternoon.'

About once in a blue moon that sort of thing happened. One of the kriegies who got within range of a censor's bag before the mail had been sorted and censored was occasionally able to grab a handful and smuggle them into the compound.

Anyway Cherub was off like a cannon shell and almost obscured by dust. He had thrown his old reserve to the winds.

When we got to the room he was already sitting on his bunk, absorbed in an open letter. The old dead-pan look was back on his face. There were long seconds of silence, though we were trying to look natural and mind our own business. Cherub looked up.

'All right, you bastards,' he said. 'It's a girl.'

He was laughing, and incidentally, blushing too. Of course everyone else was laughing too and saying it was a bit grim having two sprog fathers in the room in two days.

From that time Cherub began to emerge from his clam-like shell: spasmodically at first like the sun squinting out behind grey cloud on a dull day, but it was a start. He occasionally produced a wisecrack of no mean quality, enjoyed our applause rather self-consciously and reverted to silence once more. Yet he spent less time lying on his bunk and more time in communal activities. Occasionally he would break out into communal rowdyism and also engaged in the odd friendly scuffle. His wisecracks became more frequent and his enthusiasms grew stronger and more prolonged.

Until one day we realized that Cherub was not much worried by shyness any more.

New fathers go like that sometimes.

Chapter Eighteen

STALINGRAD

No one in the world could have followed the war with such absorbing interest as kriegies who probed every scrap of news that trickled in for signs of the silver lining. Yet after all that we didn't see the beginning of the end when it came. That was Alamein, of course, but when news of the battle and success reached us, many thought it was probably just another leg in the reciprocal motion of up and down desert warfare, though there was an interesting sidelight on the battle that created quite a stir of interest in kriegydom. It was the death of the German 'ace', Joachim Marseille, one of the most lauded heroes of the Third Reich.

A 109 pilot on the Alamein front, Marseille claimed 158 victories. There was a day, just before the battle, when he claimed to have shot down sixteen British aircraft in one day at an average expenditure of twenty rounds of ammunition per victory—a claim that is more ludicrous than impressive. The entire Desert Air Force that day lost either two or three aircraft, and that is quoting official Desert Air Force intelligence figures. Marseille's is a striking example of the extravagant claims made by the Luftwaffe collectively and by German fighter-pilots individually. In point of fact it would be virtually impossible for one pilot to have sixteen confirmed victories in one day, because confirmation of 'kills', if done properly, is an exacting process.

Marseille's claims became so fatuous eventually that the story was told that his agents offered tins of bully beef to divers captured pilots if they would say they had been shot down by Marseille. As one couldn't afford to refuse any proffered food in Germany, maybe there was something in the story.

Marseille 'bought' it in November 1942, on the day that the Germans broke at Alamein and went milling back on the long trek that led to Italy. He was fondly thought to be unbeatable and a nineteen-year-old Canadian pilot-officer knocked him down, though not quite in the way he intended because it also brought about his own downfall. He had never even heard of Marseille either, which would probably have mortified the German.

The young Canadian was Nelson Gilboe, known invariably as 'Gil'. He came from Windsor, Ontario, and is quite a character, being solidly built and rather good-looking with the plump, baby-faced bloom of youth. Gil had a slightly self-conscious smile, but there was nothing self-conscious about his flying. He had bags of guts and used to go bald-headed for anything in the sky that carried black crosses or the three fasces of the Regia Aeronautica.

He belonged to an R.A.F. Kittyhawk squadron and obstinately persisted in the idea that the Kittyhawk could turn better than it really would. This idea got him into lots of trouble because he was always spinning off by trying to make his turns too tight. Still he doggedly tried to turn his Kitty on a sixpence chasing after enemy aircraft, and kept spinning off regularly. It got to the stage that whenever a Kittyhawk was seen spinning down through the middle of a scrap, the boys in his squadron would grin in the rough and tumble of battle and say,

'There goes Gil again.'

A few moments later Gil would be out of his spin and climbing back into the fray. Like as not he would be spinning again before he was through.

His infallible penchant for tight turns nearly finished him one day a few weeks before the battle. Four Kittyhawks were out over the line looking for trouble. Gil was flying one and his bosom pal, Geoffrey Fallows, a slim, whimsical New Zealander who had joined the squadron with Gil, was flying another. About 12,000 feet they were bounced from above by three 109's. As the 109's broke away, Gil tried another of his contortionist turns after them to get in a squirt. A second later he was spinning again. One of the 109's had a squirt at him in the spin and was promptly shot down by Gil's section-leader. Gil went on spinning merrily, or maybe not so merrily for when he tried to ease out of the spin he found his rudder was locked and there is positively no future in a spin with a useless rudder. He kicked at it again and again but it wouldn't yield, so at 2,000 feet he hopped over the side and pulled his rip-cord. The Kittyhawk plunged into the deck below and exploded into flame. It happened to be No Man's Land.

As he neared the ground, Gil found that a slight breeze was carrying him right towards the furnace of the wreck of his aircraft. For some rather horrible seconds he thought he was going to land right in the middle of it—almost literally out of the frying-pan into the fire. A bit of last-minute frantic yanking of shrouds saved the day and he landed a bare fifteen yards from it, with bullets exploding from the burning Kittyhawk's red-hot guns all round him. He was struggling out of his harness when a light armoured car materialized out of a cloud of dust, a rangy New Zealand private hauled him on board and they scuttled back to the shelter of that part of the line held by the New Zealand Division, where Major General Kippenberger greeted him and poured ice-cold cans of beer into him by way of welcome.

A few days later, Gil was coming in to land at his squadron's landing-ground at Amiriya when thick black smoke billowed from under his engine cowlings and then flames appeared as a shaken Gil dived for the deck and one of the hastiest belly-landings ever seen in the desert. He just made it and scrambled out before being fried. His pal, Geoffrey, shook his head knowingly after that effort.

'They'll never kill you, Gil,' he predicted. 'You're too damned lucky.'

In the end Gil nearly killed himself, but finished by killing Marseille instead. On the tenth day of the Alamein battle, Gil went out with his squadron escorting Bostons to bomb the coast road behind the line along which the Germans and Italians were beginning to trundle back. The Bostons duly pattern-bombed effectively and then the Kittyhawks dived down to 2,000 feet, dropped the 500-lb. bombs they carried themselves and continued down to the deck to strafe. Gil was in the rear section and after having a smart squirt at a tent looked up by chance and saw a 109 about 1,000 feet above, doing a gentle dive on the leading section of Kittyhawks about 600 yards in front. Still travelling at nearly 400 miles an hour, with the momentum of his long dive, Gil eased back on the stick and went rocketing up towards the juicier target. He gave the 109 a burst from behind and below. The 109 loomed suddenly large before him as he rapidly overtook it and Gil threw stick and rudder to the right to break away. Again the Kittyhawk didn't turn quite as well as hoped and Gil had a sudden vision of the sky being full of two large black crosses and there was a 'whoomph' as the Kittyhawk smacked into the 109's belly.

Away forward in the leading flight, Geoff happened to be looking back at the time and saw Gil's Kittyhawk suddenly shoot into the air, minus one wing, while just in front of it a 109 suddenly disintegrated and dived towards the ground.

Gil's memory of the next couple of seconds is not very clear. He can recall the Kitty shooting into the air and then flicking into another spin —an inverted one this time. He wound his cockpit top back and was thrown out. He hit a broken strand of trailing aerial as he fell and got a wicked gash in his thigh.

So for the second time in a few weeks he floated down by parachute, and landed this time a bare ten yards from a group of German soldiers having breakfast. They had watched him coming down with some hostility but bound up his wound, bundled him into a truck and within a few minutes Gil found himself travelling in the stream of German transport back towards Mersa Matruh.

On the road that afternoon there was a sudden shout of, 'Achtung! Feindliche Flugzeuge!' The lorry turned and hared off the road and away as a gaggle of Kittyhawks shot past squirting venomously at the transport on the road. From the shelter of his own lorry, off the road, Gil saw them pass and recognized familiar letters on the side of the Kitties. It was his own squadron.

He was given a bed in a German hospital in Mersa Matruh that evening and about 9 p.m. two German officers called on him. They were in dusty green German Army uniforms with sand goggles on their caps and were extremely amiable. They shook hands with Gil and sympathized with him according to the old routine of, 'For you the war is over,' and 'So glad you weren't killed.' Gil spoke to them in French, which he knew well from French Canadian associations in his homeland. At last one of them said.

'Do you know Marseille?'

'No,' said Gil, a little puzzled. 'Who is he?'

'He was our German ace and you knocked him down this morning,' said the taller of the German officers. 'We are very sorry he was killed in an accident like that.'

Gil still didn't quite get the significance of it, but murmured conventional expressions of sympathy. He was not feeling very well or taking great interest either in his victory, his own downfall or the conversation, so the German officers left him.

The night before the Eighth Army entered the town, Gil was put on a hospital ship in the harbour with another captured British airman, Scotty McC——, a slim young man who had been a Glasgow schoolteacher before he became a radio observer in a Beaufighter. The ship was just sailing out of the harbour in the dawn as New Zealand armoured cars entered the town. They had the mortification of seeing their hospital ship get clear away and it took them to Greece, where they were put into a hospital in Athens.

Scotty was in rather a bad way. An Me.110 had shot down his Beaufighter quite a few miles off Alamein. He and the pilot upset their dinghy as they were scrambling into it and all the water and food went to the bottom. The pilot scrambled back on the ditched Beaufighter just before she sank and swam back to the dinghy with a water-bottle. It was empty, and then for seven unmentionable days they drifted towards the African coast. They were already bronzed enough to escape serious burning by the sun but the tortures of hunger and particularly thirst were unspeakable. On the seventh day they neared the shore a few miles behind the German lines. They were so far gone that they imagined they saw factories turning out German tanks and aircraft on the beach and thought they must get the information back.

Eventually they were washed on the beach. The pilot staggered to the shade of some stunted bushes, huskily announced that he had had it and would die where he was. Scotty struggled on inland, came upon some Germans two miles in and got them to go back for the pilot. That was about the time that the Germans pulled out of Alamein. He heard from the pilot some months later in a letter from him in England. The pilot had seen the Germans approach but had remained hidden under his bush. After a fruitless search the Germans departed and a few hours later he was picked up by British troops in the first stage of their advance.

Among the wounded who were landed from the hospital ship in Greece and were taken to an Athens hospital with Gil and Scotty was a tall New Zealand private who was put in a bed near Gil and continued to look hard at him. After a while, he said.

'I've seen you before somewhere.'

Gil looked vaguely at him, but couldn't recall the face.

'I can't place you,' he said.

The New Zealander looked hard again for a few moments.

'Were you ever up in the front line?' he asked.

'Only once,' grinned Gil. 'I pranged in a Kittyhawk in No Man's Land a few weeks ago.'

'Of course,' cried the soldier. 'I picked you up out there in an armoured car.'

And so he had.

Gil remembered him then as the dusty soldier who had yanked him into the armoured car as he was struggling out of his parachute the first time he baled out. With the private was a New Zealand major. They had both been in one of the first half-dozen armoured car's that raced on into Mersa Matruh before all the Germans and Italians had got out and while Gil's hospital ship was about to leave. Therein lies another little story, because, though people know of the rather gallant occasion when Lieutenant-Colonel Keyes' commandos nearly caught Rommel in 1942 in the dashing raid that brought Keyes a posthumous V.C., they have never heard of another occasion on which we nearly got him, because the story went with prisoners into Germany.

About the last German to leave Mersa Matruh was the almost legendary figure of Rommel. Half a dozen New Zealand armoured cars trundled into the town just as Rommel, in his own private armoured car, escorted by two German tanks, was preparing to leave. The New Zealand armoured cars sighted them and swung towards them. There was a short brief engagement before the heavier armament of the tanks told and the leading armoured cars were knocked out. From them, the major and Gil's old friend, the private, were captured.

Rommel introduced himself to the major before he went off and congratulated him on his courage in tackling the heavy tanks, commiserated with him on his capture and wished him well in captivity.

Gil and Scotty arrived eventually at Schubin prison camp near Bromberg in Poland, where Scotty casually mentioned in conversation that Gil had knocked down Marseille, 'some sort of an ace, I believe'.

'What!' shouted about half a dozen kriegies who were listening. And again 'What!' They knew all about Marseille; had been hearing about him for a long time and, in fact, were rather fed up with hearing about him. Recently there had been long screeds about his death and career and they were vastly intrigued to receive the man who brought him down. They trotted out cuttings about Marseille from German newspapers and magazines and Gil began to realize that even if he was a kriegy, he still had a considerable credit balance with the Germans.

Gil and Scotty arrived in Germany just about the time that the epic of Stalingrad occurred, and at this stage, with a wild exhilaration, prisoners at last realized that the tide had turned. The name Stalingrad is an evil memory for Nazis. Overnight the whole of Germany swung in stunned reaction from beatific dreams of approaching victory to a new and horrible reality.

As the Russians rolled over Paulus's Sixth Army and pounded relentlessly forward on the return trip to Germany, the metamorphosis of morale among Germans everywhere was quite astounding. The country literally went hysterical with shock and grief. Newspapers carried heavy black borders and were full of epic poems, eulogies, exhortations, tears, threats, and lamentations. There was never such an extravagant campaign of woe. A four-days' national mourning was declared. All theatres and cinemas were closed, endless memorial services were held with all the disciplined panoply of the Nazi spirit and Germans were practically forbidden to smile. It is a literal fact that every German who came into our camp wore a face as long as that of a spavined horse.

From Der Fuehrer's headquarters came the sad statement:

'Faithful to their oath, to the last breath, the Sixth Army, under the exemplary leadership of General Feldmarschall Paulus, has succumbed to the numerical superiority of the enemy and the unfavourable conditions. . . . Their sacrifice has not been in vain. . . . The Luftwaffe was unable, despite the greatest of efforts and the heaviest of losses, to supply them by air and the possibility of relief dwindled and finally disappeared altogether. All ranks fought shoulder to shoulder until the last round of ammunition. They died that Germany might live.'

Gloom was laid on with a trowel everywhere except in the kriegy camps where joy, as they say, reigned supreme. We were puzzled by the extent of the German hysteria as it was so obviously officially inspired. It seemed strange that the country's leaders should deliberately promote such dismal depression in a country at war.

A few days later the reason showed itself. The whole campaign of melancholy was a build-up to prepare the German people for an intense tightening of the belt. Absolute total war was announced and the country rang with the battle cry 'Alle Kräfte für den Sieg'—'Everything for victory'. Holidays became a thing of the past everywhere, further men were called up for the Wehrmacht and working hours in the munitions industry stretched right round the clock in all factories.

With the fall of Tripoli added to Stalingrad, there was, for the first time, a really hopeful ring about the perennial kriegy cry, 'Home for Christmas'. For the first time, too, they watched our armies with complete assurance as Montgomery's men rolled on into Tunisia to break the vaunted Mareth Line and finish the whole African show. This battle brought the downfall of Geoffrey Fallows who was Gil's bosom pal on the Kittyhawk squadron. He got away with his life too and surprised Gil by appearing later in the same compound. There were a lot of similar funny meetings in kriegydom.

The Mareth Battle also put an unhappy end to a series of strange meetings between two brothers by introducing one into kriegydom where the other, very sensibly, didn't follow. One, the unlucky one, was Ted B—— who was a Sydney journalist before he joined a desert Spitfire squadron. His brother, Rus, was quite a bright boy, being a B.E., B.Ec., etc. He left home in Sydney for experience of the big wide world about 1938, and when the war came was a senior Admiralty naval dockyard engineer at Bermuda. Rus had had to resign his commission in the Australian Militia when he joined the Admiralty. He tried to get back into the Army again on the outbreak of war but the Admiralty, quite rightly, would not release him, so he had to stay in Bermuda until mid-1941 before he could wangle his way back to England.

In May, that year, Ted left Sydney to complete his flying training in Canada. He knew that Rus was due to leave Bermuda early in June for England, so he wrote to him when he reached Canada. Rus's answer went astray and Ted heard next that he had probably left Bermuda early in July. In September, Ted, now a pilot-officer, went down to Halifax to get a boat across to England. About the fifth day he was there he and a couple of friends were wandering about the city looking for a drink. Now Halifax is a very dry city, and no matter how dry you are yourself, Halifax is always drier and without an intimate knowledge of the city's secret oases, you just don't get a drink. Eventually, in desperation, they turned into a café to console themselves with tea.

As they sat down in the crowded room Ted noticed a young man looking at him from the adjacent table about six feet away, and the thought casually flashed across his mind.

'Gosh! That chap looks a bit like Rus. Bit too plump, though.'

He looked away again, then suddenly looked back in one of those delayed-action double takes that are so highly funny on the films.

'Gosh!' he said. 'It *is* Rus!'

And so it was. Ted had not seen his brother for nearly five years and had no idea he had ever been near Canada, much less Halifax, but it was undoubtedly the flesh and blood of his brother. Rus finally made up his mind that the other *was* Ted about the same moment, and simultaneously, as though they worked off the same spring, each one rose, stepped forward about one pace and they shook hands and grinned foolishly between their two tables.

There is no formula for meetings like that, no stock cliché like 'How d'you do'. Each instinctively avoided the banal 'Fancy that' and had the presence of mind not to say 'Isn't it a small world?' There was a sort of deathly 'ush of the pregnant type, and then, inevitably, the Deity was invoked, not wholly blasphemously. After the shock of surprise had settled into a gentle simmer, they got things sorted out in a conversation that still bubbled with explosive pops of surprise like porridge on the boil. Rus had been delayed in Bermuda and was going on to England in a convoy, via Halifax. He had tried to get in touch with Ted but hadn't been able to find him.

The two brothers nattered away all that evening about one thing and another, never ceasing to marvel at things, and arranged to meet next day. But things started to hum early next morning and within an hour, Ted found himself on a small, passenger-carrying freighter in the basin at Halifax. They sailed shortly after. In the same row of the convoy was the auxiliary merchant cruiser carrying Rus to England too.

They did not have a chance to meet in England until months later, when Ted's squadron was posted to the Middle East and Rus came down from Scapa Flow to see him again. In the meantime Rus had been making efforts to join the Air Force, as the Admiralty wouldn't release him for the Army. He had tried three times, but half a thumb, left behind in a chaffcutter in his youth, had decided the air-crew medical board against him. On his fourth try he got through and at the same time the Admiralty offered to send him back to Australia as a liaison officer. Rus rejected it and decided in favour of the Air Force. Ted wished him luck before he sailed for the Middle East.

Weeks later in Alexandria he had a letter from Rus. The Admiralty had refused to release him for the Air Force and were sending him, instead, to—Alexandria. Just before he arrived, Ted left with the Desert Air Force on the long road from Alamein to Tripoli. When that city fell he got four days' leave and hitch-hiked back to Cairo on a Beaufighter. On his arrival he sent a telegram to Rus in Alexandria to come down and see him. Next morning he had an answer from Rus's secretary. His brother, apparently, had left Alexandria for Cairo an hour before the telegram arrived. He was on his way to Tripoli.

Ted tried to find him in Cairo, but couldn't track him down. At last he had to give up and despondently phoned R.A.F. Air Transport to book his own passage back to the front in Tunisia.

'Didn't we fix your passage a few minutes ago?' asked the anonymous voice on the other end of the wire.

'No,' said Ted, 'you couldn't have.'

'Did you say your name was B——?' asked the voice.

'Yeah,' said Ted. 'That's right.' And he spelled it again.

'Well I booked a B—— a few minutes ago. It's an unusual name and I was wondering.'

'Hell's Bells!' shouted Ted. 'That's my brother. Well, I'm damned! Have you got his address? Well, I'm damned!'

'Don't shout,' said the voice, unmoved. 'Half a mo.' There was a brief silence. 'He's at the Victoria Hotel.'

'Thanks,' said Ted, and went straight round to the hotel where he bumped into Rus coming out of the dining-room, to his brother's vast surprise again.

Next morning Rus left on the early plane for Tripoli and Ted left by the same service the following morning. At Tripoli Ted was able to see Rus again. A few days later he was back with the squadron and his first trip after his leave settled any chance of further strange meetings.

The squadron was scrambled from cock-pit stand-by to accost a formation of 109's hanging about the front line. They took off in a strong south-easterly wind and at about 10,000 feet, under a screen of alto-stratus cloud, pushed on into enemy territory, looking for the 109's. Up towards Gabes, the flak was coming up thick and fast. The sky was full of puffy, black stains and then the 109's were glimpsed scooting through the cloud behind and the squadron swung round towards them. They were back almost over the line when the 109's came at them from above and Ted's section swung up over the squadron in a cross-over turn towards the enemy, who broke off. A few seconds later, Ted saw a couple of them behind and above. They were still out of range but he called up his section-leader.

'Couple at five o'clock, Hunk. Keep an eye on them,' and then looked back over his right shoulder at them again, as another 109 came shooting out of the cloud, above and behind on the left—shooting, literally.

Ted's first intimation was that dreadful jolting that shakes an aircraft like a pneumatic drill when cannon shells smack home in quantity. He had the usual, queer, incredulous realization that he was being shot down and the shrinking expectation of a cannon shell in the back through the thin armour. The whole thing was over in a shaven fraction of a second. A couple of shells smashed through his cockpit somewhere between his legs, there were explosions crashing in his ears and the cockpit was suddenly full of black smoke. He had a flashing glimpse of shattered cockpit fittings, great chunks flew off the port wing, the engine died suddenly and quietly and then he was spinning, with the stick hard back in his stomach. He saw huge, blackened gaps in his port wing as he let the Spitfire spin for a couple of turns away from the enemy. Then he applied correction automatically, but the stick just fell forward, loose and floppy, like a broken neck, and the aircraft fell remorselessly in a curiously flat spin, with smashed controls.

Without wasting further time or height, he ripped off his helmet and oxygen mask, unclipped his harness and dived over the port side. He was half-way out when the slipstream induced by the swift fall of the aircraft, caught his body and swung him round. The seat pack of his parachute caught fast in the right-angled corner rim of the cockpit and held fast, and the slipstream forced him on his back along the side of the fuselage and held him there.

He kicked and struggled, heaved and clawed but slipstream and seat pack held him relentlessly and there was nothing in reach he could grab to help himself. The spinning Spitfire was about 7,000 feet then, falling fast, and past his left shoulder Ted could see the ground revolving round and round slowly, coming up to meet him.

He intensified his struggles, twisting his body from side to side and straining to reach the cockpit rim. He failed, and still the ground, revolving slowly, came up towards him. As other airmen have found, before and since, there is no great fear in looking closely at death. Ted's main emotion was an angry irritation as though he had spilt beer all down his tunic. The Spitfire tumbled down and down, past the 5,000 feet mark, then 4,000, 3,000, and 2,000. It must have been getting near the 1,000 feet and Ted, still lying back along the fuselage, was feeling nothing worse than annoyed disappointment as things loomed large below when he suddenly fell clear of the aircraft.

He felt curiously free and light and then saw that he wasn't wearing flying-boots any longer. They were torn off when he fell clear. For a sickening moment he thought his seat pack had been torn off too, then felt its reassuring bulk and pulled the rip-cord. There was a tug and he was hanging uncomfortably in mid-air, with a dull pain in his left shoulder and the back of his head where cannon shell splinters had hit him. Looking down, he was just in time to see his Spitfire, immediately below, make a last spin and hit the deck with a violent explosion and burn furiously. The explosion might have been only the petrol tanks going up, though it seemed too violent for that. The probability is that it was the combined effects of petrol tanks and a heavy mine, for though Ted didn't know it he was coming down in an extensive mine-field sown on the flank of the enemy front line on flat, muddy sand that stretched a few hundred yards out to the seashore. He also didn't know at the time that he had baled out just about over the middle of No Man's Land and the strong south-easter was blowing him into enemy territory. Had it been blowing the other way he would have landed in his own lines.

The ground suddenly appeared close and he saw that the wind was taking him backwards, and somewhat fast at that. He tried to twist the shrouds round but before he could get even part way round he hit, damned hard in his socks. He went over backwards, shaken and with the breath knocked out of him. He was dazed and as he fumbled to his feet his parachute bellied out in the strong wind and he was dragged willy-nilly across muddy sand that was packed tight with venomous anti-personnel mines. Still dazed and weak, he tried to undo the quick-release box of his harness but it was clogged with sand and he couldn't release it. He had been dragged about 200 yards when ahead of him he saw a rivulet of running water, and just beyond it, a line of barbed-wire entanglements.

A moment later he had opened the obstinate release catch and tumbled free of his harness as the silk canopy hit the water and collapsed. Ted wearily tried to stand up and promptly fell over again, feeling pretty shaken. He just sat up then and saw the hollow end of a rifle pointing at him, held by an Italian soldier about four yards away splashing across the stream. The barbed wire, which was the enemy front-line entanglement, was a bare ten yards away and an Italian colonel with rows of gongs across his chest and immaculate, gold-slashed riding-breeches was standing in front of it. That spot was the edge of the minefield and the colonel wasn't going any farther. A crowd of scruffy Italian soldiery was hanging about in the background.

The first soldier helped Ted stumble across the water and the colonel greeted him courteously with the old formula, 'For you the war is over'. It was about the only English he knew.

They took him along a system of low trenches to a dressing station to attend to his splinter wounds, and handed him a big dixie, half-full of fiery cognac. He took an apathetic sip as an Italian corporal came up to him and said in passable English:

'You are most lucky. That was our minefield your parachute just dragged you across.'

Ted finished the cognac in practically one gulp and after that went mournfully on into hospital and then to us in Germany, behind barbed wire, where he did *not* meet his brother again.

Chapter Nineteen

ORGANIZATION 'X'

E arlier, we mentioned what a distressingly dry place kriegydom was alcoholically after the first couple of years of war. When Germany had exhausted the supplies she had looted from France and began to feel the pinch, prisoners were well at the bottom of the list of preference for any sort of luxuries, including hooch of all descriptions. About once or twice a year—no more than that—the Germans would dole out to each prisoner about two litres of a horrible travesty of beer. It resembled the genuine article in colour only, but there wasn't a spark in a barrelful, though it was good exercise for the kidneys.

Kriegy ingenuity overcame the liquor problem with a strange and fiery concoction known as raisin wine, made with the raisins and sugar one occasionally saved from food parcels. To avoid hurting the feelings of the Red Cross we may say that only a tiny proportion of their excellent food parcels was used for this purpose.

The recipe for raisin wine is simple to the point of being elementary. Briefly, a dozen or so people would form a syndicate, save their raisins and sugar for a fortnight and put their savings into half a barrel of water with some fermented raisins as a 'starter'. This was left for about three weeks after which time all the raisins would be fully fermented. The pulp residue was then strained off through a pillow-case. This left gallons of dubious sludge called raisin wine which possessed considerable alcoholic ferocity and was sufficient to lubricate one heavy party. The hangovers were frightful but the first few hours of riotous oblivion were a refreshing anodyne to the atrophying stagnation of prison life.

Sometimes prunes, or even pumpkin or potatoes were used instead of raisins and the wine suffered accordingly. Quite often, the wine was distilled or even double-distilled into raw spirit, from which we made strange but sometimes passable imitations of apricot brandy, kummel, whisky and gin, all with a kick like an atom bomb. There was a Polish R.A.F. officer at Sagan, a chemist in peace-time, who had a secret formula for making a creditable replica of rye whisky. He used to pour a strange viscous fluid into the double-distilled spirit and then add a few grains of a mysterious white powder. Heaven only knows what his materials were or where he got them. He would never tell us, which was, perhaps, just as well. Anyway, the result was a rye that would have bluffed many black-market operators.

One of the most spectacular of these hell-brew binges was a party that took place in the East Compound at Sagan on the 9th of January 1943. For some unknown reason there was some grog left over from the Christmas and New Year's Eve celebrations and that evening a large party was staged that lasted in noisy revelry till after midnight and way past lock-up time. When at last the party started to break up people began to consider the question of getting back to their own blocks—quite a problem as the doors of all huts were locked and barred and ferrets of the armed German security staff were patrolling the camp with unpleasant alsatian dogs.

The party were in no mood to worry about such details so they began to pile out of the windows and a few others, who lived in the block where the party was held, went with them to see them safely home, among them being a couple of well-known fighter-pilots. Inevitably they encountered the ferrets and there were 'words'.

The ferrets tried to shepherd the wanderers inside but the revellers were quite happy outside and didn't want to go to bed. Eventually one of the guards fired a shot as a 'persuader' and then the party started to get rough. A couple more rifles cracked in the frosty air and then the chatter-guns opened up, sending a spray of bullets above the heads of the revellers.

The effect was immediate. There was a wild scramble for home and dark forms were tumbling noisily through windows in all directions, screeching with laughter and defiance. In less than thirty seconds the compound was clear, and as the last shape vanished through the dark square of a window-frame a final snarling rip from a chatter-gun echoed past the hut. A moment later a tousled head popped out of the window and leered alcoholically in the general direction of the gun.

'Yah! Missed, you blighter,' it said, and vanished again.

Thereafter it was ominously quiet, but ructions broke out the following day. The Kommandant was displeased. He was, in fact, hopping mad, having been pulled out of bed the previous night, but too late to play any part in the affair. He immediately stopped all further issue of food parcels—quite a serious reprisal as German rations were more a formality than a diet. Then, about noon, swarms of German soldiery descended on the block where the party had been held and took the only cooking-stove in the hut into protective custody. It was loaded with pots and pans but they took the whole lot, pots, pans and all, hoisted it on a cart and drove away to derisive cheers from unrepentant kriegies.

The Germans then nailed up the doors at one end of the hut with huge six-inch nails, though why, no one seemed to know as the other end was left open and no move made to hinder kriegy movements in and out. The Kommandant also forbade any further use of the camp theatre and imposed other petty restrictions.

Later on, after a young squadron-leader had been shot in the stomach by a guard following a party, the Senior British Officer banned raisin brews. It was a wise precaution. A lot of German guards were displaying a nasty, vindictive streak as the war turned more and more against them. After their early confidence, the horrible realization that the Fatherland was going to take the father of all hidings was a bitter pill for them and a lot of the guards developed extremely itchy trigger fingers.

But about the time of the East Compound binge, the date was approaching when nearly all East Compound prisoners were to be moved across to the nearly completed North Compound, which was to become the centre of probably the most remarkable P.O.W. escape operations of the war.

It was known for months in advance that most of us were to be transferred to North Camp, so about Christmas 1942, leading lights in the escape business began to plan for future operations in the new camp when the move should take place.

Little was going on in East Compound in the escape line just at that time because winter is the 'off' season for escape, particularly as regards tunnelling. With snow lying on the ground the problem of dispersing the sand was almost insuperable as the Germans were now watching under the huts for dispersed sand very closely. And even if people did manage to get outside the barbed wire in winter conditions were hopeless for battling one's way across several hundred miles to the safety of

Sweden or Switzerland. So there was plenty of time and energy available in East Compound that winter for planning.

The former leader of East Camp escape organization, Lieutenant-Commander Jimmy Buckley, had been 'purged' to Schubin. His place was taken by Squadron-Leader Roger Bushell, who had already shown what amounted to genius in organizing escapes. He began to plan on a scale far vaster than ever before. Where previous schemes had used twos or threes and then dozens of men, Roger envisaged hundreds who would work day and night for months if necessary and employ every cunning little trick devised in the past and a lot of new ones as well.

Roger and his cohorts were lucky in having nearly three years' persistent and mostly bitter escape experience behind them. It was a worthy framework, and on it they built well.

Around him he built a small select committee of the most ingenious, industrious, and persistent escapers. They included people like the leaders of the earlier East Camp tunnel, such as Flight-Lieutenant Johnny Marshall, who had been either playing an oboe or trying to escape since early 1941 (and his room mates wouldn't let him play the oboe very much), Crump Kerr-Ramsay, Wally Floody, nearly crushed in the big East Camp tunnel, and a couple of others.

Sometimes, when the coast was clear of snooping ferrets, they went into secret conclave in their rooms. When ferrets were about they went for 'circuit' after 'circuit', tramping round just inside the perimeter of the warning wire for hours on end where they couldn't be overheard while they mapped out the campaign.

Some important elementary points were decided. They were not going to hurry the work if it meant slip-shod methods. Even if it all took many months it was to be done with the greatest care and perfection so that there would be no slips. Security was another vital feature planned ahead. As well as keeping everything hidden from the Germans, a few vital secrets would also be hidden from the bulk of the camp as the occasional unguarded word was so hard to prevent and the Germans did so much eavesdropping outside rooms at night. Therefore security would be carried out on a greater scale than ever before. If needed they would use hundreds of sentries—and in fact they did.

They came then to the planning of the tunnel, and here the ambitious detail of the scheme becomes apparent. It was not going to be just a tunnel—there were going to be three tunnels and they would work like beavers on the assumption that the Germans might find two but one at least should be successful. Another point in favour of this was that if the Germans found an elaborate tunnel they would think they had foiled our plans completely and slacken off their searching activities for a while.

The basic policy settled, Roger's select committee settled down to dope the whole thing out in the most minute detail, providing for every contingency they could think of.

As North Camp neared completion the Germans allowed working parties of prisoners to go across there and prepare things for moving in. Roger and his committee men put themselves on some of the working parties and entered their compound-to-be to reconnoitre. Surreptitiously while they worked they paced out distances, roughly measured angles, noted good directions for tunnels and investigated the woods and roads just outside the wire for good tunnel outlets.

They also found out all they could about a sewer pipe that led away from the camp to somewhere outside. It was decided to investigate the sewer pipe as soon as they moved in. Before it received any use that pipe might save them all the trouble of tunnelling.

From these working parties before the move we knew that the new camp was about the best accommodation that the Germans had ever supplied for us—not that that was any recommendation. It contained quite a few of the scruffy, stunted pine-trees so common in Germany (and so unlike the stately pines of Canada) but generally the camp was just another barren sandy compound about 350 yards square inside the 'warning wire' which was really a light fence that ran about ten yards inside the double barbed-wire barrier that enclosed us. If you crossed that little warning fence you were on the receiving end of a bullet or bullets in about half a second. Our intelligence system found out that the Kommandant was always exhorting his guards to let us have it on the slightest breach of such regulations.

Moving day was April Fool's Day, 1943. A motley collection of kriegies and their baggage (little enough of that) tramped the few hundred yards through the woods between the two compounds (under heavy guard) and duly arrived at the new home. We were searched on the way, as usual, to see that we were importing nothing forbidden, but that was a detail and did not trouble us much. We smuggled through everything we wanted, including our precious radio, our one link with the civilized world, home, and all that sort of thing.

It was a bad day that we didn't get the B.B.C. news at Sagan. Every compound had its radio, in fact, probably every camp in Germany, though not by courtesy of the Germans. Such things were strictly *verboten* and the ferrets, who suspected we had a radio, searched industriously for it for many months but never found it.

These radios were not so difficult to come by. It was never very hard to find a German who was either dissatisfied, disloyal or greedy and with a little gentle bribery he would bring us in radio parts and other useful things. A team of underground helpers like that were worth their weight in gold, radio parts or what-have-you.

When we trudged into our new North Camp home that day we found fifteen pre-fabricated wooden living-huts each divided into about twenty rooms that were supposed to accommodate four but had to take six (and later on had to take eight and more because of over-crowding).

Prisoners slept, ate, studied, read, prepared food and generally had to do everything in their rooms. When eight people have to do that day after day *ad infinitum*, life becomes more than somewhat trying, particularly in winter when one is more or less forced to stay inside all day. The same faces, tripping over the same feet, hearing the same voices and listening to the same prejudices with never a change is not the pleasantest way of spending life and the fact that there was remarkably little friction in P.O.W. camps is an immense tribute to the self-control of prisoners generally.

The huts in North Compound even had a few wash-bowls and inside lavatories—undreamt-of luxury. There was even a cookhouse, but almost its sole function was to prepare hot water, boil potatoes and now and then prepare a soup. It was far too inadequate to cook for either all or part of the camp which was supposed to number only about 1,000 but was eventually overcrowded till twice that number were squeezed in.

All the huts were built off the ground so that the ferrets could crawl under them with torches and long metal spikes, snooping and probing for tunnels. You can therefore imagine the difficulty of building tunnels that could evade detection for months on end.

German counter-escape measures were always pretty intense—so intense that after a couple of months in occupation of North Compound they cut down all our pine-trees so as to have an unrestricted view of the whole camp in an effort to discover what activity was going on.

No time was wasted on moving day in getting to work on the long-prepared plans for escape. Before the last kriegy was through the gates, operations were under way. It was an ideal time to act. Everything was in a shambles; kriegies were dashing everywhere with baggage getting themselves sorted out and the German ferrets were not yet organized.

While sentries kept watch, the man-hole of the sewer was lifted and the concrete piping investigated. If suitable, the living-hut lavatories—the only ones connected to the sewer—were not going to be used and men would have been crawling through to freedom within a very short time.

Alas! Bitter disappointment. The sewer drew a blank. The pipe was too small for crawling operations and in any case it was discovered that there was no outlet near enough to permit of practicable operations. The man-hole was replaced and on the spot it was decided to put the three-tunnel plans into operation.

But there was yet another aspect of escape to be considered. While the new camp was in the shambles of moving in and settling down and while the ferrets were still sorting themselves out in the new location, a sort of fever hit the camp—escape fever. Taking advantage of conditions, a wave of stunt escapes were tried.

Working parties of Russian prisoners were still in the compound clearing trees and stumps, and trucks were rumbling out of the gates loaded up with masses of leafy boughs. Kriegies started climbing on to the roofs of huts and then jumping on the trucks as they passed below. It was nothing to see a couple of lads hiding behind chimneys and then, as a truck hove in sight, there would be a swift movement, a quick leap and deep in the green boughs they were whistled off towards the gate, where, alas, most were detected and were escorted outside the gate and into the 'cooler' for a fortnight of solitary meditation.

Others hid themselves in coal and ration wagons and most of these, too, were picked up at the gate by the guards. A couple of people got clear but were rounded up again before long.

A couple of days after the camp was opened the first purge of new prisoners arrived from Dulag Luft for North Compound. As they were marched up to the gates, a party of Russian workmen was marching out. As always, the guards counted the Russians. At the first gate the guard found the count correct and passed them on. At the next gate, where the new purge was waiting, the guards made the count one too many. There was a general flap. The Russians argued the point, the guards argued back and eventually a ferret arrived. New purge prisoners, wondering what was up, saw the ferret single out one of the Russians in a tattered cap and greatcoat, greet him sardonically and march him off to the cooler. The 'Russian' was an Australian pilot who had acquired a Russian cap and greatcoat and surreptitiously slipped in with the Russians in a bid for freedom. For the new purge kriegies it was an entertaining preview of the activities in store for them.

Meantime inside the compound itself, operations were proceeding apace. In all the living blocks blank lists appeared on the doors calling for people who wished to play cricket that season to append their names below. The lists were, in actual fact, calling for volunteers for escape work.

So was built the North Compound 'X' Organization, a name that was picked for security reasons and convenience. Within a few days there were hundreds and hundreds of names on its books—practically the whole camp, except a few who were sick, wounded or studying hard. Roger Bushell, at the head of the organization, was known as 'Big X' and the 'X' leaders in every block were known each as 'Little X' for block so-and-so. There was also a camp 'Big S' who looked after security, and a 'Little S' in every block.

Technicians and craftsmen were sorted out into teams. For a start there were three tunnelling teams. Wally Floody, experienced mining engineer, was chief tunnel expert. Johnny Marshall led one tunnelling team, Crump Kerr-Ramsay led another, and Johnny Bull (later to be killed) was in charge of the third. Tim Walenn, the forgery expert, sorted out his men; Tommy Guest got together a team for general tailoring and the carpenters, metal-workers, intelligence, and contact men and others built up their own branches.

This, then, was the beginning of the unflagging work of Roger and his organization. We jocularly labelled ourselves the 'cloak and dagger' men, but there was nothing much jocular about the work. It was hard, it was unremitting, often boring and tedious, and there were some bitter disappointments, as when one of our tunnels was found and another had to be discarded, but it went zealously ahead until the 24th of March of 1944—almost a year to the day after our move into North Compound —when we broke our last remaining tunnel which ended so tragically. Rather than split the strange story of these activities into several sections, we shall give you the whole account in later chapters.

Chapter Twenty

PRIGIONIERIES BECOME KRIEGIES

T hings were definitely looking up, both inside the camp and outside, at this stage of the war. The campaign in Africa came to a dazzling conclusion and many other smaller indications appeared on the scene to suggest that the Allies were going to have things very much more their way from now on.

One of these indications was the apparent increasing inability of the Luftwaffe to cope with Fighter Command's new Spitfire IX in operations over France. Fighter boy kriegies were highly delighted and also smitten with envy of their former colleagues who were flying the new Spitfire. By all accounts they were reputedly invariably on top of the Germans again—both figuratively and literally and being literally on top of the enemy is a nice place to be in a fighter.

It wasn't all a piece of cake, though, as Jimmy Abbotts found out at 26,000 feet over Holland on the 29th of July 1943. A burly, fair-haired, energetic youngster, he came from Owen Sound, Ontario, and he should have been shot, shattered, and burned, but he wasn't.

His squadron was 'delousing' Fortresses as they came back home out of Holland—that is, they were liquidating such enemy fighters as still persisted in pestering the bombers. The voice of the squadron commander came over the R/T:

'Two aircraft—nine o'clock—2,000 feet below. Go after them, white section.'

So Jimmy peeled off to port with his section and swept down towards two Me. 109's. Apparently it was the old decoy stunt. There was another 'Hun in the sun', and Jimmy was just nicely away on his attack when forty pneumatic drills started up in his Spitfire. He concluded, rightly, that he was being attacked and receiving cannon fire. In the shock of the moment his body tensed and shrank, expecting personal attention from a shell at any moment, though it didn't come. It's a nasty feeling.

Shells that punched and blasted great holes in the fuselage filled his cockpit with stinking black smoke and oil from burst pipes spurted up too, spraying him with hot glutinous filth. Jimmy slid back his perspex cockpit top in quest of air. The 'Hun in the sun' had finished his first attack, but Jimmy still saw in front of him the first two 109's he had set out to attack. He had a quick squirt at them, didn't wait to observe results, but looked for his own attacker. There he was 2,000 feet above and behind, just nosing down for another text-book squirt. It was a bad moment for the Spitfire's engine to start juddering and missing badly, but that's what it did.

It was obviously unhealthy to stick around, so Jimmy did the wise thing; whipped his throttle back, eased back on the stick, kicked on the rudder and flicked into a spin. He let his aircraft tumble like an autumn leaf for 21,000 feet, then pulled out to go home. It was a bad moment for the engine to cut completely, but it did that too. So Jimmy did the wise thing again. Quick fingers tugged out his Sutton harness clip, he shrugged the straps off his shoulders, took off his helmet and rolled his stricken Spitfire on its back, expecting to fall out.

He didn't fall, so he tried to drag himself out; fell a little way, felt himself hit something and passed out.

'The next thing I remember,' records his private diary, 'the aircraft was right side up and the heavy straps of my parachute were hooked around the radio mast behind the cockpit, while I was hanging on the right-hand side of the fuselage.

'My 'chute was open, but not open. It was just a thin string of silk trailing under the tail wheel. I tried to lift the canopy up, but couldn't make it. Then I tried to lift myself up. I got so my toes were touching the tail plane and then tried to straddle the fuselage, but the slipstream pushed me off again.

'The aircraft was at quite an angle of approach and the ground was looming up. God must have had full control. I saw the horizon disappear under the wing, a bunch of trees, a house. . . .

'I thought this was the big moment—I've had it. Dying doesn't seem so bad.'

At this opportune moment he passed out again.

He woke up in a hospital bed with bits of cannon shell in his leg and shoulder, the sound of German voices in his ears and a German girl wiping sand off his face and out of his eyes. He hurt all over, and his shoulder was a pulsing ball of fire. His mouth was full of sand and also a piece of chewing-gum. A German came in, shook a wondering head at Jimmy and said: 'One in a million'.

He told him how he had seen his Spitfire plunge into the ground with Jimmy still dangling on the side. It straightaway exploded into raging flame. People nearby had dashed up, hacked the body from the tangled parachute harness and dragged it to safety—to find it still alive.

That, incidentally, was not the last of Jimmy's lucky escapes. Nearly a fortnight later he was taken to Dulag Luft at Oberursel for interrogation. Ten minutes after he had left the train at Oberursel it blew up. When he arrived at Stalag Luft III his sole heritage of a very hectic crash was a set of shoulder muscles that would not move his right arm. A few months later even this had been repaired.

But Jimmy never lost the memory.

*   *   *

About the time Abbotts joined the motley, kriegy interest was centred firmly on the southern fringe of the European war where the Allies were preparing the storming of Sicily and Italy. A lot of people who were soon to join us were awaiting progress down there with particular yearning—they were our counterparts down south, the kriegies in Italy, most of whom had been captured in Africa.

Many of these prisoners were to suffer the most cruel frustration of hopes. They knew after Sicily and Mussolini fell that it wouldn't be long before Italy was completely out of the war. Italian soldiers round their camps were heartily sick of it all and the Italian Press was wailing with a plaintive note in sorry contrast to their earlier gimcrack arrogance.

On the invasion of Italy on the fourth anniversary of the beginning of the war, kriegies in Italy felt like packing their bags for home. On the 8th of September when news of Armistice buzzed around, the rejoicing was terrific. Unfortunately, with the news came two wicked rumours that were largely responsible for the awful anti-climax that followed. They were to the effect that Allied landings had taken place at Genoa and La Spezia in Northern Italy. These rumours convinced many kriegies that they were safe from being recaptured by the Germans. Several Italian camp commandants reassured them further on this score, so that although a few prisoners took no chances and escaped from their camps, the rest obeyed the prudent orders of their senior officers and stayed where they were.

The rumours of course were false, like most rumours in kriegydom, and that very same night a large prison camp at Bologna was surrounded by a cordon of Germans with tanks, tommy guns and searchlights. A small prisoners' punishment camp in the south of Italy was treated somewhat similarly and a field gun was trained on the camp. At Modena, unsuspecting kriegies spent a peaceful night but next day a disturbing, almost unbelievable rumour was heard to the effect that the Germans might be arriving in the afternoon. The senior British officer called a meeting and told kriegies that just in case the rumours were true they could hide in the surrounding country during the next couple of days if they so chose.

Just as the meeting was breaking up the big double gates of the camp swung open and German lorries crammed with troops and tommy guns swept into their midst. In the sickening next few minutes there was a wild scatter in which about seventy people got away, but the rest were well pinned—about 1,000 all told, including about 100 Air Force officers—and herded back towards their huts.

Scores of them then tried to hide. The roofs were crawling with fugitives, and down in the potato patch surreptitious forms were covering themselves in hastily scrabbled holes in the soil. Another covey took refuge in the woodpile and a couple more immersed themselves up to their necks in the cisterns. Most of them were rounded up and they spent three wretched days in their huts under close guard.

One morning they were marched down to the local railway station and herded into cattle trucks after a weary, thirsty wait in which two more of them escaped by pretending they were water carriers. There were between thirty and forty crammed into every cattle truck and there were about thirty such trucks. Between every six trucks was coupled a flat car carrying mounted machine-guns. From a previous trainload of prisoners taken into Germany from Bologna a day or two earlier, a total of 104 had escaped and the Germans were hopping mad about it, which probably accounts for the barbaric things that happened on this Modena train.

Each truck had only two small grilles to admit air and the prisoners crammed inside had sixty hours of stifling hell from a searing Italian summer sun on the first stage of the trip to Germany. The trucks normally would carry eight horses, which gives an idea of the cramped space inside them. There were no sanitary facilities and the prisoners were allowed but two small drinks of water during the whole of the trip. They took turns standing by the little grilles, trying to get a few lungfuls of comparatively fresh air.

Immediately the train started, escape plans started in full swing. In every truck men began to cut away the floor. Unluckily, during a brief stop a German guard beside the train noticed the damaged floor of a truck from below and a few minutes later a squad of Germans dashed into that particular truck headed by a rat-faced young Nazi in a black S.S. uniform. He was an N.C.O. only about nineteen, thin lipped, with pale eyes and sandy eyebrows. Cursing fluently he brandished a pistol at the prisoners and backed them to the end of the truck where he counted them, prodding the barrel of the cocked pistol against each chest in ticking them off.

After that he had all their gear thrown onto the track outside the truck and the soldiers then looted the kit. The little rat-faced N.C.O. found a bible in one kit and called his comrades over to sneer at it and the owner. He contemptuously tossed it aside and faced the prisoners again:

'If any of you are missing in the morning,' he said, 'I'll shoot ten of you out of hand.'

Then the squad went off and searched other trucks. In one, where they found a floorboard torn up, they strangely seemed to do nothing about it except hammer four long sharp nails across the gap left by the missing board. The prisoners in the truck were jubilant and planned to finish the job as soon as the train was under way again.

A few minutes later, one of them was allowed out to urinate and he glanced under the truck. He found there was a hand-grenade fastened near the missing board. One of the nails passed through the exploding device and it would have exploded as soon as the nail was bent or torn out.

That night while the train was stopped in a station, two South African officers in another truck cut a hole in the end of their truck, climbed out and dropped on to the rails, waiting for the train to start and leave them behind. Unfortunately dawn came first and they were caught. German guards clubbed them with rifle butts and then a burly S.S. Feldwebel (sergeant) appeared, a dark, surly-looking thug with the words 'Adolf Hitler' on his armband, indicating that he belonged to Hitler's personal S.S. Panzer Division.

Casually he ordered the guards to shoot the two officers, but before they could do so the senior British officer present, a New Zealand colonel, shouldered his way forward and angrily remonstrated with the

S.S. Feldwebel. The lives of the two would-be escapees hung in the balance for some minutes while the argument raged and the New Zealand colonel threatened the Feldwebel with vengeance to come. The S.S. man eventually gave way but ordered that the two South Africans be lashed down with wire, spreadeagled on their backs on a flat car and left there all day.

They were duly lashed there, face up, until late afternoon under the blazing Italian sun with the tortures of thirst and the wire biting into their wrists and ankles till they were torn and bloody. The incident closed with a revealing and typical statement by the S.S. man:

'I would have no more compunction in shooting all of you than I would have in swatting a fly. You are the people who have been bombing our Ruhr.'

This convenient forgetfulness of the Luftwaffe bombing of Warsaw, Rotterdam, Belgrade, London, and Coventry, was one of the strange and consistent features of the German reaction to the bombing of their own country.

Another highlight of the transfer of prisoners to Germany was the attempted escape of Lieutenant Charlie Upham, New Zealand V.C. and bar winner. He jumped out of the motor-lorry into which he and many others were crammed just after they had crossed the Po River, and made a dash for it. A couple of machine-guns in the convoy opened up on him as he ran and shot the heels off both his boots. Upham himself was miraculously unhurt and hid behind a tree. The Germans stopped the convoy and went after him. They almost missed him but the last man on the way back to the trucks happened to see him in hiding and Upham was haled back. Luckily no serious reprisals were taken on that occasion.

Upham was a man completely without nerves. On a later occasion in Germany he was abused by a German for failing to salute him. Upham, after eyeing him coldly from head to foot, told the German exactly what he could do with himself and his arrogance. Probably the German didn't fully understand the rich vernacular but there was no mistaking Upham's attitude. Eyewitnesses reported the German as being so deflated that he took no avenging action.

Among the most spectacular of the events during this transfer from Italy were the suicidal escapes of a large batch of Indians. When they found they were bound for Germany they thought they were going to certain death so they tore open the small grilles in the side of their cattle trucks and man after man took a flying header through the small hole on to the side of the track outside while the train was rattling along at high speed. After each man went out a Red Cross box of food was tossed after him.

God knows how many got away by this method but about 200 made the crazy leap and a shocking number must have been killed when they crashed to earth. Only about 100 Indians, a third of the total in the train, reached Germany.

Typically enough, German treatment of the Italians, their late allies, was even worse than that given to the British. Thousands upon thousands of Italians were herded north into Germany and the British prisoners saw dozens of cases of as many as eighty Italians crammed into the one cattle truck in unspeakable conditions. Several cases were witnessed of Italians who attempted to escape being shot on recapture. As a matter of fact quite a few British prisoners were also killed by the Germans during the move.

Ominous first taste of Germany for most of the transferred prisoners was the cosmopolitan prison camp at Moosberg where there were large numbers of Russians, Yugoslavs, French, Greeks, and men of other small European nations. One must at least be impressed with the utter ruthlessness with which, during the course of the war, the Germans threw so many millions of ordinary human beings into prison camps and left them there to rot. There were unbelievable millions of them all over the country. Moosberg itself contained well over 100,000.

The Russians there were in a very bad way, mostly from malnutrition and lack of medical attention, and when they arrived there the British prisoners were told that the Russians died like flies on working parties. There was a story to the effect that when one of them died in their crowded hut, his friends out of desperate hunger, kept the body there and drew his rations till the presence of the decomposing body became unbearable.

There was another nice story of the time the Germans planted a Russian-speaking German, masquerading as a Russian, among a batch of newly captured Russian prisoners to get information. A few days later, some of the Russian prisoners approached the German guards and said sorrowfully.

'Please come. Our friend is very sick. He has been sad lately.'

So the Germans went and found their 'plant' hanging by the neck from a beam in the hut and very dead.

The Italian prisoners at Moosberg who had just been brought up north were emphatically fed up, both with the Axis and with the war. '*Nous avons eu Mussolini*,' said one of them to a British prisoner. Translated literally from the French it means, 'We've had Mussolini,' which just shows how R.A.F. slang gets around.

From Moosberg, the ex-Italian kriegies, sick as much from disappointment as from their hardships, were soon dispersed to British camps all over Germany, and at Sagan we got about 100 Air Force prisoners who stayed disconsolately with us until Germany, too, went the way of the transgressor.

Chapter Twenty-One

THE LUCKIEST EVER

During the latter half of 1943, nights at Stalag Luft III were often disturbed by a series of prolonged and thunderous rumblings from the north-west, invariably preceded by the blood-curdling wail of the sirens. It was Bomber Command bashing Berlin, gratifyingly audible more than 100 miles away.

One of these nights as we lay in our bunks listening to the music of flak and falling 'cookies' (4,000-lb. bombs), a strange thing was happening in the air over Berlin where our thoughts were centred. It was more than merely strange. It was one of the craziest escapes from death that the unprecedented circumstances of the air war produced. If it weren't enough to be sitting on top of four tons of bombs when they went off, the star of the incident then fell three and a half miles to earth practically unchecked by parachute. And there are several more fantastic twists to this affair.

The lucky man was a bomber pilot of no mean repute, as befits the startling climax to his career. He was aged about thirty at the time, a wing-commander, D.F.C. and Bar, and one of the gen. men of Pathfinder Force. Later, in kriegydom, he heard that he had also been awarded a D.S.O. His name is Ken Burns and he is quite an impressive-looking bloke—about six feet, solidly built, forceful, and energetic, with one of those smooth pink and white complexions that are so often, as in his case, capped by fair hair, tinged with pugnacious red. His pride and joy at the time was a huge spreading moustache of the genus 'operational' that he maintained in a state of untrammelled fertility.

He was born in Oregon, U.S.A., of English parents and grew up in London. When rearmament was getting under way in 1937 he joined the R.A.F. with a short-service commission and was made a flying instructor. He was still in the backwater of Training Command when war broke out and on the inception of the Empire Air Training Scheme in 1940 he was sent, somewhat against his will, to Australia to help in getting the big training programme under way, taking a newly acquired wife with him. He spent two impatient years in Australia during which time, apart from flying, he had two main interests.

One was the devising of elaborate and audacious plans for the appropriation of a certain lavatory seat which framed a photograph of Hitler from whatever R.A.A.F. station happened to possess it at the time. This unorthodox frame was originally souvenired from the home of a well-known pastoralist near Sydney whose private aerodrome had become a flying instructors' training school. Hung, together with the original chain, in the officers' mess of the station whose personnel first 'lifted' it, the seat and picture became a sore temptation to the messes of other stations. It was purloined by officers from another mess, purloined again from them, and thereafter it rapidly developed into a precious trophy with a reputation and career like the fabulous diamonds of fiction that lead men to death and dishonour. It produced no death, but a lot of good fun.

Burns' second interest was the writing of letters pleading to be posted into the fighting part of the war. He and several friends applied earnestly and at length until, early in 1942, they were sent back to England and Ken, then a flight-lieutenant, joined a bomber squadron.

His career as a bomber pilot was brisk, business-like and considerably successful. He visited all the big targets and most of the small ones and his crew developed a sound respect for him as an energetic skipper and a pilot who left nothing to chance. It was not long before he was promoted to squadron-leader. On one trip to Turin an engine failed on the outward flight but Burns carried on to the target on three engines. Then another one was knocked out, leaving two engines to get home with the Alps in between. The Lancaster couldn't struggle over the Alps on two engines so Burns made a long detour around by way of Lyons and brought his aircraft and crew safely home. After that he got his D.F.C.

On a later trip to Pilsen, 1,500 miles there and back and the longest trip made by Bomber Command, his Lancaster was hit by flak over Kassel on the outward journey. The air-speed indicator was put out of action and the altimeter very nearly so. It might be pointed out that flying an aircraft without an air-speed indicator is about the trickiest thing in flying because you never know how close you are to stalling, and landing a heavy kite in such circumstances is somewhat terrifying.

Burns carried on to Pilsen, dropped his load and returned safely. After that they gave him a Bar to his gong.

Eventually he transferred to Pathfinders and the number of his trips mounted up and up as he progressed on his second tour. He went as Master of Ceremonies on several trips and was Deputy Master of Ceremonies on the first big effort over Berlin, when Templehof was badly hit.

He and his crew went out to do Berlin over again on the 31st of August 1943. It was his forty-ninth trip—and his last. The Lancaster headed out into an ideal night, dark and almost cloudless, and they duly arrived over the target at about 18,000 feet on the edge of midnight, about half an hour after the fireworks had started. Their job was to drop the last markers for the final wave of aircraft and in addition to flares they had 9,000 pounds of bombs on board—just over four tons —including a 'cookie' (4,000-pounder).

The Wingco was nosing the Lancaster in for the run-up when the blackness right in front of them was punctured by a frightening series of spitting orange flashes and almost before they realized that a night fighter was making a head-on attack there was that horrible pneumatic drill jolting right beside the pilot's seat as converging streams of shells from four cannon ripped up the port side of the nose just by Burns' left elbow, opened up the leading edge of the port wing-root like a tin of beans and slammed into the port inner engine. Almost in the same moment the vague, shadowy shape of an F.W. 190 slid by like a stream-lined ghost just above. From the wing near the engine fairing came a rosy glow that swiftly blossomed into ribbons of flame streaming back towards the tail. The Lancaster was obviously one of the aircraft that was going to fail to return that night. The Wingco didn't waste time in valedictions.

'This is it. Out you go, blokes,' he ordered.

The 'blokes', who had absorbed some of their skipper's swift effi-ciency, clipped on their packs and slipped through the hatch. Jock Keddie, who was bomb aimer, had previously fused his bombs.

'Shall I let 'em go, Skip?' he bawled.

'No,' yelled the Wingco. 'Leave 'em be and I'll aim the kite where they'll do some good.'

Jock obediently turned and slipped from view into the blackness. Ken shoved the nose down towards the glowing pyre that was Berlin, trimmed her to stay more or less put and unclipped his Sutton harness to bale out. He was just raising his hand to whip off his helmet when the darkness round the Lancaster was split by a blinding flash with a thunderous roar as the bombs went off. Most of what exactly happened at that moment of the Lancaster's disintegration will never be known, but among the things that did occur, three are known from deduction. They are:

(1) Against all the laws of nature and commonsense, Ken Burns was not killed—as witness the fact that he is still very much alive.

(2) His right forearm and hand were blown off just below the elbow —as witness the fact that they were there when he took off and they weren't when he came down.

(3) As the explosion blew him out of his seat like a well-oiled cork, the cord of his intercom. tightened viciously round his neck and almost choked him—as witness the cruel red weal that still streaked his throat for weeks after. That intercom. cord that almost killed him also saved his life in the queerest way, and the shock of the explosion that should have killed him also saved his life in another queer way.

It is impossible to assume anything after the explosion than that the Lancaster was blown to bits and that Burns fell some 18,000 feet to the deck practically unchecked. He was naturally unconscious.

He woke up lying on soft earth with a hazy feeling of discomfort and a great lassitude. He had no idea where he was or what had happened, nor did he care greatly. As growing consciousness exposed his senses, pain asserted itself in his right ankle and foot, and instinctively he stretched a hand down towards it. The searching fingers met nothing. He felt a little sick and a clammy fear tingled through him. No foot? Weakly he raised his head, steeling himself to look. Ah! the foot was there. It seemed all right—and then he saw his arm. It was the right hand and half the right forearm that were missing and blood was heavily caked round the ghastly mess of torn sleeve, flesh, and bone. Yet he felt no pain and his nerves did not tell him his fingers were missing.[1]

It should have been a shocking discovery, but somehow it wasn't. Nature is usually kind in such circumstances and the numbing effect of shock had insulated his mind against the full comprehension of the thing. One point only clearly penetrated his consciousness; so clearly that he repeated it aloud.

'God! I'll bleed to death.'

Instinctively he looked at his left hand. It was still there, thank God.

[1] It is a fairly well-known medical fact that people who have lost limbs sometimes have a most convincing feeling that the missing fingers or toes are still there.

So was the watch on his wrist, still ticking. It didn't occur to him to wonder at the fact. He looked at it. The luminous hands shone palely and showed 3.30 a.m. His dulled senses absorbed the fact that it was three and a half hours after he had unclipped his Sutton harness to bale out. It must be almost dawn, and without much concern he vaguely wondered why he hadn't already bled to death. Another wave of sick weakness passed through him and he realized that he must have lost a frightening amount of blood. He would have to get help, and that right quickly—or else.

He mustered all his sapped strength and forced himself to get to his feet. He was a dull ache all over and his back hurt particularly. Still there was no pain in his right arm, or what was left of it. As he struggled up, he realized that half his difficulty was because he was still wearing his parachute. It was a pilot type, with seat-pack attached. With difficulty he unclipped it and it fell to the ground. Without fully realizing the implications at the time, he saw that his parachute had not opened—naturally enough, as he had been unconscious on the way down and therefore in no condition to pull the rip-cord. The explosion in the aircraft, however, had slightly remedied the omission and probably saved his life instead of killing him, because one of the four flaps of the canopy pack had been ripped aside and a few yards of the voluminous silk had been dragged out, presumably either by the explosion or by the rush of air as he fell.

There was not nearly enough either of the canopy or of the shrouds protruding from the pack to have allowed the canopy to belly out in the approved fashion and let him down lightly. The Wingco's theory—the only acceptable one—is that the silk must have trailed out above him like a flapping banner as he fell and caused sufficient drag to take the edge off terminal velocity.

This, however, Burns did not worry about at the time. He dimly realized he must have made practically a free fall from some 18,000 feet but, for the time, remained dully unimpressed, being in no condition to meditate on miracles.

On his shaky feet at last he took in his surroundings through the quiet darkness, lightened by a rosy aura that glowed over the city's fires. He was at the edge of a sort of cabbage patch where Berliners had been 'digging for victory', and practically above his head were the tangled tops of trees, a clump of ubiquitous, spindly German pines that bordered the cabbage patch.

Across the patch he could dimly see a row of houses, some of them rather battered by that diseased decay attributable only to bombs. Near the houses was a light. He faltered a wavering path towards it, across the cabbages, until he came to a hedge which barred his further progress. The effort had weakened him further and now he was barely conscious. The light seemed to be almost above his head (actually it was a signal box and the hedge by which he stood bordered the tracks of a Berlin suburban electric railway line).

Burns called for help. He called in English but the German in the signal box could not mistake the frail urgency of the cry. He tumbled down the ladder, across the tracks and through the hedge and then the Wingco had a vague knowledge of a good Samaritan's kind support that led him a few yards along the hedge and then through a gate on to a station platform, where he was laid on a seat. There he passed out. He must have been very close to death.

He woke up a couple of hours later in the hospital at Berlin's Templehof Aerodrome, to find that doctors were just finishing a blood transfusion on him. They then bound up the stump from which the two wrist bones were protruding—an unspeakable sight.

The next few hours were vague, intermittent consciousness that came and went out of blank greyness, and hazy memories of Luftwaffe night-fighter pilots standing round his bed, questioning him and examining some of his kit they had found.

He was taken then to the Hermann Goering Luftwaffe Lazaret (hospital) at Reinigensdorf, near Berlin. Here the stump of his arm was cleaned up and in a further check, doctors discovered that one of his lungs had collapsed and was full of blood. They plunged a nozzle through his ribs and drained it off.

After a few days, the Wingco had recovered sufficiently to tell the story of his escape. It was just beginning to dawn on him how unbelievably lucky he had been; the human brain is not used to swift and full comprehension of such wild improbability. The German hospital staff could not, would not believe it all at first until the evidence forced them into acceptance of the account—the fact that their patient was there and still, though not much, indisputably alive; the discovery of his virtually unopened parachute and of the crew who had baled out earlier, and the fact that the Wing Commander's right forearm was undoubtedly missing.

The doctors searched for some explanation of it all. Undoubtedly the patient had fallen without much help from his parachute. That he wasn't immediately killed they explained by the fact that he must have come down at an angle from the velocity of the aircraft and the explosion, had hit the top of the pine-trees beside the cabbage patch, which had broken his fall, and then dropped a few feet to the soft garden below.[1] His survival of the explosion was more difficult to explain but the doctors pondered over it till they produced a most ingenious solution that is probably correct.

According to their theory, when the bombs went off Burns must have been ejected from the disintegrating aircraft at some fabulous speed, travelling with the blast so that its worst effects were partially neutralized. There was enough effect, though, to cause the usual fatal collapse of the lungs. One lung collapsed, but—and here that cruel red weal round his neck comes in—as the intercom. cord tightened round his neck as he was blasted out of his seat, the air passages of his throat were momentarily choked—just enough to protect the other lung from collapse.

So much for that. But why didn't he bleed to death as he lay for three and a half hours with his forearm blown off?

That, deduced the doctors, was largely because the terrific shock of the explosion so affected his heart that its action was reduced to an absolute minimum and its feeble pumping in the following few hours sent just enough blood through his body to sustain life. Little, therefore, was pumped away through the severed arteries. In addition to that, the doctors assumed that bits of Burns' tattered sleeve and the soft earth he had fallen on had helped to seal, at least partially, the raw ends of the blood-vessels, and, of course, coagulation of the blood had also played its part. It is all just barely medically possible.

In Reinigensdorf Lazaret, Burns slowly got his strength back, though for some unaccountable reason his back sometimes hurt very badly. The doctors discounted this and after six weeks judged that the Wingco was well enough to be sent to Dulag Luft.

A couple of days later, after an uncomfortable trip, he was ushered into one of the tiny cells at Dulag for his spell of 'softening-up' solitary confinement preparatory to interrogation. His back began to hurt him more and more until he was suffering waves of agony, and eventually he passed out in his cell. He was taken to Obermassfeld Hospital, where most of the seriously hurt captured air crew were immured, and doctors who examined him there found that he had, of all things, a broken back.

[1] The terminal velocity, or maximum speed, reached by a free-falling human body is only about 120 m.p.h., no matter from what height the body falls. This is scientifically established.

Recovery after that was a long process, even after the Germans were able to remove the plaster cast with which they protected his cracked vertebrae and which kept his energetic body so irritatingly immobilized. They gave him a piratical sort of hook to wear on the stump of his arm and it was some compensation when news came through to Obermassfeld that he had been awarded a D.S.O. for his effort as Master of Ceremonies on an earlier Nuremberg raid.

After a total of nine weary months in hospital, where, incidentally, he passed the medical board for repatriation, Burns was sent on to Belaria, near Sagan, a sort of satellite compound of Stalag Luft III, where he arrived on the 7th of June 1944, the day after the invasion started. He used to come across for treatment to our North Compound sick quarters now and then and it was here that he met his navigator and bomb-aimer, Mac and Jock, who had come to our compound months before. From them he learned that all the rest of the crew were saved, excepting the flight-engineer, who was found dead on the ground near Berlin. (Many air crew who baled out were reported by the Germans as 'found dead on the ground'. It would be interesting to know just what proportion of these landed alive and were then attacked by Nazi mobs.)

Wing-Commander Burns was repatriated to England a few months later along with other very badly wounded men, but he did not allow his injuries to cause him to be invalided out of the service. For a while he took a ground job, then he began to fly again and practised until he was once more flying four-engined bombers with his old skill. Persistent efforts with doctors resulted in his being restored to full pilot's medical category and before long he was once again fully operational and in command of a squadron, with every intention of seeing more 'ops.' over Tokyo. He joins the very select band of the R.A.F.'s limbless, operational aircrew.

Chapter Twenty-Two

ANOTHER LEGLESS PILOT

———

Some odd rumours about the legless Wing-Commander Douglas Bader started reaching us from Kolditz towards the end of the year. It seemed that not even the rigours of a 'strafelager' could subdue him and his escape attempts were seriously upsetting the Germans. So persistent did the rumours become, including one that he had been shot while attempting to escape, that it eventually became necessary for the German authorities to issue an official bulletin about him; a unique happening in kriegy life. 'The German authorities at Kolditz', the bulletin ran, 'report that Wing-Commander Bader is as fit and as happy as can be expected in the circumstances.'

It was just about this time that another of Britain's legless pilots slipped unobtrusively into our midst. He was Colin Hodgkinson, who, if not as famous as the Wingco, had the same amount of spirit. He was looking rather battered when he arrived for his face had been injured in the crash, but nothing could get him down, not even the prospect of losing an eye which, at one stage, seemed likely. Kriegies returning from hospital brought us a vivid picture of a muscular young man lying helplessly in bed with tousled bright red hair falling across his bandaged face. They said he was the most consistently cheerful patient in the whole hospital.

Most kriegies knew the story of Colin's misfortunes, for they occurred before the war, but for those who didn't, there was, in our compound, Mickey Taylor, who had something more than a first-hand knowledge. Colin and Mickey were cadets together at Pangbourne Naval College and in January 1939, were flying training aircraft with their instructors. Mickey was flying blind at the time so all he recalls was an excited shout from his instructor, the controls being taken from him, and then a tearing crash. The two aircraft had collided. Both instructors were killed and Colin eventually had to have both his legs amputated. Mickey was lucky and stepped out unscathed. He went on to complete his training as a Fleet Air Arm pilot and less than a year after the outbreak of the war he was a kriegy.

Colin was invalided out of the Navy and though he tried to become an air-gunner he was turned down. A legless airman was unheard of. It seemed as if he were destined at the age of twenty to remain inactive for the rest of his life, a hard fate for one who not only had been an outstanding rugger player but possessed more than an average share of the zest for living.

War came and before many months had passed the world was reading of the astonishing exploits of Douglas Bader. It was the chance Colin had been waiting for. He sent in an application to the Air Ministry, taking care to mention the precedent that had now been established. He was accepted, went into training and emerged ultimately as a Spitfire pilot.

In November 1943, he was escorting bombers over France when his oxygen packed up. The next thing he remembers was finding himself in the wreckage with several Germans around him. He was taken to hospital where his badly battered face was attended to. He had broken his jaw, lost several teeth, severely injured one eye and was generally bruised and bleeding. After some weeks he was sent to Frankfurt where a German eye specialist succeeded in saving his injured eye though it was a very close shave. Colin ended up at Obermassfeld Hospital, his face swathed in bandages but his spirit unimpaired. When the German doctor there learnt that Colin, though legless, was a pilot, his comment was, 'You must really hate the Germans'.

Apparently this view was general in the hospital, or perhaps it was that the Germans remembered a thing or two about how troublesome the other legless Air Force kriegy had been, for they took his legs away from him. Colin lay helplessly in bed and it was only after considerable bickering that they were returned to him.

When the Repatriation Board visited the hospital, Colin went before it, for his eye was far from better and his health generally was beginning to suffer from lack of a proper diet. Later the news reached Sagan that he was among those who had been given their tickets home.

Colin was not in time to go back with the first batch of repatriated prisoners. They left Germany in October 1943, and great was the excitement and envy thereat. It was a qualified envy, as most of the boys would have rather stayed as healthy men a little longer in barren kriegsgefangenenschaft than joined the procession of sick and maimed who were winning their release at a cost they would have to bear for the rest of their lives. Many had limbs missing or were incurably ill and it was generally a sorry sort of business all round.

Typical of the repat. boys was 'Chuck' Lark, an Australian, a short, wiry observer, about twenty-four, with light, short, crisp hair, and a puckish, snub-nosed, whimsical face. He nearly always wore an amiable grin and seemed to be winking at the world all the time, though that was only because he had an eye missing, which was how he got his ticket back.

He came from Sydney, trained in Canada, and went to a Wimpy squadron. About mid-1942, he was coming back from Happy Valley. The Dutch coast was practically in sight when a night-fighter attacked them and Chuck, on look-out in the astro dome, got a bullet in the right shoulder, another in the right hip, and a third which went in the right temple and came out of the eye socket, leaving the eyeball hanging down his cheek, suspended on stringy, bloody strips of muscle, or tendon, or what have you—not a nice sight. A great hole was blown in the side of the fuselage, one engine was put out and the Wimpy was burning fiercely. Half-blind and pretty faint Chuck baled out of the hole in the fuselage eventually, after being stuck half-way and having to squirm rather energetically.

Luck was still against him for he landed in the middle of a large, deep lake just north of the Zuyder Zee and had to swim nearly three-quarters of a mile to the shore. It wasn't till he was in the water that he felt the sharp stinging in the right eye socket, caught a glimpse of something flopping on his cheek and with his one good eye saw his mangled eyeball floating bloodily in the water by his nose.

He doesn't remember much more about that heartbreaking swim but eventually he staggered ashore and made for a nearby house, barely able to drag himself along. He knocked on the door. A woman opened it, saw the horrible sight that Chuck was, with his eye still hanging down, and wet and bloody, slammed the door in his face and fled. Chuck dragged himself to the house next door where a Dutch family of stouter nerve took him tenderly in and brought a doctor in considerable haste. The Germans took care of him then and Chuck had hospital treatment for five weeks before coming on to join us at Sagan, not greatly abashed by the loss of his eye.

Chapter Twenty-Three

HIS IRISH EYES SPOKE

Paddy Houton never claimed to be the most shaken man ever to have come to Stalag Luft III but no one would have disputed it had he done so. He had come within an ace of being lynched by an angry mob, so close, in fact, that the rope was actually about his neck. Normally, Paddy could have talked himself out of a tough spot as he is Irish with a pleasing brogue and persuasive tongue, but when a crowd is being angry in a foreign language it's asking a lot, even of an Irishman. He was lucky enough, however, to possess twinkling blue eyes under a mop of ginger hair and those eyes spoke more eloquently and effectively than ever his brogue could have done.

He left County Monaghan in Southern Ireland in 1937 to join the R.A.F. and when war broke out was a trained wireless operator with a tremendous zest for a fight. He completed a full tour of ops. in Hampdens in 1940, but not even that impaired his love for fighting. So he did another tour. And again he came back for more. He started his third tour as a member of a Pathfinder crew and was on his sixty-seventh operational flight when his luck, long strained beyond breaking-point, finally forsook him. He baled out of a burning aircraft immediately over Magdeburg which itself was a mass of flames from a thousand-bomber raid.

He left the aircraft at 15,000 feet and found himself drifting straight towards the burning city. He did some frantic pulling on the ropes and managed to change direction, but even then he landed uncomfortably close to falling 'cookies' that were making a noise like a dozen express trains.

Paddy found himself in a paddock. There wasn't a soul in sight, and having heard ugly stories of how bombed civilians sometimes reacted he decided to put himself as far as possible from the burning city. He stuffed his parachute into a rabbit hole and set off on a compass bearing. He had not gone a hundred yards, however, before a group of men came up to him. They were peasants, and while in daytime they would probably have seemed amiable country yokels, lit by the glow from the burning city they looked menacing and angry.

Grabbing him roughly they tore at his clothes, kicked and punched him. They dragged him to a barn that lay a few hundred yards down the road. Once inside they closed the door and then started in earnest to beat him. They punched him in the face until his eyes were swollen and bleeding but Paddy, suppressing every natural desire, didn't fight back. He decided to rely on his tongue.

'Nicht Englander,' he cried. 'Irlander, Irlander.'

The words had effect. They stopped beating him and a noisy argument in guttural German followed. Paddy's hopes of involving them in debate on the intricacies of Southern Ireland's neutrality were soon dashed. They started beating him again more furiously than ever. He could hardly see out of his eyes now and his body was aching with pain.

He decided to play his trump card. He pulled out a small silver crucifix but this had only a momentary effect. They shouted all the louder and he was able to catch the words 'Murder Incorporated' which one of the Germans, pointing to his back, kept repeating. They returned to the attack and Paddy fell unconscious. He revived in a few minutes and again they started beating him. This time an under-sized, unpleasant-looking German came up to him and tried to kick him in the stomach. It's more than any Irishman can stand.

Paddy kicked back and as he did so, realized that it would probably be the last thing he would ever do. But a mad, cold fury possessed him and he no longer cared.

The Germans withdrew a short distance and Paddy saw one of them draw a revolver from his pocket and hand it to the man next to him. He promptly handed it on to the next one. It seemed no more acceptable to him, however, and amid gesticulations and shouting the weapon was passed from man to man, each declining, it seemed, to accept the responsibility of shooting Paddy.

Then the door of the barn opened. Paddy saw to his amazement two women come in. One of them was aged about thirty and the other not more than eighteen. He turned his blood-stained, battered face towards them and put his heart and soul into an appealing look.

For answer the elder of the two women walked up to him and slapped him across the face. It was the disappointment that caused the pain and when the men returned to the attack he just collapsed. He did not lie on the ground for long and when he came round he felt something rough rubbing his throat. His hands went up to his neck and he touched a rope.

After that he no longer cared. He was too exhausted. He just stood waiting. But the Germans seemed as little able to agree among themselves as to who should do the job as they had been over the matter of the revolver. While they were arguing, the barn door opened and Paddy saw the eighteen-year-old girl re-enter. He had not noticed before that she was not in the barn. Much more important was that behind her came a German soldier with a revolver in his hand. Paddy was saved. His eyes had done it.

The soldier treated Paddy with the same brutality, but now that the rope was no longer pressing roughly against his throat he didn't mind so much. He was taken out of the barn and led down a farm road to a house. The sky still reflected the red glow of burning Magdeburg and for a moment Paddy thought that the mob which was following him would attack him again, but he reached the house safely and there he was taken before the local Nazi Party member for the district. Again Paddy was slapped across the face but he knew better now than to attempt to retaliate.

He waited and soon he was taken into another room where he saw his navigator suffering from a cannon-shell wound in the shoulder. Though he was scarcely able to stand up from loss of blood the navigator's wrists were tied to Paddy's with a chain and the pair of them were pushed out of the house and down the road again towards the village. Still the mob followed them. Once when the navigator fell some of the men ran up and kicked him. They smashed two of his ribs. Half-dragging, half-carrying him Paddy managed to get him to the village and they were taken into the local jail. The dirty, narrow cell seemed a haven of peace. Utterly exhausted they both fell on the floor. Outside they could still hear the shouts of the mob and the glow of Magdeburg made dancing patterns on the cell wall.

After a lot of shouting Paddy managed to persuade the guards to bring a doctor to attend the navigator who was in agony. Despite his wound, they were both packed off to Dulag next day where Paddy made a formal complaint.

Paddy was one of the lucky ones who got away with it after encountering the Hun mobs. God knows how many more there were who didn't. Many of the kriegies at Sagan knew, with varying degrees of pain, the brutality of Nazi gangs who had cheered the bombing of England by their precious Luftwaffe and who conveniently forgot all that when they were called on to endure retribution themselves.

One case worth mentioning is that of an officer of air rank who was brought down over Germany. He was an air-commodore, and after he had escaped from the crash he contacted the organization for getting shot-down air crew back to England. He was hiding up in a house in the occupied territories when the Gestapo descended on them and the air-commodore was captured.

His claim that he was an R.A.F. officer brought him scant respect. The Gestapo handled him so roughly that his shoulder was dislocated and after that he was bound with chains and flogged.

Yet the air-commodore and other kriegies who could tell similar stories were just a few of the known cases. Heaven only knows how many other ugly incidents there were that will never be known because the victims are dead.

Occasionally we heard a whisper of them. A man came in on a new purge who had seen the body of an R.A.F. sergeant hanging from a telegraph pole in Magdeburg; another three badly mauled bodies in another city. A couple of Americans who arrived saw two of their comrades thrown into the flames of a burning building after a raid. Probably there were scores—possibly hundreds—of others.

After intensive bombing started, many shot-down air crew were only saved by their guards from being murdered by vicious mobs, particularly after Goebbels' speech in May 1944, when he gave the German people *carte blanche* to wreak revenge on any airmen they found. 'Fair game', Goebbels called us. In the same spirit, they murdered the fifty.

Chapter Twenty-Four

OUT OF THE FRYING PAN

———

Like the invasion, spring seemed a long time coming to Germany in 1944. So it seemed to weary kriegies who badly wanted both. Late in March, when one of the great miracles in flying history happened, snow still mantled the pine-wooded slopes of Westfalia. Its fleecy whiteness softened the scarred outlines of pranged Ruhr towns nearby, and it was just as well it stayed late or there wouldn't have been any miracle and Sergeant Alkemade would be very dead indeed.

Fittingly enough it all happened as the air assault on Berlin was reaching its climax—another landmark in flying history—and those Berlin raids were indirectly the cause of why Alkemade deliberately jumped out of his Lancaster at a height of three and a half miles without a parachute. The direct cause was the fact that he was being roasted alive and preferred the quicker and less painful end. He woke up three hours later, seeing stars but not at all badly bent.

Alkemade was a quiet young English sergeant who took things as they came without a great deal of fuss. He took his freak escape like that. It was a week, he said, before he properly realized that it really had happened. Even then he took it composedly. He was only twenty-one at the time, a rear gunner, and when he came to us at Sagan his face was a queer mixture of clear skin and red inflamed skin. The red was a neat oval area, mostly round his eyes which were not covered by a helmet and oxygen mask. Though his lids were wrinkled and red, the fire, for some reason, had not damaged his actual eyes, which remained clear and blue. It was probably because he had screwed up his eyes when aiming.

Alkemade used to be a market gardener at Loughborough, Leicestershire, until, at eighteen, he became an 'erk' attached to Air Sea Rescue for two years. After that he got his gunner's course and eventually went to a squadron at Linton. His big moment came on the 24th of March 1944, his fourteenth trip, and the target was Berlin. They duly arrived there, dropped a couple of 'cookies' and some incendiaries, and turned for home and bacon and egg breakfast. It was a beautiful clear night; no moon but stars galore prickling the soft blackness above. There was about three-tenths cloud but it was far below as they were flying high, about 20,000 feet. It was mighty cold up in the rear turret and Alkemade was well rugged up in fleece-lined leather Irvin jacket and trousers and electrically heated boots. He even had a woollen balaclava pulled on over his helmet.

They were about half-way through the radio-controlled fighter belt, droning high over Westfalia and the silver ribbon of the Ruhr River, when there was a sudden, thunderous jolting up in the nose. The Lancaster lurched sharply to starboard, then recovered, but great tremors ran right through her as the jolting crashes continued, working down her belly towards the tail. Alkemade guessed they were 20-mm. cannon shells and looked anxiously out for the night fighter that was sending them as the crashes came nearer. There were suddenly two great bangs right in his ears as two shells hit the turret. The perspex in front of him blew inwards, a fragment gashing him in the thigh, and the pressure oil-pipes of the turret hydraulics burst and the oil, spraying out, caught fire. In that moment the sergeant saw the night fighter. It was doing a stalling, climbing attack from below, a Ju. 88, barely fifty yards away, pointing straight at him. Between its engines, there seemed to be a glowing line of white fire—the flashes of banked cannon—and reddish glowing tracer was streaming up just behind his turret.

Alkemade swung his four Brownings down and gave a long burst. As he pressed the turret controls the flaming hydraulic oil, at increased pressure, spurted up more fiercely till he was in a ring of fire that licked up to his face. In his concentration he scarcely noticed it for about five seconds as he directed a quadruple stream of bullets, almost point blank, at the 88. Then a tongue of flame streamed out from the port engine of the night fighter and she heeled over to starboard and Alkemade fell back, throwing his arms about his face to shield raw, singed flesh from the fire which suddenly struck him agonizingly. He could feel that his oxygen mask had gone all soft and squashy where the rubber was melting. He spoke quickly into the inter-com.

'Hullo, Skip. Kite's on fire down this end.'

'O.K.,' answered a laconic voice. 'Starboard wing's going the same way, too. It's opened up like a tin of beans. We'd better bale out, boys.'

Alkemade leaned far back, pushed open his turret doors and reached into the fuselage to grab his parachute canopy pack, clipped into a rack just outside the doors. With a thrill of shock he saw that the whole length of the narrow tunnel of the fuselage was blazing. Flaming petrol had sprayed back along it from split starboard-wing tanks. The flames reached right to the turret doors, and just there, embroiled in a fierce little conflagration of its own, was his canopy pack. The canvas cover was already burned off and the silk had tumbled out and was dissolving incredibly quickly in a welter of flame. Alkemade felt a tremulous quiver of dismay and fright that quickened into horror as he turned back and saw his leather Irvin trousers and jacket had caught fire.

'Oh, hell!' he thought. 'This is it.'

And curiously enough his greatest regret was that he would miss his next seven days' leave for which he was due in a couple of days. He was looking forward to making arrangements for getting married.

He didn't waste any time coming to a decision. The turret was too much like a blast furnace and getting worse all the time. His flying kit was burning fiercely now and he was choking and could almost feel himself sizzling. His burnt face was tingling queerly. Without emotion or flap, almost without any thoughts at all except the wish to make a quick job of it, he turned his turret to starboard beam and did a quick back flip through the turret doors that opened easily on to a black, cold well of space, 18,000 feet deep, allowing for a loss of 2,000 feet during the action.

He was not frightened. It was that same, queer hiatus of fear, a sort of saturation and reaction to intense emotion, that so many air crew felt just before they died, as though it were a little too much for the mind to grasp so suddenly. He felt calm. And as he left the dying Lancaster, he half-sensed, half-saw a great flash from her, and then he was away. He fell head first, as though he were nose heavy, and found himself strictly at attention as though it were a formal occasion. After a few seconds he saw the Lancaster again, going away above and streaming long banners of wicked flame.

'Funny,' he thought, 'but if this is dying, it doesn't seem so strange.'

Then soft veils gently filmed his eyes and closed over his feelings, and in blank unconsciousness his bulky, shadowy shape dropped down and down, building up to terminal velocity and turning over and over slowly.

*   *   *

Three hours later—checked by his watch—he opened his eyes and saw the soft pin-points of stars twinkling through a dark woven screen of pine branches right above him. It was quiet and rather lovely.

'Well, good God!' he murmured aloud. 'I'm alive.'

He wasn't particularly surprised. Nor did he feel greatly relieved. Mainly he was just calmly interested. There was still that mental hiatus, an insulation against intense emotion that just left the mind capable of comprehending essentials without analysing them. He just understood he was alive and had to take it for granted.

Instinctively he tested his body for damage. He wriggled his toes. They worked. Then he moved his legs, his arms and his neck. Every-thing seemed to work, though his right knee seemed a little numb. Eventually he rolled over and comprehended he was lying embedded in a thick, soft carpet of snow about four feet deep. That accounted for the cold then. Not till later did he realize it also accounted for his being alive. That, and the yielding pine branches above that had first helped to break his hurtling fall. He could see slim pine-tree trunks all around him and realized he was in a wood.

He sat up then and examined himself. There were no legs to his leather Irvin trousers. They had been burned off. The right leg of his battle-dress trousers had also been mostly burned off. His flying-boots had disappeared. His Mae West was mostly burned away and his leather jacket was badly charred. Only the chamois leather lining remained from the top of his helmet, and of his balaclava only a woollen ring that framed his face and another that was round his neck, both with charred edges. He found his wrists had been burned through leather gauntlets when he had shielded his face. And his face? He put up his hand and touched tender flesh and blood, though, curiously, it was not hurting much. He found a tender spot on his head that felt sticky with blood and concluded it was where he had hit the pine branches.

He shrugged out of his observer-type 'chute harness and then find-ing he was not only alive, but in fairly good repair, tried to stand up, but his right knee would not support him. On his side he started to drag himself across the snow to a spot where the darkness of the wood seemed a little lighter. It was downhill, which made it easier, and after only seven yards he came to the edge of the wood. Here the snow was a bare six inches deep and without thinking a great deal about it he realized the snow must have drifted up heavily on the bank behind him. Had he fallen a few yards from where he did he would have had neither trees nor deep snow to break his fall.

Alkemade did not sweat over that till a week later when full realization came. For the time, he was concerned only with the present. His feet and fingers were freezing cold but there was little he could do about it. He found his cigarette-case and matches in his pocket and gratefully lit a cigarette. As he couldn't walk and would only freeze or starve where he lay, he fished up the whistle hanging from his jacket and alternately blew it and puffed at his cigarette until a German search party, which had already found the navigator, reached him. They brought a tarpaulin, placed him on it and dragged him away, as though it were a sled. It was a rough, jolting trip as the sergeant received every bump fully through the thin tarpaulin. He found it the worst part of his experience, but eventually they came to a small village where he was shovelled into a car and taken to a hospital in the nearby Ruhr town of Maschede.

To the next bed was brought the navigator from Al's Lancaster, Flight-Sergeant Ginge C———. He had landed very heavily after he had baled out and been badly hurt. He had difficulty in breathing and they thought he was dying. He was given the Last Sacrament and then hustled off to the operating theatre. The operation was successful and after that he began to recover and was able to tell Alkemade what had happened up in the nose of the aircraft. The flash that Alkemade had seen as he tumbled out of his turret was an explosion in the aircraft that blew Ginge and the wireless-operator, Sergeant Jeff B———, right out of the Lancaster just after they had clipped their parachute canopies on their harness. Ginge doesn't remember pulling his rip-cord, but came down alive. There were no other survivors. Ginge was completely dazzled when Alkemade told him his own story in exchange.

The Germans interrogated the sergeant at the hospital and naturally wouldn't believe his story. They wanted to know what he had done with his parachute after he had landed.

'I tell you I came down without one,' persisted Alkemade time and time again.

The interpreter, a young, ginger-headed soldier just back from the Russian front, became distinctly 'aerated' when Alkemade wearily insisted on his story, and eventually the Germans angrily assumed that he had buried the contentious parachute.

After three weeks Alkemade was taken to the cells at Dulag and at his interrogation again doggedly persisted with his story. It provoked warm discussion and the actual interrogation was forgotten in the interest of the story. At last the interrogating Feldwebel said:

'Well, I still don't believe it, but I'll admit it's just possible.'

They took Alkemade before an Oberst (colonel) then, who also ignored military interrogation and wanted to hear 'your very interesting story'. He, too, wouldn't believe, but admitted it was possible.

'I'll send someone back to where you landed,' he said. 'If they find your parachute harness there, without canopy, but with the suspension straps still sealed and clipped down, we'll have to believe you.'

They let him loose then into the 'free' compound at Dulag, where air crew who had finished their time in the cells were waiting for 'purging' to permanent camps. Then, for almost the first time in history, the 'There I was' stories of just-shot-downs were hushed. No one had a tale that would stand up to Alkemade. They put him on a chair and made him tell the whole thing, which made him feel, he said, 'an awful goat' though for the first time, no one called him a liar.

Even the Americans waiting there were hushed, though one of them had a pretty exceptional story himself. He was a Lieutenant R——, a slim, wavy-haired pilot of about twenty-eight, rather short. In the U.S.A. he had been a parson, on account of which Godliness he should probably be believed, because he was very sincere about it all.

He gave up the cloth and his flock temporarily when the war came to the U.S.A. and became, instead, captain of a Flying Fortress. On a daylight raid over Germany, early in 1944, his Fortress was hit by flak at about 25,000 feet and without any warning, blew up mightily. Lieutenant R—— was hurled out of the pilot's cabin and landed on the wing, where he was jammed under the sloping bar of a mass balance with the force of the explosion, the wing snapped off the fuselage near the root and Lieutenant R—— has a hazy recollection of falling jammed on the wing, which was turning over and over, before he lost consciousness through shock, the blow of the explosion and lack of oxygen. The engines on the wing were still turning over, fed by petrol from the 'Tokyo' tanks. He came back to his senses only a couple of thousand feet from the ground but couldn't struggle free from the mass balance. Eventually he pulled his rip-cord and the parachute opened and pulled him off, only a few hundred feet up. He landed alive, but badly shaken, with concussion and a fractured ankle.

The flying parson was nothing if not fair in his judgement.

'Boy,' he told the Sergeant. 'You beat me. The stage is yours.'

A couple of days later a German N.C.O. came into the compound and went up to the Senior British Officer with Alkemade.

'We have investigated the scene of the landing of this sergeant,' he said. 'No parachute canopy was found but the harness was there. The suspension straps on it were still sealed and clipped down.'

So at last Alkemade was unreservedly accepted as a man of his word and they immediately drafted out a certificate to uphold his honour in the future. It read:

Dulag Luft.

It has been investigated and corroborated by the German authorities that the claim by Sergeant Alkemade, No. ——537, is true in all respects, namely that he has made a descent from 18,000 feet without a parachute and made a safe landing without injuries, the parachute having been on fire in the aircraft. He landed in deep snow among fir-trees.

Corroboration witnessed by,

(*Signed*) ⎰ Flight-Lieutenant H. J. MOORE (Senior British Officer)
⎱ Flight-Sergeant R. R. LAMB
⎰ Flight-Sergeant T. A. JONES

25-4-44.

So, thankfully alive but a little suspicious of his luck, Alkemade came to Sagan. For want of something better, he put his freak escape down to Divine Providence and is a little more religious than he used to be. But he still expects to slip on a banana skin, as soon as bananas get around again, and break his neck.

*   *   *

It was somewhere about the same time that another similar fantastic freak escape occurred. This time it was a man who was blown up and fell 22,000 feet without a parachute and still lived. In broad outline, the story is a parallel to the classic of Wing-Commander Ken Burns.

We do not know the exact date of the affair because the human freak who figured in it, a Scottish flight-sergeant, had lost most of his memory—which was not surprising—and as he did not come to

Sagan from Dulag, we have had to piece the story together from the reports of several officers who got the story first hand from the flight-sergeant at Dulag himself. It is not possible for us to prove the story here and now on paper, but the officers who came directly from him informed us that the Germans confirmed the story. The flight-sergeant himself can give us little information on the point as he was unconscious for eleven days after his aircraft blew up.

His name was Mac——, as befits a Scot, and he was mid-upper gunner in a Lancaster (all the best parachute stories seem to come from Lancasters). He used to be a professional boxer, but for some time before the war he had deserted his native Scotland to fight in the rings of England. He was a slim, wiry young man with a lean, slightly hard-bitten face.

At some time in the early months of 1944 (he cannot remember the date) he and his crew took off in a Lancaster to bomb a target (he cannot even remember what the target was). He has a vague memory of being briefed and then of flying over occupied territory sitting lonely in his upper turret. He was wearing observer-type parachute harness but the actual canopy pack was stowed away in the fuselage in its usual rack.

At some time on the trip, the Lancaster suddenly blew up. Mac has just the haziest idea of the disintegrating explosion. The Germans later confirmed it for him.

Eleven days later he recovered consciousness in a hospital near Brussels. The Germans told him it was the fourth hospital he had been in and that when they had picked him up there was no sign of his parachute, apart from the harness he was wearing. Mac himself had recovered sufficiently to realize that when the aircraft exploded it would be the height of nonsense to assume that he would have had any chance to delve down into the fuselage for his canopy pack and clip it on before being catapulted into the blackness.

His left arm was broken badly and the flesh of his head and face was badly split open. It was stitched together for him and it healed up, but dreadful scars run across his head and forehead and down both sides of his nose. He was still much too sick in hospital to pay much attention to what the Germans told him and this, combined with his elusive memory, has resulted in his being uncertain exactly where he was found or what broke his fall.

At Dulag he was content to live quietly, getting back his strength without letting his mind dwell too much on what had happened. He sometimes wondered at his miraculous escape but could not be bothered about finding out exactly what had happened. All he knows is that there was no possibility that he was able to get his parachute canopy and clip it on and that when he looks into a mirror now he does not recognize himself—in which it is not his memory that is to blame, but his scars.

Chapter Twenty-Five

MID-AIR MIRACLE

June, and the Invasion! Kriegies talked of little else for the next six months, until towards the end of the year at Belaria, satellite compound of Stalag Luft III, in walked Joe Herman, latest and greatest of the nine-days wonders.

Joe was the brassbound ultimate among all the people who should have died but didn't. People like Sergeant Alkemade, Ken Burns, and others who came down without parachutes have to give precedence in the matter of illogical luck to Joe Herman. He was blown out of his aircraft at more than 17,000 feet without a parachute, but bumped into a friend about two miles lower down, joined forces with him and they finished the trip to earth together. He arrived in about the last purge of the war to reach Stalag Luft III, a fitting climax to the procession of dolorous, lucky-to-live newcomers since 1939.

Joe is an Australian, a twenty-two-year-old flight-lieutenant from Hughenden, in North Queensland, where he had been a gold miner before he joined the R.A.A.F. He is rather a good-looking bloke, tallish and slim with a very brown skin, a pair of keen hazel-grey eyes and a good, dimple-cleft chin. He captained a Halifax on an Australian squadron in England and met his downfall on the thirty-third trip.

He and his crew took off from Driffield in about five-tenths cloud at 4.30 p.m. on the 4th of November 1944, bound for Bochum in Happy Valley. Darkness closed in as they headed out across the North Sea and shortly after that Joe saw a couple of aircraft nearby collide and then spin down towards the water. The crews of other aircraft nearby in the darkness saw the same thing and thought one of the collided aircraft was Joe's Halifax, which accounts for a peculiar sequel that the affair had.

211

An hour or so later the bomber stream was converging on Bochum. At this stage of the war the German defences had been considerably weakened and the opposition, even over the Ruhr, was generally not quite as awe-inspiring as it used to be. On this night, however, for some unknown reason, Bochum was a hot spot. There was a tremendous ring of searchlights round the place and masses of flak were shooting up, winking spiteful red eyes all over the sky.

Joe looked it over warily, decided not to waste time in that area and headed the Halifax in for the run-up, straight and level over the target. Within ten seconds he was coned by several searchlights that lit up the interior of the Halifax like day, almost blinded Joe and gave them that awful naked feeling that you get in a bomber when searchlights find you. He peeled off violently to port, pulled up again and found he had slipped the beams of light. So far so good, and the Halifax once more headed in to bomb.

A few seconds later they were coned again by another group of searchlights and again Joe violently peeled off, twisted, turned and pulled up to find that once more the Halifax was enveloped in protecting darkness. He felt the perspiration starting up on his skin and his mouth was dry. Getting twice out of being coned like that was rather unusual and more than a little lucky. That sort of thing mostly spelt 'curtains'. Once again the Halifax headed in towards the target. Flak was still bursting all round and with some queer premonition, Joe felt impelled to do a thing he had never done before. He called up the crew on the intercom. and said:

'Better put your parachutes on, blokes. I don't like this.'

So for the first time on ops. the crew of the Halifax clipped their canopy packs on their harness. All except Joe, who was wearing observer-type harness too but was much too preoccupied with the air-craft to carry out his own advice. His own pack was clipped in a rack back in the engineer's compartment. He held the Halifax steadily on course and a minute or so later the bomb-aimer got rid of their 11,000-lb. lethal cargo, reporting shortly after, 'Got a wizard photo, Skip'.

Joe carried on out of the target area without delay until the worst of the flak and searchlights had dropped behind and then he turned on to their course for home. They had been briefed to lose height after leaving Bochum so he eased the nose down a fraction and the altimeter needle began to slip back very gently. They had lost about 300 feet and there were only a few isolated bursts of flak when a sudden heavy thud in the fuselage shook the heavy bomber frighteningly. It was a direct hit from flak just behind the rear spar of the wing but Joe didn't know for the moment whether it was flak or fighters. His mind immediately leapt to fighters as most of the flak had ceased, and he peeled off violently to port and called up the gunners to see if they had found anything. Both of them came back promptly over the intercom.

'No fighters in sight. Must be flak.'

As he pulled the Halifax up again from her twisting dive, Joe saw on his windscreen the reflection of flames in the fuselage behind him and felt a cold little wave shoot through him. In the same moment the engineer called up.

'She's burning behind the main spar, Skip.'

'Right. I can see it in the perspex,' said Joe. 'Duck back and see what you can do about it, Harry.'

Sergeant Harry Knott, the engineer, stocky, unemotional Londoner, grabbed the fire extinguisher and before he unplugged his intercom. called up the pilot again:

'Do you want your 'chute, Joe?'

'No,' he answered. 'Not yet. Go and look after the fire.'

Joe started the Halifax on mild evasive action, weaving from one side to the other. The fire behind him didn't seem to be getting any worse when suddenly, in quick succession, two more weighty thumps shook the aircraft. Either the flak was uncannily accurate or their luck was completely out. One shell smacked into the wing, just behind the port inner engine. The other exploded just behind the starboard outer. In both cases the wing petrol tanks burst open and exploded into flame. In two seconds it seemed as though the whole aircraft was a mass of fire. Tests have shown that when a bomber's wings start to burn like that, there is, on an average, about a minute's grace before they fold back and come away, so Joe wasted no time.

'Hell's bells!' he shouted into the intercom. 'We've got it in the wings.' And then three times—'Bale out! Bale out! Bale out!'

Back over the intercom., very faintly, came the voice of Flying-Officer 'Irish' Vivash, mid-upper gunner from Tamworth, New South Wales.

'I think my leg's broken, Skip. Can you help me?'

Joe couldn't leave his seat. He had to keep the aircraft straight and level while the crew got out. He looked back along the fuselage, saw a ragged torn hole in the 'dust-bin' of the mid-upper turret and also saw Harry Knott, the engineer, spraying his fire extinguisher at the flames by the rear spar. He called back over the intercom.:

'Can't leave my seat, Irish. Get Harry to give you a hand.'

He heard a faint 'Going out', presumably from the rear gunner, and then the intercom. faded out completely, probably burned out by the fires. Up forward, Joe saw the escape hatch open and the navigator about to go out. He still had control of the aircraft which was flying steadily enough, and nosing down slightly.

When he looked again, Joe saw the front compartment was empty and presumed both the navigator and bomb-aimer had left. He remembered that Harry the engineer had probably unplugged his intercom. before the 'bale out' order was given so he tried to waggle the aircraft's wings to attract his attention. He swung his control wheel both ways but there was absolutely no response. Lateral controls evidently burned out. There was no point in waiting any longer in his seat. He slipped off his Sutton harness and went back to get the engineer and mid-upper gunner out and also to pick up his own canopy.

He had just stepped on to the engineer's little control platform when he saw the mid-upper gunner crawling down the fuselage, dragging one leg painfully. Practically in the same moment, out of the corner of his eye, he saw the entire starboard wing suddenly tear off the fuselage and fold back.

In a flash the heavy bomber whipped on to her back and started to spin. Joe was thrown to one side and he was putting up his hands to brace himself against the fuselage roof when the Halifax, just completing the first turn of her spin, suddenly blew up.

Joe remembers reaching up towards the roof and then the roof wasn't there. His hands touched nothing but there was one big flash, a moment of utter mental hiatus and then he found himself falling and falling.

It was not quite dark, thanks to a three-quarter moon and the searchlights and he could see a few dark, shapeless objects near him that didn't seem to be moving very much. He realized after a moment that they were pieces of the aircraft, falling with him.

Suddenly a horrible piercing chill went through him. His parachute! He didn't have his canopy. Only his useless harness. For a few seconds he almost panicked and struggled in the air with a dreadful helpless feeling and then strangely the crisis passed and he accepted his plight almost without emotion. O.K., so he didn't have his parachute. O.K., so he was going to die. O.K., so what?

He went on falling, falling and then his mind began to think of what was going to happen when he stopped falling. It was a frightful thought and he couldn't escape it. The feeling of chilled horror, almost unreal, began to return. His imagination was working overtime and wouldn't stop. He wished his mind would go blank or that some of the nightmare quality would leave. One split second he found his mind wouldn't believe it all and in the next fraction he knew it was true and he had to face it and couldn't get away from it. There was nothing he could do. He might fall for another thirty seconds and then. . . .

Suddenly he thought his canopy pack might be among the debris of the aircraft falling all round him. Just a faint, absurd chance that it might be within reach. He looked. There were a couple of dim shapes near him but not his canopy pack. It was nowhere. He felt his body was prickling with sweat. He seemed to have been falling for minutes and minutes.

He found he was slowly turning over and over in the air. One moment he was looking at soft stars and next moment he was looking at the ground—how far away he could not tell. It was not so much the ground he saw—that was just a black void—but the silver ribbon of a river that straggled across the country. He had a sudden thought that he might fall in that river and began to hope, a frail, desperate yearning, that he would hit the water. It was possible, just barely possible that the water might break his fall and save his life. He clung to the hope but knew it was useless, a chance in God knows how many million.

Brutal imagination returned in full strength and he fully and finally realized that in a few seconds he was going to die very horribly. He felt like screaming 'Oh, God! Don't let me die like this', but doesn't remember whether he spoke the words or not.

A second later he hit with a stunning thump.

He had another moment's utter mental hiatus and then a queer floating feeling. He thought he had hit the ground and been killed and then he thought: 'If this is death it can't be too bad.'

Then he heard a voice. It was almost in his ear, and he recognized it.

(At this stage Flight-Lieutenant Herman's experience becomes frankly almost incredible. Believe it or not as you wish. We can only say that R.A.A.F. interrogators believe it and so do we, the authors, who lived with thousands of shot-down airmen for years and know that these things *do* happen. We also know Joe Herman and have not the slightest doubt that his account is perfectly true.)

Joe heard the voice, and recognized it as the voice of 'Irish' Vivash, his mid-upper gunner. It said:

'Is there anybody around?' (Silly, isn't it, but what would *you* have said? And remember it was dark and both were dazed and hurt.)

Joe came slightly out of his mental void and found he was hanging on to a pair of legs with fierce strength, both arms wrapped tenaciously around them. He said:

'Yes. I'm down here.'

'Where? Where are you?' It was Vivash's voice again.

'Here. Just below. I'm hanging on to your legs,' said Joe.

'Be careful of my right leg, Joe,' said Vivash. 'I think it's broken.'

(His leg wasn't broken, as a matter of fact. But there were seven nasty flak wounds in them and for the time being they were quite numb which explains why the dazed Vivash didn't realize that Joe was clinging on to them.)

'O.K.,' said Joe. 'Are any of the crew around, do you know?'

'I think the navigator and wireless operator are above somewhere,' said Vivash.

'Good show,' said Joe, and for a few seconds they fell in silence.

If you think they should have expressed amazement or gratitude over their mid-air meeting, don't forget the circumstances were more than a little unusual and that the human mind can usually adapt itself so much and then, for a while, no more.

They worked it out later that Vivash could only just have opened his parachute when Joe arrived. He can't remember actually pulling the D-ring (very few people can after baling out) but he must have been swinging considerably in the shrouds as is normal just after a parachute opens when Joe fell on top of him at the end of one of the swings. Instinctively he must have grabbed Vivash's legs as soon as he touched him. Vivash was probably still falling fairly fast as his 'brolly' had only just opened and Joe's momentum was probably checked by falling on top of Vivash which explains why Joe's grip was not torn away. Both men say they hit with a terrific thump and Joe Herman says he was winded by it. As far as they can roughly calculate, the meeting took place at about 5,000 feet, so Joe had fallen free for over two miles, from between 17,000 and 18,000 feet.

While they gently descended in a sort of dazed silence, Joe found that he could not think straight and had a hazy idea he was dreaming it all. His arms were beginning to ache and then Vivash spoke:

'When we get near the deck, d'you think you'll be able to drop off?'

'Maybe,' Joe said, then looked down and saw the ground coming up. He saw the tops of trees sweeping sideways beneath them and realized the parachute was still swinging. His arms were getting terribly tired and he felt he couldn't hang on much longer.

'Look out,' he said. 'The deck's coming up.'

It seemed to rush up the last few feet and then he felt his body lightly brush the side of a treetop, felt his feet touch the earth and tried to let go and roll clear but there wasn't a hope. Vivash landed heavily right on top of his chest and then they rolled apart and lay gasping.

Joe recovered first and rose to his feet. He felt sharp piercing pain in a couple of places in his chest. (No wonder. He had two ribs broken when Vivash landed on him.) He found his left boot was missing, the left leg of his trousers was in tatters and the leg itself cut and bleeding. His face and ears were split open and bleeding, he was covered in bumps and bruises and his arms ached intolerably. He saw they were in a tiny clearing a few feet across in a pine wood and the parachute was drooping from one of the treetops.

Vivash rolled under the trees. The numbness was passing away from his legs and he was in agony. Joe gave him what attention he could and managed to stop the bleeding with rough silken bandages torn from the parachute canopy.

After a while Joe saw torches flashing near the wood and decided they had better get clear of the spot. They headed towards a small hill, Vivash painfully hopping along, supported by Joe. From the hilltop they heard what sounded like someone turning over strips of metal and Joe guessed it was probably the wreckage of his aircraft. Later on, when the sounds stopped, he crawled over in that direction and found the battered hulk of part of the fuselage. Two hundred yards away he found the starboard wing and right at the wing-tip, by a fantastic coincidence, there was his navigator's left flying-boot, standing up. He knew it by the name printed inside. As Joe was lacking his left boot he tried it on. It was a shade small but beggars could not be choosers and he walked back properly shod again.

They made a game but abortive effort to get into Holland and contact 'The Underground Organization'. They half-walked, half-hobbled west for three days. It was bitterly cold and they slept in barns and woods, steadily growing weaker from hunger and the cold. One of the barns they slept in was visited during their stay by a labourer with a pitchfork who tossed some of the straw outside. He was working within a couple of feet of them and while they were lying quaking beneath some of the straw, Joe felt the luckless Vivash give a sudden twitch as a couple of prongs of the pitchfork sank into his rump. He stifled the cry in his throat and a few seconds later the labourer unsus-pectingly walked out.

The 8th of November brought a bitterly cold night. They were within a few miles of the Rhine, but in desperation, with frost-bitten feet, had to go to a farmhouse to try for some food and shelter. The police were sent for and they spent the night in a dungeon. The follow-ing morning, the local Gestapo chief came into the cell and threatened them with a pistol while he lashed them with a cane. After that little episode it was the usual programme—a fortnight in hospital, interroga-tion at Dulag and then to Belaria.

There was an unusual sequel to this affair which Joe discovered a few months later after liberation. Some months before he was shot down he had married Betty, an English girl. His squadron friends believed that Joe had collided with another aircraft over the Channel on the night he was shot down and regretfully reported their fears to Betty. Like many another wife, Betty refused to believe that her husband was dead.

Then shortly before she heard that Joe was a prisoner of war, she had a dream. She dreamed that she saw an aeroplane crashing into the sea, but as it hit, TWO men climbed out TOGETHER and walked off on to the land.

Funny, wasn't it?

PART II

THE ESCAPE

*And by strange ways they tried
to get out again*

IN MEMORIAM

F/Lt. Henry Birkland, R.C.A.F.

F/Lt. Edward Brettell, D.F.C., R.A.F.

F/Lt. Leslie Bull, D.F.C., R.A.F.

S/Ldr. Roger Bushell, R.A.F.

F/Lt. Michael Casey, R.A.F.

S/Ldr. James Catanach, D.F.C., R.A.A.F.

F/O Arnold Christenson, R.N.Z.A.F.

F/O Dennis Cochran, R.A.F.

S/Ldr. Ian Cross, D.F.C., R.A.F.

F/O Haldo Espelid, R.A.F. (Norway)

F/Lt. Brian Evans, R.A.F.

F/O Nils Fugelsang, R.A.F. (Norway)

Lt. Johannes Gouws, S.A.A.F.

F/Lt. Alastair Gunn, R.A.F.

F/Lt. William Grisman, R.A.F.

F/Lt. Charles Hall, R.A.F.

F/Lt. Albert Hake, R.A.A.F.

F/Lt. Anthony Hayter, R.A.F.

F/Lt. Edgar Humphries, R.A.F.

F/Lt. Gordon Kidder, R.C.A.F.

F/O Reginald Kierath, R.A.A.F.

F/Lt. Anthony Kiewnarski, R.A.F. (Poland)

S/Ldr. Tom Kirby-Green, R.A.F.

F/O W. Kolanowski, R.A.F. (Poland)

F/O S. Z. Krol, R.A.F. (Poland)

F/Lt. Patrick Langford, R.C.A.F.

F/Lt. Tom Leigh, R.A.F.

F/Lt. J. L. Long, R.A.F.

Lt. Neville McGarr, S.A.A.F.

F/Lt. George McGill, R.C.A.F.

F/Lt. Romas Marcinkus, R.A.F. (Lithuania)

F/Lt. Harold Milford, R.A.F.

F/O Jerzy Mondschein, R.A.F. (Poland)

F/O K. Pawluk, R.A.F. (Poland)

F/Lt. Henri Picard, C. DE G., R.A.F. (Belgium)

F/O P. P. J. Pohé, R.N.Z.A.F.

Lt. Bernard Scheidhower (France)

F/O S. Skanziklas, R.A.F. (Greece)

F/Lt. Cyril Swain, R.A.F.

Lt. Rupert Stevens, S.A.A.F.

F/O Robert Stewart, R.A.F.

F/O Denys Street, R.A.F.

F/Lt. John Stower, R.A.F.

F/O P. Tobolski, R.A.F. (Poland)

F/Lt. Ernest Valenta, R.A.F. (Czechoslovakia)

F/Lt. G. W. Walenn, R.A.F.

F/Lt. James Wernham, R.C.A.F.

F/Lt. George Wiley, R.C.A.F.

S/Ldr. J. E. A. Williams, R.A.A.F.

F/Lt. J. F. Williams, R.A.F.

A memorial to the fifty murdered officers, designed and built by fellow-prisoners, now standing in the small cemetery at Sagan

Chapter Twenty-Six

TUNNELLING UNLIMITED

———

On the night of the 24th of March 1944, at the very moment that Sergeant Alkemade was making his fantastic three and a half miles free fall from his exploded Lancaster over the Ruhr, another strange affair was taking place in North Compound Stalag Luft III, hundreds of miles to the north-east.

Thirty feet under the ground, along a cramped, 350-foot tunnel, scores of Air Force officers were travelling by a home-made railway towards freedom outside the barbed wire. The Berlin raid from which Alkemade was returning had upset some of the escape arrangements, but it was too late to postpone the break and the great climax to over a year's hard work by about 500 men was under way.

We go back a year to pick up the threads of the escape story again, back to early April 1943, just after the move to North Compound from the East Camp had taken place.

In these first few days, North Camp population was about 700. About 500 of them were R.A.F. and Dominion Air Force officers—a few score Poles and some other European countries being represented in the R.A.F. complement. There were about a hundred other-ranks prisoners as orderlies for camp maintenance and cookhouse duties and also about a hundred U.S. Air Force officers. The American prisoners were just starting to arrive in numbers from the U.S. Air Forces in Britain and the Middle East. They were new, of course, to escape work but all of them were keen and adaptable and were rapidly co-opted into the Organization.

We have previously recorded the fact that plans for mass escapes from North Camp had already been in preparation for three months before the move and that the first provisional scheme to utilize the sewer pipe as a tunnel had had to be discarded.

Squadron-Leader Roger Bushell, the escape genius known as 'Big X' and leader of the 'X Organization', set about putting the rest of the scheme into operation.

Roger was an unusual-looking chap in an impressive way that accorded well with his unusual personality. He was tall, nearly six feet, and well built, but it was his eyes that were so remarkable. They were a light grey-blue, with heavy rings under them and in some uncanny way they seemed to probe right through you. One couldn't analyse the reason but got the impression there was a terrific amount of thinking going on behind that penetrating, almost lowering and sinister look. South African born, he was a rising London barrister when war came and as an Auxiliary Air Force squadron-leader, he re-formed a last-war fighter squadron that was later to lead the R.A.F score of 'kills.' Roger was shot down before that, however, over the beaches of Dunkirk.

After the sewer pipe had to be washed out as a possible tunnel, he called a meeting of the Big Four and other departmental heads. The Big Four were the tunnelling kings, Wally Floody, Johnny Marshall, 'Crump' Kerr-Ramsay and Johnny Bull. Wally, tall, very slim and with almost an Indian darkness of skin, had been a mining engineer in Canada and was a priceless asset for technical advice. He was in effect, technical adviser for the projected three tunnels. Johnny Marshall, who had been in the Air Force for donkeys' years, tall, rather dark and good-looking, a little thin on top and with perfect white teeth, was put in charge of the first tunnelling team. Crump, shortish and stocky, took the second team and Johnny Bull, dark, well built and good natured, took team number three.

It was decided to go ahead immediately with the three tunnels and bank on being successful with at least one.

For security reasons they were to be known as 'Tom', 'Dick' and 'Harry', as Germans from the censor's and interpreter's staffs had a habit of sneaking into the compound at night and listening outside the black-out shutters. People in the rooms never knew when they might be there, so among countless other security precautions the word 'tunnel' was never used in the camp.

Sites for the three tunnels were finalized from data which we had been collecting for months on working parties to the new compound and from a new survey made after our arrival there. 'Tom' was to be dug from barrack block 123, 'Dick' was to go from block 122, and Harry's origin was to be block 104. At this stage a description of the camp lay-out is obviously necessary.

North Compound was in the form of a square, each side being about 350 yards. Around it ran the orthodox two barbed-wire fences about seven feet apart and about seven feet high, with coils of barbed wire crammed between them. Just outside the northern boundary wire was part of the German 'vorlager' where they built a sick quarters for the camp and also a 'cooler', the inevitable cell block for us. On the other side of these buildings ran another double barbed-wire fence, making the north side of the camp doubly secure. Outside all the fences and rarely more than twenty or thirty yards away, were thick pine woods which effectively screened any view of the outside world. About ten yards inside the boundary wire ran the warning wire, across which it was usually fatal to step.

The gate of the camp was in the north-east corner, facing north. The second fence outside the 'vorlager' also ran past this section so there actually had to be two gates and each one was always guarded. In addition, two of the big sentry towers were stationed there. These sentry towers, built about fifteen feet above the ground, were placed at intervals of about 175 yards all round the wire. Each was fitted with a searchlight, not to mention sentry with rifle, mounted machine-gun and field-glasses constantly on watch, day and night.

The southern half of the compound had been cleared of trees for a playing-field but the northern half was dotted with scores of the ubiquitous, spindly pines of Germany. For a couple of months after moving in, these trees gave quite good cover for nefarious work, until the Germans cut them down for that very reason.

Among these trees were arranged the living-huts—fifteen of them—running in three rows of five from east to west. The huts themselves were each about 100 feet long, aligned north to south, and divided into sixteen living-rooms, a small kitchen, a washroom, a small lavatory and three small rooms at the ends for senior officer prisoners. The larger rooms, about sixteen feet square, accommodated first six and later on eight kriegies, and the small rooms took two, and later on four. The blocks were prefabricated of wood, with double wooden floors.

The first east-west row of five barrack blocks near the northern boundary wire was numbered 101, then 103 to 107. The next row (east to west) was numbered 112, then 110 down to 107, and the last row was numbered 119 to 123.

Block 123 therefore was next to the western boundary wire, about 150 feet from it, and the tunnel 'Tom' was to be dug from it due west until it was under the fringe of the wood outside the wire, at which point it would go up into the shelter of the wood and break clear there. It was block 123, incidentally, which housed nearly all the Polish officers in the camp—about seventy of them. Block 122 was next to 123, but separated by it from the wire. 'Dick' was to be dug from 122 towards 'Tom'. If necessary it could be taken all the way to the wood, or, in the event of any trouble with 'Tom's' entrance shaft, 'Dick' could join up with 'Tom' as an alternative entrance.

'Harry' was to be a couple of hundred yards away on the northern side of the camp, dug from a room near the northern end of block 104. It was then to lead under the northern wire, under the cooler, under the far 'vorlager' wire and so on into the wood—a long way but nevertheless one of the more practicable routes.

The great difficulty about tunnelling was that the entrance trapdoors could only be hidden by digging from under a living block. This discounted any digging towards the south as that half of the camp was bare. As the Germans built the huts about a foot above the ground, the problem was decidedly ticklish because of the blue-overalled German security guards—the ferrets—who were always present in the camp, night and day, in numbers ranging from one to a dozen, and averaging about three. They patrolled ceaselessly, peering through windows, walking through huts, constantly on the look-out for any signs of escape activity. They carried torches and long steel spikes and they used to crawl under the huts through special trapdoors in the base of the walls, looking for tunnel entrances, hidden trapdoors and also for dispersed sand from tunnels.

They got to know they were called ferrets after a while and the story goes that the Kommandant looked up the meaning of the word in an English dictionary, being considerably incensed when he discovered that a ferret was a form of pole-cat. He was not a bad type, this Kommandant, Oberst (Colonel) von Lindeiner. He was tall, quite dignified and of very erect build, considering his sixty-odd years. He wore an Iron Cross, first class, and was reputedly an Aide to the Kaiser in the last war. When this war broke out he was on Goering's personal staff. He was generally not an unreasonable man while things went smoothly, but showed unmistakably the Nazi spirit and a furious

Facing this page: Above—A map of the camp
Below—A sand-laden trolley from the face being transferred at half-way house

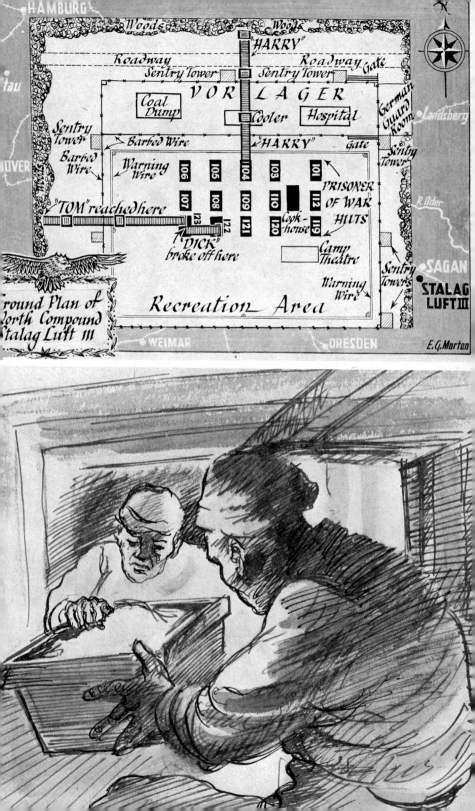

temper whenever escapes were made. He literally *did* froth at the mouth, go crimson in the face and threaten indiscriminate shooting whenever a 'break' occurred. There was a story, and it appears to have had more than the germ of truth, that he was due for promotion to general on two occasions and lost it both times because of two mass escapes that were staged from North Compound at the crucial moments.

The Germans made one mistake when they built our barrack blocks. The washrooms and kitchens had concrete floors and right around these rooms there were brick and concrete foundations that, of course, rose as high as the floors. The same building method applied to one corner of each living-room where stoves for heating were installed over a small section of floor that was concreted and tiled. Therefore, all these little sections as well as the bathrooms and kitchens were sealed off under the floor from the rest of the blocks and ferrets crawling under-neath searching for tunnel entrances could not investigate those parts. Obviously, these were the places to start our tunnels.

There was one more serious tunnel complication we knew we would have to face. The soil of the compound was very sandy. It would be soft and easy to dig but at the same time it was going to be decidedly crumbly. The tunnellers had had experience of this same crumbly sand in the East Compound so it was realized from the start that tunnelling was going to be dangerous because of falls. Not that this dissuaded any-one but it meant that we would have to shore the whole of the tunnels with wood. This meant finding an awful lot of wood from somewhere because timber merchants are not found in prison camps. However, ways and means would be found.

A few days after we had moved into North Compound on April Fools' Day, 1943, the 'X Organization', so long planned in detail, had taken material form. Blank lists appeared on doors in every block, calling for the names of people who wanted to play cricket in the coming summer, for others who wanted to play softball, or to help in building a swimming-pool or a theatre. The lists were quickly filled and that was how Roger, 'Big X', got his first nominal role of volun-teers. Everyone, of course, knew that neither cricket nor softball had anything to do with the lists.

As soon as the lists were complete, the chief 'X Organization' repre-sentative in each block (he was always known as 'Little X' for block

---

Facing this page: Sand en route for secret dispersal, reaches the tunnel entrance

so-and-so) went round to all the volunteers in his block to take a census of any special qualifications among his flock. People who knew anything about mining usually went on to tunnelling teams, those who spoke German well were allocated to the 'contact' and intelligence branches, artists found themselves attached as a rule to the forgery factory, tailors went on to Tommy Guest's clothing factory staff, carpenters and fitters went to special departments, and so on, and the scope of experience and ability revealed by this census was quite amazing.

Before long departmental heads had their staffs completely organized and briefed, temporary rooms were chosen to work in and operations were under way. People new to escape work or without any specialized ability were either put on to sand-dispersing gangs or on 'stooging' teams—'stooges' being the Organization security name for our own sentries who kept up constant watch in shifts over all illicit activities to give warning of the approach of ferrets or other German staff.

At the head of the stooges was Colonel Clark, tall, rangy American who was known as 'Big S'—the 'S' meaning 'security'. He looked after all camp general security and had as first lieutenant another American, grey-haired George Harsh, who was in the R.A.F. and had been a Chicago journalist. George looked after nearly all the special tunnel and factory security. Each block then had a 'Little S' who organized stooges for his block.

Considering the barrenness and comparative smallness of the compound and the fact that the ferrets were constantly snooping around, the security people had an immense job in keeping all our operations hidden. They became easily the biggest branch of the Organization and for the next year, from dawn to lock-up, day in and day out, we had between 200 and 300 stooges working constantly in shifts. This 'stooging' was a boring business, so monotonous that it was sometimes hard to keep one's attention from wandering, but the ferrets never succeeded in tripping our stooges successfully.

The first sentry system started by the stooges—within a couple of days of moving into the camp—was the 'duty pilot', who was stationed near the camp gate through which all in-and-out traffic had to pass. He was really two people; one was watcher and the other was his runner, and their job was to keep tabs on any and every person who came into the camp—particularly, of course, ferrets. Lists were kept showing the times everyone came in and the times that they left so that at any time of the day, 'factory' workers could know the 'state' of the camp, that is, who was in, where he was, and quite often, why he was there. This 'duty pilot' system was kept up in shifts practically without a break until we were evacuated from the camp in January 1945, nearly two years later.

As well as the two watching by the gate, other members of the 'D.P.' staff were stationed at various vantage-points of the camp, and a system of innocent signals was devised whereby every quarter of the camp that needed to know could tell at a glance how many ferrets were wandering about. By an incinerator near the gate the 'duty pilots' kept a coal scuttle and a cardboard Red Cross food box. They were always there and they looked innocent enough, no matter in what particular position they happened to be, but if the coal scuttle alone was lying carelessly on the small incinerator, kriegies would know at a glance that a couple of administrative German staff (fairly harmless people) were wandering about. If the cardboard box was casually tossed on the incinerator, everyone knew that a couple of ferrets were in and were consequently wary.

There were different combinations and positions for numbers and types of Germans so that the exact 'state' of the camp was always available at a glance. Where huts or trees blocked the view of these signals, the other 'D.P.' relay stations reflected them at their posts. Most important of these was at the south end of block 110. From it, stooges for the tunnels 'Tom' and 'Dick' and for the forgery factory could know at a glance the strength of Germans in the camp.

At this station there was another watcher and runner, and signals from the gate were reflected on shutters that covered the window of a lavatory at the end of 110 that was not used in the daytime. If the camp was clear of ferrets, which was a rare occasion, both shutters would be wide open. One ferret in the compound was indicated by a shutter closed, two ferrets by both shutters being closed; three ferrets or more, or a particularly dangerous ferret like Oberfeldwebel (Staff Sergeant) Glemnitz, chief of all the ferrets, or his deputy, Unteroffizier (Corporal) Karl, known far and wide as 'Rubberneck', were shown by both shutters closed and a soiled handkerchief hanging innocently from one of the shutter hinges.

Once the 'D.P.' system was established, Roger and the Big Four felt the coast was clear to go ahead with the tunnels. They had already decided that the best places were in those sections of the blocks where the brick-and-concrete foundations kept out the ferrets snooping under the floor, and the great problem that then remained was to build hidden trapdoors that would not be found by ferrets in their periodical full-scale searches of the blocks. They were thorough, those searches. The ferrets would turn out all the occupants and with the proverbial fine-toothed comb go through all the rooms, upsetting everything generally, prying through beds and wood-straw palliasses, lockers, food cupboards and stoves; they would examine and sometimes tear part of the walls down looking for secret hidey-holes, go over the floor inch by inch for trapdoors and crawl around on top of the ceiling, looking not only for tunnels but 'verboten' tools, civilian clothing, even civilian buttons, nails and in short anything that kriegies could possibly use in escape activity.

Problem, then, how to make trapdoors that the ferrets couldn't find? Kriegy ingenuity, backed by three years of weary experience in contriving essential gadgets with inadequate tools, found a way, and Polish R.A.F. officers started to put it into execution about a week after the move to North Camp.

For the entrance to 'Tom' in block 123 near the western boundary wire, the Big Four picked on the concrete flooring of a tiny passage about five feet long that led into a room next to the kitchen. A chimney with a stove on the far side was at the end of the tiny passage and the solid foundations carried right through underneath the floor to the centre of the hut. They picked on a tiny, two-foot square of the concrete passage floor in the corner next to the chimney where light did not easily fall.

The seventy-odd Polish officers of the R.A.F. who lived in block 123 were nearly all pretty gifted in making gadgets and did a lot of brilliant work in the tunnels and the engineers' section. One of the top-notchers was Gucio Gutowski, whom we have mentioned before as the freak who baled out at about 150 feet. His parachute didn't open and he fell on a pile of beet leaves that softened the blow and saved his life. Gucio was duly seconded with a team of Polish helpers to manufacture the traps.

By a stroke of luck the Germans, in building the camp, had left behind, among odd items of spare building material, a quantity of cement. It was no generous gesture on their part, but merely an oversight. Sufficient cement was promptly acquired by Gucio and his cohorts. They very carefully measured the area that the trapdoor was required to cover—about two feet square—and with a wooden mould they had made they cast a concrete block to these exact dimensions. In casting this slab they inserted about midway along the side two metal staples, so that the heads were barely protruding, being almost flush. To these were attached two pieces of fine strong wire with looped ends. Sufficient play was allowed in attaching them so that both pieces of wire could be pulled up or laid down flat along the sides of the slab.

From then on the work demanded the utmost security, and 'Big S' and his assistants doped out an exhaustive plan to ensure that the workers got it. Block 123 was the block in the camp farthest from the gate, which promised to make matters a little easier. The camp was arbitrarily divided into two sections by an imaginary line running down the side of block 110. East of that line to the fence, that is the section of the camp nearest the gate, was known then as 'Safe Zone'. West of block 110, including the area of 123, was known as 'D (danger) Zone'. From that time on work was only carried on at any comparatively exposed places while ferrets were in 'Safe Zone'. As soon as they crossed the dividing line into 'D Zone', work automatically packed up. All workers, and particularly 'duty pilots', were briefed on the new procedure.

At the same time all 'duty pilots' were instructed that if any collection of three or more ferrets should suddenly come into the compound, indicating that a 'snap' search might be about to take place, the pack-up signal should immediately be given and the runner sent immediately to warn the craftsmen.

Then, with infinite care, Gucio and his assistants, working with illegal cold chisels they had acquired from somewhere or other, cut from the concrete floor in block 123 at the chosen spot, a square of similar size to the one they had made themselves. Under the floor, as they lifted up this cut-out section, they found loosely packed rubble. Below the rubble, they knew, was soft sand, ideal for quick digging and treacherous for falls, but just for the moment they were not interested in that. The cut-away section, with its chipped and broken sides, was useless but suspiciously revealing, so it was quickly smashed up and made unrecognizable.

After a painstaking fitting-in process, involving shaving off a little here and there till the coincidence was perfect, the new slab was gently fitted into the hole, so that it rested on the rubble below. The whole job was so painstakingly done that the sides were flush and scarcely evident. The looped tops of the two wire toggles attached to the sides of the slab were sunk into the crack just below the surface, but could be reached with the blade of a penknife and fished up. To lift the slab out again the workers merely put two little pieces of wood through the loops of the toggles, a firm heave, and the slab came smoothly out. Once it was replaced again, though the borders were barely evident, no chances were taken and the tiny crack on all sides was packed with cement. The whole floor was then dusted over lightly with sand.

So perfectly was this trap made that when diggers later on reported for tunnelling they were shown the tiny corridor where the trap was and invited to point it out. Few of them ever did it by eyesight alone, though they knew to within a couple of feet where it lay.

Next item on the programme then was 'Dick's' trapdoor in block 122, and it was here that the Big Four, with Gucio and his Poles, produced probably the most cunning trapdoor in the history of kriegydom. There was little chance that the ferrets would ever have found it. (In point of fact, they never did.)

In the middle of the concrete floor of the block washroom was an iron grating about eighteen inches square, through which all waste water ran down into a little square concrete well about three feet deep. About a foot up from the bottom of the well a pipe led out to carry off all waste water. There was, therefore, always a foot of water in this little well, up to the edge of the pipe.

While stooges kept vigilant watch outside, Gucio and his boys removed the iron grill and baled out the bottom of the well with empty tins. They mopped it dry with old rags—mostly discarded long under-pants, which were about the only clothes one could ever be sure of getting in kriegydom—and cordially hated they were.

That done, Gucio chipped away with his cold chisel one whole wall of the concrete well till the complete slab could be lifted out. The soft earth revealed at the side was duly inspected and found fit for tunnel-ling. When the slab was replaced in the side of the well, liberal applica-tions of soap were applied at the cracks till they were completely sealed, the iron grill was replaced, the taps set running until the well was again full of water up to the pipe, and 'Dick's' modest portals were ready.

'Harry's' trap was next, and a few complications set in here. In room 23 of block 104, that is, the big room nearest the northern boundary wire of the camp, the tall heating-stove was moved from the tiles on which it stood—while once again stooges kept their monotonous watch. The whole tiled area, about four feet square on a concrete base, was taken up tile by tile and the concrete scraped off the bottom of the tiles. A solid wooden frame was made and the tiles re-cemented into this. The frame was then placed back over the gaping hole, resting on supports under the floor. It was an excellent fit and the tiny crack was dusted with cement.

It looked perfectly innocent except that five of the tiles had been cracked in the process. That was not good enough for the exacting Roger and the Big Four. They smuggled a note across to the East Compound and in answer received a smuggled parcel a couple of days later. It contained a complete set of new tiles whipped from East Camp cookhouse. The cracked tiles were taken up, new ones put in, and 'Harry's' doorway was complete.

With all traps finished, everyone drew a long sigh of relief. They had been a gamble, as the large chunks taken out of various floors would have been impossible to hide successfully in the event of any serious search. In 'Harry's' trap, notably, the floor was up for about ten days and just covered with a spare palliasse when ferrets wandered nearby. It would never have passed undetected in later days, but in the first few days of the North Camp occupation the ferrets were not well organized, so the gamble came off.

All this work was completed by the end of April 1943, and the stage was then set for the serious business of tunnelling to go ahead.

Chapter Twenty-Seven

FORGERIES TO ORDER

In the meantime, other 'X' departments were becoming thoroughly organized. Tim Walenn, chief forger, was using an empty room in block 120 as production centre for a variety of highly faked but extremely convincing documents. Before the war he had been divided between his duties as a flying instructor, which was his official occupation, and his leanings towards art, for which he ran a small studio in London. He was a most polite bloke and quite good-looking until he grew a monstrous moustache that hid nearly half his face.

Among his chief assistants were Gordon Brettell, an up-and-coming fighter-pilot before he was shot down and quite a promising pre-war racing driver; Dicky Milne, who had been Wingco at Biggin Hill fighter station till his downfall; Henri Picard, a Belgian with Croix de Guerre, and Cas Cassie, an embryo psychologist as well as a first-class artist, with a tousled mop of ginger hair that fell over his eyes like a Skye terrier and a raggedly ambitious ginger moustache and beard.

Gordon Brettell was actually missing for the first few weeks of forging. Just before the move occurred he and a Canadian, Kingsley Brown, changed places with two orderlies in a working party for North Camp, then drifted off and hid in an empty hut. The camp was searched and Hauptmann Pieber, the rather innocuous German compound officer, actually looked through the room they were hiding in, but Gordon and Kingsley were concealed in palliasses on the bunks.

They got away at night through the unguarded wire of the still empty compound, but were picked up some days later by a stroke of rather bad luck. At Chemnitz they asked for a railway ticket to Nuremberg, not knowing that travel to Nuremberg was 'verboten' because of a recent bombing raid. This raised German suspicions, and though they tried to bluff it out with a prepared story and forged papers, the Gestapo was called and Gordon and Kingsley finished with three weeks solitary confinement before being ignominiously returned to us.

Among the papers that Gordon carried with him on that occasion was one of the early faked typewritten sheets. The whole thing had been done by hand in the East Camp with infinite care, the text purporting that Gordon was a French worker *en route* to his homeland on leave. As an instance of the minute detail observed in these things, the forgers had hand-drawn some of the letters as though they had been overtyped, and others were done as though the typewriter shift-key had not completely returned, showing an impression of one letter slightly above the line and another slightly below. It was so convincing that the Germans who closely examined it never woke up to the fact that it was not actually typed.

For security reasons the forgery factory was named 'Dean and Dawson', after the passport and travel agency of that name in England. No implications of forgery, of course, were made against the original firm; it was just to avoid having to make any direct mention of the work of producing papers. In common with all other 'X' factories and schemes, the papers and forgery work generally were never mentioned inside any of the living blocks and workers also undertook never to carry on them any bits of paper carrying details of 'X' work or names.

All such details committed to paper, all finished and partially finished documents and passports, all materials such as 'verboten' inks, pens and stocks of drawing-paper, were kept hidden in secret panels in the walls. This hiding of materials naturally applied not only to 'Dean and Dawson' but to other factories throughout the camp, such as the map and compass makers.

The sides of the huts were prefabricated double-wooden walls with a space of about five inches between. To make the hidey-holes, 'X' carpenters would remove a section of, say, half a dozen boards in one piece and fit this panel with hidden clips so that it could be lifted on and off the wall at will without leaving any outward trace that it had been tampered with. The five-inches-deep space behind was fitted with shelves and there was the hidey-hole—easy to use and exceedingly hard to find, unless one knew exactly where it was.

Tim and his forging gang had brought across from the East Camp a small stock of inks, pens and papers that they had obtained through bribing German guards. The guards at Sagan were all Luftwaffe men and most of them were either last-war veterans, C3 physical types or simple peasants who understood little about the war and wanted only to get back to their families. Specially selected specimens were assiduously cultivated by our German-speaking 'contact' people and when reduced to a proper state of amiable co-operation they could nearly always be persuaded to bring in little things for us.

Much of this morale undermining was done by inviting the guard in question into a room for a cup of coffee and biscuit. We had coffee from our Red Cross food parcels and the Germans hadn't seen real coffee for years, so they never turned down these invitations if they could help it.

Once they sat down with a cup of coffee in their hands, the contacts started on the most persistent propaganda campaigns. In the most friendly way they sympathized with the guards who had to fight Hitler's war for him, they played upon his lack of freedom and the spying Gestapo and above all kept up a flow of insidious logic showing that Germany could never win the war.

It was the only chance the guards had had for years to speak their minds on politics and the war in general and they invariably took it with open hands, or rather, loose tongues. They talked, found a sympathetic audience, and half the battle was over. After a few weeks of this treatment the contact would casually suggest that he needed some ink and a pen for his art work. He wanted to do pen-and-ink sketches— he had to do something to pass the time or go mad. Would the guard see if he could get him a bottle of ink and a nib or two. He could pay the guard in chocolate, said the contact.

Chocolate! The guard hadn't seen any for years. Nor had his children. He knew we got good chocolate in our food parcels, had occasionally been given a small square. The temptation was too great and there was little fear of being caught. Yes. He would do it. He would do it once, then a second time, then it became a habit and he would keep on doing it, bribed by chocolate and cups of coffee.

With several contacts doing this, several guards bringing in contraband for month after month, we built up stocks of many things that we needed for our work. There were pens for different work, different-coloured inks, papers of various qualities; there were magnets to help make compasses, radio parts to build our receivers for B.B.C. news (and later a transmitter that we didn't get a chance to use). There was a camera and photographic equipment for taking our passport photographs and developing and printing them. We got various items of clothing, tools such as hammers, saws, pincers and pliers, maps in detail of the surrounding district (and in fact the whole country and adjacent countries)—in short, a hundred-and-one little 'verboten' articles that the Organization needed.

With the stocks he brought over from East Camp and successfully hid from the routine search on the way, Tim and his forgers had barely enough material to start with. With new supplies brought in by bribed guards they pretty soon had enough for full-scale operations. Stooges were posted at each end of block 120 where they had their workroom and 'Dean and Dawson' set to work every day of every week on the exacting, highly skilled job of hand copying printed documents.

They had to have plenty of light for the job and their tables were set up by the west windows where the afternoon sun came pouring in. Whenever ferrets came near the block there would be a quick 'rat-tat-tat' on the door. Within ten seconds the wall panel would be opened, a lot of interesting materials stowed safely away and the panel replaced. Should the ferret wander by, all he would see would be a small party of studious young men paying assiduous attention to a lecture on psychology or maybe motor-car maintenance or some such subject. 'Coast clear' would be reported by the stooge as soon as the ferret was out of the way. Then out would come the work from behind the panel and the forgers would carry on.

For most of their documents they had actual, official documents to copy from. They made, for example, specimens of the German soldier's paybook, the 'sohlbuch', which was also a soldier's official identity card. For this there was no trouble in getting a close look at an original. Guards influenced by contacts were only too glad to show or lend their 'sohlbuchs' for hours at a time. They also produced other forms of German identity cards for us to copy, and before long there was an excellent selection of official documents and passes at our disposal. Probably they did not realize that the forgers could copy them so convincingly. It got to the stage when even one or two of the ferrets, supposed to be doing everything in their power to foil kriegy escape work, would, without asking, hold out their 'sohlbuchs' and say:

'Here, use mine if you like, but let me have it back before I leave the compound.'

Once the first copies of a new document had been made, we had that document available at will for the future, but reproduction of them was an incredibly finicking job. Some of the documents were covered with line upon line of close print; some had a background of fine, whorled lines almost like a banknote, and it all had to be reproduced with the most exhausting, snail-like care with pen and ink or brush and paint. One document for instance, the 'urlaubschein', used in crossing frontiers, took a skilled forger working five hours a day every day, a whole month to make. Consider that quite a few of these documents had to be made; consider that on the night of the tunnel break the escapees had a total of about 400 forged documents, and you have an idea of the magnitude of the organization and of the work done by 'Dean and Dawson' alone. That factory alone employed fifty forgers and stooges three to five hours a day for a year on the tunnel escape.

After starting in North Compound, the first job for 'Dean and Dawson' was to prepare papers for a different kind of mass escape. In addition to the tunnel prospects, the brains of the Organization planned a trick walk-out. About thirty keen workers were chosen to take part in the show and a complete security black-out was imposed on the scheme. Though the chosen thirty made their preparations, not even the people in their rooms knew that something was brewing. Tim's forgers began preparing papers for them, but only Tim himself knew what was in the wind.

This complete security silence was one of the finest features of the Organization. Even when the tunnels were hundreds of feet long, many prisoners in the camp did not even know what blocks they were in. Tunnel workers had been asked not to breathe a word of the tunnels and non-workers had been asked not to show any curiosity in them, so the work went on in silence. Most people in the camp did not even know in which block our radios were hidden—nor did they inquire. It was not desired, and that was enough.

One of the first instructions issued to new kriegies when their purges arrived at the camp was that they were never in any circumstances to take any notice of any strange activity in the compound. If they saw a man doing the most extraordinary things they were to ignore it and not draw undue attention to it. Thanks to such security in no small measure was the Organization able to hide its mass operations from the Germans for so long—a remarkable feat considering that it was only a smallish, barren compound and that always, night and day without a break, ferrets were snooping about the place looking for signs of our activities.

Much the same conditions that held for the work of 'Dean and Dawson' also held for other factories. In a northern room of block 103,

Al Hake, a dark, rather hirsute and good-looking Australian, was making compasses while stooges kept guard outside.

In a variety of rooms Tommy Guest and about sixty of his sewing experts were making civvy clothes. Some of them were rather make-shift conversions from uniforms, and others were really well-tailored garments. One of their first big jobs in these early weeks was the making of three German uniforms, almost exact replicas of the clothes worn by a Luftwaffe Unteroffizier (Corporal). 'Almost exact replicas', because exact replicas of German uniforms would make escapees wearing them liable to be shot as spies or saboteurs. According to the Geneva Convention, however, an escaping prisoner could wear a home-made imitation uniform of the detaining power, so long as it was not exactly the same—not that the Germans were particularly punctilious about observing such niceties of the Convention. There was always the good possibility of being promptly shot by the Gestapo or S.S., no matter what you were wearing when picked up.

In these early days of North Camp it was not so difficult to find quiet locations for working, as the camp was only half-full and nearly every block had a few vacant rooms.

Among the first departments to get under way was the general engineering branch, which covered carpentry, metal work and the design and manufacture of a queer variety of essential gadgets. Presiding genius of the engineers was John Travis, short, thick-set, ruddy of complexion and always immaculate. He had been a mining engineer in South Africa and was invaluable for supplementary advice on tunnels, but he was such a wizard with his hands that he was diverted from tunnelling to look after engineering. He had several gifted assistants—notably two inseparable pals, Morrison and Welsh, who later nearly stole a German aircraft and flew it home, 'Digger' MacIntosh, an Australian, Ken Campbell who had commanded a fighter squadron, and a good-looking English lad, Bob Nelson.

One of their first jobs—indicative of the ingenuity of their work—was the manufacture of three imitation German service rifles out of wood. They got their measurements for them by sneaking up behind German guards with calipers and surreptitiously measuring parts of the rifles slung behind their backs. Out of hunks of wood, John and his gang carved the rifles in exact detail, and then stained the wooden parts with tan boot polish. The wooden parts that were supposed to be of metal, barrel, breech-bolt and so on, were leaded with pencil and then polished till you couldn't tell the difference. Leather slings were fitted and the rifles were good enough to pass the German guards on the gate when the time came.

These rifles were not for use in the projected tunnel breaks, but in that other secret stunt escape that Tim Walenn and his forgers were preparing papers for and for which Tommy Guest and his tailors were making German uniforms.

It should be made perfectly clear that the 'X Organization' by no means limited itself to one or two big escape attempts. Small escapes in ones and twos and threes were continually being organized and to help these an escape assistance committee was set up in the first few days at North Compound. It consisted of Roger Bushell, 'Conk' Canton his adjutant, Colonel Clark, the security organizer, known as 'Big S', and Lieutenant-Commander Norman Quill. When a kriegy got an idea for a small escape by means of guile he would take his plan to his block 'Little X' who would discuss it with him, and if it sounded practicable 'Little X' would take him along to the escape assistance committee. If they decided that the scheme was a sound idea they would help the prospective escaper plan it in detail, brief him on procedure from their camp intelligence data and organize assistance from all 'X' auxiliary departments, so that the escaper would be equipped with maps, compass, forged papers, iron rations, clothes as required, maybe a little money, and so on—all from camp stocks and all acquired or made within the camp.

By the end of April, too, Wally Valenta, intelligence and 'contact' chief, had his staff sorted and apportioned to their duties. Valenta was a Czech in the R.A.F. and had been a lecturer at Prague Staff College in the old days. Dark, plump of face and with a neat moustache, he knew practically all one man could absorb of the geography, politics and history of Europe and was reputed to have done official underground work previously. He spoke fluently a fine selection of languages, including Russian and German.

His staff were all fluent German speakers and each man was appointed to a ferret or one of the German administrative staff, his job being to cultivate him and look after him generally. This could not be construed as collaboration with the Germans, or even as fraternization. If anything, the effects were that the Germans collaborated with us.

Whenever a ferret entered the compound, his appointed 'contact' (though of course the ferret didn't know that) would shortly wander out and greet him and engage him in conversation. Shortly afterwards as a rule the contact would invite the ferret, or maybe it would be an administrative clerk, into his room for a cup of tea or coffee and a biscuit. Other members of the room were briefed always to co-operate and special stove facilities were given to contacts so that water could always be heated for the brew.

The effects of this procedure were threefold. First, the ferret was diverted from his snooping and this gave factories a clear run for their work. Secondly, the German, in course of conversation, continually let drop little snippets of information as to what was happening in Germany and what was happening in the Kommandantur, the German administrative compound, particularly as regards anti-escape plans directed against us. This information was always promptly reported to the departmental head, and from all contacts' reports, he built up a continual picture of what was happening outside the wire.

To illustrate the value of this, the 'X Organization', after a few weeks in North Camp, always received prior warning from well-trained ferrets as to what searches were planned, when they were to take place and what huts were to be searched. That information alone was invaluable. Also they told us what suspicions, if any, were held officially in the Kommandantur as to the form and progress of our operations.

The third purpose of this 'fraternization' was the cultivation and then the bribing of the German staff to bring us in the little bits of equipment that we needed for our work.

As an intelligence organization it functioned with unbelievable smoothness and efficiency and we always knew far more about the Germans than they knew about us, which gave us a comfortable advantage in our work.

Within the first week or so of the move into North Camp, the map-making department was also functioning, headed by Des Plunkett, a shortish, sandy-haired, industrious bloke with a fierce moustache. Apart from teams of stooges he had about half a dozen mappers working with him, making tracings of a variety of maps they had acquired and getting ready to run them off on a home-made mimeograph.

At this time Charlie Hall was also trying to organize his photographic section so that we could take our own passport photographs. Camera, film and developing and printing materials were being 'ordered' from bribed guards by 'contacts'.

By the end of April, then, just less than a month after the move into North Camp, the 'X Organization' had taken shape and settled down to its various tasks. The tunnel trapdoors were built and from rough trigonometry calculations, distances, directions and angles of digging had been settled. The way was clear for tunnelling to commence.

According to their usual practice, the Germans had sunk sound-detectors round the boundary wire. The 'X' intelligence men had discovered this months before the camp was ready and 'Big X' and the Big Four had planned to overcome them. Thirty feet underground they knew the detectors could not pick up the sound or vibrations of digging. Thirty feet deep then the tunnels were going to be.

The Big Four had found from experience that tunnels were easier to work if the shafts went straight down and then the tunnel branched straight out. It was decided then to dig straight down thirty feet and carry on from there. Before digging started, however, three more departments had been co-opted for auxiliary duties. 'Big S' first turned on extra teams of stooges to watch, during working hours, all approaches of all three huts that sheltered the incipient tunnels, and the 'duty pilot' and his runner were briefed to be particularly conscientious. Stooges on duty at the tunnelling huts were to work in shifts so long as tunnelling continued, and for a start this meant from morning appel (German counting parade of all prisoners) which was about 9.30 a.m. to evening appel, about 5 p.m.

Then the sand-dispersing teams were called into action. It was their job to collect the sandy soil as it was dug from the shafts and dispose of it secretly in the compound. It was one of the trickiest problems of all. Unbelievable quantities of sand, tons and tons of the stuff, were excavated from the tunnels, and to dispose of it within the comparatively small barren compound without being detected by the ever-present and ever-watchful ferrets was made doubly difficult by the fact that the sandy soil dug from below was invariably a different colour from the top-soil. It was a sort of bright yellow and showed out glaringly against the dun-coloured ground of the compound.

Unfortunately, after the tunnel in East Camp when a huge quantity of sand had been disposed of under a couple of huts, the ferrets had decided not to be caught the same way again. Every time they crawled under the living-huts in North Camp, which was frequently, they looked carefully for any spots where sand might have been dumped, and under-the-blocks dispersal had therefore to be ruled out as too risky.

A scheme was devised for a cunning new method of dispersal and the dispersing teams and their special equipment were prepared accordingly. These dispersers were always known by the security name of 'penguins'.

The final detail was the provision of shoring-frames for the shaft, and framed supports for the trapdoors when the earth below was dug away. Carpenters and gadgets men had been working on these for weeks and when the diggers were ready to go ahead, the carpenters announced themselves as ready also.

They had had a ticklish job and had carried it out with typical kriegy ingenuity. The shoring-frames and trap supports had to be of timber. But among the things that the Germans did not supply to prisoners, timber ranked high. They wouldn't even give us wood to make food-shelves or book-shelves, so they certainly were not going to provide thousands and thousands of feet of cut timber for escape activity. Obviously, we had to find our own timber.

There were two sources. We had wooden beds and the barrack blocks had double floors of wood. Both were used.

At this time the camp was equipped with about 600 beds. They were simple, double-decker jobs made to a pattern standard to practically every barrack-room in Germany, including their own Wehrmacht. A post about six feet high at each corner, planks screwed along the sides and shorter planks screwed across the ends about eighteen inches from the floor; similar planks screwed at the level of about five feet. Then, between these planks, both top and bottom layers, were laid slats of wood, and on these slats one laid a rough palliasse of woven paper that looked like hessian, filled with wood wool—fine shavings of wood. They were firm and strong but not particularly comfortable.

The slats of wood laid across and on which the palliasse rested were fifty centimetres long. Excellent. An ideal length for each side of a tunnel frame. A small levy was promptly made on every bed in the camp, taking for a start two bed-boards from each bed. The small gap left was not noticed through the palliasse (the noticeable effect came later after about the fifth or sixth levy and the bed under the palliasse was more space than board). This gave the carpenters more than 2,000 feet of good timber, cut into handy lengths and averaging about twelve centimetres in width. It was plenty to go on with, and from this wood they prepared a stock of shoring-frames and trap supports.

Early in May, then, a start was made with the digging. Teams of stooges kept watch outside the huts, the carpenters stood by with their frames and the penguins stood by with their containers. The traps were removed, blankets were spread around them so that incriminating sand should not fall on the floor to give the game away, and in all three shafts the first sods were turned.

Chapter Twenty-Eight

A NEAR TRAGEDY

For a start the shafts were dug mainly by the experienced Big Four, together with just a few chosen veteran tunnellers like 'Conk' Canton, who was Roger Bushell's adjutant, Henry Birkland and 'Cherub' Cornish. Their implements were first the little coal shovels with which barrack blocks had been equipped, but they were soon found to break too easily, so John Travis, the engineering chief, made much better ones from iron plates which he appropriated from block cooking stoves.

'Dick' was fairly easy to start. They just had to tunnel into the soft soil at the side of the concrete well where the washroom waste water of block 122 flowed. The hole there was made about two feet square and firmly frame with the levied bed-boards. From that position, the shaft could be dug straight down.

'Harry' was rather more complicated. Under the trapdoor in block 104 there were solid brick and concrete foundations that went down about two feet to ground level. This all had to be laboriously chipped away with a pick that the Organization had acquired. It was a nerve-racking job as the pick rang on the brick with a suspicious din that could be heard yards and yards away. The space so cleared was ideal for the top of the shaft.

'Tom' was still more complicated. The rubbish beneath was supporting the concrete slab of the trapdoor and when that was cleared away a new support had to be put under it immediately, and it had to be so well constructed that the slab would still fit perfectly as part of the floor. Johnny Travis and his engineers made a hollow built-up frame which covered the gap to the earth, and on top of it they fitted a deep, hollow lid packed with sand so that the slab would not ring with

242

a hollow sound when a ferret's jackboots clumped over it. It was done so well that the slab was fitted perfectly back into the floor.

The Big Four and their helpers reported to their respective shafts each morning after appel. They dug then with only a short break for lunch till evening appel at about 5.30. As the sandy soil was excavated it was passed out in buckets to the waiting penguins who had the tricky job of dispersing it. For this they had sewn together the sides of dozens of small hand-towels, making cloth cylinders about two feet long and about four inches in diameter. Each penguin had two of these which he hung on each end of a piece of string. The string was slung round his shoulders under his coat and the two cloth cylinders passed down inside his trouser-legs. The bottoms of the cylinders were both closed with pins and a string attached to the heads of the pins led up inside the trouser-legs into the pockets.

The cylinders were then filled with sand and the penguin donned his greatcoat so that his abnormally fat legs should not be noticed by snooping ferrets. When stooges reported the coast clear they wandered out to selected sandy patches of the compound where special diversions were staged. There would be a boxing match there, or maybe a game of volley ball, and crowds of 'diversionists' would be standing around. The penguins, casually wandering about with their hands in their pockets, mixed with the crowds and then pulled the string in their pockets that released the pins holding together the lower ends of the bags of sand down their trouser-legs. While the sand flowed out over their boots they shuffled about in the crowd and kicked the sand into the top-soil.

One of the main difficulties about this dispersing was that there were only a few spots in the compound where the normally dun-coloured soil was of even vaguely the same lightish yellow colour as the sand dug up from feet below the ground. There was still a difference but the chance had to be taken. Later on, when these areas could not take any more sand without the additions becoming too obvious, other methods of dispersal were worked out, but Bushell, Floody, and their fellow-Brains were never completely comfortable about the dispersal problem. As a ferret once said to one of our contact men: 'You'll never get a tunnel out of here until you find a way of destroying sand.'

Well, we didn't ever destroy sand and we got our tunnel out, but we knew what he meant.

The shafts were to be about two feet square, but the diggers in excavating the soil would make the hole a little larger than that. After they had excavated to a depth of about six inches the carpenters would pass down the components of a box frame—four pieces of bed-board matched for width and about two feet long. Half the ends of the boards would be cut out into grooves and the other ends would have a tongue protruding. The four boards would then be assembled in the form of a square in the space dug, the tongue-and-groove joints fitting tightly. Soil would then be packed in behind until the frame was tightly held. Another few inches would then be dug and another box frame fitted. As the shafts became deeper, ladders were nailed to one side of the box-framed walls to allow workers to climb in and out.

Then the problem of light had to be faced and this was solved very satisfactorily. An offshoot of John Travis's engineering branch were the 'gen men' on electrical work. They collected some odd bits of wiring left by the Germans in building the camp and supplemented this by surreptitiously rearranging the camp electric light wiring to their own specifications, saving quite a few feet of cable in the process. With the cable so acquired, the barrack block wiring was tapped at a hidden point behind the double walls. Still hidden from prying eyes, the cable was taken under the double floors and into the shafts under the traps and so down to the base. Lamps were appropriated from block corridors and so we had bright warm electric light in the shafts.

Sometimes the Germans would not turn on the power for us during the day and on those sad occasions the shaft diggers had to use home-made lamps. They were made from old tins filled with margarine from which the water had been boiled out. Pyjama cord was used as wicks and the lamps, if a little odorous, at least gave an adequate light.

While the shafts were rapidly descending to the thirty-foot level, John Travis and his metal workers—they were always known as 'tin-bashers'—were busily making air pipelines which were essential for working in stuffy confined tunnels. For these pipes they used empty milk-powder tins from food parcels. The tins were about four inches in diameter and about four inches deep. The 'Little X' in every block collected these tins as they were emptied from every room in his block and they were taken to the room that the 'tin-bashers' were using as a workshop. In the usual secrecy with stooges posted all round to keep them warned of prying ferrets, the 'tin-bashers' set about assembling the pipeline. First the bottoms of the tins were cut off, leaving a clean metal cylinder. The rims of the tins where the lid fitted were a fraction smaller in circumference than the rest of the tins and this smaller section fitted very neatly into the base of the next tin, the joint then being wrapped in paper. As the pipeline was never submitted to any movement once it was laid down, this wrapped joint made an adequately strong and air-tight connection. Feet after feet of the piping were made and smuggled across to the tunnel blocks.

At the top of 'Tom's' shaft in block 123, a short excavation was made under the floor to lead up into the chimney which stood beside the trap. The pipeline was led into this and earth repacked around it. As the summer was approaching and no coal was available, the chimney was not being used and the air intake was therefore in no danger of being fouled by smoke. Foot by foot the pipeline was then led down the shaft.

For 'Dick's' air intake in block 122 washroom, one of the diggers burrowed his way through the rubble under the floor about ten feet to the corner of the washroom where another chimney stood. The pipe was led up into the chimney and then taken back to the shaft under the floor, the rubble being repacked round it. It led them down the shaft. 'Harry's' pipeline intake in block 104, like 'Tom's', was led into the adjacent chimney and so on down the shaft.

Just as the shafts were completed, there was a nasty accident in 'Dick' that very nearly had fatal results. The shaft was being enlarged at the base and Wally Floody, Crump Kerr-Ramsay and 'Conk' Canton were down below doing the job in the confined space when one of the frames higher up began to leak sand. The leak became a torrent in a matter of a few seconds and then the frames started to twist and give way and sand from thirty feet up began to collapse in a flood into the narrow shaft.

By a sheer stroke of luck the ladder held for a few vital seconds. Crump and 'Conk' Canton went scrambling up it, closely followed by Wally Floody, but the sand filled the shaft with incredible speed and in a few seconds, before he could get clear, Floody was up to his waist in sand and rapidly being submerged. Crump and 'Conk' just got their hands to him in time and hauled him clear with all their strength. Within thirty seconds of the sand leak starting, 'Dick's' shaft had filled in with sand almost to the top.

It was a confounded setback but the tunnellers did not brood upon it. Without delay they set to work again, excavating the fallen sand, digging out the box-frames and assembling them again and then packing the sand firmly behind the frames again—a big job as the earth walls of the shaft had just collapsed and masses of sand had to be packed tightly again. It was a wonder the whole washroom floor didn't fall.

Eventually the task was finished and all three shafts were ready again. So far so good but the actual tunnels could not be dug out towards the wire yet. First, the underground working chambers had to be excavated. There had to be three at the base of each shaft. First were the air pumping chambers which were dug in the same position at the base of all three shafts. Facing the direction that the tunnels were to go, they were dug at right-angles to the left, about six feet high, three feet wide and about seven feet along. By the time these were dug in all shafts John Travis and Bob Nelson had the air pumps ready to install.

The pumps were a development of the pump used in the East Compound tunnel the previous year, for which the first idea came from designs in a popular mechanical magazine that had somehow found its way into the camp. The bellows were made of kit-bags kept distended by fitting wire hoops inside them. Intake and exhaust valves were fitted and the contrivance mounted on a wooden frame with runners so that the kit-bag bellows could be pushed in and pulled out by a handle on the front. By pushing, one exhausted the air in the bellows through the exhaust valve. By pulling out, more air was sucked in through the intake valve. A sliding seat like an oarsman's seat in an outrigger was fitted in front and the pumper sat on the seat, held the bellows handle and worked the pump as though he were rowing. The intake air pipe-line was connected up and, Hey Presto! out of the exhaust valve and into the base of the shaft came a constant rush of fresh air.

When this was done, work in all tunnels became easier to hide from the Germans. With constant supply of fresh air down below we could afford to seal up the trapdoors on top while work progressed, and from then on interruptions from wandering ferrets became almost negligible.

The 'temporary soil dispersal' chambers were also dug at this time and these were also in the same position at the base of every shaft. They were rather smaller than the pumping chambers—about six feet high, a couple of feet wide and about four feet long—and were excavated leading back in a straight line from the direction the tunnel was to take. In these chambers sand dug from the tunnel was to be stored as it came back on the trollies and then cleared away by dispersal gangs of penguins in the evenings after the day's digging was completed. Like the shafts all the underground working chambers in all three tunnels were shored with solid wooden walls made from bed-boards.

The third of the working chambers were the general equipment chambers for storage of underground gear and manufacture of tunnel

The ingenious air-conditioning plant, made from discarded milk tins,
kit-bags and scrap wood, which pumped air to the workers in the tunnel

Tunnel workshop thirty feet below the surface

installations. Facing the tunnel direction this was at right-angles to the right and about the same size as the temporary dispersal chamber.

All this work was completed by about the middle of May which is some indication that workers were by no means slacking. Now that actual tunnelling could begin, all the digging teams were brought into organized action, with regular working hours.

There were about thirty of these permanent tunnel workers all told for a start, divided into three teams of ten each and each team divided into two shifts.

Johnny Marshall, with the first team, took charge of the digging of 'Tom', Crump Kerr-Ramsay was in charge of 'Dick' with team No. 2 and Johnny Bull took command of 'Harry' with team No. 3. Practically all the diggers were experienced burrowers and had a fair idea of the stamina and nerve they would need for the job. They knew—none better—that in the crumbly, sandy soil, easy though it was to dig, there were going to be a lot of falls with an uncomfortably large chance of being buried alive down below. There was the sticky incident in 'Dick's' shaft to impress the point even more deeply on them.

Among them were some very distinctive characters who were not unduly perturbed even when falls were occurring later on at an average rate of one every day. There was for instance 'Shag' Rees, tough little Welshman, short and nuggety with a thick cap of curly black hair and a nose that had been broken so often it was getting to be a habit. Shag was so tough he had even been known to play rugger after a night's binge on raisin wine—than which there can be no greater praise. Then there was Danny Krol, a Pole, shorter than 'Shag' and reputed to be a sabre champion, with the most perfect physique imaginable. There was 'Conk' Canton, Roger Bushell's adjutant, sturdy, square-jawed and a persistent escaper; 'Red' Noble, red-headed Canadian continually doing solitary confinement in the 'cooler' for upsetting the Germans in a variety of ways, and by no means least Henry Lamont, wiry New Zealand Sunderland pilot known as the 'original mole' after his extraordinary effort in the East Compound when he burrowed his way under the wire in a few hours from an anti-escape trench that the Germans had dug between the warning wire and the boundary fence.

Once tunnelling was under way, the work progressed smoothly and rapidly. The three duty shifts of four men went to the trapdoors as soon as morning appel was finished. Stooges arrived at the same time as well as a report from the 'duty pilot' as to the numbers and whereabouts of ferrets in the camp. As soon as the coast was clear and stooges

247

were on watch, the traps were raised and four underground workers scrambled down the ladders of each shaft. The traps were closed above them and most of the stooges could then dismiss. One stooge, however, was retained at the top in the vicinity of each trapdoor to give warning by knocks if ferrets should come wandering close by in the block. The reason for this was that muffled sounds from the workers below might occasionally be heard from above, and no chances were taken.

Down at the base of each shaft, the four workers would be stripping for action. One man seated himself at the pump and began his monotonous pumping job, two men crawled into the tunnel proper to dig and the fourth man collected the earth as they excavated it and stored it in the temporary dispersing chamber. He also worked in the equipment store and workshop, cutting out shoring-frames and assembling air pipeline from the materials already smuggled down there and sending the stuff up to the diggers as required.

Picking the accurate direction in which each tunnel had to be dug was done by compass bearings taken up above and checked carefully at the base of every shaft. (The 'X Organization', incidentally, possessed a couple of very fine prismatic bearing compasses acquired by intelligence department contacts.)

As soon as the tunnels had been dug a few feet out from the bases of the shafts there would, in each one, be a No. 1 digger reclining almost full length on his side and one elbow hacking away at the working face with a small shovel and pushing the excavated sand back towards his feet. Digger No. 2 would be lying facing the other way, his legs overlapping No. 1's legs. As No. 1 pushed the excavated sand back, No. 2 collected it in specially made boxes and passed it on to the man waiting in the shaft.

The tunnels themselves were about two feet square, but as diggers excavated them they dug out a section a little over two feet square. As soon as a digger had progressed about six inches, the shaft worker would pass up the four ready-cut bed-boards of a box frame and No. 1 digger would then assemble it and fit it into position. Earth was then packed very solidly round the back of the frame so that it was held tightly by pressure of the soil. For this reason there was never any need to nail or screw the frames together. Box frames had to be fitted as soon as a few inches were dug because of the readiness of the sandy soil to fall.

Meantime, as the tunnels were dug the air pipelines were taken along them, buried under the floor. A channel about nine inches deep was dug in each tunnel keeping pace inch by inch with the excavations at the actual working face. Just before the floorboard of the box frame was fitted, a short length of pipeline would be fitted into the last section of the channel. Always at this end of the air line there was a transferable nozzle which led out of the little pipeline trench and up by the shoulder of the digger to keep a flow of fresh air close to him and to prevent any sand getting into the air-line in the trench. It was taken off for a few seconds while a new section of pipe was fitted in and paper wrapped round the joint. Then the nozzle was inserted once again, sand was packed round the pipeline in the trench till the trench was filled in, the floorboard of the frame was fitted over it and work carried on.

At the base of the shaft the pipeline led out to the exhaust valve of the pump and thus a constant flow of fresh air was fed to the cramped working face of the tunnel. In the shaft itself an exhaust pipe for surplus air led up to a hidden outlet in the barrack block.

As soon as each tunnel had progressed a dozen or so feet the railways were installed. These railways were most essential for easy tunnel transport and particularly, of course, for passing boxes of sand back from the face to the base of the shaft. It was no longer practicable for digger No. 2 to hand the boxes of sand back to the shaft man.

The tunnel railways were really first-class installations. The rails were made of lengths of wood which were originally beading strips at the junctures of ceilings and walls in the barrack blocks. These beading strips were collected from rooms all over the camp and the carpenters split them lengthwise to make strips about an inch wide, half an inch thick and a few feet long. They were nailed to the floor boards of the tunnels about a foot apart and made firm, smooth rails.

John Travis, the wizard with his hands, made the trollies—made them so well that they ran like beer down a stoker's throat. He carved the wheels from lumps of wood and painstakingly cut the flanges for the rails all round them. The wooden rims of the wheels he fitted with metal strips cut from old food tins, and the hubs of all the wheels—his *pièce de résistance*—were fitted with smooth-running ball-bearings fashioned out of wood. For axles, Travis used rods which he took off cooking stoves in various barrack blocks. He ground down the ends (also, of course, with tools brought in by tame guards) and then securely fitted the wheels on. The trolley bodies were strong wooden frames tailored to take two sand boxes at a time to and from the working face.

Ropes at each end of the trollies were the motive power, and rope signals were used as the tunnels lengthened and distances became greater. As digger No. 2 filled his boxes he placed them on the trollies and gave the tow-line a sharp tug. The shaft worker would haul away and at the shaft base he would empty the sand into either a barrel or kit-bags kept in the temporary sand-dispersal chamber for the purpose. The line on the other end of the trolley would still be retained at the working face by digger No. 2. A sharp tug on this from the shaft man and digger No. 2 hauled the trolley back with the sand boxes. Without the ball-bearing hubs and the metal tyres, the railway trollies would never have stood up to the amount of solid work they received in the tunnels.

Now that the temporary sand-storage chambers were operating in the shafts, intensive digging operations could go on all day without having to worry about opening up the trapdoor and dispersing sand out in the compound as it was dug. It made the job so much easier and in particular, so much safer from detection, which, after all, was the main consideration.

Operations then fell into a smooth routine. Every day from morning appel till evening appel—from about 9.30 to 5 or even 6 p.m.—the trapdoors were all securely closed down and thirty feet underground in all three tunnels the shifts were working continuously. The boys used to take their lunch down with them—really it should be printed thus, 'lunch'. It was rarely anything more than a nominal meal in a German prison camp, even with Red Cross food parcels. The average lunch would be a slice of black bread thinly spread with margarine and jam, and maybe a biscuit. If the ration position was exceptionally healthy there might even be a couple of thin slices of black bread and a couple of boiled potatoes, but such good days were fairly rare. Quite often 'lunch' would be such a nominal quality that the boys wouldn't bother to take anything down.

Before the tunnels became too long we had enough cable to supply electric light at the working faces. Shaft lighting cables were extended and taken up the tunnels attached to the roof corners of the box frames. When the power was not on during the day, fat lamps were used. These were avoided wherever possible, however, as they made the atmosphere even more stifling down below. They burned up a lot of oxygen, gave off sooty fumes and generally got in the way. The light they gave was adequate, but no more.

The diggers at the face never crawled along the tunnel if it could be avoided. One was too prone to bump one of the bed-board frames in the confined space, knock it slightly aside and the invariable result was a fall of sand that was dangerous, highly uncomfortable and had to be laboriously repacked behind the replaced frame. Usually when the diggers were travelling up to the face for the day's work, No. 1 would balance himself precariously on his stomach on the trolley and pull himself up to the working face with his hands, like a swimmer doing dog-paddle. When he had arrived he would signal with a tug of the tow-line and No. 2 would haul the trolley back. With the tow-line attached to the other end, No. 1 then hauled him up to the face.

The diggers used to work either stark naked or in the hated heavy underwear—thick vests and long underpants. These dreadful garments were the only things we were never short of. Normally, nearly all kriegies detested wearing them but supplies kept coming into the camp and most of the time one just had to wear them.

Doting mothers and wives who sent us clothing parcels every three months rarely seemed to realize we mainly wanted light summer underclothes, and it got to the stage where a kriegy couldn't give away his stacks of long underpants and found it very hard to get light underclothes. Long underpants are not good for a young man's morale.

The tunnels were so small that only a few of the shorter people were able to turn round in them. Often, when No. 1 digger wanted to change places with No. 2, they would have to go back to the shaft on the trolley and change places there. It was tiring work lying on one's side and hacking away at the face with one outstretched arm. Digging, too, had to be done so carefully if a fall of sand was to be avoided. The sides and roof had to be carefully and smoothly scraped out—particularly the roof which was invariably cut in a concave shape like a low archway. When the top board of the box frame was fitted, the space above it was then gently packed with sand till the fit was perfect.

The sectional shape of the tunnel was not perfectly square. Frames were cut so that the base was about fifty centimetres long and the top board about forty-six centimetres, so that the sides sloped slightly inwards. This was done so that the weight of the sand above would press down and in on the frames and lock the four boards firmly together. Using this system, the tongue-and-groove joints of the frames were quite sufficient for strength and no nails had to be used. In point of fact it would have been practically impossible to insert frames already nailed together or to nail them after being fitted.

It was surprisingly warm working below, particularly at the face, where space was so cramped and the work so strenuous. Diggers were constantly in a sweat and the cold blast of fresh air coming continually through the air-line close by was rather treacherous from the health point of view. This was accentuated whenever a ferret wandered near the traps. There would be a quick 'rat-tat-tat' from above and all work would stop while the underground staff lay quiet and still. This might last for several minutes and one's body became cold and stiff, particularly with the stream of cold air playing over the sweaty diggers. Later on, when the tunnel working faces progressed farther from the shafts, there was no need for the diggers to worry about the warnings as they were too far away to be heard from near the trapdoors.

A few minutes before evening appel, work was packed up. The diggers trundled back from the working face, slipped off their heavy underpants and vests and changed into their ordinary clothes—very 'ordinary' really, they were usually rather ragged—which were stored during the day in the workshop chamber at the base of the shaft. Invariably too they would don a cap as their hair was suspiciously full of sand. At this same specified time every day, teams of stooges would report to all trapdoors to keep watch while they were opened up. As soon as this was done, all tunnelling shifts clambered out and went straight to the washroom of the blocks where a rough shower had been fixed up to wash off the conspicuous traces of the day's work. A few minutes later they were innocently on appel.

As soon as evening appel was over, the second shift of all three tunnelling teams took over. Stooges again reported in strength to the traps, the second shifts went down, stripped for action, and the second phase of the day's operations began. This phase was quite different for it was at these times that dispersal of sand dug during the day took place.

For this operation all traps had to be kept open while the sand was hoisted up from the temporary dispersal chambers below. As ferrets were usually less in evidence after evening appel, the time was ideal for the purpose.

Immediately the traps were opened, penguins began to appear, each with his cloth cylinders concealed in his trousers. Their inflow and exits were controlled by the penguin chiefs—'Hornblower' Fanshawe, a naval lieutenant-commander who was in charge of penguin security, and McGill, McGarr, and Gouws, who were in charge of penguins at the three tunnels. This had to be done so that suspicious numbers of people should not be continually trooping in a body in and out of the three particular barrack blocks that housed the tunnels, and also so that operations could be stopped when ferrets came too near.

As each penguin received his signal he made a nonchalant entry and reported to the shaft entrance of his tunnel, where blankets had been spread over the floor: this, of course, to avoid any of that glaringly yellow sand from being spilt around the trapdoors and thus giving the whole show away. Zinc water jugs were filled with sand from the dispersal chamber below and hauled up on ropes. The sand was poured into the penguin's trouser bags, he was given the 'all clear' and nonchalantly he wandered out again to get rid of it. When that was done he came back for another load.

By this time so much sand was excavated every day that about 150 penguins had to be employed to dispose of it. This dispersal was the main factor in the speed of tunnelling. They could only dispose of so much sand in a day and only that amount therefore could be excavated. This amount was invariably dug by the first shift and so very little digging was done at night. While a couple of men of each second shift brought up the sand from the temporary dispersal chamber below, the other two did maintenance and installations work. The air pump had a daily inspection and then the railway tracks were extended along the section dug during the day. The air-line was checked on the new section of tunnel and the lighting cable taken further along.

Generally the tunnels were extended about seven or eight feet a day, a distance which soon adds up to a pretty respectable total when work is going on seven days a week. It was important from the point of view of evading the sound-detectors on the wire and of digging up and out at the far end, that the level of the tunnel remain constant. To ensure this constant checks were made along the tunnel floor with a spirit-level—another of John Travis's ingenious makeshift productions. As a matter of fact he made two of them and they worked perfectly.

For the first thirty or forty feet of each tunnel, the shoring was all solid box framing, with no spaces in between. After that, because of the wood supply problem, it was decided to space the box frames about a foot apart and pack boards between the gaps. The reason was that bed-boards were most suitable for the box frames and the supply was not inexhaustible. Already all the beds in the camp had surrendered a couple and when a couple more had been levied the effect was going to be felt in less comfortable sleeping. The need, then, was for economy in the use of bed-boards.

For the spaces between box frames the Big Four and John Travis planned to use floorboards. Travis's carpenters then set to work and pulled up the lower section of double floor in some of the block rooms. The wood was smuggled down into the workshops at the bases of the shafts and cut into lengths of about eighteen inches. From this time on—it was only a week or so after the actual tunnels were started—box frames were placed about a foot apart and the lengths of floorboard were fitted in behind so that the ends overlapped behind the sides and tops of the box frames. Earth was packed tightly behind after they were inserted.

The spaces in the floor between box-frames were not boarded, and this meant that diggers during the day did not have to worry about extending the air-line. The evening shift, after that, dug the trench between and under the box frames and inserted the extra few feet of pipeline, so that it was all ready for the next morning.

254

Chapter Twenty-Nine

'TOM' IS FOUND

As soon as the system of spacing box frames was introduced, falls of sand became both more frequent and worse. By the new method, the tunnel face had to be dug forward about two feet completely unshored before the new frame could be put in. No matter how carefully the diggers carved away the sand from top and sides, the soil was so crumbly and unstable that falls were occurring every day. They were treacherous affairs. There was never enough warning. No. 1 digger would be working away when there would be just the slightest crepitation and before he had time to move an inch, down would come the roof on top of him. Luckily the sand as a rule only fell for about three or four feet above the tunnel, but it was always bad enough. A mass of earth weighing hundreds of pounds came away, leaving a dome several feet high over the spot where the roof was supposed to be.

Digger No. 1 from his waist up would be buried under the suffocating mass, sand in his eyes, mouth, and ears—in fact quite an effective small-scale grave, and not the worst feature was the invariable smothering of the fat lamp and air-line. Digger No. 2 then had to work fast. He had to grab his No. 1's feet in inky blackness and with the utmost difficulty in the cramped conditions, haul him back and clear of the fallen sand.

Then the heartbreaking job of clearing up the mess. First another fat lamp was sent up from the shaft. The air-line was cleared from under the sand and then the fallen mass had to be cleared a few feet back. The fallen section was then box-framed solidly and most of the fallen earth packed laboriously above the frames until the dome on top was filled tightly. The job sometimes took a couple of hours in miserably uncom-

255

fortable conditions, with No. 1 alternately spitting out sand and curses with prolonged and earnest disgust.

These falls tended to slow up progress, but it was still a fairly bad day that the tunnellers did not push on a further seven feet in each tunnel. Though there was so much to be done, there were so many willing workers that by the end of May all three projects were about seventy feet long, the distance being checked by measured pieces of string. Accuracy and direction were also constantly checked by the bearing compasses and by sighting along the tunnel walls.

Prospects appeared so good that Roger Bushell and the Big Four went into a huddle and decided to concentrate all forces on 'Tom', which had less distance to go for success than either 'Dick' or 'Harry'. We were on the verge of summer, which is the ideal season for escaping as most of the escapers would have to travel on foot overland, sleeping out, living off the land and generally keeping to the byways rather than the highways. There was, too, a further cause for hurry. With new purges, there were now about 300 Americans in the camp and they were due to be moved to a new all-American compound that was being built on the other side of our southern boundary wire. Many of them had put in a lot of work on 'X Organization' and it would be damned bad luck for them to be moved before the tunnels were ready. As far as our contacts could discover it would be about six weeks before the new compound was ready for them. Six weeks! There was just barely time—maybe—to finish 'Tom' and stage the break, but it cut it mighty fine.

'Dick' and 'Harry' were sealed up, the diggers all combined to work in three shifts on 'Tom', and a little of the excessive caution was relaxed in the pressing need for speed.

'Tom' forged ahead, and about a week later the first half-way house was built. These half-way houses were to be built every hundred feet, so that working in the tunnel, and particularly working the railway, should not become too complicated.

They were all to be made in slightly bigger sections than the main tunnel. Boards to shore this first half-way house were taken from the end frames of our wooden bunks, all being about six inches longer than the usual bed-board. The little chamber so built was about ten feet long and six inches wider and higher than the tunnel, so that diggers could now find room to manoeuvre in it without having to go back to the shaft. No rails were laid in the half-way house. Instead, two extra workers were stationed there, one lying with head towards the working face and the other lying towards the shaft. There was a trolley then for each stage of the tunnel. One half-way house man pulled the trolley with sand back from the face, took off the sand-boxes and passed them to his comrade, who put them on the next trolley and signalled the shaft man to pull. This raised the number of underground workers in each shift to six and sometimes seven, depending on how many were working in the shaft.

Calculations showed that 'Tom's' half-way house was just about under the warning wire. About a hundred feet further on outside the boundary wire was the edge of the wood that surrounded the camp. Just inside that wood was the target.

Meantime, the tailors, forgers, and woodworkers had completed their sets of special equipment for a stunt walk-out escape in mass that had been planned months before.

The germ of the idea was found in the periodic delousing parties that were taken out with bundles of clothes for delousing showers. 'Why not', reasoned Roger Bushell and his fellow-Brains, 'put on an unofficial delousing party of our own?' Give them forged gate passes, put them in charge of a couple of kriegies disguised as Luftwaffe corporals with uniforms and imitation rifles, as escort, and as soon as they get on the road to the showers outside the compound, let them filter into the woods and away.

By early June the rifles, uniforms, and forged papers were ready. Some of the papers were practically genuine, because a contact had persuaded one of the German administration staff to bring in some of the official forms used for gate passes. Tim and his forgers filled in the particulars and signed them. Everything was ready, when suddenly the Germans started to issue the Luftwaffe corporals with pistols in holsters instead of rifles when they came into the compound.

The incident provides a perfect illustration of the attention to detail that Roger Bushell gave all his plans. The rifles that John Travis and his assistants had made were temporarily discarded and they set about making imitation pistol holsters out of cardboard, treated with boot polish. These were practically completed when another contact persuaded a German to bring in three genuine holsters. The pistols didn't matter, as they couldn't be seen in the holsters anyway.

One afternoon two apparently genuine Luftwaffe Unteroffiziers (corporals) collected twenty-four kriegies, all carrying bundles wrapped in towels, and marched them to the gate. Guards duly inspected the Unteroffiziers' identification 'sohlbuchs' and gate passes as per routine, and passed them through. The party swung on to the road through the woods outside and in a couple of minutes had quietly vanished into the woods.

A few minutes later a select party of six senior officers escorted by another Unteroffizier reported at the gate. Among them were Wing-Commander Bob Tuck, rather famous fighter-pilot, tough Bill Jennens, the camp adjutant, a couple of American colonels, a Pole, and Nellie Ellan, who organized the camp radio service. They were going, they said, for a requested interview with the Kommandant in the Kommandantur. The guard passed them through the first gate. At the second gate another guard examined the papers of the Unter-offizier, who was Flight-Lieutenant Bob van der Stok.' A year later he was one of the three who reached England safely after the great tunnel break.

By the foulest of luck a similar stunt walk-out had been tried a couple of days earlier in a neighbouring compound, and we had not heard of it. Only that morning, a special extra mark of identification had been placed in the 'sohlbuchs' of the German guards. 'Unteroffizier' van der Stok (a Dutchman and fluent German speaker) did not of course have the new mark in his 'buch'. The party was held for investigation, and the game was up. Suspicions were aroused by the departure of the previous party. It was soon discovered that no authority had been given for it and a special appel was called.

The Kommandant came across, livid in the face, and made the 1,200 odd people in the compound stand out on appel for nearly seven hours while the Germans tried to find out who was missing by an individual photograph check. A terrific hue and cry was made for the missing twenty-six and most of them were soon rounded up and brought back. An exception, who took longer to find, was Johnny Stower, a veteran tunneller, thick-set, good-looking, and exceedingly tough. He had lived for years in the Argentine and spoke fluent Spanish.

He was nearly picked up when he was questioned by a guard half an hour after leaving the compound. Producing forged papers stating that he was a Spanish worker, Johnny bluffed his way past. He was wearing rough civilian clothes, and set out to walk the ninety kilometres to the Czech border. Keeping to fields and woods he duly arrived in a Czech border town a week later, made friends with some Czechs in an inn and they gave him money and a smarter suit of clothes. From there he boarded a train and travelled nearly to the Swiss border. He set out to walk across, and, without knowing it at the time, actually crossed a narrow strip of land that was Swiss territory, and then walked out again into Germany and was nabbed by a frontier guard.

After an unpleasant spell in a Gestapo prison, Johnny was sent back to us. It was unbelievably bad luck, particularly considering the tragic sequel, because Johnny was among those who escaped from our successful tunnel the following year and was among those shot by the Gestapo.

Morrison and Welsh, the two inseparable pals on John Travis's engineering branch, were another two on the walk-out and they didn't come back to us at all. They got to a nearby aerodrome, sneaked their way into an old Junkers training aircraft and were just starting the engine when a German pilot came along—quite unsuspectingly—to fly the aircraft. He thought Morrison and Welsh were German ground staff for a moment but then realized his mistake, and the two escapees were nabbed. The Germans took a typically spiteful view of what was very nearly a brilliantly successful effort. They nattered about sabotage for a while and kept the two kriegies cooling their heels in a cell for some weeks. There was talk of a German court-martial for them, but eventually the Germans packed them off to the strafelager at Kolditz.

That was the end of the delousing party, but it left us a small heritage in the shape of the three imitation rifles that were made for the break but not used on it. Shortly after, another similar escape was tried at night and the rifles were successfully used by several kriegies who bluffed their way through the gate disguised as German soldiers.

Meantime, the tunnellers in 'Tom' were burrowing their way rapidly towards the wood.

To speed things up, digging was now sometimes done on the evening shift as well, and to keep pace, the dispersing of sand could not be done quite so painstakingly. A few chances had to be taken. Some of the sand was buried in little patches of garden under the overturned top soil.

Chief of the ferrets at this time was Oberfeldwebel Glemnitz, and on the approach of summer he had taken it for granted that the kriegies would be up to something. He was a considerably cunning fellow, Glemnitz, a fluent English speaker with a lined and seamed face you could crack a diamond on, it was so tough. He spurred his ferrets on to search every inch of the compound, and one of them, digging around with his metal probe, found freshly dispersed bright yellow sand under the top soil of one of the little garden patches.

Another lot was found by another ferret who was kicking around in a sandy patch by the camp theatre, which was then being built by us and nearing completion just south of blocks 119 and 120.

Ructions promptly set in with considerable vim. Glemnitz immediately staged an anti-tunnel campaign. Blocks were searched every day, and that was always a nuisance. You would come off appel and find your hut all barred up with half a dozen ferrets inside giving the whole place 'the works'. Everything was turned upside down and inside out while the ferrets probed about for about three or four hours.

Ferret activity was redoubled everywhere. They were always crawling under the blocks, hiding in the ceilings when we went on appel, and generally trying every known trick of the trade to trap us.

In reply we instituted thorough searches of the camp after every appel, because while we were away on the parade ground we could never know where the ferrets might have hidden themselves. After every appel then, kriegies peered under the blocks and climbed up through the ceiling manholes, and no activity went on until the camp was reported 'all clear'.

There was one pleasant little incident when Glemnitz was located under a hut and didn't know he had been spotted until an amiable voice spoke near the trapdoor in the base of the wall.

'My dear Glemnitz, *do* have a cup of tea and a biscuit. You must be terribly hot and dirty under there.'

He actually offered the tea and biscuit, but Glemnitz, a delicate pink flush over his not so delicate features, left rapidly by another wall trapdoor and was not seen again that day.

The next move was a horde of guards who came in with axes and began to chop down the pine trees that grew in the northern half of the compound. They disposed of the whole lot in a few days. Then we found that Glemnitz, his chief assistant, Unteroffizier 'Rubberneck' Karl, and other choice ferrets were spying on us with field-glasses from hidden vantage-points in the woods outside the compound—the idea of course being that if we didn't know we were being watched but thought the coast was clear we would work more openly and give away the location of operations.

Roger Bushell, Colonel Clark and George Harsh immediately countered this with patrols of stooges who walked round the 'circuit', just inside the warning wire, looking for the spies in the woods.

Then 'Rubberneck' made an effort to hide in the cookhouse one evening and spy from there without being seen. The 'duty pilot' soon discovered he was lurking somewhere in the camp. He had 'Rubberneck' down on his list as having come in and he had not been checked off as having left the compound. Rubberneck was on the 'dangerous' list so an immediate search was made and he was located. All the shutters of the cookhouse were promptly closed from the outside and shortly afterwards 'Rubberneck' discreetly gave it up and left the compound.

Move and counter-move rapidly followed one another on each side and life and work in the compound were becoming decidedly tense and interesting. The Germans knew there was no point in getting tough and knocking kriegies about. They had to get definite evidence of the presence of the tunnel and they had to do it by guile. Although all the tunnel huts were among those searched, nothing was found in them.

Glemnitz and his ferrets then started to spring a series of surprise night searches on us—evidently in the hope of catching us working by night. A feature of ferret vanity was that if they couldn't find us working by day, then they thought we must be doing it at night. One would be fast asleep and dreaming sweetly about two o'clock in the morning when there would be a thunderous clattering of German jackboots in the corridor, the delightful cry of 'Aus! Aus!' and we would have to pile out of our rooms and wait, sleepy-eyed and irritable, while a gaggle of ferrets searched leisurely through everything. After every block had had a couple of those nights, Glemnitz was not exactly popular.

Still the tunnelling of 'Tom' went on apace. A few feet past the first half-way house the supply of electric cable for tunnel lighting ran out and the diggers had to work by smoky fat lamp all the time. That was a detail of only nuisance value. It meant that the diggers were continually spitting black saliva—lamp black that they had inhaled during the day—but they didn't let that worry them.

About the end of June, the Big Four calculated that 'Tom' had reached under the edge of the wood. They immediately started to build another half-way house there and on completion of that they were going to dig up the thirty feet to the surface and break clear. Then one day, without warning, a horde of German woodchoppers gathered along the edge of the wood and began to chop the trees back.

Apparently it was not specifically directed against 'Tom'. It was sheer coincidence, because the Germans were going to build another compound there. Within a few days the wood opposite Tom had been chopped back about fifty yards, which left just that distance still to cover before 'Tom' could break in the security of the wood. The

South Compound, where the Americans were to be moved, was nearing completion, and it was obviously not going to be long before the move took place.

No time was lost in crying over spilt milk. Roger and the Big Four decided to push on. They would break 'Tom' out a few feet short of the wood and the escapees could crawl the rest. It would be far enough, they calculated, from the sentry boxes round the wire to give a reasonable chance of getting out without detection.

But the dispersal problem was now acute. All the ferrets were looking for dispersed soil all round the compound. They had already found the two lots of fresh yellow sand and if any more were spread about in the usual places they would probably find that too before wind and weather mixed it with the dun-coloured top soil and harmonized the glaringly different colours. The problem was discussed by Roger and his advisers earnestly and at length. Then someone had a bright idea.

'Why not,' he said, 'put it down "Dick"?'

It was a gem of an idea and the point was promptly settled. 'Dick' was opened up, the penguins received new instructions, and from then on during dispersal times in the evenings a carefully controlled stream of penguins went from 'Tom' in block 123 to 'Dick' in block 122, carrying the excavated sand. Tunnelling proceeded at a cracking pace in 'Tom' and so much sand was pouring out of it that the Big Four thought that 'Dick' would not be able to take it all. Time was getting shorter, the sand had to be put somewhere, so further chances were taken.

Cardboard Red Cross food boxes were one of the commonest sights in the camp. Most people had several under their beds filled with various belongings. Why not store sand in some of them in various blocks? Why not, indeed? Further penguins after that strolled casually out of block 123 carrying the common or garden Red Cross box and made their way to various blocks in the compound. A day or so after this started, an undiscovered ferret spying on the camp with field-glasses from the woods outside, noticed what he considered to be an undue exodus of men carrying Red Cross boxes from 123.

Our first warning of the discovery was the following morning when a horde of ferrets and guards came in, accompanied by the Kommandant and other officers. They roped off the western end of the camp, which included block 123, searched all the huts, and started to probe the ground all round with long steel spikes. Others of the horde dug a deep trench between block 123 and the warning wire, presumably trying to unearth a tunnel, but 'Tom' of course was far too deep to be located like that.

The result of their day's work was a complete blank. The Kommandant and Glemnitz departed, looking very worried.

Roger, the Big Four and the other Brains were also a little worried and decidedly wary. They decided to seal up Tom for a few days and cease work to try and allay suspicion. The tunnel was now a total of 260 feet long, within a few feet of the end. Even with stopping work for a few days they should still have a good chance of breaking out before the Americans left.

In a couple of days there was another critical development. Glemnitz and his ferrets searched block 103 and found dozens of Red Cross boxes full of sand. Glemnitz nearly exploded with fury. Here was proof enough for anything. He bellowed some dark threats and stormed out of the compound. A few minutes later some transport wagons came trundling through the gate and began to drive all over the camp, particularly around the walls of the blocks. They wrecked most of our gardens but did not collapse any of the tunnels. The rest of the day passed quietly, but tensely.

Roger Bushell made the next move. It was a bluff move and started a bluff campaign. He got together strings of kriegies to wander at various times all over the camp carrying Red Cross parcels, knowing well enough that ferrets outside with field-glasses were watching every move as well as the ferrets inside.

Next morning Glemnitz and his ferrets descended on block 119 where a lot of the Red Cross parcels had been taken. The search found nothing, but specially briefed contacts spoke to Glemnitz and told him he was being made a fool of. They hinted vaguely that there was actually no tunnel and that it was just a camp stunt to pull the legs of all the Germans.

Then for the next couple of days special stooges were appointed to trail Glemnitz and 'Rubberneck', laugh openly in their direction now and then, and generally to ridicule them. 'Rubberneck', who was rather touchy on the point, promptly had one of these stooges turfed into the 'cooler' for a fortnight.

After a couple of days of this, Glemnitz apparently began to believe that the whole thing just *might* be a leg pull—probably because he preferred to believe that than to have the worry of a mass break hanging over his head.

He decided then on a last investigation of block 123. He brought in another gang of ferrets, ordered the occupants out, and went through the block again. They were almost finished when a ferret called Herman, never a very hostile specimen, jabbed his probe into the edge of 'Tom's' trapdoor. As far as we know, it was done more or less by accident as he was idly jabbing at the stone floor. At any rate he noticed that the floor was not as it should be, called to his brother ferrets, and that was the end of 'Tom'.

They couldn't find out how to open the trap, so it was broken in, and Glemnitz and the Kommandant were severely shaken men when they saw how close 'Tom' was to completion and the elaborate and solid nature of the construction. Later that day, incidentally, Herman disclosed that if the search had revealed nothing, Glemnitz was going to conclude that either the whole tunnel was nothing but a bluff or that at least the suspicious activity around block 123 was a blind to cover work elsewhere.

The loss of 'Tom' was a sickening blow and a mass meeting of 'X' workers was called in the camp theatre which had just been completed. It had been built, incidentally, completely by kriegies in the camp and also paid for by us.

Wing-Commander Day, then Senior British Officer of the camp, and Roger Bushell both gave pep talks. The gist of it all was that work would go on. 'The Kommandant,' said Prickie Day, 'wants to retire as a general.' It was our job to see that he was retired, but not as a general.

A few days later a German soldier came in, put charges down 'Tom' and blew the poor old fellow to smithereens, along with part of the roof of block 123. Surprisingly few reprisals had been taken by the Germans over the whole business. There was a certain amount of unpleasantness about Red Cross food cardboard boxes and for a while we were not allowed to keep them, but on the whole they seemed to be so pleased at discovering 'Tom' that they were willing to let bygones be bygones. One incomprehensible feature of the thing is that though they presumably knew that bed-boards were used for shoring the tunnels, they never did anything about it. No one knows why. They just didn't. Sometimes the Germans were surprisingly obtuse and at other times they would lash out with petty little restrictions that succeeded in making prison life even more uncomfortable but did little to hamper escape activities.

Shortly after this, towards the end of August, the Americans moved *en masse* to their new compound which bordered our southern boundary wire. There was a great raisin-wine party to send them off, which ended in most of the senior officers in the compound being thrown into the stagnant water firepool, clothes and all. There was nothing acrimonious or disrespectful about it; it was just robust kriegy humour, and after each senior officer had climbed out he usually helped in the ducking of his colleagues.

The Germans allowed no communication between the two compounds so we organized a system of semaphore signalling from hut windows for the purpose of swapping various tit-bits of information.

As soon as the general flap over the finding of 'Tom' was over, Roger Bushell went into a huddle with the Big Four and other departmental heads to plan future operations. In view of the fact that winter was approaching and that the ferrets were still watchful for tunnelling activity, they decided to leave 'Dick' and 'Harry' alone for some months and resume work on them during winter, the 'off' season for escape, when the ferrets would not be so watchful. Meantime the 'X' Organization would foster a series of smaller escapes in ones, twos, and threes, and all departments for manufacturing incidental escape equipment would carry on at full pressure.

Chapter Thirty

'X' VERSUS THE FERRETS

This state of affairs was to last for four months, in which time a couple of dozen escape attempts were made. Several people managed to get outside the wire but all were eventually rounded up and turfed back into the compound after a few weeks' 'solitary' in the cooler.

'Wire jobs' were the most common of these attempts. Briefly the system was for a couple of kriegies to wait for a foggy night or an air raid in our area, when the boundary lights would all be turned off. They would crawl out of their huts, hope to God they wouldn't strike the night guard strolling around with his half-wild Alsatian dog, and make for a part of the boundary wire well away from any sentry box. The idea then was to cut one's way through the wire with wire clippers obtained through contacts—and there was an awful lot of wire to cut one's way through—and then away into the darkness. Very few ever got clear as on nights like that the Germans had hosts of sentries patrolling the wire.

The programme for attempted escapes like that was usually 'Out of the hut, up to the wire, down to the guardroom with hands in the air and pistol poking into the back and then into the cooler.'

One of the gamest of these attempts was made by Jacky Rae, a New Zealand Spitfire pilot who had done rather well on Malta, and Rex Probert, a Canadian. Instead of going to a part of the wire near the huts they decided to crawl on their bellies across the open parade ground to the far side where no German guard would expect to find an escapee. The area was constantly swept by a searchlight and the only shelter was a slight dent in the ground where the Germans had been thinking of putting a road. They had to be so careful that it took them nearly seven

266

hours to crawl the 250 yards to the wire—an extraordinary feat of patience—and they were duly picked up at the wire. They were given such a stiff term of 'solitary', well over a month, that Probert got fed up with the cooler and made a dash for it. He was promptly shot and wounded rather badly, but eventually recovered.

Most of these escapers were equipped with papers, maps, compasses, and other aids to ambitious prisoners made by 'X' factories which were still all hard at work.

'Dean and Dawson', Tim Walenn's forgery department, worked like Trojans and did the most amazing work under severe difficulties. One trouble about their concern was that the artist-forgers had to work next to a window so as to get proper light. This made them rather vulnerable to ferrets wandering along beside the blocks, peering in windows. Their stooges therefore had to be particularly vigilant and ferrets became suspicious of a couple of men they always saw hanging around near block 120 where Tim was working. This question of hiding stooges was one of the trickiest things the security people had to contend with because after a while ferrets became suspicious of any block where they thought they saw sentries on duty.

One ferret in particular began to hang around block 120. He was named Adolf, a little rat-like man with a large nose and tiny moustache that gave him a caricature resemblance to the late arch-Nazi of them all. Adolf was continually wandering around the block, so Tim and his gang moved across to the canteen in the cookhouse. Muslin was spread over the windows, ostensibly as fly protection, but actually to prevent ferrets seeing too closely through the window. A stool was then put about fifty yards in front of the window near another block and a stooge in the canteen continually watched the stool. Whenever a ferret wandered near the canteen another stooge casually appeared, removed the stool and the stooge in the canteen gave the warning. The work was covered in a matter of seconds and an innocent lecture was in progress.

Just next to the canteen in another room, the camp orchestra was continually practising and whenever 'Rubberneck' or some other dangerous ferret approached, the work was packed in a violin case and the stooge walked confidently out with it as though he were just coming away from music practice. This worked well until Adolf whipped round the corner of the canteen from the blind side one day and peered through the muslin over the windows before warning could be given. Apparently he could not see sufficiently clearly because he gave no alarm, but Tim and his gang thought the place was getting a bit too hot and moved across to the church room in block 122.

Stooges were posted at each end of the block and it was not long before the nemesis Adolf was watching them suspiciously and continually wandering up and down by the block windows so that the forgers had to pack up work time and time again. Then the stooge system was changed. The conspicuous men at each end of the block were taken off. One sat in the sun fifty yards away by another block and the other was another fifty yards away in another direction. In these positions they could see every approach to the church room side of block 122. A third man sat near the church room window with a book, in a perfectly natural position. Whenever a ferret approached, one of the two outer stooges lazily stood up and blew his nose. The stooge by the window spoke a quiet word without looking round and the work was stowed away.

This put Adolf off the trail for weeks and work went ahead fairly smoothly until a new ferret began to become suspicious of the man always near the block with a book. He was a most industrious ferret with a long thin nose and was quickly labelled 'Keen Type' and put on the dangerous list. Then a contact cultivated him and within a month 'Keen Type' had lost his zest. Whenever he came into the compound he went straight to his contact's room, knocked on the door, poked his head round it and said '"Keen Type" here. Can I come in?'

In he went then, got his brew and biscuit and let the interests of the Reich go to the devil. In this way some, but not all of the ferrets had their stings removed.

By this time, Tim's 'Dean and Dawson' forgers had a fine supply of inks, brushes, pens and paper and were turning out some amazing work that could not be distinguished from genuine documents without very, very close examination. All of them were stamped by official Nazi stamps, bearing the eagle and swastika. The stamps were very cunningly done. Tim used to paint the design on rubber boot-heels and a couple of squadron-leaders carved them out with bits of razor blade. Al Hake, the compass maker, did a lot of this work too and the forgers had a dozen or so selected stamps for various documents.

They also had, by this time, a fine selection of official papers to copy. These were a couple of genuine passports, leave passes for foreign workers returning to their homes, German soldiers' paybooks with identification card, French and German identity cards, cards for workers on Wehrmacht property, special gate passes for the compound and quite a few others. If they ever wanted something special that they didn't possess, they would often design it themselves, like a letterhead for a nearby Focke Wulf aircraft factory which was embossed—the embossing being done by pressing a toothbrush handle on the back of the hand-painted 'print' against a pad of paper. The result was exactly like genuine embossing.

Some of the genuine papers had been obtained by bribing Germans, some had been purloined from Germans inside the compounds, such as the foolish German staff officer who left his car in the compound while he inspected the camp and later found his maps, papers, torch, and tools missing. Quite a few were obtained from foreign workers while some of the kriegies were temporarily loose after escaping. Bit by bit the collection was built up.

Getting reproduction of typewritten forms was quite a problem for a long time. Doing enough of them by hand was a long business and all the typewriters in the compound were on parole and therefore couldn't be used. Eventually a way was found. A little administrative staff German was assiduously cultivated by a contact and after a while he consented to help. It was amazing how many German soldiers, ostensibly perfectly patriotic, could be persuaded to help. Tim would draft out the sheets showing where every letter and dot were to go. The form would then leave the compound hidden in the German's boot, and eventually it would find its way to Hamburg where his wife had a typewriter. She would type stencils of the form and return them to her husband who smuggled them back into the compound again. Tim and his gang made a makeshift printing press with a roller made of a hunk of wood covered with a strip of blanket. Printer's ink they made from lamp black from margarine lamps and neat's foot oil and then hundreds of the forms were run off.

In their search for suitable paper for various documents, Tim and his staff occasionally swiped fine art papers from Bibles. If they couldn't find the right stuff, they made it or faked it, like the stiff linen-covered folders for certain passes. Tracing linen was glued and pressed over thin cardboard, then painted the right colour and necessary lettering painted over that. You couldn't pick them from the genuine article.

It was Adolf again who drove 'Dean and Dawson' out of the church room by becoming suspicious of the stooges, and continually hanging around and causing interruptions to the work. This time, Tim and his forgers moved to the library room in block 110, where they worked in intermittent peace and danger until the big break occurred.

Other factories were less unfortunate in being troubled by ferrets as they did not have to work such long hours in exposed positions next to windows.

Des Plunkett had a staff of map copiers dispersed in various rooms throughout the camp. Through the camp contacts they had collated an extraordinary amount of detailed information of the surrounding country and conditions and could produce accurate, detailed maps of any area within hundreds of miles on demand.

For reproducing their maps they made a mimeograph, after ingeniously overcoming the lack of proper gelatine. By hook and by crook they got hold of some fruit jellies, but the big problem was how to extract the sugar so that they could be used for reproduction. Kriegy resource soon found a way. The jellies were cut up finely and soaked in a little hot water. This mess was wrung through a handkerchief. The sweet fruity solution that streamed out was tasted until it was no longer sweet. Then left in the handkerchief was the gelatine, sans sugar, ready to use. It was melted and poured into a flat tray made from old food tins.

The maps for reproduction were drawn with ink made from the crushed lead of indelible pencils. Such pencils were 'verboten', but we got dozens of them from bribed Germans. These maps were pressed against the gelatinous top of the mimeograph and then hundreds of copies were run off the impression so left.

Tim Walenn used the same system on occasions to run off copies of certain forged documents.

By this time, Charles Hall, rather a good-looking young Englishman, had his photographic studio well organized with camera and equipment supplied by bribed guards. There would have been hell to pay from the Germans had they ever found this equipment, so it could only be used inside the huts. This made it necessary for Charles to do time exposures, and only on a bright day at that, but the results were quite good enough for passports.

His sitters had them taken in a variety of civvy clothes supplied by Tommy Guest's tailors shop and many of them couldn't resist the temptation to be photographed in some of the German uniforms that the tailors had made with painstaking care. There was, for instance, a very fine shot of 'Unteroffizier' Roger Bushell, of the Luftwaffe, staring out of the picture with a most sinister look.

The tailors were also dispersed in various rooms about the compound and their security was not too difficult a problem. Their main difficulty was in getting suitable cloth. They used old uniforms, the linings out of greatcoats, bits of cloth smuggled in from outside and generally anything they could get their hands on. If a cloth was too thick or coarse they shaved the nap off with a razor blade. If it were of a suspicious R.A.F. blue or khaki colour, they dyed it with dyes made from boot polish or from the covers of books soaked in water or in some other weird and wonderful way. Little incidental items of German kit, like uniform buttons, badges and braid were brought in by bribed guards, often under the pretext of being wanted for 'souvenirs'.

Al Hake, the Australian compass manufacturer, was turning them out almost in quantity production. He made the casings of his compasses out of smashed and melted down gramophone records, the heated and malleable composition being pressed in a mould. Camp artists painted the points of the compass accurately on little circles of paper which fitted neatly into the base of the casings. A gramophone needle sunk into the centre of the base was the needle pivot and the needle itself was part of a sewing-needle, treated by rubbing against a magnet which had been smuggled into the camp by tame guards.

A cunning pivot point was designed and attached to all the magnetized needles, the solder for this work being made from melted down silver paper out of cigarette packets or from the tops of bully-beef tins. Resin for soldering was dug out of the couple of pine trees left in the camp or from the resinous wood that was used in hut walls and our wooden bunks.

Glass for the compass tops was taken from bits of broken window— there was never any dearth of broken windows in the camp. Hake had a system of cutting the glass under water to stop it from cracking and chipping. Next the rims of the compass casing were heated till they were soft and semi-melted, the glass tops were squeezed in and there they set, tight and waterproof. For this local heating and for solder work generally kriegy workmen made dozens of little blow-lamps from fat lamps and little bits of small calibre pipe rolled out of empty food tins. Through the little pipe, the worker blew a tiny jet of air against the flame and then played the small tongue of flame against the point that needed heating.

One of the neatest things about Al Hake's compasses was the inscription he carved in the base of the mould for the casings. When you turned the finished article over, there on the base was neatly and professionally engraved 'Made in Stalag Luft III'. He had what was virtually a mass-production line working in his little factory and by the time of the big break, after working day in and day out for about a year, he had made something like 500 neat, efficient and waterproof compasses.

As the various factories turned out their aids to escape, forged papers, civvy clothes and German uniforms, maps, compasses, passport photographs, and so on, all the stuff was hidden away in special hidey-holes. By about the end of summer for instance, there were about a dozen secret wall cupboards hidden behind panels of the double wooden walls of various blocks. No trace of them could ever be found on the outside of the walls and short of tearing down the walls, the Germans had little chance of finding them. Masses of stuff were mounting up in these store cupboards. Other stuff was hidden in the roof of an outside lavatory hut, which it did not occur to the Germans to search, though they were consistently going through our living-huts with Teutonic though not particularly imaginative thoroughness.

A lot of the bulky clothing produced by Tommy Guest's men was stored up in this roof. There was so much of it that the secret panel cupboards could not take it all. It is a most impressive fact that up to the time of the big tunnel break, the compound tailors had manufactured a couple of hundred sets of non-kriegy clothing from all sorts of makeshift materials that were always in short supply. 'Dick', the old tunnel that had been mostly filled in to take 'Tom's' dispersal sand, was also opened up and what was left of the shaft was used as a storeroom and a very secure storeroom too.

With the advent of winter, cold weather, and snow, the problem of concealing stooges became most acute. It was too cold for many people to be outside and so the stooges stood out like sore thumbs as they loitered in roughly the same spot in the snow hour after hour every day guarding the approaches to factory huts. There was also the problem of reasonable conditions for the stooges. Kriegy food, clothing and leaky boots did not fit them for long vigils in the open in blizzardy weather.

As Christmas 1943 approached, Adolf the ferret was again causing trouble. As before he was particularly the *bête noire* of the 'Dean and Dawson' forgers. He suspected the conspicuous stooges standing outside block 110, in the library-room of which the forgers were working. He began to pay uncomfortable attention to the block and though he never got successfully past the stooges before warning was given, he caused frequent and annoying interruptions of work. It was decided to pump him to see what he knew.

Adolf then was invited to have a couple of glasses of raisin wine at one of the Christmas parties that were staged. After a couple of potent slugs he thawed and began to talk. He said he knew there was something going on in block 110. 'But', he said, 'your postens (guards) are always there and I know they always warn the workers before I get there.'

That gave Tim Walenn an idea. 'Take the postens away,' he said. 'Adolf will think work has stopped there and won't worry us.'

The idea was considered, debated and finally adopted. The stooges were given a holiday and lo and behold! Adolf's attentions promptly ceased as he saw no stooges at work.

For a week the forgery work went ahead like a house on fire with no interruptions from wandering ferrets. Then one afternoon one of the forgers looked up and saw Adolf's thin and bony face peering through the window.

'Oh, hell!' he said. 'Look!'

There was a horrible electric silence and then Tim quietly said:

'Go on working as though nothing unusual is happening.'

Adolf continued to peer through the window but Nature was on the side of the forgers. With the intense cold outside and the heat of the room inside, moisture had condensed on the window and was running down the glass. It apparently blurred the window sufficiently so that Adolf could not see properly what was being done. He must have assumed the workers were writing letters or studying, because after a couple of minutes his face vanished. In a few seconds all the documents were safely stowed behind the wall panel in the room and the forgers had dispersed.

Obviously the stooges now had to be replaced and obviously they had to be stationed in hidden spots, but the problem was how to do it and still cover all possible approaches to the workroom so that warning and pack-up could unfailingly be finished within a matter of seconds.

The trouble was that if a ferret suspected a certain hut he would approach it under the cover of other huts then suddenly dart round the corner and up and down, peering through all the windows.

There would possibly be ten seconds for warning to be transmitted and the work to be concealed. This might happen to a suspected factory a dozen times a day, and no matter from what direction the ferret appeared, the warning would have to be given right on the dot. Timing had to be perfect, vigilance had to be unremitting and now all stooges also had to be hidden and at the same time all approaches covered without loss of security.

'Dean and Dawson's' solution was fairly typical, quite involved and very effective, and other factories used somewhat the same system. The library-room in which the forgers worked was midway along the western side of block 110. There was a door to the corridor and two windows facing west to be covered. One stooge took up position in a window at the end of block 103, facing the northern end of 110 so that he could see down both sides and around the near end.

Another stooge stood by an east window in block 109, facing the factory room in 110, so that he could see past both ends of that block. A third stooge was put in the room next to the library-forgery room. It was no good putting him in the actual workroom because the forgers themselves were all clustered round the window. This third stooge could see any ferrets approaching from the west. All the outlooks of all three stooges were overlapping for double security and all approaches were thus doubly covered.

Whenever the stooge in block 103 saw a ferret approaching, he opened his window. The stooge in block 109 immediately observed this and casually placed a folded newspaper against his window, and the stooge in 110 next to the workroom immediately caught the signal, knocked on the wall and the stuff was out of sight behind the secret panel within a few seconds.

The system worked well, the stooges were more comfortable and the ferrets' suspicions were lulled. Winter, the 'off' season, had arrived; there would be little escape activity (so reasoned the ferrets) and, ostensibly at any rate, the kriegies needed no special watching.

Chapter Thirty-One

'HARRY' IS READY

That, reasoned Roger Bushell and the Big Four, was the time to start work again on 'Harry', the last remaining tunnel.

As 1944 dawned they began to plan a 'blitz' campaign to finish the tunnel and break clear as soon as the weather was good enough for escape and cross-country treks. The Germans would not expect them to have a tunnel completed early in the season and would be caught off their guard.

'Harry' was the only tunnel now available. 'Dick' had been nearly filled up with 'Tom's' dispersal and in any case the Germans had started to build another compound where 'Dick' would have broken out.

Dispersal of excavated sand was again the great problem and this time it was more of a problem than ever. Snow lay heavily on the ground and obviously no sand could be spread there. The Germans still kept a wary eye under huts for dispersal, so they were again ruled out as being too risky. This time the organizers wanted to take no chances. There was no particular need for hurry and 'Harry' was our last chance.

One of the Brains had another bright idea.

'Put the stuff under the theatre,' he said. 'They never look under there.'

It was true. The Germans never did look under the camp theatre. As a matter of fact they couldn't very well do so because we had built it ourselves and hadn't supplied investigation trapdoors in the base of the walls. Had the ferrets possessed any sort of intellectual elasticity they would have found some way of getting under, but for some unknown reason they never bothered. Probably Teutonic experience had never found dispersed sand under theatres before so Teutonic imagination did not visualize it.

We had built the theatre even longer than the normal barrack block and had excavated a lot of soil for the foundations. Under the floor therefore was a long empty space about two feet high—a perfect spot that could take tons and tons of sand. The 'X' engineers modified a seat in the back row of the auditorium so that it swung back on hinges and then they cut a trapdoor in the floor below.

At this time of the year, because it was the 'off' season, the Germans were allowing us to walk between huts after dark, and this meant that dispersers could carry sand from 'Harry' to the theatre under cover of the night. Everything was working out perfectly. Not the least of the advantages of the situation was that we would be able to work with little danger of arousing German suspicions.

Digging teams were assembled again; about thirty diggers being chosen, including all the old veterans, and divided up into three shifts. 'Harry's' trapdoor in the northern end of block 104 was opened up and work started again about the 16th of January. About seventy feet of 'Harry' had already been dug so there was no trouble or time lost in preliminary installations.

The first teams went down immediately after morning appel and work carried on without interruptions under the closed trap. The second shift took over after evening appel till about 9 p.m., and the third shift resumed the following morning. That meant that tunnellers worked one shift on and two off.

Johnny Marshall, Johnny Bull, and Crump Kerr-Ramsay led the shifts and again Wally Floody was in charge of operations. Exactly the same system was used as before, with the trap sealed down during the day. Two diggers, No. 1 and 2, working at the face, passed the sand back on the trollies to the shaft, where it was stored in kit-bags in the temporary dispersal chamber.

Dispersal now was easier than ever. As soon as dusk fell, the trap was opened and kit-bags of sand were hauled by rope up the shaft. At the top, about fifty penguins were continually reporting in ones and twos, taking charge of the bags of sand as they arrived. To avoid any possible chance of detection the most thorough system of security was started.

George Harsh, former Chicago journalist in the R.A.F., was now 'Big S'. He stationed himself in a room near the trap together with the penguin security chief, and there they received continual reports of the whereabouts of all ferrets in the camp. Runners constantly came from the 'duty pilot' with accounts of all incoming and outgoing Germans. Every ferret who entered was immediately tailed by two people—one as watcher and one as runner, so that at any time, George knew where they all were. All contacts were ordered to entice their ferrets to their rooms as soon as they came in and keep them there. While they stayed, their two trailers stayed outside and as soon as the ferret emerged, one kept on tailing him and the other reported the move to George Harsh.

As he collected his bag of sand at the trap, each penguin reported to George in the next room for orders. When the coast was clear he slung his bag over his shoulder, nipped out of the door, across to block 110 and reported to another control there. If the coast was still clear, he continued on his way. If not, the kit-bag was slung under a bed and he waited till the 'all clear' was reported, when he took up his bag of sand again, passed out into the darkness and so on into the theatre.

Here a man stood over the trapdoor in the auditorium and passed the bags down to a team of half a dozen men working in the flickering light of fat lamps under the floor who crawled away with the sand to the sides, poured it out, stamped it in and returned the empty bag. Back then went the penguin for another load. The system worked smoothly and quickly and massive quantities of sand were being dumped every night under the theatre floor.

So easily was the sand being dispersed that further digging could be done in the evening shift, and as a result the tunnel forged ahead quicker than ever before. In a good day's work, some ten to twelve feet further were excavated and shored and the railway and air-line extended.

The North Compound arch-ferret at this time was Unteroffizier 'Rubberneck' Karl. Glemnitz of the plug-ugly features had been transferred to foil escape operations in the South Compound. 'Rubberneck' was a youngish man with a slightly sullen red face, rather lean and with a long thin neck. He was smart, keen, and incorruptible and therefore distinctly a menace. Luckily he rarely came into the compound of an evening and we did not expect to have much trouble from the other ferrets. Then, like a bad penny, Adolf came back from leave and began to prowl round while dispersal operations were under way.

Adolf was not a friendly soul and contacts found it very difficult to cultivate him and practically impossible to lure him into their rooms out of the way for a brew and a 'natter'. It looked for a time as though Adolf was going to be a considerable nuisance until one of those incomprehensible 'Acts of God' occurred and Adolf suddenly developed a friendship for a tall, red-bearded Scot called Jim Tyrie. Jim happened to be a fluent German speaker but had made no particular attempt to cultivate Adolf. However, it is an ill wind and so on and Jim used to get Adolf into his room for coffee and biscuits and Adolf would be safely out of the way while work progressed.

By the end of January, Harry had grown to a length of 100 feet and the first half-way house was built to the same pattern as the half-way houses in defunct 'Tom'. It was about 10 feet long and 2 feet 6 inches wide and high. So many levies had been made on the camp for bed-boards by this time that many kriegies disposed of their few remaining boards and made themselves new supports for their palliasses from bits of string, wire, and strips from old food tins.

This first half-way house was named 'Piccadilly' and was practically under the cooler, which was about ten yards on the far side of the boundary wire. Beyond the cooler there was another double boundary wire and then a road. Beyond that again was the wood that encircled the camp and it was there that 'Harry' was intended to break clear. By rough trigonometry the Big Four had calculated that we would have to tunnel 350 feet to be reasonably sure of coming up in the shelter of the trees. It was a long way but not, it was thought, too long.

We had had enough electric cable to fit electric light in the first part of 'Harry', but after that there was no more and the fat lamps were again called into play. Working at top pressure the diggers were leading highly uncomfortable lives. The ground below was cold and damp but they were mostly in a sweat, and whenever they eased off for a while to rest (one couldn't work without a break in those cramped conditions) they became cold and shivery. Later, when they came up above again, they had to walk under an icy cold shower under midwinter conditions. As a result practically all the diggers suffered from miserable colds all the time.

Then again, as the tunnel progressed the air became worse, even though it was constantly pumped up to them. Nothing could be done to improve it and often the air was so bad in the tunnel that the fat lamps would scarcely burn. This meant poor light and constant headaches for the diggers.

There were lots of little aggravating difficulties they encountered. Sometimes the margarine for the lamps had not had the water completely boiled off and the lamps would go out anyway and refuse to light again.

Falls still kept occurring nearly every day and these were enough to fray the nerves badly. Every time they had to be monotonously cleared, the whole area box framed and earth laboriously packed behind the frames. Diggers seemed to be spending nearly all their lives in a semi-buried state, hunched in a stuffy cramped tunnel, dressed in filthy, sweaty long underpants and scrabbling almost blindly at a grimy, crumbly face of earth that seemed to stretch into infinity and kept continually falling in and half-suffocating them.

There was always the chance of a really bad fall behind the diggers that would bring down yards of the tunnel and trap the face workers for hours. Operations were so well planned, however, that had this happened it is doubtful whether any grave result would have followed. As the air-line was buried under the floor, fresh air would still be pumped up to the trapped workers at the face and surplus stale air would (it was devoutly hoped) seep away through the dome over the tunnel left by the fall. A special party would have worked like beavers then and dug the face diggers out. Thus all would end well (theoretically).

'Harry' kept forging ahead and about mid-February the next 100 feet had been completed and another half-way house was built. This one was named 'Leicester Square' and was just about under the far boundary wire. A little more than 100 feet to go and 'Harry' was there.

About this time there was a stroke of luck for the diggers. Some German workmen came in to fix up a loudspeaker in the compound so that German radio propaganda could be administered to kriegies. They were putting up several hundred yards of wire to connect it with the master set in the 'vorlager' and while they worked, dumped a couple of reels of wire a few feet behind them.

It was reported to 'Big X' in a matter of minutes and 'Conk' Canton was dispatched with a team of diversionists to collar some of the wire.

They concealed themselves behind a nearby block and began to plan an elaborate disturbance that would divert the attention of the workmen and allow one of them to sneak up behind and grab some of the wire.

Just then the compound gate opened and in came 'Red' Noble, one of the veteran diggers who had been unable to work for the past few weeks. In point of fact he was just returning from his latest spell of 'solitary' in the cooler for trying to sneak into a block that was being searched. Red wandered up the dusty path carrying his blankets over his shoulder, and a quiet gleam came into his eye as he saw a coil of wire about fifty yards in front. He changed course just a fraction and without faltering walked up to the coil of wire, scooped it up on his arm and walked on. The workmen ten feet away didn't notice a thing.

A minute or so later, 'Conk' Canton's men also struck while the iron was hot. They staged a mild scrap in the open and while the workmen looked on with interest, another coil of wire vanished.

At night the wire was smuggled over to 'Harry's' block. There was about 600 feet of it, and within a couple of days the Organization's electricians had light in both 'Piccadilly' and 'Leicester Square' half-way houses, and another lead going up to the face.

The German workmen were foolish enough (probably too scared) to omit to report the loss of their wire and later paid for the omission very heavily.

Meantime, 'Rubberneck' was due to go on leave, and either because of that or because somehow he sensed that something was going on, a spate of intensive searches started. Particular attention was paid to the huts nearest the wire where tunnels were more likely to be started. What was worse, particular attention was apparently being paid in rooms to the tiled squares over which the stoves were placed. One such square of tiles was the top of 'Harry's' trapdoor. Block 104 was among those searched, but nothing was found.

Roger Bushell sent an extra warning round the camp for everyone to tighten up on security. Particularly there was to be no talk whatsoever in the blocks about operations. Ferrets were crawling around under the huts by day and interpreters listening outside the shutters at night. Roger himself, knowing that he might be suspected, cleared out the secret panel in his room where various things like civvy clothes and papers had been hidden.

Next day a couple of guards walked on to the parade ground during appel and meandered towards Roger's section. Doing some quick thinking, Roger decided to take no chances and pulled out of his pocket some papers carrying plans for the coming mass break. His fears were justified. The guards beckoned him forward and as he shouldered his way out of the ranks he surreptitiously pressed the papers into the hand of the man beside him. The guards noticed nothing but took him back to his room where he was searched. They found nothing on him of course and then turned their attention to the room. With their probes they happened, by sheer luck, to spring the panel that covered Roger's hidey-hole in the wall, and pulled it out. Like Mother Hubbard's cupboard, it was bare. Twenty-four hours earlier it had been crammed full of stuff.

A couple of mornings later another extra batch of guards marched on to the appel and called out about a dozen people, who were immediately marched off. Among them were Wally Floody, chief tunnel executive; George Harsh, security chief; 'Hornblower', penguin security chief; a couple of diggers and other key workers and also Jim Tyrie, the bearded Scot who had kept Adolf out of the way for some vital nights.

Without even a chance to go to their rooms, the whole lot were searched and then marched out of the gate to Belaria Compound some miles away. There they stayed.

As it precluded them from the tunnel escape, it probably saved some of their lives—but no one appreciated that at the time.

This was decidedly a blow. It was bad enough losing the key men. Even more unpleasant was the certainty now that the Germans were definitely suspicious and would make things awkward for the rest of the work to be done.

There was one bright spot. A couple of days later (this was the first week of March) 'Rubberneck' went on a fortnight's leave. Without his evil direction, the ferrets were not quite as intent on their work for the next fortnight as they otherwise would have been and work was not seriously hampered.

The diggers went to work like furies on the tunnel. There were now two men at the face, two in 'Leicester Square' half-way house transferring sand to the centre stage of the railway, two more in 'Piccadilly' dispatching the sand on the last lap, and the pumper, storer, and frame-cutter at the base of the shaft.

The day they burrowed out under the road brought a shock for 'Shag' Rees, tough little Welsh digger. There was an awful rumble just over his head it seemed and he cringed, expecting the whole tunnel to come crashing down. The rumble passed and then he realized what it was—a heavy cart passing above on the road. Often after that the same rumble was heard in the tunnel and always the diggers thought their last moments had come. They knew it was only a cart, but nerves were very edgy. The workers in 'Piccadilly', incidentally, could sometimes hear the clump and ring of German jackboots on the concrete floor of the cooler above them. It was an intriguing position.

By the 8th of March, the final 100 feet were finished and in the next two days a third half-way house was completed, this one the biggest of all, being about eighteen feet long. The three separate laps of the tunnel of a little over 100 feet each, plus the three half-way houses were found to measure a shade under 350 feet. According to calculations, the end of the tunnel should now be under the wood and the way was clear for the upward shaft to be dug.

This promised to be a highly tricky job, and was dug by the more experienced Big Four ('Conk' Canton had filled the gap left by the departure of Wally Floody). Their home-made spirit-level checks of the floor of the tunnel indicated that they would still be about thirty feet below ground-level. They decided then to dig up about twenty-eight feet, support the remaining two feet with boards and leave it at that till everything was ready for the break.

As they dug up they fitted solid box framing, and when the working face was dug up out of reach they nailed sections of ladder to the side of the shaft, stood on that and dug up further. To prevent bad falls they dug on one side of the shaft at a time with boards balanced on the top box frame covering the other half. In four days they had come to pine roots in the soil, judged they were near enough to the surface so they boarded over the top of the shaft to support the surface soil and left it at that.

This was all completed on the 14th of March and the tunnel sealed up to wait for milder weather and a night suitable for the break. The trap was closed and the cracks round the sides cemented up.

It was just in time. 'Rubberneck' came back next day and that afternoon a gaggle of ferrets suddenly poured into the compound, made a beeline for block 104 and conducted an exhaustive search. They paid particular attention to fireplaces and in the room that sheltered 'Harry's' trap one of the ferrets ran a probe round the concrete that sealed the edges of the trap. It held, and he wandered off to search elsewhere. The whole search passed off without a hitch.

The sigh that followed that unsuccessful search was one of considerably qualified relief. The determined attention paid to block 104 was a pretty serious affair and obviously that would not be the end of it as far as the ferrets were concerned. Preparations for the break were therefore pushed ahead at full pressure with all the factories turning out escape equipment.

The 'X Organization' executives conducted a secret ballot to determine the lucky men who would take part in the escape. About 500 kriegies had worked on the whole project in various departments and obviously not all of them could go. It was estimated that at the most only about 220 would be able to pass through the tunnel in one night when the time came. To give an extra chance to people who had done most work, Roger Bushell picked the first thirty himself and then seventy more names were drawn out of the hat. Roger then picked a further thirty and seventy more names were drawn blind. Twenty more names were then chosen of deserving people who still lacked a place. People were to go out in the order chosen or drawn.

The lucky ones were informed and began their preparations. Roger checked over as many of their plans as possible and arranged briefing lectures for the remainder. Every escapee had to have a story which could be backed up by forged papers and they were also required to plan their proposed routes.

In one way and another, the Organization had enough money to allow about forty people to go by train, buying their tickets and arranging accommodation and so on. The rest would have to go 'hard-tail' across country by foot. The train people's plans were all checked by Roger and he gave general lectures on procedure with helpful suggestions to all the 'hard-tailers'. Johnny Stower, who had reached the Swiss border after the delousing party walk-out, gave lectures on his procedure and experiences and Johnny Marshall spoke on how to get through the tunnel without coming to grief.

As most of the 'hard-tailers' planned to strike down into Czechoslovakia (the border was only about fifty miles south of the camp), Johnny Vesley, a Czech in the R.A.F., lectured on the border mountains which they would have to cross.

Roger and the Big Four also doped out a foolproof system for getting the 220 people unnoticed into block 104 on the night of the break and for getting them through the tunnel without a hitch and out at the other end without confusion.

Meantime, all factories were in full production. Johnny Travis's engineers switched to the manufacture of metal water-bottles. Old food tins were cut into sheets according to patterns and a squad of solderers, drawing heavily on stocks of silver paper, solder and resin, got to work with home-made blow-lamps and turned out neat flat flasks by the dozen.

Des Plunkett and his mappers set up their mimeographs and ran off maps by the thousand until the total products of his department totalled something like 4,000 maps.

Stooges all over the camp were working overtime on protecting all these hectic activities and, by the grace of God, no slips were made that week and the suspicious ferrets were given nothing further to intensify their misgivings.

Al Hake continued making his excellent compasses almost till the last minute and Charley Hall had his scores of photographs ready for the forged papers.

'Dean and Dawson', Tim Walenn's forging gang, were working at furious pressure. They had the hardest job of all because everyone's papers had to be prepared to fit their stories and intended identities. Names, individual particulars, and photographs—everything had to be in the right place on the right papers. Altogether they had prepared about 400 forged papers of various kinds for the escape. Everyone was to have at least one official paper of some kind, most had two and the men with elaborate identities like Roger Bushell and some of the German speakers had as many as half a dozen, including letters of credit and incidental forged personal letters, just for effect. The forgers kept special folders for each of these people.

They had so many papers and so much depended on them that Tim was unwilling to leave them in the secret wall cupboards. He put them down the shaft of the old tunnel 'Dick', which had been mostly filled in. As it was partially flooded down there, the 'tin-bashers' of the engineering branch produced four large metal cans with sliding lids which were quite waterproof when smeared with vaseline or margarine. The tins had to be brought up every day for extra work on the papers. This meant extra stooges to guard over the opening of 'Dick's' complicated trap. The iron grating in the centre of the washroom floor was removed, the concrete well below bailed out, cement sealing strips chipped off the cracks and the side slab lifted out. When the papers were taken out they were hidden under a box of potatoes and carried across to the forgery room while the slab was replaced in the side of the well, cement sealing mixture applied again to the cracks, water poured into the well and the grating replaced.

When the forgers broke off for a spell and a meal the papers were taken back under a box of dirty clothes to the washroom that harboured 'Dick'. Once again while stooges watched, the complicated procedure of opening the trap was followed and the trap was closed again. After the meal the trap was opened once more and out came the papers again, and when work finished, the same thing again. Four times a day every day in this period were stooges summoned to 'Dick' while the same laborious procedure was gone through. It is a detail that gives an indication of the passionate and tireless care that was taken on all points of the whole fantastic 'X' project.

Tim's forgers worked long hours in those days—worked till their heads were splitting and the points of their nibs and brushes and the letters they were forming seemed to jump and wriggle under their eyes.

Most of the prospective escapers were travelling as foreign workers and the forgers filled out identification cards and passes representing most of the countries of Europe. Tim himself, for instance, was going out as a Lithuanian. What matter if he couldn't speak the language? Any German who questioned him probably wouldn't be able to speak it either and bluff stood a good chance of doing the rest. In that spirit, the boys were ready to have a crack at anything. Just to be outside the damned eternal barbed wire!

Chapter Thirty-Two

THE GREAT TUNNEL BREAKS

———

Just after appel, on the morning of Friday, the 24th of March, Roger decided that the escape would take place that night. Word flitted round the camp to all essential workers and the Organization swung into hectic under-cover activity.

The decision was a surprise and some of the 'hard-tailers' felt a little tremor of dismay because snow was still lying six inches deep on the ground. For them it was going to be tough, but there were reasons for the sudden decision.

The sun was shining, the day was mild and spring was evidently in the air. The escape required a dark night and the moon at the present stage was practically non-existent. Hall, the compound meteorological expert, thought there was a chance of a slight wind in the night that would help to drown suspicious noises. Most important of all, 'Harry's' trapdoor was developing a slight wobble, so much had it been used. Unless the current no-moon period were used, they would have to wait a month till the moon had vanished again. With the ferrets so suspicious of block 104 and the trap so shaky it would be too much to expect that the tunnel would continue to evade detection for another month and to lose everything now when success was so close and after all the work that had been done would have been heartbreaking. And 'Harry' was now the only tunnel left. So to-night was the night.

There was a tremendous amount still to be done. First and most important, the tunnel had to be finally prepared. Crump Kerr-Ramsay gathered a team of workers and vanished down the tunnel. He went up to the top of the far exit shaft, removed one of the boards that sealed it off and gently probed into the earth above with a stick to see how far they had to dig to break out. It should be about two or three feet. He

286

got the shock of his life. After sinking in for three inches the stick poked through into the open and a speck of daylight showed. Crump hurriedly withdrew his probe, gingerly replaced the board and left it alone. At least there should be no delay in getting out.

Then the tunnel preparations started. Blankets were spread over the floor of the tunnel near each end to deaden the sound of operations that night, and more blankets were laid in 'Piccadilly' and 'Leicester Square' half-way houses so the trolley haulers working in them that night would not have their escape clothes covered in dirt. Planks about five feet long were nailed on the flat frames of the trollies so that escapers could lie more securely on them as they were hauled to the exit with all their bulky equipment. Other workers began the tedious job of installing extra electric light lamps along every twenty-five feet of the tunnel.

Meanwhile, above in the compound, the 220 chosen to go out that night were making hectic last-minute preparations. They had refrained from making obvious preparations earlier for fear the Germans would find them. All over the camp, iron rations were being prepared. Grated chocolate, oatmeal, crushed biscuits, vitamin pills, sugar, milk powder, and other concentrated foods were boiled and baked into heavy, nourishing cakes, and then packed in tins.

Shortly after lunch the 'Little X' of every block called together the men in his block who were going out that night and gave them final briefing. He handed them water-bottles, compasses and maps, gave them final directions on how to pack their equipment and how best to manage the tunnel. They were also given directions on how and when they were to go to block 104 without arousing German suspicions. This part had to be very carefully controlled. The escapers went back to their rooms after final briefing and started to pack all their special kit into extra pockets they sewed inside their greatcoats and coats. Many of them had even made little fat lamp heaters for brewing coffee and cocoa on the coming cold trek across snow-clad country.

Special squads of stooges were out all day to conceal the sudden extra activity. Under their protection, Tommy Guest's clothing department raided their secret stores and smuggled the stuff according to pre-arranged directions to scores of people throughout the camp who were to wear the clothes for the break.

Tim Walenn's forgers had the most hectic day of all. They had the job of date stamping all their papers—a job that couldn't be done till the date of the effort was known, as all papers had to be endorsed to cover certain limited periods. Particularly did this apply to travelling permits. After that, all papers had to be sorted and distributed. The forgers worked all day, practically up till the time the tunnel was opened, before they finished the job. They used a date stamp made inside the camp from rubber boot-heels.

By evening appel, the tunnel workers still had not finished their preparations. They came up for a breather, went on appel and then dived down the tunnel again. Operations were to start about 9 p.m. and not until just on 8.30 did they finish the last job, fitting newly-woven rope (three thicknesses of thick plaited string) on to the trollies to ensure there were no hitches in the hauling. On one trolley they were able to use genuine rope that contacts had arranged to be brought in. Some of these late workers were among those chosen for the break and they had to go like scalded cats to get themselves ready in time.

Round about 7 p.m. when it was quite dark, escapers began to drift in to block 104. They went by a tortuous route. Each had a particular minute to leave his room and right on the second they drifted out into the compound, dark bulky figures with blankets and masses of kit concealed under their greatcoats. Some of them, notably the train travellers, carried attaché cases and were wearing immaculate civilian clothes beneath their coats.

Keeping well away from block 104 they walked swiftly to the south end of block 109 and reported to a room where a marshal let them go in spaced ones and twos out of the north door, across the camp road-way and into the south door of 104. Each man had a particular room to go to where he was to sit or lie down, keep quiet and wait till his turn to leave.

Crump Kerr-Ramsay and Jimmy Davison were to control the evacuation through the trapdoor in the block, and about 8.30 p.m. Crump announced that the tunnel was ready for operations.

While the first few were making their last-minute preparations to leave, the Senior British Officer of the camp, Group-Captain Massey, came in to wish them Godspeed. Not very much was said. The atmosphere was too tense and somehow it was the wrong time for panegyrics. The Group-Captain himself was shortly to be repatriated because of a badly injured leg, so he quietly shook hands and made dates to meet any successful escapers in London when they got back. He was exceedingly proud of the whole effort and didn't hesitate to say so.

Facing this page: Sectional drawing of Escape Tunnel 'Harry'

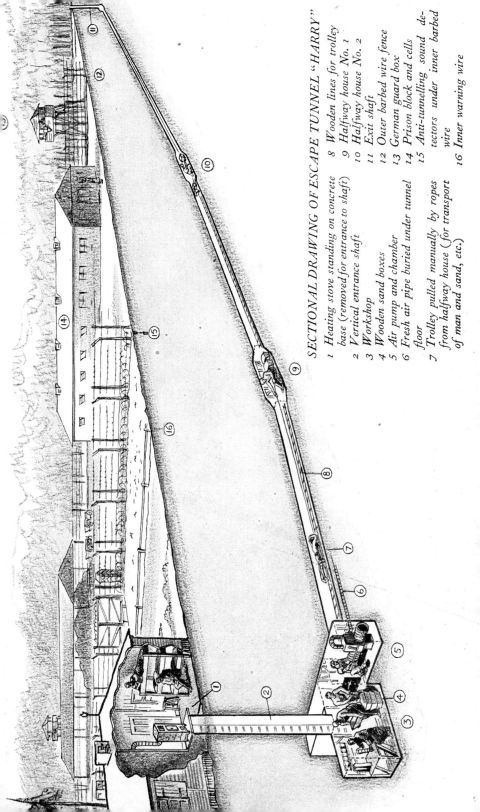

SECTIONAL DRAWING OF ESCAPE TUNNEL "HARRY"

1 Heating stove standing on concrete base (removed for entrance to shaft)
2 Vertical entrance shaft
3 Workshop
4 Wooden sand boxes
5 Air pump and chamber
6 Fresh air pipe buried under tunnel floor
7 Trolley pulled manually by ropes from halfway house (for transport of man and sand, etc.)
8 Wooden lines for trolley
9 Halfway house No. 1
10 Halfway house No. 2
11 Exit shaft
12 Outer barbed wire fence
13 German guard box
14 Prison block and cells
15 Anti-tunnelling sound detectors under inner barbed wire
16 Inner warning wire

By 8.40, Johnny Marshall and Johnny Bull were climbing down the shaft into the tunnel. They had the job of excavating the last couple of inches of the exit shaft and controlling the first few out. Johnny Marshall was immaculate in civvies and attaché case. He was to travel first-class by train. Johnny Bull was going third-class and was dressed like a workman. Roger Bushell, Bernard Scheidhower, French Fleet Air Arm pilot, and Wally Valenta, the Czech, followed them down. Roger looked like a successful business-man in a grey herringbone lounge suit, smart black overcoat and dark felt cap, carrying an attaché case. He was calm and very confident, chatting gaily to everyone. Before long, fourteen men had descended, a figure that included the air pumper, the controller at the base of the first shaft and a hauler in each half-way house.

In the end half-way house, next to the upward exit shaft, half a dozen men were crammed—the first five who went down plus Sydney Dowse, the hauler. Two blankets had been hung across the far end so as to keep out the light from the shaft when it was opened up. You crawled past one blanket, let it slip back into position blanking off the light, then crawled past the other.

Johnny Bull went through, clambered in darkness up the ladder to the top and started to open up. He even had a small shovel, specially made of wood for the final excavation so as to make less noise. The remaining five in the half-way house waited in tense silence for the 'okay' from Johnny Bull. Minutes passed; they seemed to drag like hours and still no signal came. Johnny Marshall crawled past the blankets and called softly up the shaft.

'How long?'

'Can't loosen these damned top boards,' Johnny Bull answered. 'They're wet and they seem to have jammed. Must be swollen with water.'

He worked on in the darkness, standing precariously on the ladder and trying to lever out the unseen, tightly packed boards that enclosed the top of the shaft. Before long the sweat was pouring off him and the strain of anti-climax was telling on the waiting men below. Johnny kept on tugging and straining and an unbearable half-hour passed. At last he came down the ladder exhausted.

Facing this page: The tunnel exit less than fifteen yards from a sentry-box. The escapee, just emerging from the hole, is being guided to cover by a rope held by a 'controller' hidden in the undergrowth

'You have a go,' he told Johnny Marshall. 'I'm done in.'

In the cramped confines of the half-way house, Marshall stripped off his smart suit and clambered up the ladder. He couldn't risk getting into a first-class train compartment in clothes covered with dirt. They would have made him suspect immediately. He worked in his shirt and under-pants at the top of the ladder for a quarter of an hour in growing ten-sion until at last he had loosened a board and tugged it out. The rest came easily and then he clambered down the ladder to dress again while Johnny Bull went aloft once more and gently scraped away at the last couple of inches of soil covering the top. He felt his little shovel break out above and then cool fresh air caressed his upturned, sweating face. Within a minute he had the shaft fully open, could see a couple of faint stars above—a glorious sight and an epic moment—climbed the last couple of steps up and put out his head.

He got the shock of his life. Calculations somehow had just missed out. They were not quite so far as they had intended to be. Instead of being just inside the edge of the wood he saw that he was out in the open and a few feet short of the dim line of trees. Worse still, looking back towards the compound he saw the shaft mouth was in full view of the sentry tower standing outside the wire.

The tower was a bare fifteen yards away, complete with sentry, mounted machine-gun and searchlight. Softly he turned and felt his way back down the shaft.

There was a moment of shaken silence in the half-way house when he broke the news. For a moment it looked as if the whole project were going to end in failure—a ghastly thought. All those 500 men working every day for over a year! The burning ambition to escape of men who had been behind barbed wire for up to five years! Just for a few seconds there was a sickening dismay.

It did not last. The men who had planned and laboured so long for their freedom were in no mood to be stopped at the last moment by an unexpected hitch. Coolly and dispassionately they talked it over.

Their evacuation plans had provided for a man to lie alongside the top of the shaft, and when the coast was clear he would silently signal the next man out by a pat on the head as he stood at the top of the final ladder. A rope was to lead from the opening about seventy yards into the wood. Each man as he came out was to crawl along the rope to the end where his party would assemble. Then they would hare off into the night.

Obviously a man could no longer lie alongside the hole with the sentry tower only a few yards away. Against the white snow he was bound to be seen sooner or later—probably sooner.

'We've got two courses,' said Roger. 'We can go ahead with it now and get as many out as we can before we're caught. The only alternative is to put a couple out now, let them close up the outside, and then we'll have to dig on a few more feet till we're properly inside the wood, put up another shaft and stage the break then. That can't be till the next no-moon period—about a month.'

The position was quietly discussed. No one liked the idea of calling it off for a month while they dug on. It would be a horrible anti-climax, but that was nothing compared to the very acute danger of the whole project being discovered. The shaky trapdoor and the suspicious ferrets' interest in block 104 was in all their minds. To lose the whole thing now would be unbearable.

Someone thought of something else.

'We can't put it off now,' he said. 'All the papers are date stamped. In a month's time they'll be no good. A lot of us won't get far without papers. We'll have to go to-night and chance it.'

That decided it. The mass break would go on as per programme.

The next problem was to amend the evacuation procedure. It was going to be difficult to find a workable way, but of all people, the ferrets, as it happened, supplied the answer.

'Listen,' said Johnny Bull. 'Just about ten feet from the hole, by the edge of the wood, I saw one of those spy fences the ferrets put up.' (They were little brushwood barriers behind which the ferrets used to spy on the camp with field-glasses. The idea was to catch us napping when we thought there were no ferrets about to watch us.)

'Put the outside control behind the fence,' said Johnny. 'Give him a rope from the hole for signalling and he can still control the boys coming out.'

It was so obviously the solution that Roger agreed on the spot. He scrawled the new procedure on the wall of the half-way house with a pencil and told the hauler to warn all escapers as they came through. Johnny Bull scrambled up to the top of the shaft with a long coil of rope which he tied to the ladder, gently eased himself out on to the snow and crawled noiselessly till he was behind the shelter of the ferret fence, paying out the rope as he went. He lay for a while to get the lie of the land and see what the sentry situation was. The man in the tower did not seem to be worrying about the woods behind him but merely kept playing his searchlight along the barbed wire boundary fence and over the compound.

Then Johnny Bull heard a man approaching from the west along the boundary wire. He saw him dimly, a German soldier muffled in great-coat and carrying a rifle. He walked up to the sentry tower, turned and walked back. A moment later another walked along the wire from the east, reached the sentry tower, turned and walked back. A couple of minutes later both of them reappeared again. Obviously they were tramping a beat along the northern boundary of the camp.

As soon as they had both gone, Johnny tugged sharply on the rope and in a couple of seconds Johnny Marshall snaked over the edge of the hole, keeping one hand clutched around the rope that led from the ladder to Johnny Bull behind the ferret fence. The rope was to serve both as a means of direction in the dark and as a means of warning from the controller should any German appear.

Behind the little fence, Marshall collected the rest of the coil of rope from Bull, shook him quietly by the hand, wished him luck and crawled off into the wood, paying out the rope behind him. About seventy yards inside the trees he tied the end of the rope round a tree and waited to be joined by Wally Valenta, with whom he was travelling. Johnny Bull was staying behind the ferret fence to control the first twenty people out, when he would be relieved by No. 21 and then crawl away himself to freedom.

One by one the others silently emerged from the shaft after getting the 'all clear' tug from Johnny Bull and, keeping the rope always running loosely through one hand, they crawled past the barrier and on to the end of the rope. There they waited for their No. 2's or the rest of their party (most people were travelling in pairs), and then slunk off into the darkness. Marshall and Valenta went, then Bushell and Scheidhower (Roger spoke French fluently as well as German and was travelling as a French worker) then Tim Walenn, the forger, accompanied by Romas Marcinkus, a Lithuanian R.A.F. officer.

They were all going by train and they headed due north through the wood to where Sagan railway station lay only about a quarter of a mile away. Time-tables had been smuggled into the compound through bribery and everyone knew what train he was to catch, and what alternative trains existed if he missed it. They were going in all directions—some south-east to Hirschberg and Czechoslovakia, some south-west through Leipzig towards France, some north-west to Berlin and then on to Stettin or Danzig, heading for Sweden.

As much information as possible had been collected from guards about the approaches to the railway station and all train travellers had been briefed that when they got to the far side of the wood they would come to a road that bordered the railway line and station. By a certain fence there was the entrance to a subway that led under the tracks to the booking-office and platforms.

Unfortunately a shed had been built over the subway entrance as a shelter from the weather and it was unrecognizable in the dark from the description given. Kriegy escapees who arrived there could not find the entrance and went tramping up and down the road looking for it. More and more kriegies arrived until there were a dozen or so walking up and down searching for the subway. It was a strange twist to the adventure. There were muffled curses and English voices asking where in the name of so-and-so the damned subway was. By the grace of God no Germans were around and the escapees had the scene to themselves as the search for the subway went on. At last, in desperation, Johnny Marshall and Wally Valenta decided to barge into the shed and see what was there. A couple of trains had come and gone and matters were getting serious. They walked into the shed, dimly saw another door down a flight of steps and were about to try it when the air-raid sirens went. They hesitated then and a few seconds later a German poked his head into the shed with a torch. He was a railway official.

'What are you doing here?' he said. (Valenta spoke German fluently so there was no language difficulty.) 'Don't you know the siren has gone and you must take shelter.'

The two kriegies mumbled something then brushed past out into the road again and away from the German. There was one train left that they could catch. It meant a dubious change of trains later on and in any case the train might be held up by the air raid. If the escape were discovered early, the train was bound to be searched. Was it worth waiting for?

'No!' said Valenta. 'Let's strike down on foot for Czechoslovakia. It's not so far and I can get help there.'

They turned back into the woods, heading for the road that ran south past the western boundary of the camp. Several other intending train travellers that night did the same thing because of that unfortunate camouflage over the subway. Had they been able to catch their trains, some might have got back to England, instead of getting a Gestapo bullet.

Chapter Thirty-Three

A RIFLE SHOT

Back in block 104 and the tunnel, matters were also going somewhat awry.

There had been a long and nerve-racking wait for the shaft at the other end to be opened up. In the hut, by the trap and in the first parts of the tunnel people did not know what was wrong. They just knew 'something' was wrong. It was due to be opened at about 8.45, but at 9.15 the workers had been down nearly forty minutes and still 'no joy'.

People in the block were restless and tensed. They played a couple of gramophones and tried to keep normal conversation going so that any Germans outside would not sense that anything unusual was happening. The hut was crowded with twice its normal complement, so movement was cut down to avoid too much noise. Strict orders were in force to prevent the slightest veiled reference to the night's activities in case of eavesdropping Germans and it was practically impossible to talk of anything else.

The block corridor was kept fairly empty and stooges were fairly plastered around the block to give warning of any approaching Germans. The rooms were strange sights. Instead of scruffy kriegies lolling about in them there was a queer collection of beings. There were well-dressed civilians, poor working men, a few sinister thugs in makeshift 'civvies' who in trying to disguise themselves had managed to make themselves look like the most suspicious of criminals. Others again were in barely camouflaged R.A.F. uniform, trusting to keep out of sight by travelling at night through woods.

One or two were in German uniform, as Davison found out when he left his post at the trapdoor for a moment to go into the room next door with a message. He opened the door and jumped with shock.

Sitting facing him was a German Obergefreiter (lance-corporal) in Luftwaffe uniform. Davy thought for a horrible moment that the game was up and felt sickening dismay. Then he saw it was Tobolski, the Pole, who was going out that night with Wing-Commander Day.

Just after 9.30 the tense and anxious controllers standing around the trap felt a sudden blast of cold air come shooting up out of it. It could only mean one thing. They had broken through, and there was a faint muffled cheer. The news flashed round. A little of the anxiety lifted from everyone's mind but a lot of the tension remained. Everyone realized they weren't going on any picnic. The coming trek across snowy hostile country was going to be tough and call for every ounce of endurance and guts. Most would almost certainly be caught, there would probably be a few S.S. and Gestapo beatings and a term in a wretched Nazi dungeon after that.

A few minutes later, Crump, who was now controlling at the base of the shaft, signalled Davy to send the next man down. The exodus had started.

It was all done systematically according to plans designed to provide against any conceivable hitch. At a table in the block corridor, Squadron-Leader David Torrens sat with a list of names in order of projected departure. Against each name was the room to which the person had been allotted while waiting in the block and as a man's turn to go approached, a runner called him from his room. He muttered a brief farewell to the other people still waiting, struggled into his kit and went out to join the little queue of about half a dozen waiting outside the door of room 23 where the trapdoor was situated.

As Crump called from the bottom of the shaft for the next man, Davison, at the trapdoor with another list, called out the next name and gave him the stock patter designed to eliminate 'flap'.

'Sit on the edge of the trap, feel the ledge a foot below with your feet. Stand your right foot in the far corner, feel the top rung of the ladder with your left foot. Let it take your weight, the ladder is strong. Turn your body round and down you go.'

So they reached the bottom of the shaft where Crump helped them to lie on their bellies on the trolly, told them how to hold their kit, signalled the hauler in 'Piccadilly' half-way house and away they went.

A shuttle service was kept up so that all half-way houses had a man waiting in them to go on the next stage. When a kriegy crawled out of the exit shaft, the hauler at that end signalled back to 'Leicester Square' where there was a hauler and also another waiting escaper who had already pulled back the trolley from the far half-way house. The waiting man climbed on, gave a sharp answering tug and the hauler at the far end pulled him up to the end of the tunnel.

Meanwhile, the hauler in 'Leicester Square' signalled down to 'Piccadilly' for the next man up, eventually got his tug signal back and hauled the trolley and man up to 'Leicester Square'. The hauler in 'Piccadilly' signalled back to the starting shaft and when he got his signal in return, hauled the next man up to 'Piccadilly'. As a man reached a half-way house, he crawled off the trolley, squeezed past the hauler and himself pulled the next trolley back from the next half-way house.

All the haulers had been experienced tunnel workers so that if anything went wrong underground they could take care of it. All of them were due to go out so they worked in shifts.

After each hauler had pulled ten people past him, the eleventh, twelfth and thirteenth men successively took over the ropes in the half-way houses while the old haulers continued on down the tunnel and out. The controller outside the hole behind the little ferret fence looked after the exit of twenty men and then the twenty-first man took over from him, and so on.

Shortly after 10 p.m. a German guard came round as usual and locked and barred the doors of all the huts, including of course, block 104. He never bothered to look into huts during this duty but the kriegies breathed a sigh of relief all the same when he had passed on his way.

It soon became fairly clear that operations were going to be considerably slower than was hoped for. Barring hitches of any kind Roger Bushell had aimed at getting a man out every two or three minutes, but the first hour settled any hopes of evacuation at that speed. For a start, the first thirty-seven people on the list were all train travellers and all carried attaché cases or larger suit-cases. Nearly all of them found a lot of trouble in handling these cases while they lay on the trolley, which was not designed for passenger and luggage transport in the first place.

The pace dropped right down and the average became more like a man every five or six minutes. People became stuck and had to be eased through—very gently indeed because any sharp knock or strain against the side of the tunnel was liable to bring out a box frame and cause a disastrous fall of sand.

Occasionally there was a clear run and half a dozen kriegies would shoot through in about ten or twelve minutes; then someone else would become stuck and there would be a long hold-up. These long delays were nerve-racking affairs. Most of the times the people up on top by the shaft and in the block did not know what the trouble was and the tension of waiting became almost unbearable. Kriegies chewed their nails, shuffled their feet and talked in jerky nervous whispers. They just couldn't help fidgeting. To keep still and quiet was impossible.

The tension was so great that even experienced tunnel workers who had ridden up and down on the trollies scores of times found they were fumbling and getting themselves tangled up in half a dozen ways. The worst part was the constant derailing of the trollies. Whenever that happened, space was so cramped in the tunnel that the men on the trolley could do nothing about putting it back on the rails. The hauler in the half-way house would feel the rope tighten and then became too hard to pull. After diagnosing the trouble he had to crawl down the tunnel and get the traveller on the trolley to take his weight on his hands, then the hauler had to fit the flanged trolley wheels back on the rails and painfully crawl backwards to return to his half-way house.

Time and again, the men carrying cases lost control of them as they were being hauled and sometimes the haulers had to crawl down to them, fix the case once more in their arms which they held out in front of them and then get back to the half-way house to haul them forward.

About 11.45 p.m. the sirens suddenly sounded and out went the lights everywhere, including, of course, the lights in the tunnel. It was a disaster of the first order. Down below, everything was in complete and utter blackness and the difficulties they were contending with became completely impossible. Everything stopped at once but the contingency had been envisaged and provided for. Fat lamps kept in the block and down the shaft were immediately brought out and lit and then they had to be passed by stages along the tunnel to the half-way houses.

While this was being done, the men in the tunnel had a really unpleasant time. The confinement, the stuffiness and discomfort, combined with complete ignorance of what was going on in utter darkness and the fear of moving for fear of causing a fall gave them an agonizing wait and the tension was rising towards snapping point.

Not until half an hour had passed were the lamps in position in the tunnel for operations to proceed. They could only be put in the half-way houses, which meant there was practically no light in the tunnel itself. In the half-way houses the light was adequate but no more and it did not help to make the work any faster.

Up in the block the time had come for camp 'lights out' at about midnight, and the prearranged 'lights out' procedure was followed. Blankets were laid over the floor of the corridor to deaden sound and also over the floor of the trapdoor room, No. 23.

Three heavy lockers were hauled across to cover the view of the trapdoor from the windows and then all black-out shutters round the block were opened as they always were after midnight. So that ferrets or guards passing by the block would not see an extraordinary number of people packed into the rooms, those on the first half of the list left the rooms and sat or lay on the blankets in the corridor. There were nearly a hundred of them. The remainder of the people who stayed in the rooms got into the bunks so that nothing would appear unusual. Batches of stooges were posted at various windows to give warning when any guard should approach, particularly the guard who always patrolled the compound at night with the big Alsatian dog. He was known as the 'hundfuehrer' (dog leader).

Then, far away, we heard the bombs start to fall. The sirens had heralded a raid on Berlin which was over a hundred miles away, but when the R.A.F. 'heavies' plastered it the tremendous explosions were enough to rattle the huts at Sagan. Usually it was music in our ears but on this night the raid was not heard with particular joy. It was a rather unfortunate coincidence as there had been no major raid on Berlin for several weeks. As it was it hindered operations and also held up trains which may have been responsible for several of the train travellers not getting sufficiently far enough away before the alarm was sounded and trains searched.

Most of the people who were late on the list to leave had realized by this time that they had little chance of getting out before dawn when operations would have to cease. Already the exodus was well behind schedule.

As soon as the margarine lamps were in position, escapers started to move through the tunnel again. The suit-case men were still going through and still having trouble. Between 'Piccadilly' and 'Leicester Square', Tom Kirby-Green, who had been squadron-leader in an R.A.F. Czech squadron, was stuck. He was a huge bloke, about fifteen stone and over six feet, with shoulders like an ox. He tried to squeeze himself gently through, then unluckily knocked a box frame, dislodged it and the first bad fall occurred. For about four feet the roof gave way and sand came cascading into the tunnel. It was a nasty moment. In three seconds Tom was practically buried under the sand that flooded out and very effectively blocked the tunnel. Then the sand stopped falling and there was a dome nearly three feet high over the roof. Tom luckily had his head just clear of the sand so he could breathe, but his hefty body was buried.

Henry Birkland, who was hauling in 'Leicester Square', immediately guessed what had happened and crawled down the tunnel to the accident. He slowly pulled Tom clear and Tom crawled over him up to the half-way house while Birkland set about the trying job of patching up the tunnel. He worked like a frenzied beaver with sweat pouring off him, refitting the box frames and one side of the roof boards, packing sand up to fill in the dome and then putting in the rest of the boards and packing them tight. It was three-quarters of an hour before he had finished and operations could proceed again.

The next man to stick was the 'Dodger', game old Army major with the last war D.S.O. and M.C. who had always been for some unknown reason with the Air Force prisoners and had already escaped several times. He was swaddled in so much clothing and kit that he was like a cocoon and too bulky for the tunnel. He stripped some of it off before he went down but still had trouble in getting through. Luckily no fall occurred.

'Pop' Green was another who had to strip off some of his bulky clothes and had bother in negotiating the tunnel. Like the 'Dodger' he was a last war veteran with the M.C., and when this war came along he wangled his way into the R.A.F. as an air-gunner, though he was well into his fifties. Tom Kirby-Green, the 'Dodger' and 'Pop' Green were among a party of fifteen travelling as workmen by train towards Hirschberg and then into Czechoslovakia.

When all the train and suit-case men had gone, the pace became a little quicker. The 'hard-tailers' carried only a blanket, folded according to instructions and tied on the chest, and they had a little less bother with the tunnel, though there was still some difficulty. By this time men had been going through for nearly four hours and only about three hours were left till dawn. Less than a quarter of the 220 prospective escapers had passed through and it looked as though the hundred mark would not be reached.

About 2 a.m. the electric lights suddenly came on again, though the air raid had long since ended and the 'all clear' sounded. The men in the tunnel heaved a long sigh of relief. Stinking fat lamps were put out and placed on one side and operations became easier and less unpleasant.

Now that the 'hard-tailers' were going through the system outside the hole was slightly different. At the far end of the rope leading into the wood, men waited until a party of ten had assembled, one of whom had been particularly briefed on leading the party through the wood, round the side of the camp and on to a little road leading south towards Czechoslovakia.

The number out was around the fifty mark when the second bad fall occurred. 'Cookie' Long was being hauled on the first stage and was within twenty feet of 'Piccadilly' when he became stuck. Bob Nelson, who was hauling in the half-way house, tried to pull him gently through but a box frame suddenly came away and 'Cookie' was practically buried under a flood of sand. He dragged himself off the trolley and crawled up to 'Piccadilly' and Nelson crawled down to the fall and set about patching it up. He, too, worked like a beaver, but it meant another valuable half-hour wasted.

There were a couple more incidents about that time; two more kriegies were stuck and once the hauling-rope broke, so after the fifty-seventh man had gone, the controllers upstairs in the block felt they had to take drastic steps. They ordained that from then on all blankets would have to be left behind. Escapers could take their great-coats, but no more. It was a desperate expedient to speed up operations and it worked. There was little more trouble in the tunnel and men began to go through fairly swiftly.

Just before 4 a.m., No. 60 went through. He was 'Lang' Langlois (never called anything but 'Lang') and he relieved the outside con-troller behind the little ferret fence. Lang duly brought two men out of the exit and then guards started to tramp along the road, only about seven or eight yards from the hole. They tramped past in ones and twos but did not seem to have anything on their minds, and Lang realized that it was guard changing. This meant another hold-up. For the next twenty minutes guards were continually strolling back along the roadway after having been relieved and Lang got only about two people out in that time. Then the flow of sentries ceased and again the exodus quickened.

About 4.30 a.m. the worst moment of all occurred. The German sentry in the sentry tower about fifteen yards away from the hole suddenly called out to one of the sentries who were patrolling up and down the wire. The patroller climbed up into the tower and the search-light sentry came down and turned straight across the road towards the hole.

Lang nearly had heart failure. The German kept coming straight

300

towards him, seemed to reach the hole and then casually turned away as though he wasn't worried about it. A bare four feet from the gaping black opening in the white snow the sentry busied himself with the functions of nature. The exit was just to his side and he took absolutely no notice of it. Lang, who was a bare ten feet away, burrowed down behind the ferret fence. He could hardly believe his eyes but it was a fact that the German *did not see the opening.*

He must have been blind—possibly his eyes were affected by the searchlight he had been operating. A broad black trail led away from the hole where kriegies had crawled out and away, and out of the hole itself Lang could see, against the glare of the searchlight, a thick column of steam rising from the damp earth, a peculiarity of all newly-opened tunnels.

For five minutes the guard was there within four feet of the exit; then he casually strolled back to the sentry tower and the patroller who had taken his place up there came down and resumed his monotonous walk. Lang breathed again for the first time in five minutes.

Back in block 104, the number passed down was nearing the eighty mark. They were going through fairly well now and there seemed to be fewer hitches. Crump came up from the shaft to keep an eye on the light outside.

About five minutes to five he thought he noticed the snow outside the windows getting a little lighter. He called Davy across who said he thought it was getting lighter too. It was time to pack up.

'Get the next three down,' said Crump. 'Then we finish. If we can get 'em all out of the way without being found, the Huns won't know a thing till appel and the boys will have an extra four hours before the hunt is on.'

So the last three went down—Michael Ormond, tough New Zealander who made a most attractive 'popsy' on the stage of the camp theatre, 'Muckle' Muir and Tim Newman.

Newman was just vanishing up the tunnel on the trolley when a rifle shot cracked crisply across the snow. It came from outside the wire in the direction of the tunnel mouth.

Chapter Thirty-Four

'THE KOMMANDANT IS VERY CROSS'

Just before ten minutes to five, a tall hefty air-gunner called Reavell Carter climbed out of the hole, went crawling past Lang behind the ferret fence and followed the rope on into the wood till he came to the rendezvous tree where the rope was tied. He was to lead the next party of ten through the wood to the road leading south away from the camp.

A couple of minutes later, 'Oggy' Ogilvie, a Canadian, emerged in answer to Lang's 'all clear' tug and went crawling on up to the tree. Next was Mick Shand, tough, amiable New Zealand Spitfire pilot. Len Trent,[1] the next man, had just crawled out of the hole when the German sentry who had been patrolling along the eastern part of the wire hove in sight again.

This time, for some unknown reason, the sentry was walking on the near side of the road along the edge of the wood. If he kept going he must walk across the hole.

Lang saw him coming and went even colder than his long vigil in the snow had made him. He gave two sharp tugs on both ropes. Mick Shand, half-way to the tree behind Lang, and Len, just outside the hole and directly in the path of the oncoming German, froze where they were and didn't move a muscle. The German kept steadily on. He was ten yards away and Lang, watching him, felt that his eyes were sticking out like organ stops. The German was seven, six, five yards away and still he came on and still he hadn't noticed anything. He seemed to be half asleep—left, right, left and then he put a boot down within a foot

[1] Squadron-Leader Len Trent, V.C., D.F.C. He got his V.C. for more or less suicidal determination on the trip when he was shot down and captured —a very sticky affair when his whole Ventura squadron was wiped out.

302

of the edge of the hole and *still didn't see it*, and his next foot just missed by a couple of inches treading on Len lying doggo and quaking by the hole. *Still the sentry didn't see him*. It was unbelievable.

He took another pace—and then came out of his coma. He must have noticed the broad black track through the snow made by the bodies as they crawled up to the tree. With a muttered exclamation he swung round towards it and in the same moment shrugged his rifle off his shoulder and into his hands at the 'ready'. Then he must have seen Mick Shand lying on the track. He lifted his rifle, was about to fire, when Reavell Carter, who could dimly see the drama from the tree, took swift action. He leapt up into sight and waved his arms.

'*Nicht schiessen, Posten!*' he bawled. '*Nicht schiessen!*' ('Don't shoot, sentry! Don't shoot!')

His sudden appearance out of nowhere gave the German the shock of his life. He jerked his rifle upwards and fired. The bullet went wild, but things suddenly happened in all directions.

Mick Shand bounced up from where he lay on the track and made a crouching dash for freedom, dodging in and out of the pine trees. 'Oggy' Ogilvie jumped up from behind the far tree where he had been burrowing into the snow and did the same thing, tossing away excess kit as he ran.

Reavell Carter came forward—there was nothing else he could do—and then, right beside the guard and still unseen, Len slowly and sheepishly got to his feet. The guard saw him, jumped about a foot in the air and then stood still, staggered with shock. He was a rather bovine peasant type and he was completely speechless.

A second later, Lang—with no option—also stood up behind the ferret fence about ten feet away. The guard saw him and shook his head unbelievingly, and then he saw the hole in the ground, right at his feet, and his mouth opened and shut like a fish.

For about three comically wretched seconds he stood stock still, and then he recovered. He whipped out a torch and shone it down the hole. There just below the surface, hanging on to the ladder, was Bob McBride, who was to be next man out—the eightieth.

The sentry fished up a whistle and blew it shrilly then pointed his rifle at McBride and beckoned him up out of the shaft. He crawled sheepishly out and the sentry covered the four of them with his rifle—Lang, Reavell Carter, Len, and McBride. Hoarse, unintelligible sounds were bubbling out of his throat like porridge on the boil heard through an amplifier.

The sentry in the nearby tower was heard frenziedly telephoning the German guardroom, and then along the road from the guardroom by the compound gate a couple of hundred yards away a horde of German guards came running. The sentry by the group of four yelled to them and they fanned out into the woods. The first sentry prodded his rifle at the four and beckoned them to get going along the road to the guardroom. They turned, and with hands in the air, trudged off.

*   *   *

Back in block 104 a sudden hush had followed the shot. Around the trap in room 23 there was a tense silence of about three seconds. The three or four people in the room looked at each other, startled. The silence was broken. Someone said quietly:

'That appears to be a shot.'

'That was indeed a shot,' said someone else.

'Damn!' said Crump. 'Someone's got it. I'll get the blokes back from down the tunnel.'

'Right. I'll burn these lists,' said Davison and dashed off to get a fire going in the block kitchen.

Crump clambered down the shaft in nervous haste, knowing that the people in the tunnel probably had not heard the shot and would still be travelling through.

He was about seventy-five per cent right. Most of the people down below hadn't heard the shot and didn't know anything had happened, but in the far half-way house at the base of the outward shaft, Squadron-Leader Denys Maw, No. 81, had been just about to follow Bob McBride up to the exit hole when right above his head and echoing down the shaft came the shattering crack of the rifle. One awful thought flashed straightaway through his mind.

'The B——s! They've known all along and they're plugging each bloke as he crawls out.'

Then he realized that couldn't be so or they'd have heard it before. He realized the hole had just been found and he turned back into the half-way house where two other people, the hauler and the next man out, had reached the same conclusion.

'Let's get back out of here,' Maw said and the other two needed no persuading. One man lay on the trolley and propelled himself back to 'Leicester Square' and then the trolley was hauled back to the end half-way house. The next man propelled himself back to 'Leicester Square'

304

and Maw then hauled the trolley back and set off himself on the return journey.

So the trolley shuttle service was reversed as the escapers started to scurry like moles back towards the compound. For a few minutes, however, the people in the first section of the tunnel still didn't know the 'flap' was on. They did not find out till the people started to scuttle back from the exit end, and meanwhile, Crump, at the base of the shaft, was trying to inform them.

Peering up the tunnel, Crump could just see the trolley up by 'Piccadilly' half-way house with a bulky shape lying on it. He howled, 'Come back! We've been spotted! Pass the word along.' His voice was blurred and muffled in the long narrow space and the man on the trolley couldn't make out what he was saying. A vague muffled shout came back to Crump in reply.

'Come back! Come back!' Crump howled again. 'It's all up. The tunnel's been found.'

Again the muffled, indistinguishable answer. A shouting match developed and neither man could make out what the other was saying. Crump grabbed the trolley rope and tried to haul it back with the other man still on it, but the man on the trolley wasn't having any. He was on his way and he wasn't coming back for anyone. He grabbed hold of the rails and held the trolley firmly. Crump shouted again and hauled back more strongly. He heaved and heaved and then the rope suddenly snapped.

Crump realized there was no point in crawling up the tunnel after him. People at the far end would soon find out the game was up and come pouring back. If he crawled up the tunnel he might only cause further congestion. He clambered back up the shaft to see what was happening up above. He found the block in a mild uproar of destruction. Fires were going in the kitchen and various rooms. People were burning forged papers and maps, crushing compasses, stripping off civilian clothes and generally destroying or hiding the evidence of their escape intentions.

From the trapdoor then, Crump heard the sound of a trolley returning along the tunnel. He peered over and looked down. Tim Newman's head appeared out of the tunnel at the base of the shaft. He scrambled out and came clambering up the shaft ladder.

'We've been spotted,' he said. 'I think ferrets are coming down the tunnel from the other end. There's someone just behind me.'

There were more sounds in the tunnel and Muckle Muir's head appeared. He too came clambering up the shaft.

'It's all up,' he gasped. 'They've found the hole and I think ferrets are coming down. There's someone just behind me.'

More sounds in the tunnel. Mike Ormond appeared and came breathlessly up the shaft.

'They've found us,' he said. 'I think ferrets are coming along.'

One by one people appeared from below, panting, sweating, and excited after their pell-mell return. They all had the same story, and as the last few came climbing up the shaft each one burst out excitedly:

'Look out! There's a ferret just behind me!'

Each time it was only another kriegy, but things were getting rather exciting.

The last three back were 'Red' Noble, flaming-haired Canadian who had been hauling in 'Piccadilly', Denys Maw and 'Shag' Rees, nuggety, tough Welshman who had been hauling in 'Leicester Square'. Shag had had a nasty moment. When he heard Denys Maw, the last man, returning from the far end, Shag did not know whether it was a kriegy or a ferret. He took the light bulb out of its socket in his half-way house and squeezed himself against the wall. Unable to stand the tension any longer he called out: 'Who's that?'

Maw answered reassuringly and said he was the last man. Back they both scuttled along the tunnel, Shag expecting a bullet from behind at any moment.

When they emerged at the top, the trapdoor was closed down and the stove moved back over it. Everyone set to work to clean up all traces of the operations. All blankets were taken up and tossed on beds, lockers that had shielded the trap were moved back, and all over the block kriegies were burning, hiding and destroying their papers, money, compasses, maps, 'civvy' clothes and all escape paraphernalia. Though it was still camp lock-up time a few leaped out of windows and dashed back to their blocks, risking bullets from the sentry towers and patrolling guards. They found their beds occupied by people who normally lived in block 104 and had been moved out for the night of the escape.

Smoke from little piles of burning equipment was issuing from nearly every window in block 104 about 5.30 a.m. when the door of the block was unbarred and in walked the 'hundfuehrer' with pistol drawn and his Alsatian dog. The 'hundfuehrer' was distinctly bewildered and rather scared. He hadn't the faintest idea of what to do. The circumstances were not provided for in the German book of rules.

For a couple of minutes he wandered disconsolately up and down the corridor and eventually told everyone to go back to their rooms. They did so cheerfully and all the 'hundfuehrer' could think of to do next was to take all the coats hanging in the corridor, pile them in a heap and sit his dog on them.

About this time, Crump, in room 23, heard a faint scratching and scuffling under the trapdoor. The ferrets had arrived. As they had found their own way there, Crump decided to let them find their own way out again.

Now that the show was over the main tension had relaxed and kriegies who had not been able to get out of the tunnel—there were about 140 of them—sat around in the rooms talking and laughing and generally letting off pent-up steam after the excitement of the night.

Meanwhile, in the German guardroom near the gate, the four kriegies who were caught at the tunnel mouth, Lang, Len, Reavell Carter, and McBride, were getting a 'strip' from the Kommandant. Poor Kommandant. This was going to break him and he knew it. He was purple in the face from passion and practically uncontrollable. Little flecks of foam flew off his lips as he screamed at them in a mixture of German and English. He was so incoherent with rage that they could make out only a little of what he was saying.

'So you do not like my camp!' the Kommandant mouthed at them in one of his more coherent passages. 'You do not like my camp! So! I will give you to the Gestapo and they will shoot you! I will give you all to the Gestapo! They will get rid of the whole lot!'

And so on and so on. The captured four kept straight faces, which was probably just as well as the Kommandant was definitely in a shooting mood.

Shortly after six o'clock, hordes of Germans descended on the compound; a long column of about seventy of them with coal scuttle helmets, tommy-guns, mounted machine-guns and general equipment possessed by the normal riot squad. A large gaggle of ferrets came in and then a clump of German officers.

The guards fanned out over the compound closing all the shutters round every window in every block. Others formed a ring around block 104 and two or three squads set up machine-guns on tripods covering the block doors. The affair was beginning to look rather too businesslike. A couple of ferrets clumped into the block yelling '*Aus!*

Aus! Efferybody aus!' ('Everybody out!')—the traditional cry of the prison camp guard.

The 140-odd kriegies left in the block began to shuffle out of the doors into the snow, half expecting the machine-guns to open up and mow them down as they emerged. A menacing reception committee awaited them—ferrets, guards, and tommy-guns. About a dozen ferrets were the first people to greet them. As each man emerged, a ferret grabbed him and made a thorough search on the spot. Each man had to strip in the snow, boots and all, while every article of his clothing was minutely inspected.

Anything that looked as though it could possibly be an escape aid was promptly confiscated, and what was worse, any article of clothing that had been even slightly modified to look like civilian wear was also tossed aside on a pile. Some of the kriegies were deprived of their pants and coats and were left standing up in their underpants. The position began to have its slightly funny side, but it wasn't so funny that people felt like laughing. If they had felt so it would have been distinctly unwise to do so. There was a considerable amount of uncertainty as to what was going to happen but from the look on the Germans' faces it was not going to be pleasant.

The search was taking a long time and while it was still going on, the German adjutant, Major Simoleit, short, dark, and bandy like a little brown ape, but always ten times as spruce in an immaculate uniform, bounced into the compound and went haring along to the room of burly Bill Jennens,[1] who was our own compound adjutant. He roused Bill out of bed. Flapping like an agitated hen, Simoleit implored him to get dressed, hurry and 'komm'. Unteroffizier Pfelz was down the tunnel and couldn't get out. He would die. He would suffocate. Herr Major Jennens was to come at once and get him out. (Charlie Pfelz was not a bad type, as ferrets went, and was the only ferret who ever had the nerve to go down a kriegy tunnel.)

Squadron-Leader Jennens, big, red-faced and tough, was not exactly popular with the Germans. He shouted and banged his fist at them too much. It was quite amazing what he got away with but it is a literal fact that he had the German staff completely bluffed. He demanded of Simoleit what the hell Charlie Pfelz thought he was doing down the tunnel and then bluntly told him what he thought of him for bursting into his room so early in the morning. Finally, he said he would come.

[1] He got an O.B.E for the way he bluffed Germans into frightened respect.

Simoleit took it like a lamb—there wasn't much option with Bill Jennens. The German was hopping up and down in his agitation. Would Herr Jennens be good enough to hurry? Unteroffizier Pfelz might be suffocating!

Bill leisurely dressed and leisurely followed Simoleit down to block 104 where a couple of ferrets were frenziedly trying to find the trapdoor. No one would tell them where it was. They said they didn't know. Jennens collected 'Red' Noble and they went along to room 23 and opened the trap. Down below at the bottom of the shaft a relieved Unteroffizier Pfelz blinked up at them and scrambled up the ladder.

Outside the block, complications had set in. The Kommandant had arrived. He was purple in the face as he stalked up to the Germans and kriegies by the hut in an awful silence. All the Germans stiffened to attention. There was a quickfire succession of salutes and a rattle of boot-clicking as they paid homage. They all immediately became noticeably tougher and more industrious. All the ferrets drew their pistols and became considerably more officious.

Almost immediately there were a couple of minor incidents that almost ended in shooting. 'Rubberneck', the arch-ferret, was in a shocking mood and his red face was redder than ever and rather splotchy. He was immediately responsible for anti-escape measures in the compound and this was the saddest smack in the eye the ferrets had ever had. 'Rubberneck' knew he was going to get it right in that long neck of his and was not happy. When he saw 'Red' Noble and 'Shag' Rees he bristled. They were practically his personal enemies and he had had trouble with both of them before (so had nearly every other ferret). At least a couple of times each he had sent them to the cooler.

He made a beeline for them as they were being searched, grabbed their coats as they were trying to take them off and generally pushed them about. Both 'Red' and 'Shag' wrenched themselves away and turned defiantly out of his reach. A guard swung his rifle down and raised it at them. 'Rubberneck' held his pistol ready and for a moment the incident was on the verge of ending with a couple of shots. The moment of tension passed and 'Red' and 'Shag' slowly stripped in peace. The guard took their trousers and slung them aside, leaving them to stand in their underpants.

The Kommandant had watched the incident and his face became a shade richer in colour.

'Cooler,' he said. (It was funny how even the Kommandant used that word.) Not long after, 'Red' and 'Shag' were duly removed to the cooler.

At last the search was finished and the kriegies were left standing in the snow, lined up in threes under heavy guard. The Kommandant still remained with his ire no whit abated. Standing still in the snow the would-be escapers began to feel decidedly cold and those who had lost coat and trousers were shivering. There wasn't much humour left in the situation until a fair-haired former Spitfire pilot from Kenya with a reputation for playfulness on appel began to make funny mocking noises in his throat.

The Kommandant saw and heard him.

'Cooler!' he said tersely, with a face like thunder, and Johnny was duly marched off.

At that, a young London bomb-aimer, not long out of school, couldn't hide a grin, and the Kommandant saw him too.

'Cooler!' he said again with the same black look, and Horace was marched off to the cells.

The Kommandant spoke to a few kriegies near him.

'If there are any disturbances here, I will personally shoot two British officers.'

There wasn't much doubt that he would do it, so for the rest of the time the kriegies stood patiently and discreetly. Every ferret now had his pistol in his hand and the machine-guns and tommy-guns were constantly trained on them. A complete photographic identity check was made of them all and after that they just stood there and shivered while a photographic check was made in every block of the compound to discover who was missing.

After about two hours, the group of would-be escapers by block 104 was marched over to the compound gate and there they stood again in the snow. It looked as though the Germans didn't quite know what to do with them. Undoubtedly they wanted to put them all into the cooler, but there just wasn't room.

Hauptmann Pieber, the German compound officer, at last spoke to them. Pieber was a queer type; one of the earliest Nazi Party members (though an Austrian) and with a face covered in duelling scars, he was nevertheless a most innocuous man. He was always meek and mild as a church mouse and almost ingratiatingly polite. Most people said he was a complete hypocrite but that may be unjust, though by this time he was consistently telling us (in confidence) that the Nazi Party was not what he had expected it to be. (That, however, was a common German practice when the end became obvious.)

At any rate, Pieber went up to the kriegies by the gate and, blinking meekly through his thick-lensed glasses, said:

'Ah, shentlemen, shentlemen! You should not do this. It only makes trouble. The Kommandant is very cross; very angry indeed. I do not know what he will do with you! Ah, I would not like to be in the Kommandant's shoes.'

And shaking a disapproving head, Pieber wandered dolefully away.

Half an hour later, the Germans had made their decision. They decided they couldn't do anything with the people they had found in block 104 so they let them return to their blocks, where the rest of the camp was waiting, bursting with impatience, to hear all about the night's events.

Chapter Thirty-Five

GESTAPO HEADQUARTERS

W hile all the flap was going on in the camp, most of the people who had got out of the tunnel during the night were making good headway on their journeys. This brisk progress did not last, because in a matter of hours the whole countryside was roused and out searching for them in what was one of the biggest man hunts in Germany throughout the war.

The German radio warned all civilians, and in addition masses of troops and auxiliaries were out on the job. For a hundred miles around the camp the country was literally thick with Germans of every description, searching and watching for the escapees. Trains were searched, all kinds of vehicles examined, roads were patrolled, houses, hotels, and farms investigated. On the job were thousands of men from the S.S., Gestapo, the Army, Luftwaffe, and various branches of the numerous German police systems. Out from their homes for miles around came decrepit old men of the Landwacht and Landwehr (a sort of Home Guard) to patrol the area night and day. Far away in ports like Stettin and Danzig the Kriegsmarine (Navy) was called into the hunt, together of course with the inevitable S.S. and Gestapo, to prevent any escapees slipping across to Sweden on the ferries.

After the first few hours of the escape then, the hue and cry was fairly on and the boys who were out had the searchers as well as the snow and slush to contend with. The only way to cover their activities is to give a few typical stories of experiences.

Little was ever discovered in the camp of the progress of most of the train travellers, as only three of them ever came back to us. There was a large party travelling third-class as workmen who caught their train and went down through Breslau and on to Hirschberg, near the Czech border, where they were caught. Two of that party eventually came back to the camp, one of them being 'Pop' Green, game old last war veteran.

Paul Royle, a tall slim Australian, with an R.A.F. short-service commission, and 'Hunk' Humphries, who had been years in the R.A.F., were No. 54 and 55 out of the tunnel. Both had been prisoners since 1940 and were more than somewhat keen to get back. They came up out of the hole about 3.45 a.m., sweaty and shaking with nerves, and crawled along the rope to the end by the tree where they waited till about ten people had arrived. They were led away then by the leader who had been briefed on the route, passing between a bomb dump and a camp of Jewish prisoners, then on past a nearby French compound, across a road that led to it and along a few hundred yards to a railway line that led south. They turned south and followed this for nearly a mile, and then one by one the twos and threes who had decided to travel together dropped out. Paul and 'Hunk' sat down, rearranged their kit and struck off in a south-easterly direction till they came to some woods in which firebreaks had been cut. They walked along the firebreaks where the going was fairly easy. Snow was still about six inches deep there but it was fairly dry. They were aiming to reach and cross the Berlin-Breslau autobahn which ran roughly east-west about twelve miles south of Stalag Luft III.

Several times they had nasty shocks when they heard loud and menacing barking near them. They thought they were being trailed by dogs till they remembered being told on the briefing lectures a few days before that they would find plenty of deer in the woods that barked just like dogs and invariably frightened the life out of all kriegies who escaped and travelled through those parts.

At dawn they had not reached the autobahn but came to a wood of young trees about twelve feet high, found a ditch, and prepared to spend the day there. (There must have been a couple of dozen kriegies hiding up in that young wood that day.) Paul and 'Hunk' had brought a little fat lamp heater to heat water from their water-bottles for a brew, but it wouldn't burn properly so they gave it up and tried to sleep. The sleep wasn't very successful either. Each managed to sleep for barely an hour during the day. They still felt lively and awake, but were very cold.

At dusk they pushed off again and came out into open country. For a time they tried to walk across the fields but the snow was slightly thawed and the going was too slushy, so, rather unwillingly, they turned on to a small road leading south. The policy of nearly all kriegies was to leave roads severely alone as far as possible, particularly after the first night, because the Germans were bound to be watching the roads once the hue and cry started. The only person they saw was a man who came on to the road from a field and crossed to the fields on the other side. They were pretty sure he was a kriegy but took no chances and hid while he passed. A couple of hours later they came to the autobahn. For a time they watched it warily, expecting to see Germans lurking in wait, but there was no sign of life so they went a couple of hundred yards down the autobahn away from the crossroad and then quickly nipped across. They tried to strike off through fields again but it was slushier than ever and with soaking boots they returned once more to the little road leading south and warily walked along it. They passed through a little village and then another small hamlet.

A party of Germans was heard coming and they nipped off the road and hid while a group of men ambled past. They were half way through the next village when another party of Germans was heard and they took cover in a small haystack. Before they were out of that village a car was heard coming and they just had time to half-conceal themselves behind a pump. The headlights of the car played on their faces but it swept on past them.

A couple of miles further on they saw a man and girl coming towards them on bicycles and they dived and took cover under a small bridge that crossed the road at that point. They were just coming out again when the man and girl rode back again and once more they dived back under the bridge. Eventually they came out and walked on their way but about 200 yards further on suddenly saw three Germans in front of them. It was too late to hide or go back. They had to try and walk past and bluff it out. They tried it—and the three Germans suddenly closed around them. One had a rifle, one a shotgun and the other a pistol. The rifle and shotgun were prodded into their ribs with a few gruff and unintelligible German commands. There was quite obviously no future in the position so Paul and 'Hunk' raised their hands. Neither spoke German to any extent and as they were in barely disguised R.A.F. uniforms they knew there was no chance of bluffing their way any further. Their captors were so obviously waiting and expecting escaped prisoners. In the darkness, the two kriegies could just make out that the three Germans were rather senile members of the Landwehr in green uniforms. In the background were the man and girl on bicycles and it was fairly obvious they had warned the Landwehr veterans about them.

314

One of the Landwehr called and shortly a policeman appeared, and then a soldier.

The soldier was very friendly. The policeman and the Landwehr men were not, and waved them to march on down the road. The party walked on, Paul and 'Hunk' chatting with the soldier in broken German while the other four kept grimly silent.

'Don't worry about them,' said the soldier. 'They're not fighting soldiers like you and me. They don't count. We fighting men understand each other.' He couldn't have been more sympathetic.

After a couple of miles they came to a village with a small jail and Paul and 'Hunk' were thrust into a tiny cell about seven feet square. There was already a ragged little Polish boy of about twelve sleeping on a bunk there but the Germans told him to clear out. Paul and 'Hunk' sat down rather disconsolately, tired and disappointed. They were just considering the question of sleep when the cell door opened and in came Johnny Marshall, Wally Valenta, and 'Shorty' Armstrong.

Marshall and Valenta, among the first few out of the tunnel, had had to abandon their train programme and take to the road. They had been caught nearby in much the same circumstances as Paul and 'Hunk'. They, too, had found that they had to travel on the roads because of the slush and that once guards detected them they were so obviously looking for escaped prisoners that there was no chance of bluffing through.

The five in the cell, jammed in like sardines, had a unanimous rise in morale at finding company. It was warm in there in contrast to the bitter cold they had felt for the past couple of nights. They munched chocolate from their hard rations, yarned for a while and then slept, exhausted.

In the morning they looked out of the tiny cell window and saw an old Landwehr man on guard with an old carbine slung over his shoulder. The local Nazi Party chief was strutting up and down in a resplendent party uniform. A little later the cell door opened and about half a dozen S.S. stood in the doorway. They were blustering and menacing, pushed them out of the cell into a van, told them to keep quiet, not to move and not to smoke.

They were driven right back to Sagan along the road they had travelled. The van pulled up at Sagan civil gaol. They went through a courtyard and into small cells upstairs for a few hours and were then taken out for a fairly elementary interrogation which did not last long. During Johnny Marshall's interrogation the telephone rang in the little

315

office. He heard the guard who answered it repeat in German into the mouthpiece: 'Yes, yes. Six at Hirschberg, yes, and four at Danzig. Good.'

Johnny had no trouble guessing what it meant. He knew that four of the kriegies had planned to go by train to Danzig and then cross to Sweden by ferry. The mention of Hirschberg could only mean they had caught at least some of the party who were going third-class as foreign workmen down into Czechoslovakia by way of Hirschberg.

They were all taken then to a large, filthy cell downstairs where there were a few three-tier beds without blankets. The whole place smelt and was bug-ridden. Tired, hungry and not particularly cheerful, the five tried to sleep.

Not so very different was the experience of 'Oggy' Ogilvie, who was with Reavell Carter by the tree in the wood when the guard discovered the break. 'Oggy' ran for it into the wood, fell heels over head a couple of times, threw away a lot of his impedimenta and eventually found himself breathless on the road leading south. He found the firebreaks in the wood and headed along them. He came across several sets of footprints, guessed they belonged to kriegies and was considerably cheered. When it was completely light he branched deeper into the woods and made a nest in the snow with old leaves. He found he couldn't sleep so he ate some chocolate and just waited.

At nightfall he carried on. He was tired and very cold. Several times the deer, barking like dogs, gave him the fright of his life. Eventually he came to the autobahn, expected to see hordes of Germans but there were none there so he walked across and tried to get through the woods on the other side. He ran into slushy, almost swampy ground and had to turn back several times. Like the others, he eventually had to take to the road—a course that led to the downfall of nearly all the 'hardtailers'. He passed a couple of villages and once was accosted by an old man who fired some question in German at him. 'Oggy' knew a few German words but couldn't think of the right ones, so he just said 'Aw nuts!' and passed on.

He kept on going for some time and then another old man loomed out of the darkness on a bicycle and before 'Oggy' knew what was happening there was a pistol sticking in his ribs and the old man was telling him to walk on and no tricks. He escorted 'Oggy' to a nearby village, took him first to a hospital and then across to an inn, where he very gratefully relaxed in warmth, feeling he could sleep for about a week.

A few minutes later, Charles Hall and two other escapees walked in, escorted by three armed Germans. One of the kriegies was arguing in French with one of the Germans, obviously trying to bluff his way through, and 'Oggy' just had the presence of mind to look blandly at all three as though he'd never seen them in his life before.

The next couple of minutes were funny. The French-speaking kriegy was trying to pass himself off as a French worker returning home, but the German spoke considerably better French than he. The German was shooting questions at him and 'Oggy' felt he was going to burst out laughing as he saw the kriegy, whom he knew particularly well, slowly repeat each question and then frame a stumbling answer. At last he gave it up.

'O.K.,' he said. 'You know who we are.'

They did, and shortly a police car came and took all four back to Sagan jail where they were put through the same procedure as Marshall, Valenta, and the others, and were eventually taken down and turfed into the stinking big cell where they found quite a few of their friends. The cell now contained about a dozen kriegies.

Another kriegy to end up in that cell was Bob Nelson, rather good-looking English lad who was sixty-fifth man out of the tunnel. He reached the young pine wood just before the autobahn soon after dawn and made a bed from young pine branches. They made a terrific crack as he broke them off the trees and shortly after he heard a few similar cracks several hundred yards away. He guessed it was probably another kriegy, but thought it was not wise to investigate. (He found out some days later that it was 'Shorty' Armstrong, also making a bed for himself.)

Bob spent a cold and miserable day, part of which time it was snowing. At dusk he pushed on through thicker snow and came to the autobahn. It was so dark he thought the road was a canal, went down on his hands and knees and crawled up to it to put a hand in the water. He got a shock when he touched the road and then realized where he was. He crossed over and then, like the others, ran into trouble. There was snow and slush up to his knees, and patches were just like miniature lakes.

He kept making continuous detours but realized that he was thus making little headway south. In the early morning he came to a barn on the edge of a village. Sopping wet, he crawled up on to the straw and lay there all day. That night there was a blizzard but he made a sortie down to the village and had a drink and a wash from a pump that seemed to clank with a terrific noise. He went back to the barn and was going to spend the day there but in the afternoon the farmer and several civilians came in and searched the barn with hayforks.

They found Bob lying under the straw and the old farmer marched him off to the village of Halbau in front of the hayfork, where the burgomeister duly arrived with a car and flourishing a revolver. Bob was driven to Sagan jail, interrogated and then pushed into the same big noisome cell as the others.

All the kriegies' escape food had been taken from them and the jail guards did little to make up for the loss. Two thin slices of dry black bread was the daily ration and the prisoners were beginning to feel really hungry. They had been given no clue as to what was to happen to them but assumed that they would eventually be taken back to the camp for a spell in the cells and then be returned to the compound. Now and again the door of the cell opened and a couple more escapees came in to join the cheerless company. Nearly all had been picked up on the trek south where snow and slush conditions forced them on to the roads and into the hands of waiting patrols. A couple of hours after nightfall the number of recaptured people in the cell had reached nineteen. There was not much conversation. All of them were tired and hungry and suffering acute discomfort from the cold, as no blankets whatsoever were supplied.

About midnight there was a tramping of feet outside and the cell door swung open. In marched a collection of the nastiest thugs any of them had ever seen, shouting the familiar and hated '*Aus! Aus!*' They were Gestapo guards and they looked exactly like the Hollywood idea of typical gangsters. All of them were wearing heavy and rather flash overcoats, together with black felt hats pulled low over their eyes. Without exception they had vicious, villainous faces, with the odd scar here and there, and all of them were loaded down with tommy-guns.

They shepherded the nineteen outside into a large covered truck which shortly moved off. At first the kriegies thought they were going back to the camp which was only a few minutes' drive away, but the truck kept on going and they soon discarded that idea. The next theory was that they were being taken to another prison camp, but could get no information from the guards except grunts and ugly looks. They could not see outside the truck very well and it was dark anyway, so they just had to sit quietly. They travelled for nearly three hours until about 2.30 a.m., when a few people who could see out over the tailboard made out that they were running into a largish town. Dimly they saw cobbled streets in the darkness and a row of nondescript houses, and then the truck slowed and turned under a heavy, rather grim stone archway. A few yards further on it braked to a stop.

Within a few seconds the Gestapo guards had piled out and formed a rather sinister cordon round the lorry. There were more loud cries of '*Aus! Aus!*' and one by one the kriegies piled over the tailboard and dropped down. In the darkness they made out that they were in a cobbled courtyard surrounded on all four sides by gaunt stone walls about three stories high, pierced at regular intervals by a lot of little windows. Across the windows were iron bars! Evidently they were in a jail. Not so good!

Still menaced by Gestapo tommy-guns they were herded through a door and along gloomy stone corridors, up a couple of flights of stairs and then were pushed, four at a time, into tiny cells about six by nine feet. Three-quarters of the floor space in each cell was covered by a wooden platform about a foot high, which was supposed to be the communal cell bed. Exhausted and hungry, the fours in each cell crowded together for warmth on the 'bed' and slept.

They were all woken shortly after first light and presented with 'breakfast'—a thin slice of black bread and a cup of 'tea', ersatz and horrible, without milk or sugar. Spirits that morning were surprisingly high. They hadn't the faintest idea what was going to happen, but for the time being no one let the uncertainty perturb him.

In the morning light they inspected their new quarters. There wasn't much to see. Four bare stone walls of a dirty white, a concrete floor, a thick steel door and high up in the tremendously thick walls a small window, heavily barred. All the cells were the same. The kriegies all relaxed back on their wooden platforms and began to yarn about their experiences since the break. It was the first real chance they had had and in the lively accounts of their adventures, treated with universal lightheartedness, their spirits rose further and they passed an uneventful but decidedly hungry day.

For sanitary facilities they were allowed out of their cells to a room at the end of the corridor. Truth to tell there wasn't enough room left in the cells for the usual primitive bucket that German ideas on sanitation ordained. The long corridor outside the cells reminded Paul Royle of the interior of a submarine—it was narrow, dank and grey, with the forbidding steel doors inset at regular intervals. The only people they saw for a while were a few drab uniformed guards carrying bunches of enormous keys for the stout, old-fashioned locks on the cell doors. To a man they were distinctly unfriendly.

Later on, a doddering old German and a young Polish boy, a slave worker, only about fourteen years old, came round and perfunctorily cleaned out the cells. In several cells they tried to get the Polish boy to talk, but he seemed to speak little German and the only thing he said, with a frightened sidelong glance towards the corridor, was 'Deutschland kaput.'

Supper was brought round—a treat this time, two slices of black bread, and a small bowl of thin, watery soup. The kriegies felt they were feeding like kings, but still felt ravenously hungry after it. Most of them were still in fairly good spirits and the general conversation was still brisk, but in Paul Royle's cell, Wally Valenta, the Czech, was worried. Among the other prisoners, only Johnny Marshall knew that Valenta had done intelligence work some time previously before joining the R.A.F. As a former regular Czech officer, Valenta knew the German and Nazi methods only too well and would not be reassured as to the prisoners' subsequent well-being. The night was again uneventful, though most of them slept only fitfully.

The following day German guards several times entered various cells and took a prisoner out. None of them knew where or why they were being taken, and nerves were a little on edge.

Each one, as he was taken out, was escorted out of the gaol by a German guard into the town streets. They walked about half a mile to a grey stone building about four stories high near the centre of the town, which, they were told by their guards, was Görlitz, about forty miles south of Sagan and not far from the Czech border. What the kriegies did not know was that Görlitz was a Gestapo centre and the grey stone building was the Gestapo district headquarters.

When Paul Royle was taken out of his cell into the streets he thought it was one of the finest moments of his life. To be out in the open again after the uncertain close confinement of the cells was sheer exhilaration. It was the first time he had walked openly in a public place for four years and he took in the sights of normal life about in the streets with an almost pathetic zest.

At the Gestapo and police building he was taken up several flights of stairs into a comfortably furnished office where he had a surly reception from a villainous-looking German interpreter with a strong American accent. The only other occupant of the room was an elderly grey-haired man in civilian clothes sitting behind a large desk. Through the interpreter, Paul was asked a variety of fairly harmless questions. 'Where were you heading for?' 'What were your plans?' 'Where is all your equipment, your compass, and maps?' 'What sabotage directions did you receive?' 'What information were you to collect on the way?'

Paul answered simply and disarmingly. He laughingly denied any sabotage directions or any directions for collecting information. He just wanted to get home again. He had been four years behind the wire and he was fed up with it. Wouldn't the interrogator be fed up if he were in the same position?

As far as Paul could gather, the interrogator was not a Gestapo man but seemed to be some sort of civil police official. He did not seem particularly hostile, and after a while the interpreter said to the interrogator in German, 'This man is obviously all right.' Paul knew just enough German to understand the statement and began to feel fairly secure. The interview ended and he was escorted back to the jail, but this time was placed in a different cell. As every man came back from his interrogation he was returned to a different cell, where he found other kriegies whom he had not seen since the night of the break. Evidently the Germans had brought more of the escapees to Görlitz than the one truckload from Sagan.

This procedure went on for about four days. Kriegies were therefore being shuffled about from cell to cell all the time and everyone eventually met practically everyone else.

Johnny Marshall had a rather trying interrogation from officials considerably more hostile than those who interviewed Paul Royle. As soon as he was pushed into the interrogation room at the Gestapo office in the town, a swarthy, heavy-featured English-speaking German rose from a chair, walked across to him, stopped six inches in front of him and said ominously:

'You'll never see your wife and children again.'

It was not an encouraging start but it was so obviously meant to intimidate that Johnny became very much on his guard and decided to play dumb. The interrogator behind the desk was a brisk, businesslike type and shot out questions abruptly via the interpreter.

Johnny replied innocently to the same standard questions that had been asked of Paul Royle, but the interrogator was hard to satisfy. He insisted on knowing what Johnny had done with his papers. (Like all the kriegies he had, of course, thrown them away as soon as he was caught and before he was searched.)

'Papers? What papers?' asked Johnny, stalling and playing dumb as hard as he could.

'The papers you got in the camp,' said the interrogator through the interpreter. 'You got papers there, didn't you?'

'Oh, heavens, yes,' Johnny said. 'We got the *Völkischer Beobachter* —that's Goering's paper isn't it, and the *Deutsche Allgemeine Zeitung* and the——'

'No, no,' snapped the interpreter. 'Papers—forged papers and identity cards. You all had them, didn't you?'

Johnny looked vastly surprised.

'Did they? Lord, I wish I'd had some. Where did they get them? I wish I could have got some somewhere but where do you think I'd be able to get hold of an identity card——' and so on and so on. He talked and talked garrulously, aimlessly, 'misunderstanding' questions, deflecting others, branching off on to a new subject and generally giving the impression of an amiable and voluble dimwit.

It was the same when they asked about maps. (He'd had about half a dozen first-class detailed maps.)

'Maps?' said Johnny. 'Yes I had a map. I made it myself from a war map of Europe in the *Völkischer Beobachter*. It wasn't much good. I think that's why I was caught——' and off he went again on a long monologue about nothing in particular.

It was the same with his clothes, which had once been a uniform but were well converted by the compound dyers and tailors into a creditable civilian suit.

'You realize you can be shot as a spy for wearing civilian clothes round Germany,' said the interpreter. 'Where did you get them?'

'Oh, Lord, this is a uniform, not a civilian suit,' Johnny said with an ingratiating laugh. 'See, I re-cut it, put boot polish on it and changed the buttons, that's all.'

'No,' said the interpreter menacingly. 'That's a civilian suit and you can be shot as a spy.'

Johnny cheerfully denied it all as though he hadn't a worry in the world.

'Bring in someone who knows about cloth and they'll tell you this isn't a proper suit,' he said.

The interrogator brought in his stenographer from the next room. She was a horse-faced fräulein, so plain that she'd probably never had a smile from a man in her life.

Johnny Marshall fought down his better feelings and flashed her one of his nicest smiles. She looked faintly surprised and then smiled back. Invited to inspect the clothes she felt them briefly and gave a verdict for Johnny. They were, she said, not proper civilian clothes but had seams where one usually found them on uniforms.

The interrogation went on for a while longer but the prisoner's endless talk exasperated the Germans so much that the interrogator abruptly stopped the whole performance and let Johnny go back to the jail.

The business of interrogations lasted for four days till everyone had been questioned, and as the time passed, the prisoners' spirits became lower and lower. They were in complete ignorance as to what was to happen to them and could get no clue whatsoever from any of the hostile jail guards. Rations were three to four slices of black bread a day and a little watery soup, so that acute hunger was already tormentingly with them. Conversation in the cells grew less and less until by the fourth day there were hardly three words spoken in an hour in any cell. There was just nothing more to say and nothing to do except lie there and think about hunger. They couldn't even look out the window, or rather, they could but were told they would be shot if they did.

On the fourth afternoon, after all the sorting out process of prisoners leaving one cell and being put back in another, Paul Royle found himself in the same cell with Johnny Marshall, 'Oggy' Ogilvie and Mac McDonald, a Scot with a lined and patient face and an imperturbable outlook. That evening, when the cell door was opened to admit their 'supper', they saw a big white 'S' had been chalked on the door.

'Good show,' said one of them. 'S. for Sagan. That means we're to be taken back to the camp.'

'Maybe it means *schiessen* (shoot),' said one of the others dryly and there was a slightly hollow laugh. They were beginning to realize it could just as easily mean either.

The following morning there was some busy tramping along the corridor, the sound of abrupt voices and then an opening of several cell doors and a further shuffling of feet. Ogilvie had the door of the cell opened on the pretext of going to the lavatory and in the corridor he saw a party of eight of the kriegies being escorted out by several heavily armed Gestapo agents, as grim a set of plug-uglies as Ogilvie can ever recall seeing. They had the same vicious scarred faces and the same black felt hats pulled over their eyes. The Gestapo seemed to affect sinister black hats in mass.

He managed to get a few whispered words with a couple of the party as they went, and they said that they believed they were going for a second interrogation. Ogilvie and the other three risked a spray of bullets to stand up on their platform 'bed' and watch out of the window as the eight were loaded into a closed van together with their guards and driven away.

Shortly after, the four in the cell marked 'S' heard more tramping feet and shouting in the corridor and then more cell doors opening. They heard another party go past their door down the corridor and, looking out of their tiny window again, saw half a dozen more kriegies herded into a covered truck with guards and vanish out through the courtyard archway. Later in the morning they heard yet another party, and from their window saw a further eight being taken away.

They passed another tedious day waiting for their turn but it didn't come. In the evening three Luftwaffe guards arrived in the jail and slept the night in the cell opposite them. They told the four kriegies they were to take them back to Sagan in the morning.

They spoke the truth. About 9 a.m. next day the four were escorted to the station by the three guards and taken by train back to Sagan where they were immediately turfed into the cooler for three weeks' 'hard', which meant no Red Cross food, no cigarettes, no books and would also have meant solitary confinement except that the cooler was so full that everyone had company in his cell.

Chapter Thirty-Six

OUR BLACKEST HOUR

A day or so later, eight more kriegies came back from Görlitz. Of the rest, no sign.

By this time the Germans had the cooler full, almost to overflowing. The four who were caught when the tunnel was found, Lang, Len, McBride, and Reavell Carter, were languishing there, and also the four, including 'Shag' Rees and 'Red' Noble, who displeased the Kommandant in the snow outside block 104 after the discovery of the escape.

Then 'Pop' Green and Douglas Poynter arrived from Hirschberg. They had been part of the workmen's party travelling by train. For some unknown reason they were returned and the others were not seen again. Straight into the cooler they went. Another inmate at the time was Ronnie Baines, a fairly innocent young Australian who paused while walking round the compound the day after the break and looked through the window of the room in 104 where the trap had been with a cheerful grin. As he peered happily through the window he looked straight into the irate face of the Kommandant, who was inside conducting investigations. The Kommandant almost exploded, pointed and said, 'Cooler.' Whereupon two ferrets dashed out and lugged the Australian off.

Then Desmond Neely arrived back. He was a quiet little fair-haired Fleet Air Arm bloke and had had a considerably exciting time. Within forty-eight hours of climbing out of the tunnel he had arrived by train in Stettin, intending to catch the boat to Sweden. There he obtained help at a French hospital whose staff hid him in the rear of the building and gave him food. Then the hue and cry started in Stettin for the escapees and of course the Sweden ferries were watched like hawks. Neely was informed of this and decided to lie low for a while, but in the thoroughness of their comb-out the Gestapo descended on the hospital and Neely got out of the back door as they were going through the front of the building.

He went to the station and got a train to Munich, by sheer good luck avoiding any identification check on the way as the whole country had been roused and some trains were checked by the Gestapo up to three or four times a night. In Munich his luck gave out and he was nabbed and returned to Sagan and the cooler.

The score at this stage was seventy-six out of the tunnel and clear away, of which fifteen had been returned. In North Compound there was violent excitement and curiosity. As each man came back he was seen from the compound, which was next to the cooler, and he usually tried to shout a little news across the wire before he was told to keep his mouth shut by the guards and hustled into his cell. A couple of notes were smuggled across from the cooler by bribed guards and from them we learned about the capture of the rest of the kriegies seen at Görlitz. But why hadn't they come back too? People thought that maybe they had been sent to another camp. No one for a moment guessed the real reason. Up till that time the Germans had never had the nerve to murder British officers (at least, not openly) though we knew of the callous brutalities they practised on people of the small, defenceless European countries.

Meantime, all half-dozen compounds of Stalag Luft III were in a state of unprecedented excitement and tension. The excitement was because of the tunnel and the tension was both waiting for news of the escapees and waiting also for the German reprisals. There were bound to be reprisals. We all knew that. The escape had broken a world's record for the length of a kriegy tunnel and another world's record for the number of officers escaped. That was bound to be interpreted by the Master Race as a direct insult to The System.

Then some rather amusing things happened that diverted German attention from the thought of reprisals.

A few days after the break, a team of Gestapo and special S.S. men descended on the camp to investigate the affair, and then we heard that the Kommandant and Oberleutnant Breuli, the chief German security officer of the whole establishment, had become ill and taken to their beds. While rumours were flying round about this development, the Gestapo and S.S. came in to search North Compound. Now neither Gestapo nor S.S. were ever popular with ordinary German troops and in this case their unpopularity was accentuated by the fact that all the ferrets were uneasy both because of their failure to find the tunnel in time and because they were more or less superseded by the Gestapo. They knew that if the Gestapo found anything that they had been unable to find, they would be in a spot. On the other hand, if the Gestapo didn't find anything, the ferrets would be partially vindicated.

So the ferrets virtually came over to our side for the next few days. As far as they could, without going too far, they offered the Gestapo no help at all but a considerable amount of passive resistance. The Gestapo searched the compound for a couple of days, but lacking experience of 'X Organization' methods and without any help from the ferrets, they found precisely nothing of any importance, though when they went they left behind a couple of deftly purloined torches that later came in very handy to us.

Next they descended on all the other compounds, both British and American, and went over the whole lot thoroughly, again finding nothing of importance. Lamentably then, both Gestapo and S.S. were faced with an abject failure of their mission—an unthinkable position for them. In true German fashion they decided to search their own people, the German camp staff in the Kommandantur.

And, lo! Success was theirs. They unearthed a black market racket run by.... Guess! The Kommandant, the chief German censor officer, von Masse, and a Luftwaffe major who was flying transport aircraft from Denmark. The major, who was related to a German officer in the camp, used to fly choice wines and rare foods from Denmark and the racketeers had a store of the stuff under the Kommandantur cookhouse, which the Gestapo very astutely found, allegedly because some of the German staff knew of the racket and 'split' on the Kommandant. The next report that reached us was that the Kommandant, reputedly feeling very ill indeed now, was removed from the scene, together with von Masse, for court-martial.

The Gestapo got three more victims in their stay. They could not understand how we had obtained about 600 feet of electric cable for the lighting system in 'Harry'. Being Gestapo they could only imagine one thing. Someone had betrayed the Reich. They looked through the stock list of the camp electricians and found that about 600 feet of cable had been lost. Useless for the electricians to protest that the cable had been purloined from them while their backs were turned. The Gestapo had been soaked in natural suspicion for years. They took the two electricians and also the chief electrician who had been too scared to

327

report the loss of the wire and the next thing we heard was that they had shot all three.

Then the new Kommandant, Oberstleutnant (Lieutenant-Colonel) Korda, appeared on the scene. He seemed to be a fairly inconspicuous fellow who kept mostly to his office in the Kommandantur. Apparently, as the break had not concerned him and as therefore his own personal dignity was unimpaired, he did not go to any extremes of reprisals. He shut our camp theatre for a while and thereafter wouldn't let us keep cardboard Red Cross boxes or old food tins. Then for a time we had three appels a day, but these were all half-hearted reprisals and we began to think we were getting off fairly lightly. We were still rather curious about the escapees who had not been returned to us but no one dreamed for a moment that anything serious had happened to them. The popular theory was that they had been sent to another camp—possibly Kolditz 'strafelager' (punishment camp).

The Gestapo finished their investigations which had cost three German lives, a lot of German lamenting (on the part of the old Kommandant and von Masse) and caused no trouble to kriegies in the camp at all, and then they left. The ferrets, after pouring sewage down one end of 'Harry' and blowing up the other end, entered once more upon their old duties in the compound. They were somewhat more vigilant now and 'Rubberneck' had a nasty gleam in his eye, but no one cared a damn about that except the other ferrets who became more wary in their 'leadswinging'.

Poor 'Rubberneck' had had to do a lot of explaining to the authorities as to why he had not found the tunnel in time. His explanations were quaint. According to a voluble ferret who told the whole thing to one of our contacts, 'Rubberneck' said the prisoners must have finished the tunnel months before and just bided their time to break out from it. No dispersed soil had been found. They couldn't have hidden it under the living-huts as they were constantly checked for fresh soil and they couldn't have dumped it on the snow. So the tunnel, said Rubberneck, must have been dug about the same time as the old tunnel, 'Tom'.

The authorities also wanted to know how 220 people could cram into block 104 on the night of the break with all their kit without being detected by the ferrets. 'Rubberneck' is said to have mumbled a bit over

---

Facing this page: Forty men and their kit are crammed into a cattle-truck for the journey across Germany

this one and then said that we must have a small tunnel from a nearby hut leading into block 104. As a matter of fact this suggestion was even taken seriously and the ferrets staged several surprise searches of the nearby huts to find the tunnel that existed only in 'Rubberneck's' frustrated mind.

A fortnight after the break it seemed as though matters were quickly returning to normal when one morning, early in April, the innocuous Hauptmann Pieber called on Group-Captain H. M. Massey, Senior British Officer of North Compound. Massey was a grand old 'regular', with an M.C. from the last war (as a pilot) and a D.S.O. from the Palestine fighting in the 'thirties. He was thick-set with a rugged, strong face, possessed masses of dignity and used to hobble about with a stick, and one foot in a flying-boot. That foot had been hurt when the Group-Captain crashed in flames in the 1914–1918 war and the injury was aggravated years later by a sniper's bullet in Palestine. Still full of fight the Group-Captain had been shot down on what was to be his last 'op' in this war, one of the early thousand-bomber raids. His foot was injured again when he landed heavily after baling out.

Pieber went to the Group-Captain's room and saluted politely. Would the Group-Captain be good enough to wait on the new Kommandant in the Kommandantur at 11 a.m., together with his official interpreter?

'What does he want?' asked Massey. 'Is he going to announce the programme of reprisals against us?'

Pieber's face was very solemn as he answered:

'I cannot tell you, Group-Captain Massey, but it is something very terrible.'

Even with that formidable warning there were no particular grounds for worry as Pieber was universally regarded as an old woman who took all minor setbacks with a show of great distress.

Just before eleven o'clock, the Group-Captain was escorted over to the Kommandantur, accompanied by his personal interpreter, Squadron-Leader 'Wank' M—— (who, you will remember, was captured in the first week of the war and was taken to be interviewed by Goering). After waiting a few moments they were shown into the Kommandant's office, a normal barrack-room, but with a carpet, a leather chair and a large desk, above which on the wall were the two standard items of

Facing this page: Arrival at 'Marlag' near Bremen. A rainy six-hour wait outside the camp

equipment for all Luftwaffe officers—photographs of Hitler and Goering.

The Kommandant was standing behind his desk to greet them. He was a fairly tall man of about fifty with a rather athletic figure, fair thinning hair and the Iron Cross, First Class, on his chest. Normally, on these occasions when the Kommandant and the Senior British Officer met officially, there was a formal handshake and the usual military courtesies. This time there was no handshake. The Kommandant gave a slight, stiff bow and indicated to the two British officers to sit down on two chairs that had been placed by the desk. Simoleit, the German adjutant, and Pieber were standing beside the desk, staring with downcast eyes at the carpet.

The Kommandant stood up and said in German:

'I have been instructed by my higher authority to communicate to you this report . . .' he paused and 'Wank' translated his words so far to the Group-Captain. The Kommandant continued:

'The Senior British Officer is to be informed that as a result of a tunnel from which seventy-six officers escaped from Stalag Luft III, North Compound, forty-one of these officers have been shot while resisting arrest or attempting further escape after arrest.'

'Wank' felt himself going red in the face. Unbelieving, he asked:

'How many were shot?'

'Forty-one,' the Kommandant replied. 'Wank' slowly translated the passage to the Group-Captain.

The Group-Captain listened in silence and made almost no sign that he was hearing, except that he stiffened slightly in his chair and the lines of his face became hard and set. At the finish, he said briefly:

'How many were shot?'

'Wank' answered: 'Forty-one.' He felt that his face was crimson and the scene in the room took on an air of unreality for him.

There was a long heavy silence in the room that lasted with almost unbearable tension for nearly a minute. Neither the Germans nor the British officers moved or spoke.

At last the Group-Captain spoke.

'Ask him,' he said, 'how many were wounded.'

'Wank' put the question to the Kommandant. The German looked in embarrassment at a paper on his desk and then looked out of the window. He hesitated, then said:

'My higher authority only permits me to read this report and not to answer questions or give any further information.'

Group-Captain Massey repeated his question: 'Ask him again how many were wounded?'

The Kommandant looked acutely uncomfortable, paused, and then slowly said:

'I think no one was wounded.'

'No one wounded?' asked the Group-Captain. 'Do you mean to tell me forty-one can be shot in those circumstances and that all were killed and no one wounded?'

'I am to read you this report,' said the Kommandant, 'and that is all I can do.'

All three German officers seemed to be disliking their position intensely. Simoleit and Pieber were still silent with downcast eyes.

The Group-Captain asked for the names of the dead.

'I can't give them to you,' said the Kommandant. 'I haven't got them. I have only this report which I am to read to you.'

'I would like to have the names as soon as it is possible to get them,' said the Group-Captain.

'Yes, I will do that,' answered the Kommandant. 'I must remind you that I am acting under orders and may only divulge what I am instructed to by my higher authority.'

'What is this higher authority?' asked the Group-Captain.

The Kommandant made a futile little gesture. 'It is just higher authority,' he said.

'I require to know what has happened to the bodies so that I can arrange for burial and the disposal of their effects,' said the Group-Captain. 'I demand that the Protecting Power also be informed.'

The Kommandant said that this would be done. He would let the Senior British Officer have every possible scrap of information as soon as he received it, but reminded him that he was always limited in action by his 'higher authority'.

He rose to his feet: 'I think that is all, gentlemen.' Stiffly the two British officers withdrew, and as they emerged into fresh air again the Group-Captain said to 'Wank':

'Don't mention this dreadful thing to anyone till I have released it in the compound.'

'Wank' still felt that his face was crimson. Neither man felt like speaking and the Group-Captain's face was still grimly set.

On the way back to the barbed wire, Pieber joined them. He seemed nervous and distressed.

'Please do not think that the Luftwaffe had anything to do with this dreadful thing,' he told the Group-Captain. 'We do not like to be associated with it. It is terrible.' Pieber may at times have been a hypocrite but he certainly was not on this occasion. He was a considerably shaken man.

Half an hour later, back in the compound, word was sent round requesting the senior officer of every room to report to the camp theatre for an announcement from the Group-Captain. With the order was a rumour to the effect that 'something dreadful' had happened. We all assumed that reprisals in the camp were going to start in earnest. At the time we were not particularly worried about the 'something dreadful'. The camp was always hearing rumours like that and it was largely discounted. We were slightly uneasy and very curious over the coming reprisals, but these reprisals rarely had much more than nuisance value.

About 300 senior officers crowded into the theatre for the announcement. The Group-Captain walked on to the stage, paused for a few seconds while the rustling died down, and then said without preamble:

'Gentlemen, I have just come from a meeting with the Kommandant in which he told me the unbelievable, the shocking news that forty-one of the officers who escaped from the tunnel on the 24th of March have been shot.'

There was a stunned silence. People were utterly horrified. Mass murder was something new in the quiet backwater of British prison camps, however unpleasant the life was. Shaken to the core we could not believe our ears. A lot of the kriegies felt suddenly sick.

The Group-Captain went on to describe the meeting very briefly. Names of the victims would be announced as soon as they were available and burial arrangements had to be made. More than that there was little he could say. There would be a memorial service on the coming Sunday.

Still in a stunned silence we filed out of the theatre and within two minutes the news had spread to everyone in the camp and there was a hush over the whole compound. Many flatly refused to believe it. 'I know', they said, 'the Huns are murderous bastards, but they've never been game so far to murder British people openly in mass and there seems no point in starting that sort of thing on relatively harmless prisoners.'

They decided that the whole thing was a bluff; that the forty-one had probably been removed to another camp and that we, believing they were dead, would be intimidated into stopping all escape activity.

332

Nearly half the camp tended to believe that and the other half was inclined to take the gloomier view.

Everyone, however, realized that it might be no bluff at all. We knew the Nazis were capable of callous murder on any scale but the whole thing was so barbarous, so unbelievable and the people in the escape were all so well known to us that we did not want to believe, and sheer wishful thinking induced many to discount the whole affair as a bluff.

None the less, we could not get away from the fact that the Germans had officially announced the shootings and there was a passionate anxiety throughout the camp to know who, if it were true, had been killed among their friends who escaped.

Meantime, with the official intimation of the deaths, a memorial service was held and every man in the compound sewed a little black mourning diamond on his sleeve. Afraid that there might be some sort of demonstration or revolt, the Germans exhorted all the guards to extra watchfulness and ruthlessness at the first sign of any trouble. When some of us were a little slow in getting into our hut at lock-up time a bullet from a sentry tower came whistling just over our heads as a gentle persuader. When the air-raid siren went, early one afternoon, a few of the kriegies were a little slow in getting back inside their blocks where everyone had to stay during raids. One of the Germans emptied his magazine at them, missed them by a few inches and several people sitting in block 109 were unpleasantly surprised to get a couple of the bullets in the wall by their chairs. They ringed the bullet holes with pencil and labelled them 'Easter eggs, Sagan, 1944'.

A couple of minutes after this a guard got an American sergeant standing innocently in the doorway of his block in the adjoining American compound. The bullet went in his mouth and he died instantly. It was not so very unusual for a trigger-conscious guard to kill one of the kriegies, but this was an unfortunate time for another killing and more and more people began to think the forty-one were really dead.

A list was brought into the compound a few days later and pinned up on the notice-board. It contained the names of the escapees who had been shot. They were counted. They were not forty-one names, but forty-seven.

Faced with the actual names of those dead, we got back that same stunned feeling of horror that had followed the first announcement. It was a terrible list. Many of the finest people in the camp were on it.

333

There were many of the leading lights of the 'X Organization' (a perfectly legitimate organization as escaping attempts from prison camps are fully permitted in the Geneva Convention, which lays down that no harsh penalties shall be imposed on prisoners who attempt to escape). Many of those on the list, too, were only youngsters, a year or two out of school, and there could not have been the slightest suggestion that any of them had been engaged in espionage or sabotage work.

Roger Bushell's name was on the list. That was not unexpected as he had escaped several times and the Germans suspected him of being responsible for escape activity in North Compound.

The ever-courteous Tim Walenn, chief of the 'Dean and Dawson' forging factory, was on the list. So were Gordon Brettell and Henri Picard, two of his assistants. So were Al Hake, the compass maker, and Charles Hall, the compound photographic expert. 'Hunk' Humphries was there (he had been Paul Royle's travelling partner) and Tom Kirby-Green who had been stuck passing through the tunnel. Johnny Stower was another, a particularly tragic one because in the delousing party walk-out of the previous year he had reached the Swiss border and actually crossed into Switzerland for a while before he unconsciously walked back into German territory and was recaptured. Denys Street was on the list too. He was a son of the Permanent Under-Secretary for Air. The Germans certainly were not discriminating. Many of the compound's veteran tunnellers were among those shot and, this was particularly noted, all except one of the Poles who escaped from the tunnel. Also on the list was Wally Valenta, who had been so uneasy in his cell at Görlitz.

The closest friends of all of them were among the kriegies left in the compound and for days the whole camp was clouded with grief and fury. Then another list went up on the board. It contained the names of three more who had been shot. It brought the total up to a round fifty. That later provided the only clue to the reason for the shootings.

A few days later another group of badly wounded prisoners was taken from the camp for repatriation back to England, and among them was the Senior British Officer, Group-Captain Massey, who was being repatriated because of his almost unserviceable foot.

About two hours before they left the compound, the Germans did a peculiar thing. They called for all the clothing and kit of the fifty officers who had been shot. Apparently it was a rather senseless sort of bluff. They knew that the repatriates would reveal the full story of the escape and shooting when they returned to England and presumably the Germans thought that the demand for the kit of the missing fifty would induce the repatriates to believe that they had not, after all, been shot, but had been removed to another camp. It was just an effort to throw doubt on the matter of the shooting but how the uneasy Germans meant to cover the atrocity up ultimately is a mystery.

The whole affair so far was shrouded in mystery. The Germans had advanced no reason for the shooting other than the patently absurd story that they had been shot attempting to evade capture. That had never happened in other mass breaks, and as the Group-Captain had implied, why were they all killed and none wounded? We had all been wondering and worrying ourselves sick over the affair for weeks trying to read some sense into it when the few escapees who had returned came out of the cooler and back into the compound. Eagerly we pumped them for news of what had happened.

They had heard about the fifty being shot while they were in the cooler but most of them point-blank refused to believe it. They had seen the people at Görlitz being taken out for second interrogation and knew they were perfectly all right then. It must be a German bluff. They must have been taken to another camp.

The returned escapees told us all about Görlitz and about the impossible conditions for the 'hard-tailers' on the escape. It was more than interesting and we lapped it up, but still there was no clue as to the shooting. Why should they shoot some and send the others back for no particular reason? There was another puzzling detail. One of the people who returned from Görlitz knew that a friend of his who was in his cell there had been taken to hospital after the first couple of days with badly frost-bitten feet. He couldn't walk, and yet he was on the list of those shot. That obviously disposed of the theory that they were shot attempting to escape again. It must be, we decided, it *must* be a bluff to dissuade us from escaping. The supposedly shot men must have been taken to some other camp.

Then the Germans returned the kit of the fifty which they had taken out on the morning that the repatriates went. Shortly after, they brought in some of the personal belongings that the missing fifty had been carrying when they escaped, such as watches and photographs. Some of the stuff was bloodstained.

We were all severely shaken. If this were a bluff, it was a distinctly convincing bluff, even taking Teutonic thoroughness into account.

The issue was more or less put beyond all doubt a couple of weeks later when the Germans brought in urns carrying the cremated ashes of those who had been killed. No need to ask why they had been cremated. It destroys the evidence of the manner of death.

On each little urn was marked the locality where death had taken place. Four were marked 'Danzig', and just four of the escapees had been making for Danzig. Two more were marked with the name of a town down near the French border and others came from scattered parts of Germany, including several from Hirschberg and a lot from Görlitz. They testified to the widespread net that the Nazis had put out to trace the escapees and to the fact that a lot of the escapees had given them a good chase for their money before being rounded up.

Information brought in by guards from time to time eventually led us to believe that the staggering figure of 5,000,000 Germans had to spend some of their time looking for the prisoners. Many thousands of them had to be put whole time on the job for weeks and this in itself made the break in one respect a considerable success because escape attempts from prison camps are made not only to get people back home, but also to cause the diversion of part of the enemy's manpower.

The stories of the people who had come back were examined over and over again to try and find some reason why the fifty had been shot and others returned to us. Every little scrap of information we had about the affair was taken into account and the history, careers and activities of all the fifty were checked and cross-checked. No common factor could be found anywhere to indicate why some were shot and some were returned. There seemed to be a complete lack of logic about it. Some of those shot were old hands at escape, but on the other hand a couple of those who returned were similarly notorious with the Germans. So it was with all points checked. Nowhere could we find the one common factor that would give a clue. It seemed to be just another senseless German mass killing, which, as a theory, was not so unacceptable at that.[1]

One possible indication only was there to an explanation. The number killed was the round number of fifty—neither more nor less. If, then, the Germans wanted to deter us from escape, what more typical Nazi method than to pick out fifty men at random and shoot them out of hand. It was the only possible theory we could devise.

[1] The Nuremberg Trial has confirmed this. The decision for the murder of the fifty was apparently made by Hitler and Himmler themselves, and Keitel and Goering were also involved. The fifty were made to climb up one by one on the top of cars and then were shot by Himmler's precious thugs.

With vengeful grief we set about building a memorial vault to the fifty in a nearby cemetery, where already there was a row of graves of other victims from the camp. The Germans let small working parties of kriegies go out to the cemetery to build the vault, and while it was taking shape we wondered how many more of the tunnel escapees had died, and if any of them had run the whole gauntlet and reached home. Seventy-six had got clear on the night of the break. Fifty, we knew, had been shot, and a total of fifteen had come back to us from Görlitz, Hirschberg, and Munich. That left eleven still unaccounted for, including Wing-Commander Day, the 'Dodger', and Plunkett, who had been chief of the map department. We waited for news and hoped.

Meanwhile, Crump Kerr-Ramsay and 'Conk' Canton were busy in the compound. As old escape veterans, they had been chosen to stay behind in the camp instead of escaping. As they knew all the ropes, theirs was the job of rebuilding the 'X Organization' after the rest of the experienced 'X' leaders had gone through the tunnel. They had not liked the idea of staying behind one little bit, but their loyalty to the job probably saved them from sharing the fate of the fifty.

If the Germans had planned on frightening the North Compound out of escape operations, they made a prime psychological bloomer. Had they possessed the intellectual resilience of a cannon-ball they should have realized that such an intention made it a matter of high principle for the kriegies to carry on. Which they did.

A couple of months later, a reformed 'X Organization' was working at full pressure again and 'George', our next tunnel, was reaching out towards the wire from under the theatre.

EPILOGUE

In June a letter came to Sagan from England, written in Spanish and signed with a pre-arranged fictitious name. Flight-Lieutenant Bob van der Stok, Dutch pilot in the R.A.F., had made it back home from the tunnel. The Spanish letter was his way of letting us know and North Compound was considerably cheered.

Then a postcard arrived from Sweden, signed with two more fictitious names. 'Rocky' Rockland and Jan Muller, both Norwegians in the R.A.F., had made it safely.

That made three home (all of whom spoke German fluently) and eight still to be accounted for.

We didn't know at the time and didn't find out till we got back to England, but those eight had all been caught and were in various concentration camps around Germany and the occupied countries. At least one was in Buchenwald. Later, five of them were collected and sent to Oranienburg Concentration Camp, just north of Berlin. This five consisted of Wing-Commander Day, the 'Dodger', James and Dowse (all English) and van Wymeersch, a Belgian. The Germans told them fifty of their comrades had been shot after the tunnel escape and furthermore said that the five certainly wouldn't get any chances to escape from Oranienburg.

'Prickie' Day promptly organized the digging of another tunnel which they worked industriously upon till they successfully finished it and escaped again. It was a considerably game effort after knowing that fifty had been shot because of the other tunnel and knowing that the chances were they would be caught again. In point of fact they were all caught again but for some unknown reason the Germans still didn't shoot them.

Back at Sagan, North Compound, the Klim Club had been formed. Some fanatical Nazi guards had made a few nasty cracks about what they were going to do to us when the war finished, so the new Senior

British Officer, Group-Captain Wilson, and the military experts of the camp doped out a counter-scheme of self-defence. The compound population was split up into sections, platoons and companies and each man had his job for which he did a little secret training. The security name was the 'Klim Club'—Klim being a popular brand of milk powder in the food parcels. There was a special commando company for use as shock troops, if needed, and various courses of action were planned for various emergencies.

Laboriously, over the weeks, everyone saved up a little food by stinting their already stinted rations. Some was hidden in their rooms and some hidden down 'George'.

'George'—the new tunnel—was making good progress. It started from a trapdoor near the stage of the camp theatre and the sand was being dispersed, as with most of 'Harry', under the auditorium floor.

While 'George' was being pushed out towards the wire, it was decided that it was time to start again on small-scale escapes by guile. Mac——, a rabid Left-wing amateur politician, had an idea about concealing himself under a pile of empty tins in one of the garbage carts. He would risk being stabbed by the iron spikes with which they probed all such carts at the gate, looking for people like Mac. He was given permission to go, but a couple of hours before the time for trying his idea, a message came into the compound.

A German stenographer in the Kommandantur, disgusted at the shooting of the fifty, decided she wanted to help the kriegies and damn the Third Reich and damn Der Fuehrer. She sent a message by a tame guard that she had heard through her work that all kriegies who escaped henceforth were to be shot.

The 'X' leaders rubbed their chins reflectively and told Mac he'd better not go. Mac lay low for a few days, then said he thought he could get away with it and wanted to risk it. After a bit more chin rubbing they let him go.

He was back in the cooler a few hours later, but still alive, and eventually he came back into the compound again. It did not necessarily mean that the stenographer had sent in a 'phony' message. Mac was just lucky in keeping out of the hands of the Gestapo.

Meantime, whether escapees were to be shot or not, 'George', the tunnel, went creeping out towards the wire. Winter came and further escapes had to be postponed till the 'off' season was over. They didn't want people out in the same impossible conditions as last time. 'George', by this time, reached to just outside the wire.

The 12th of January 1945: The Russian offensive started and the East Front came sweeping towards Sagan like a hurricane. In a few days we would either be evacuated or freed. Oh! the tension and hopes of those days.

We were evacuated! The whole six compounds of Stalag Luft III, nearly 10,000 aircrew, mostly officers, marched out into a foot of snow on the 27th and 28th of January. Everyone started in poor physical condition as for four months we had been on only a half parcel of Red Cross food a week to supplement insignificant German rations. North Compound, now about 2,000 men, force-marched thirty-four kilometres the first night and day, carrying all food and possessions possible. Many people knocked up rough sleds.

Next night the temperature dropped to twenty-two degrees below zero. We slept (or tried to) in barns. A German guard who wasn't relieved and foolishly stayed at his post had to have a foot amputated through frostbite.

We force-marched nearly thirty kilometres the next day to the town of Muskau, where the guards were so exhausted the column had to stay for three days, quartered in a riding school, a stable, two factories, a cinema, a laundry and a small French P.O.W. cage.

The thaw came and we had to discard sleds and march to Spemberg, about twenty-five kilometres, where the Germans at last produced a meal for us—a cup of barley soup; the first 'meal' they had given us for six days. We were crammed into cattle trucks—forty to each truck, which is quite a squeeze. One can't lie down. One can barely even sit. Thus we travelled in acute misery for thirty-six hours without water, then got a cupful each of filthy water from the locomotive. Then another half-day's cattle-truck travel and a march to Marlag, a naval P.O.W. camp near Bremen, where we waited several hours outside in rain and slush to be searched before entering. Many kriegies had reached the end of their tether and collapsed.

So, after eight days of a highly unpleasant journey we were crammed up to eighteen in a room in a compound that had already been condemned for human habitation. About seventy-five of our number were missing—about half of them left behind at various places through illness and half just 'missing', maybe escaped or maybe shot. Of the remainder, seventy per cent were sick. Everyone had lost weight, up to two stone.

Rations were further cut, Red Cross food parcels were uncertain and the Germans could not even supply blankets.

Then the Western Front offensive started. Again there were rosy dreams of liberation—till the 10th of April, when we were marched out again, heading north.

This time it was a picnic compared to the previous evacuation. A few kriegies were shot by trigger-conscious guards, a few more were killed by strafing aircraft, but the weather was fine and we were able to acquire food by trading with Red Cross coffee, soap, and cigarettes. We acquired food, too, by plain, common or garden variety 'pinching', about which no qualms were felt.

We crossed the Elbe by ferry and continued north. There were strict orders *against* escaping now. It was better for the whole crowd to stick together according to the old tag, 'United we stand, etc.'

Sheltering in barns near Lübeck, we heard the barrage as the British Army crossed the Elbe. Two days later, on the 2nd of May, there was firing just down the road, and at 11.45 a.m. two tanks rumbled up the road from the south. Through the trees we couldn't see whether they were British or German. The tension was painful—and then two Tommies hopped out of the hatch of the leading tank and we ran to them screaming hoarsely.

The first kriegy to reach them was Dave D——. If you recall chapter five you will remember he dropped some mines under the *Tirpitz* in Wilhelmshaven in 1940 and then made about the lowest pull-off non-fatal parachute jump in history.

He frenziedly pumped the arm of the first Tommy out of the tanks.

''Ow long 'ave you been in Germany?' asked the Tommy.

'Five years,' said Dave.

'Blimey!' said the Tommy. ''Ave yer?'

His accent was Cockney. Sheer, unadulterated Cockney, straight from London. And in Dave it rang a bell. He suddenly realized he was free.

So we were liberated.